The Knitter's Guide to Sweater Design

Carmen Michelson and Mary-Ann Davis

 INTERWEAVE PRESS
306 North Washington Avenue
Loveland, Colorado 80537

Design by Linda Seals, B. Vader Design/Production
Layout by Mary Daline

Photography by Joe Coca, ©1989 Interweave Press, All rights reserved.

Yarn for the sample sweater in the section following page 298, designed by Jean Scorgie, is NZN, color B, and was graciously donated by Ironstone Warehouse. Special thanks to Katie Swanson and Jackie Truelove for their sweaters in the color section.

Interweave Press
306 North Washington Avenue
Loveland, Colorado 80537

Library of Congress Catalog Number 87-46352
ISBN 0-934026-33-5
First printing: 15M:389:ARC:CL

Library of Congress Cataloging-in-Publication Data
Michelson, Carmen, 1948-
  The knitter's guide to sweater design.
  1. Sweaters. 2. Knitting—Patterns. I. Davis,
    Mary-Ann, 1942-   . II. Title.
    TT825.M53 1989   746.9'2   87-46352

CONTENTS

About This Book   v

Developing Your Ideas   1

Introduction   1
The Idea and the Start of a Plan 1/ *The Scrap File* 2

The Shape   3
Selecting a Basic Shape 3/ *Flat or Round?* 3/

The Fabric   4
The Test Swatch: Determining Your Gauge 4/ *Stitch
Patterns* 5/ *Color Patterns* 8/ *Getting Patterns to Work Out on
a Garment* 10/ *Choosing Yarn* 13/ *Color
Theory* 23/ *Yarn First or Color Scheme First?* 28

Pulling It All Together   29
Getting the Design to Work with the Figure 29/ *Fitting* 29/
Refining the Idea 30

The Charting Preliminaries   33

Taking Measurements   33
The Tape Measure in Action 33/ *Potential Fitting Problems* 35

Determining Ease and Other Adjustments   36
Ease 36/ *Seam Allowances* 38

The Test Swatch Revisited   38
More than One Swatch 39/ *Pattern Repeat Gauge* 40/ *Aran
Sweater Test Swatches* 40/ *Biasing* 40/ *Swatches and the
Sweater-in-Progress* 41

Yarn Requirements   41
How Much Yarn? 41/ *Too Much Yarn* 43/ *Not Enough Yarn* 43

Charting Tools   44
Pocket Calculators 44/ *Standard Graph Paper* 44/ *Knitting
Graph Paper* 45

Picture Knitting   46
Charting a Picture 46/ *Scaling a Drawing to Size* 48/ *A Light
Box* 48

Charting Your Pattern   49

Charting Arithmetic   50

Basic Charting Formulas   51
Gathers 51/ *Tapers* 52/ *Slopes* 56

Body and Yoke Shaping   57
*Classic Body with Set-In Armhole Shaping, and Standard
Shoulder Shaping, labelled CB* 57/ *About the
Formulas* 57/ *Enlarged Sweater Front* 63/ *Blouson
Body* 65/ *Tapered Body* 67/ *Double-Tapered
Body* 69/ *Reverse-Tapered Body* 69/ *Cinched-Waist
Body* 74/ *Dart-Tapered Body* 76/ *Bust Darts* 76/
Alternate Set-In Armhole Shaping 80/ *Semi-Raglan Armhole
Shaping* 80/ *Shaped Yoke* 82/ *Extended Shoulder
Shaping* 86/ *Basic T Yoke* 86/ *Modified T Yoke* 89/
Saddle Shoulder Yoke (Standard and Modified) 89/ *Standard
Raglan Yoke* 92/ *Modified Raglan Yoke* 95/ *Round Yokes
(Large and Small)* 98/ *Full-Fashioned Shoulder Shaping* 104/
Vest Armhole Shaping 107/ *Summer Tops* 113

Necklines   113
General Information 113/ *Round Neckline* 117/ *Alternate
Round Neckline* 120/ *Traditional V Neckline* 120/ *Blunt V
Neckline* 122/ *Square Neckline* 127/ *Boatnecks* 130/ *Draped
Neckline* 136/ *Optional Back Neckline Shaping* 140

Cardigans   141
Styling 141/ *Buttonholes* 141/ *Cardigan Necklines* 144/ *Chart-
ing a Cardigan* 146/ *Front Finishes* 149/ *Non-Overlapping
Cardigan Styles* 176/ *Cardigans with Shawl Collars* 177

Sleeves and Sleeve Caps   189
Sleeve Ease 189/ Shorter Sleeves 189/ Set-In Caps 189/ Tapered Sleeve and Classic Set-In Cap, labelled TS 197/ Lantern Sleeve 200/ Bishop Sleeve 203/ Bell Sleeve 206/ Leg o' Mutton Sleeve 206/ Straight Sleeve 209/ Funnel Sleeve 209/ Gathered Cap 211/ Expanded Cap Shaping 214/ Pleated Cap 214/ Box Cap 218/ T-Square Cap 221/ Designer's Choice Cap 224/ Standard Saddle Shoulder Cap and Band 233/ Modified Saddle Shoulder Cap and Band 235/ Semi-Raglan Cap 239/ Standard Raglan Cap 239/ Modified Raglan Cap 243/ Basic and Modified T Sleeve Bind-Offs 247/ Modified T Sleeve with Gathers or Pleats 247/ Folded T Sleeve 249/ Cap Sleeves 249

One- and Two-Piece Garments   251
General Information 251/ T-Shapes 255/ Dolmans 257

Finishing Details   268

Neckline Finishes   268
General Information 268/ Round Necklines 270/ V Neckline Finishes 281/ Square Neckline Finishes 295/ Boat Neckline Finishes 299/ Combinations of Neckline Finishes 300

Hoods   302
Separate Rectangular Hoods 305/ Separate T-Shaped Hoods 312/ Attached Hoods 319

Plackets   325
Keyhole Openings 328/ Seam Openings 335

Pockets   344
Patch Pockets 344/ Inset Pockets 349

Favorite How-Tos   360

Blocking   360

Assembling Instructions   361

Seams and Joins   363

Increasing, Decreasing, Beginning, and Ending   366

Buttonholes   375

Turning Ridges   377

Curve Guide   378

Appendix   380

Knitting Ethnic   380

Hats   383

Knitters' Graph Paper   387

Measurement Chart   388

Yardage Chart   389

Standard Measurements   390

Acknowledgments   394

Index   395

Charts

100 Stitches on Needle   5

Working with Different Weights of Yarns   14

Compound Yarn/Needle Chart   21

Measurements   35

Ease for Adult Garments   37

Converting Fractions to Decimals (and Vice Versa)   44

ABOUT THIS BOOK

A handknit sweater is special: it is often worn, cherished, and admired long after whole wardrobes of mass-produced garments have been discarded. As a knitter, you probably already know the satisfaction of telling someone, "I knit it myself." When you master the simple skills in this book, you will be able to add, ". . . and I designed it myself, as well."

Every sweater evolves in three distinct stages. In the *design stage,* the seed of an idea takes root. This is the stage of choices, of exploring separate elements and bringing them together in a pleasing way. Decisions are made about yarn, color, stitch patterns, and general garment shaping, resulting in an image or actual sketch of how the designer would like the eventual garment to look.

In the *charting stage,* stitch and row gauges are combined with body measurements and allowances for ease to provide the numbers necessary for knitting. The original idea may need to be further refined so the stitch patterns or designs work effectively with the numbers.

In the *knitting stage,* the garment comes to life. Skeins of yarn leave shelves or boxes and travel across a knitter's needles to become a prized wearable.

Most of us have, at some point in our knitting careers, skipped over the first two stages and knit from patterns designed and charted by others. Many knitters remain at this level, believing they are neither "creative" nor privy to the "mysterious secrets" of design and charting.

It is our sincere hope that you, as a knitter—even if you're a beginner—will learn that you *are* creative and that you *can* master the simple techniques necessary to produce your own creations. In fact, you're already one-third of the way there. You've mastered stage three. You've learned how to cast on, bind off, and make knits and purls. Once you understand stages one and two, you will find that it's easier and more rewarding to knit your own designs than to follow printed patterns.

The Knitter's Guide to Sweater Design will introduce you to the fundamentals of knitwear design and charting. You will be able to select from a vast array of sweater shapes and styles, and you'll learn how to arrive at the essential numbers for knitting them. You'll no longer need to knit to a specific gauge, or work with a stitch pattern or yarn selected by someone else. You'll be able to see a sweater in a magazine or store and knit one like it for yourself or a loved one. And you'll gain the confidence to make your own unique ideas a reality.

What's more, since you will work from individual measurements, *your sweaters will fit!* (We also provide standard measurements, of course, so you can make special sweaters for people who aren't within reach of your tape measure.)

This book will give most knitters a lifetime full of design possibilities. Since you can combine various body, neckline, sleeve, and sleeve cap styles, no two sweaters need ever be alike. In planning this book, we've researched not only current styles but also interesting variations from the past to help feed your own creative process.

Our writing may appear to be oriented toward the hand knitter, but this book is for our machine-knitting friends as well. While the techniques of knitting by hand or machine may differ, the basic design and charting techniques are the same for both. Machine knitters will also find special tricks here that meet their particular needs.

We highly encourage experimentation. If you're a cautious knitter, you'll find enough hand-holding here to develop your skills and assurance, plus examples of work by other knitters—including our students—to inspire you. If you're adventurous, you'll use our guidelines as a jumping-off place for your own imagination. In either case, you'll soon find you've earned the title of *designer.*

Happy knitting!

THE PARTS OF A SWEATER

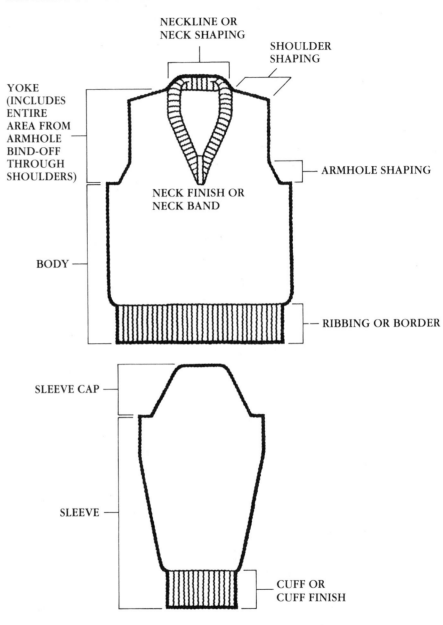

NECKLINE OR
NECK SHAPING

SHOULDER
SHAPING

YOKE
(INCLUDES
ENTIRE
AREA FROM
ARMHOLE
BIND-OFF
THROUGH
SHOULDERS)

ARMHOLE SHAPING

NECK FINISH OR
NECK BAND

BODY

RIBBING OR BORDER

SLEEVE CAP

SLEEVE

CUFF OR
CUFF FINISH

Developing Your Ideas

INTRODUCTION

The Idea and the Start of a Plan

Knitters are by nature creative. It's not surprising that so many eventually express an interest in design. There is immense satisfaction in knowing that you alone are responsible for a garment, from its initial conception through its first wearing.

Each sweater begins with *an idea*. The design process gives that idea substance. Your idea for a sweater may be utilitarian, or it may qualify as "wearable art," but above all a garment is meant to be worn. A successful garment is one which works visually, practically, and comfortably. As the designer, you make that happen.

Your idea may center around a yarn you fall in love with, a skirt that needs a dressy complement, a particular cable-stitch pattern, or a four-year-old's sketch of a goldfish. Before you begin to chart the numbers of stitches to cast on and to plan where decreases will occur, you will need to fine-tune your idea by filling in other essential elements. If you have a yarn, you'll need a shape, a stitch pattern, and other details. If you have the shape, you'll need the yarn and so forth.

While the actual charting of a garment requires only a knitted swatch and some body measurements, the best sweater design requires an understanding of many topics, including:

- garment style selection,
- shaping techniques,
- yarn (including fiber content, thickness, texture, and care),
- stitch patterns,
- color,
- body measurements,
- figure problems, and
- ease,

to name a few. All of these factors work together, forming an interwoven body of knowledge to be applied to each individual project.

Paying close attention to one area at the expense of another could leave you with a finished sweater that is less than satisfactory. Before you pull out your knitting needles and yarn and cast on for the ribbing, take the time to become familiar with the material in this section. We will cover all the topics listed above—and more—and will explain how they relate to your special creations.

While mastering all these areas at once may seem daunting, in fact you can begin to design successfully when your understanding is in an early stage. Your knowledge and confidence will grow with each additional garment. Knitting is rich in tradition and possibility, and as a designer you can tap into this wealth.

You will come to understand all the components of sweater design—individually and as they affect each other. You'll develop a familiarity which allows you to take them into account as if by second nature. Some compromises may be necessary along the way, and that's where the challenge of designing comes into play.

Even more important, you will consider these choices as they relate to the *person* who will wear the sweater. So begin by asking yourself some simple questions about the garment you have in mind, and think about how the answers relate to the elements you must refine. This may help the sweater take shape in your mind. For example:

Who will the garment be for?
Man, woman, child, or infant? Does the person have strong personal preferences in colors or styles? Is the person allergic to any yarn fibers? Is ease of care and cleaning important?
How will the garment be worn?
Indoors, next to the body? Layered for a combination of indoor and outdoor wear? Strictly outdoors? In what type of climate? Will any yarn fiber or thickness be best? Would a hood or pockets be important or practical?
Is a particular body shape or style most appropriate?
Will the sweater be classic, ethnic, or high-fashion? Pullover or cardigan? Dressy or casual? Is styling more important than comfort—or vice versa?

Should certain aspects of the figure be accentuated or diminished?
Are any decorative or styling elements of primary importance?
Is the yarn most important? Or are the stitch patterns? Pictures or symbols? Novelties, such as buttons, beads, sequins, or feathers? Pleats? Gathers? A special neck finish?

Other questions may come to your mind, or your own questions may come in a different order. We'll consider each of the issues raised above in more depth as we proceed.

You'll find that each sweater you design takes form in a unique manner, to meet its own set of requirements. That's why the sweaters you design will be the most successful sweaters you'll ever make.

The Scrap File

Ideas do not appear magically from nowhere. They grow, like plants, from tiny seeds. Every designer—for fashion, advertising, interiors, or industry—develops a scrap file of ideas relating to his or her particular area of expertise.

You are going to be a designer of knitwear. Perhaps your garments will be for yourself or your immediate circle of family and friends. Perhaps your dreams are more ambitious, and include designing for craft magazines, specialty shops, or the fashion industry. Perhaps this second type of success will evolve from your achievements closer to home, as people see and admire your sweaters.

Whatever your eventual plans, now is the time to start an idea file. Even if you already know what you want your first sweater to look like, this file will be an indispensable source for ideas down the road.

You can use a simple folder or make a special scrapbook. Consider starting with a photo album which has self-adhesive pages; you can easily collect notes and clippings without having to deal with tape or glue.

Be on the lookout for exciting uses of color and pattern, mixes of texture or stitches, and interesting shaping techniques. Keep your eyes open for unique collars, sleeves, and pockets. Trim photos and sketches from magazines and catalogs—but don't limit yourself to pictures of sweaters. Cut out photos of interesting blouses, dresses, and coats sewn from commercially knitted or woven fabric. You can convert many styles and details to knitwear.

If you see a striking garment in a store or worn by a friend, make a note or simple sketch of the details which caught your attention. If certain images or color combinations intrigue you—a photo of a landscape or a sunset, a child's drawing of a spaceship or an animal, a swatch of wallpaper or giftwrap—include them in your record. Perhaps you can interpret them in yarn.

Most importantly, your file should contain a record of your own garments. Include sketches and photos, charting information, and graphs. Attach a sample of the actual yarn—the yarn wrapper can also be useful—and note how many skeins you used. Copy the stitch-pattern instructions from your pattern source. Add comments on problems you encountered and how you, the designer, resolved them. Everything you save here will be invaluable in your future designing, and you'll enjoy watching your creative abilities expand as your portfolio grows.

THE SHAPE
Selecting a Basic Shape

Knit fabric lends itself to a great variety of garment shapes. These shapes are formed by the addition or subtraction of stitches—through increasing, decreasing, casting on, binding off, and working short rows. Any basic shape can be considered for a sweater, a jacket, or a coat. All styles can be constructed as pullovers or cardigans. Whatever your choice, you can dress it up or down with your choices of yarn, stitches, and detailing.

Your selection may be made because a particular silhouette is currently in fashion, or because it enhances a particular person's body shape, or because it's comfortable (raglans and dolmans often rate high marks here). Sometimes a specific style will work best for an important design element—for example, you may want to carry a vertical sleeve panel design across the shoulders, so a saddle band will be appealing.

At times tradition may help you determine a sweater's final form. Two simple shapes have long histories and remain popular today. Fishermen's sweaters from many parts of the world fall into the *square* or *"T"* styling, while Scandinavian and Icelandic knits utilize *round yoke* shaping. These sweater shapes endure because they work well for the presenta-

tion of color and stitch patterns and are comfortable to wear. We'll talk more about traditional sweater design later, and you'll find these shapes in our charting instructions.

Perhaps you want to update a classic silhouette with ideas of your own. Or you may want to try something you once felt was beyond your capabilities but which you are now ready to explore.

If a style for your first sweater isn't already firmly planted in your mind, we'd like to offer a suggestion. We've met several knitters who limit their charting to Ts and dolmans for only one reason— they're afraid to tackle a sleeve cap. In fact, a sleeve cap is not difficult to design, but you won't believe us until you do it yourself. So if you are hesitant to chart a set-in cap, approach this challenge early. Set yourself the goal of conquering the set-in styles—start with the standard set-in cap and move on to the gathered or pleated version. We will go into great detail on the whys and hows of getting sleeve caps to work when the time comes—we've developed a formula for charting which works, even for machine knitters.*

Facing this (or any other) challenge head-on will allow you much greater design freedom as your experience grows. Be brave! Don't hold back your visions.

---

*Hand knitters have a luxury unavailable to machine knitters—they can measure a sleeve cap against the yoke as the work progresses. Machine knitters must chart their caps completely before they knit them, and can't measure the fabric until it is finished. Our formula allows both hand and machine knitters to chart the numbers before they cast on.

CIRCULAR-KNIT BODY, FLAT-KNIT YOKE

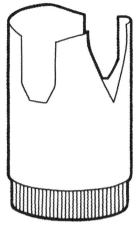

FLAT-KNIT BODY AND YOKE

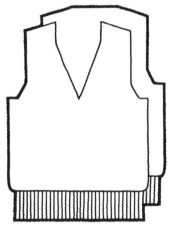

Flat or Round?

Sweaters can be knit in one of two ways: *in the round* (also known as *circular knitting*) or *in rows* (*flat knitting*). Each knitter develops a preference for one of these methods, but as a designer you will become more sensitive to the strengths and weaknesses of each approach. You'll find yourself choosing the method which best meets a given sweater's requirements.

A garment is knit in the round on a circular needle, or on four or five double-pointed needles. The right side of the garment always faces the knitter; the work is not turned at the end of each round. This means that in stockinette fabric, no stitch is purled; all are knit. The main benefit of this method is that seams can be eliminated. A garment can be knit entirely in one piece, and some knitters say they can knit much faster when they work in the round. However, styling options are limited, especially at the yoke, which in our terminology means the area between the shaping of the armholes and the shoulders.

Flat knitting is worked on two straight needles, or back-and-forth on a circular needle. The work is turned at the end of each row, so the knitter works alternately from the right and wrong sides of the fabric. In stockinette fabric, equal numbers of stitches are knit and purled, worked in alternating rows of all-knit and all-purl. Most flat-knit sweaters have a back section, a front section (or two half-fronts, for a cardigan), and two sleeves. These are completed and joined with seams, and then the finishing touches are added. The styling options are immeasurably increased over those available in circular knitting.

If you presently knit from patterns printed in magazines, booklets, or most books, you are probably accustomed to working flat. And that's how our step-by-step guidelines are written. Knitters who are familiar with circular knitting and who prefer to work portions of their garments in the round can easily adapt our instructions by eliminating the seam stitches.

You're in charge now!

THE FABRIC

Many elements contribute to the look and feel of the fabric you will make for your sweater. These include the color and texture of both yarn and fabric, the use of stitches and knit-in patterns, and the draping or insulating qualities of the fibers you choose. As you think about your garment's design, you will need to decide what type of fabric will work best.

In this section we'll talk about different fibers, and the sizes and types of yarns, as well as stitch and color patterning. We'll also give some general guidelines for making your yarn and pattern choices work with the basic shape you've chosen.

Wherever knit fabric is concerned, the subject of gauge comes up. We're pretty sure you're familiar with the idea. If not, we'll introduce you. Gauge is the key to successful knit fabric.

Gauge refers to the number of stitches in a horizontal inch of your fabric (*stitch count*) and the number of rows of stitches in a vertical inch of your fabric (*row count*). As a general rule, a fine yarn will have many stitches and rows per inch, while a bulky yarn will have few stitches and rows per inch.

Your gauge will be affected by the size and type of your yarn, the stitch pattern you choose, the composition and shape of your needles, and your knitting "touch." Gauge is as individual as finger-prints, and determining an accurate gauge is essential to proper fit whether you work from commercial patterns or from your own designs.

As you plan your fabric, you'll get a lot of information from your gauge swatch, or sample piece—which must be worked by you, on *your needles* (the actual ones you'll be using for your sweater), and with *your yarn*.

The Test Swatch: Determining Your Gauge

To establish your gauge, knit a test swatch in the stitch pattern and on the needle size you intend to use. If you plan to use stockinette stitch, knit your swatch in stockinette. If you'll be using a lace, a slip-stitch pattern, color-stranding, or cables, work your swatch in that pattern. A miscalculation of even a quarter-stitch per inch can throw off the finished size of a sweater substantially, so make your gauge swatches at least 5″ square. On your first swatch you may have to guess how many stitches you'll need, so cast on more than you think necessary, rather than less.

To determine the best needle size for the yarn you have chosen, begin with a swatch worked on the size recommended on the yarn wrapper. Then knit two more swatches, one on needles a size larger and one on needles a size smaller. Larger needles will give you a looser, softer fabric, while smaller needles will make tighter stitches and a firmer fabric.

Block the swatch (see "How Tos") to get a sense of the true hand (drape and feel) of the fabric. If your finished garment will be laundered by machine, run your swatch through cycles of your washer and/or dryer. If fabric shrinkage occurs, you will need to take that into account in your calculations.

Decide which swatch you like best. Since you're designing your own sweater, you don't have to match a specific gauge and have the option of selecting the tension you prefer. The feel of the fabric can be your guide.

Once you have chosen the best swatch, measure the number of stitches and rows per inch accurately. Use straight pins to mark off 4″, both vertically and horizontally. Count the number of stitches in 4″, and the number of rows in 4″. Divide each result by four. Include any fractions in your calculations. For example, if your swatch has 21½ stitches in 4″, you will find that $21.5 \div 4 = 5.37$. Your stitch gauge is 5.37 stitches per inch. Treat the row count in the same way.

If your body stitch pattern is complex, work a separate swatch in stockinette stitch. Block and measure it, as you did the pattern swatch, and use the stockinette gauge for charting ribbing or other borders.

Some special applications of swatches will be explained when we get down to serious charting. For clarity, and because these are fairly standard measurements for good fabrics made with knitting-worsted-weight yarns, our examples will use a stitch gauge of *5 stitches per inch* and a row gauge of *6 rows per inch*.

The importance of measuring gauge accurately is shown by this chart. Notice how a difference of even one stitch per inch affects the fabric width. While the variation is greatest in coarse gauges (thicker yarns), a miscalculation in the fine gauges (delicate yarns) can also affect your sweater's finished size.

100 STITCHES ON NEEDLE

Stitch Gauge (stitches per inch)	Fabric Width (in inches)
2	50
3	33.3
4	25
5	20
6	16.6
7	14.4
8	12.5
9	11.1
10	10

Stitch Patterns

Many wonderful books are available which contain collections of stitch patterns—creative ribbings and borders, textured knit/purl combinations, bold cables, delicate laces, multicolor mixes. Other books examine the history and stitches associated with individual geographic areas—there are books on Guernsey, Aran, Shetland, Fair Isle, Spanish, and other knitting traditions.

Books of both sorts are invaluable sources of information and inspiration, and can be readily obtained through libraries, yarn shops, book stores, and mail-order sources. Several stitch-pattern resources should be in every knitter's personal library.

It is not our intention to explore an area so thoroughly covered by other authors, but we would like to add a few general comments that may relate to your designing, charting, and knitting.

Borders on knitwear serve a functional as well as a decorative purpose. They prevent the edges of a garment from curling, and both strengthen and visually finish these edges. A fabric made of all knit stitches (stockinette) tends to curl forward at its lower edge and backward at the sides. A fabric made of all purl stitches (reverse stockinette) tends to curl backward at the lower edge and forward at the sides. For this reason, borders are worked in a combination of knit and purl stitches, so the curling tendencies cancel each other out and the edges lie flat.

Two of the most popular borders are 1/1 and 2/2 ribbing. Other ribbings can also be selected, but many are not as elastic as these familiar, traditional ribs. Where elasticity is not a factor, borders are commonly worked in seed, double seed, moss, and garter stitches. Lace edgings can be used for hems, cuffs, and necklines of dressy sweaters.

Brocade knitting, made by combining knit and purl stitches in more complex patterns, can result in lovely embossed symbols and designs. This type of patterning has been made popular by Guernsey-style fishermen's sweaters. The groupings of knit and purl stitches form herringbones, checkerboards, chevrons, and diamonds. The purl-stitch shapes stand higher than the knit-stitch shapes, producing both pattern and texture.

The stitch and row counts remain similar to those in stockinette stitch for your yarn, needles, and personal knitting tension—about 5 stitches and 6–7 rows per inch for worsted-weight wool. Brocade designs are suited to all weights of yarn, and display their texture best when

STABLE STITCHES FOR BORDERS

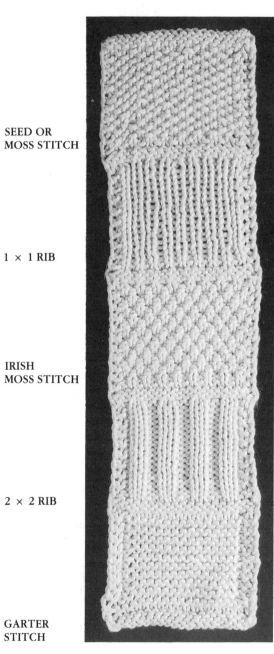

SEED OR
MOSS STITCH

1 × 1 RIB

IRISH
MOSS STITCH

2 × 2 RIB

GARTER
STITCH

BROCADE KNITTING

*Patterns are formed by combinations of knit
and purl stitches.*

DESIGNING WITH CABLES

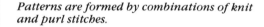

*One cable can add interest to an otherwise
simple garment.*

worked in smooth yarns of uniform
color.

You'll find brocade patterns in books
on Guernsey knitting and elsewhere, but
be creative in your search for ideas. An
often-overlooked source of designs can be
found in patterns for Fair Isle and Icelandic sweaters. These sweaters depend
on color patterns, rather than texture, but
the snowflakes, stars, hearts, crosses,
animals, and other figures can frequently
be worked very nicely in one-color
brocade. Use knit stitches in place of the
first color, purls in place of the second
color, and experiment.

The **Brioche** patterns include the
familiar Fisherman's Rib; they are worked
by knitting at regular intervals into the
center of a stitch on the row below the
one being worked. (When you insert the

right-hand needle through the center of
the stitch in the preceding row, below the
stitch which would ordinarily be knit
next, both stitches are knit at the same
time.) Brioche stitches are easy to work,
but can be tricky to unravel.

The stitch gauge for a brioche pattern
is much looser than that of stockinette
worked with the same yarn and needles.
The row gauge, on the other hand, is
compressed because the stitches from two
rows are regularly knit together. Brioche
patterns require more yarn per square
inch of fabric than does plain stockinette.

From simple eyelets to complex
designs, **Lace** patterns result in some of
the loveliest knit fabrics imaginable. Some
lace patterns lend themselves to use over
an entire sweater, while others work best
as elegant panels. Lace is beautifully

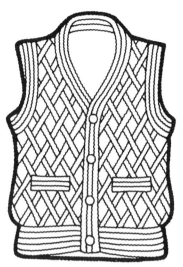

The entire fabric can be composed of cable repeats.

Portions of cables can travel across the fabric, and cables can interact to form more complex designs.

Different cables can be worked in panels across a garment, as in fishermen's knits.

suited to dressy women's sweaters, and to infants' and children's wear. However, don't let these suggestions limit your imagination.

Knitted lace is made by combining decreases and yarn-overs. To yarn-over, the working yarn is wrapped around the right-hand needle between stitches, making an extra loop in the row. On the next row, this loop is worked as if it were a stitch, creating a small, decorative hole in the fabric. The placement of the holes and the angles of the decreases used to eliminate the resulting extra stitches are the basis for lace designs.

The size of the holes is critical to the pattern, and depends on the yarn and needles you select. If the needles are too small, the holes will close and the airiness of the lace will be lost. If the yarn is too

textured or fuzzy, the effect will be the same. Fine, smooth yarns best suit the delicacy of lace patterns.

A lace fabric requires less yarn than a comparable stockinette fabric; how much less depends on the openness of the work.

A **Cable** is made by crossing a stitch or group of stitches over or under its neighbor(s)—a simple procedure, if you haven't tried it yet. From a technical standpoint, it's no more difficult to knit an Aran sweater, full of intricate cables, than it is to knit a single simple cable. The complexity in an Aran design lies in keeping track of panels and rows—and making each cross at the right time.

Cables can be used by the designer in a variety of ways.

1. One cable, or a small group of cables, can add visual and textural interest to an otherwise simple garment.
2. The entire fabric can be worked with repeats of a single cable design; honeycomb, lattices, and basket cables are good examples of possible all-over patterns.
3. Portions of cables can travel across the fabric.
4. Neighboring cables can meet to form entirely new designs; you can plan these cable "road maps" on graph paper.
5. Different panels can be combined across a garment, in the manner made familiar through fishermen's knits from the Aran Isles.

While a single cable will not slow you down much, heavily cabled sweaters can be time-consuming. Not only does the process of slipping stitches to a cable needle involve an additional step, the fabric is drawn together by the crossing stitches and thus requires about 20 percent more stitches (and yarn) than the same amount of fabric worked in stockinette. While the result is worth the effort, consider this fact if you are planning a quick or inexpensive gift!

Cables are the most dramatically sculptured of stitch patterns and look their best when made of smooth yarns in light colors. The smooth yarns don't distract from the cabling, and light colors display the shadows made by the stitches and enhance the depth of the design.

Worked in thick yarns, cabled fabric is firm, heavy, and ideal for layered outerwear for all ages. In finer, more delicate yarns, intricate cables can embellish a dressier garment.

Color Patterns

The easiest way to introduce color into your fabric is with horizontal **Stripes**. There are tricks which will make the working of different types of stripes easy for you.

When you are working with two or three colors and changing colors frequently, it may be simplest to carry the extra yarns up along the side edge, instead of breaking off and beginning again with each color change. Interlock the unused yarns with the working yarn at the end of every two rows, so you won't end up with long, loose strands at the seams. Carrying too many yarns along the edge can be bothersome; you may choose to break off the less essential color(s).

Stripes with an odd number of rows are easy to work on circular needles, whether you're knitting in the round or flat. When knitting in the round, simply use each color for as many rounds as you choose and then change colors. When knitting flat, work back and forth on a circular needle. After working with color A, slide your fabric back to the beginning of the row and work color B.

For example, to work one-row stripes in stockinette stitch, begin by working a knit row with A, then slide the fabric back along the needle, and work another knit row with B. Now both colors are at the same edge—the "end" of both rows just worked. Turn your work, as if you were on straight needles. Purl a row with A, slide the fabric back along the needle, and purl a row with B. This method of working stripes is useful if you need to blend yarn in two closely related dyelots, or if you want to avoid a piebald effect when working with a variegated yarn.

Colored stripes can be accented or supplemented by textured stripes. Two-row stripes in garter stitch create a purl ridge when worked across a stockinette fabric. This can be an effective way to work in a yarn of a different thickness, or to showcase a highly textured yarn. Stripes worked in reverse stockinette stitch in a different color from the main fabric give an interesting effect; the interlocking of the purls breaks up the hard line of the color change, and gives the fabric a woven appearance.

How much yarn do you need for each color in a striped fabric? Calculate the percentage of the garment which will be knit in each color. You can determine the number of square inches of fabric to be knit in each color by multiplying the width of a stripe by its depth, and then adding up the number of stripes in that color.

There's a delightful method of color knitting which combines stripes and slip stitches to create **Slip-Stitch Patterns**. When you work certain stitches and slip others, the colors of the stripes are broken up and mingled. Texture can be added by having the right side of the fabric contain both knits and purls.

Many color slip-stitch patterns can be used to incorporate yarns of varying thickness into a fabric. To succeed in using substantially thicker or thinner yarns in a slip-stitch pattern, limit the number of rows of the odd yarn (don't use more than one or two rows at a time), and maintain a fabric background of uniform thickness.

Mosaic knitting belongs to this category of color work. The elaborate geometric designs must be worked in yarns of consistent thickness. They display their pattern most clearly if the colors contrast enough for one to become the background and the other to appear as the pattern. Two colors are used throughout, worked in alternating two-row stripes. The fabric can be based on either stockinette or garter stitch.

Color slip-stitch fabric takes more yarn than a comparable stockinette fabric, because the fabric draws together slightly when the stitches are slipped. To determine yarn requirements, pay close attention to how much yarn you use in your swatch. Weigh your sample if you need to, and calculate the percentage of each color used in the fabric.

There are several ways to figure how much yarn you've used. The easiest is to measure a length or weight of yarn, knit it up, and then see how many square inches were produced. If you've already knit your swatch, you can measure it and then unravel to find out how many yards of yarn you used.

In deciding how much you'll need of different colors, you can either unravel and measure, or you can count the number of rows in each color and translate to percentages. For example, in mosaic knitting you'll use two colors and each will contribute half of the yardage. As another example, a pattern with a repeat containing two rows of one color and three rows of the second color will require two-fifths of the first color (40 percent) and three-fifths of the second (60 percent).

Stranded-Color Knitting goes by many names—Fair Isle, Jacquard, and Nordic are a few—but the technique is always the same. Unlike slip-stitch knitting, every stitch is worked on every row. Where slip-stitch patterns can contain both knit and purl stitches, stranded-color knitting is worked entirely in stockinette stitch. All of the colors which will appear in a row are carried, or stranded, along the wrong side of the fabric. Yarns are

picked up and used in turn, as their colors are called for in the design.

Working instructions generally come in the form of a graph. The design can be shown in colors, or by symbols which designate the colors. When you plan a stranded-color design, it's easiest to limit the length of the unused strands on the back to between ½″ and ¾″, so they won't be snagged when the garment is pulled on. If your design calls for longer floats, you will need to weave in the loose strands on the back side as you knit.

Stranded-color work produces a thick fabric, because the carried yarns form a second layer. A garment knit entirely in a color-stranded pattern requires nearly twice as much yarn as the same garment knit in plain stockinette. A sweater worked in this technique will be warm—perhaps too warm, if worked in a chunky yarn.

The gauge of a color-stranded design is often different from that of a comparable stockinette, one-color fabric. When you plan to combine single-color stockinette and color patterns, work a swatch in each type of fabric. You may need to change needles in order to maintain an even tension throughout the garment.

Tapestry Color Knitting, often called intarsia, enables the knitter to work blocks of a number of colors into a garment without carrying the strands across the rows. In intarsia, each color of yarn is worked back and forth only in its own section.

Each color is carried on its own bobbin, and the fabric is traditionally worked in stockinette stitch. At the points of color change, the adjacent yarns are interlocked to prevent holes from forming in the fabric. The designs, like those for stranded-color knitting, are planned on graph paper. (See "Picture Knitting" for information on graphing your own designs.)

Because the yarn is carried to the left edge of the fabric on the first row of knitting, and needs to return from that point on the second row, tapestry color changes don't work well for knitting in the round. In order to knit a tapestry design on circular needles, you would have to cut and rejoin the yarn on each round—something most knitters like to avoid.

Figure the amount of each color as you would for stripes, by calculating its percentage of the total garment.

Argyle knitting belongs in this category of color work. Argyle patterns have diamond shapes, interwoven with a diagonal grid. They're challenging, and can be fun to work not only because of the color combinations (which are infinite), but because you can vary the shapes of the diamonds. If you change the diamond shape on every row (adding one stitch to each side of every other diamond, and subtracting one stitch from each side of its neighbors), you'll get a flatter, more horizontal set of diamonds. If you change the diamond shape on every other row, you'll get a taller, more vertical set of diamonds.

Getting Patterns to Work Out on a Garment

To design effectively with stitch patterns, you will need a clear understanding of **Multiples and Repeats**. These terms are used in written instructions and in stitch-pattern collections, and they relate to the number of stitches needed to work a particular pattern stitch. They mean almost—but not quite—the same thing. If you understand the basic idea, you'll be able to turn cartwheels with any pattern you want to use.

Most stitch-pattern dictionaries list the number of stitches required for the pattern at the beginning of the written instructions. You'll see something like, "Multiple of 7 plus 2." The repeat for a pattern with this notation is seven stitches; this is the number of stitches needed to work one unit of the design. The "plus 2" indicates extra stitches needed to balance the pattern and keep it symmetrical. (For example, a pattern of P2, K2, P1, K2 repeated will not be completely balanced at the end of the row unless a final two stitches are worked P2.)

You can work the pattern in our example if you have on your needle any multiple of seven stitches, plus the two extras.

> 51 stitches will work:
> $(7 \times 7) = 49 + 2 = 51$
> 79 stitches will work:
> $(7 \times 11) = 77 + 2 = 79$

and so forth. The multiple and plus (balancing stitch) numbers remain the same, no matter how many repeats you use in your garment.

Graphed instructions will clearly bracket, or otherwise mark, the repeat. When you want to work a stitch pattern from a magazine or leaflet which does not designate the repeat, you can find it by totalling the number of stitches between the asterisks or parentheses. Count the additional stitches outside the repeat in order to find out how many stitches are required to balance the pattern.

For more on the nuts and bolts of making stitch repeats work with your sweater design, see "The Test Swatch Revisited."

There are many ways of **Combining Stitch Patterns** within a garment. Most garments utilize at least two stitch patterns—one for the border and another for the body.

You can choose to combine any of the different types of stitches. Patterns from the same general category are often worked. You may want to use panels of cables, a selection of brocade stitches, or a handful of complementary lace patterns. You can also cross these categorical boundaries with great success, and use cables with lace, cables with brocade patterns, or stockinette with just about anything.

How you arrange the stitches is also open to your imagination. You can make panels with different stitches running horizontally, or you can place them vertically. You can make a patchwork effect with squares, rectangles, or triangles. Or you can work half of a sweater in one stitch, and the rest in another.

Regardless of how you plan to combine different patterns, one rule of thumb applies. Make a test swatch for each stitch pattern, and pay very careful attention to the stitch and row gauges.

If your swatches do not block to the same gauge, you will have to compensate when you chart your sweater. If the stitch gauges vary, you will have to cast on a different number of stitches for each pattern in order to obtain similar widths. If the row gauges are different you will need to keep your fabric length constant by working short rows in the section which requires more rows per inch. If you place different patterns above and below each other, you can decide to increase or decrease stitches or to change the size of your needles in order to keep the garment width constant.

These adjustments take place in predictable ways, at regular intervals. When you understand stitch and row gauge, and have your sample swatches in hand, you will be able to combine stitches liberally, and with impeccable results.

When you plan to work the body of a garment in a pattern stitch, you may also have to adjust the number of stitches you cast on for the border. The ribbing or border can be based on the stitch gauge of your stockinette swatch, or you can work a swatch of the border pattern on appropriately sized needles. Either method will help you determine whether you need to increase or decrease stitches between the border and body stitch patterns.

You'll also need to check how your stitch patterns work with your **Garment Shaping**. Will a pattern repeat work with the charted numbers? In particular, what will occur at the seam edges? Will you have only a partial lace repeat, or a portion of a cable, at the edges of the yoke after the armhole or neckline shaping is complete?

If you have a pattern on a cardigan back and want to repeat the pattern on the front sections, what will happen at the center, where the button and buttonhole bands will be worked? Will the bands crop off a portion of a critical design element?

We can't emphasize enough how important it is to plan ahead! A little forethought can prevent a lot of frustration. Consider the way that simple adjustments can be made to work in your favor. Will an additional stitch or two solve a problem without affecting the garment's size to any degree? Will a change in needle size—and hence gauge—help? Will different placement of a stitch pattern, or the use of a different but similar pattern, eliminate the difficulty?

As you explore the options for pattern placement, consider what design role, if any, a pattern can play within garment shaping. For instance, you can carry a lace panel or cable along the edge of a raglan yoke or sleeve or of a V neckline by working the decreases to the inside of the pattern edge, instead of at the seam edge.

Can you simplify the garment shaping to work better with your pattern stitch? Set-in armholes and sleeve caps have curves, which can cause difficulty when you need to decrease a complicated stitch pattern. You may want to select either the basic or modified T shaping or the semi-raglan, all of which have angular lines.

As you contemplate the fine points of your design, you will discover that creating a sweater is an organic process. Each decision affects the others—that's part of the challenge, and the pleasure.

Sometimes you'll want to work a sweater with **Stitch Patterns Worked in Both Round and Row Knitting**—perhaps making the body in the round, then dividing stitches and working the yoke sections in rows. There are minor details in charting the garment's shape which you'll need to keep track of when using both methods in the same garment; we'll discuss these when we get to charting. And when you want to use the same pattern stitches with both methods, you'll need to think ahead about getting the pattern stitch to work both ways.

Most written or charted pattern stitches, for either texture or color patterns, can be used with either circular knitting or flat knitting. There are some exceptions—tapestry or intarsia charts are an outstanding example—but you'll learn to spot them, partly through trial and error on your swatches. Making a gauge or sample swatch of the stitch you're considering will teach you a lot about converting pattern stitches.

First, you need to be familiar with your pattern stitch. Your approach to converting from round to flat or vice versa will depend on whether you're working from written instructions or a chart.

Although a small number of *written instructions* for stitch patterns ask that you work in rounds, most stitch instructions are for flat knitting. The majority of

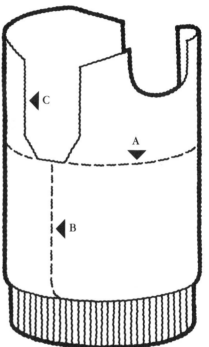

In order to combine these types of knitting successfully, you will need to plan the start of your armhole shaping so that complex pattern maneuvers (like cable crossings) occur on right-side rows (a), to use markers for imaginary "side seams" (b), and to remember that you will probably need to include extra seam stitches at the sides of the yoke (c).

patterns are worked over an even number of rows, and the even-numbered rows are planned to fall on the wrong side of the fabric. Since circular knitting keeps you on the right side of your fabric at all times, these wrong-side rows need to be reversed—both in the *direction* the pattern is read (right to left, instead of left to right) and in the *way* the stitches are worked (knits become purls, and purls become knits). It's not as hard as it sounds. Practice—and writing out a revised set of directions—will help you keep it straight.

Charted designs for texture patterns and for color patterns other than intarsia are a little easier for round than for flat knitting. If you work from a chart in flat knitting, you will work from right to left on the odd-numbered rows and from left to right on the even-numbered rows. If you're familiar with the symbols for knits and purls and accustomed to reading charts, you'll cope with changing the type of stitch on each row with ease. When you work from a chart in round knitting, you will always read from right to left across one line of the chart for each round.

Charts for intarsia designs cannot be worked in the round, but can be used for the parts of your combined-approach sweater which are worked flat, for instance the yoke and possibly the sleeves.

Again, take care when you *plan the placement* of your pattern repeats. Chart your garment body flat, but without the two extra seam stitches which you will normally add to pieces that will be worked flat. Lay out your pattern based on the required number of stitches. When you knit the body on the circular needle,

ADAPTING PATTERNS TO CIRCULAR KNITTING

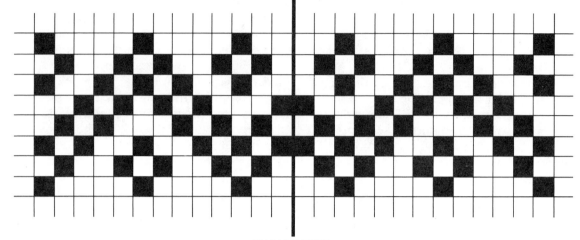

SEAM MARKER

When you are working a pattern with a regular repeat and the stitches on either side of the imaginary "seam" markers are partial repeats, these stitches must appear as mirror images of each other.

place stitch markers to separate the back from the front. When you are working a pattern with a regular repeat and the stitches on either side of one of these markers are partial repeats of your pattern, they must appear as mirror images of each other.

Partial repeats of some patterns may be difficult to work. (You'll find this in both circular and flat knitting, and when you shape any piece.) You may choose to knit any extra stitches in stockinette, or in a pattern stitch which is simpler than your main pattern, but compatible with it.

Watch your gauge carefully, since it will very likely change when you move from flat to circular knitting. Work a swatch in each method, so you'll be sure that the stitch gauge will be consistent throughout the garment. Most knitters will find their knitting is slightly looser when worked flat, so you may need to use needles one or two sizes smaller in the flat section than you use for the circular work.

If you plan to work the body on a circular needle and the sleeves on double-pointed needles, be sure that your needles are of the same size and brand, or prepare to adjust your gauge again. Needles made by different companies are not always exactly equivalent and could produce slightly different gauges.

The easiest way to see if your needles are identical in size is to punch one needle through a piece of paper, then stick the second needle through the same hole. Does the second needle feel about the same as the first did, or looser? If it felt the same, continue your test. Put the first needle back in the hole; does its fit feel looser than it did a moment ago?

Choosing Yarn

Today's yarn shops are wonderlands of colors, textures, and fibers. No longer is the knitter limited to basic sport and worsted weights in a small selection of hues. The variety is extensive—and perhaps confusing.

Making the right choice can seem overwhelming until you understand what's available and how your decision will affect the way the garment looks and feels. While many yarns may be right for your project, just as many may be wrong and may leave you with a final product which is less than satisfactory. When you think about yarn choices, you'll have questions like:

Which yarns can withstand heavy wear, and which need gentle treatment? What kind of care is required for the fiber? Is warmth important? Which yarns are unsafe for infants' wear? Which will display specific stitch patterns to their best advantage?

Taking time to learn about yarns and how they can affect your design will help you make an intelligent final decision.

Yarn is available in a wide range of thicknesses. We've broken down the **Sizes of Yarn** into three broad categories—fine, medium, and heavy—and will talk about the general characteristics of each.

Fine yarns are generally worked on small needles, with many stitches per inch. Thin yarns produce thin fabrics. They are usually used for infants' garments, lightweight sweaters, and dresses. Because of the fine gauge, actual knitting will take longer than when you use thicker yarns. If you have the same fiber spun in two weights of yarn, the finer yarn will produce a fabric which will drape better, will accept greater extremes of gathering, and will allow you to make smaller pleats.

The finer the yarn, the more detail you can get, in both picture knits and stitch patterns. With fine yarn, more repeats of color patterns or textured bands (such as cables) can be worked across a given width of fabric. Lace is displayed to best advantage in fine yarns.

If you want to work with fine yarns, look for fingering weight in handknitting yarns; this is a broad term for many yarns which are finer-than-average. Fine—and even finer—yarns are also available on cones for both machine knitters and weavers.

Medium yarns include the familiar sport and worsted weights. This group of yarns is very versatile, and is used to make knitwear for all ages. Sport yarns are finer than worsteds; they are com-

monly found in children's sweaters, vests, indoor garments, summer-weight garments, and sweater dresses. Worsted-weight yarns produce heavier versions of the same items. Both of these weights are popular for cabled sweaters, like Arans, and can be used for lace, although much of the daintiness of a lace pattern will be lost in a worsted-weight yarn.

Fabrics made with medium yarns will not drape as well as those made with fine yarns, and gathers won't be as effective, but pleats remain an excellent option. Think in terms of tailored shapes as you design.

Heavy yarns, also called bulky or chunky, work best in jackets, coats, heavy sweaters, and vests. These yarns knit up quickly—a good thing to know if you're in a hurry.

The fabric will be firmer than one made in a lighter-weight yarn. Gathering and delicate draping become infeasible, but pleats are still possible. However, you'll need to consider the thickness of the fabric in the pleated sections—there will be three layers of fabric at those points.

Cables work well, but extensive cable work can make a very heavy fabric—maybe too heavy for the garment's intended use. You can produce color pictures and patterns in heavy yarn, but don't try to achieve a lot of detail. Remember that if you're stranding colors across the back, your sweater will be twice as heavy as a comparable garment in stockinette. Try combinations of knit and purl stitches—they can add texture when you're working in a plain yarn, without increasing the fabric's bulk.

WORKING WITH DIFFERENT WEIGHTS OF YARNS

Yarn Thickness	Recommended Needle Size (American)	Stitch Gauge (stitches/inch)
FINE		
Very fine	0–2	9–10
Fingering	2–4	7–8
MEDIUM		
Sport	4–6	6
Worsted	6–8	5
HEAVY		
Bulky, Chunky	8–10	3½–4
Super-bulky, Extra-bulky, Extra-chunky	10–15	1½–3

These categories are not technical terms; they imply an approximate weight of yarn. The thicknesses and number of yards per pound of yarns within each category will vary.

Individual **Fibers** for knitting yarns come from one of three sources: animal, vegetable, and chemical. The animal and vegetable fibers are commonly referred to as *natural fibers* and the chemical products are called *synthetics.* Animal fibers are also called *protein* fibers and vegetable fibers are called *cellulose* fibers, after their primary chemical components.

ANIMAL FIBERS are grown on or produced by specific animals. As a group, they are strong, elastic, insulative, and nonflammable.

Wool, shorn from sheep, has been used in knitwear for over two thousand years. It remains very popular for many reasons. Where warmth, strength, and durability are required, it is the fiber of choice. Each wool fiber has *crimp,* a wavy formation, which gives the wool yarn resilience and high bulk—it's fluffy.

Wool can absorb up to 30 percent of its weight in moisture without feeling damp, and retains its insulating qualities even when wet. It resists wrinkling, retains its shape well, and withstands hard wear. It takes dyes well—and even dark colors are usually colorfast. Wool is flame-resistant; the fiber will sizzle and quit burning when it is removed from the source of ignition, so it can be safer for children (and adults) than other fibers. Because each animal produces a relatively large amount of fiber, and because there are lots of sheep in the world, wool is less expensive than other animal fibers.

Some wools are softer than others. The fiber comes in a wide range of qualities, from coarse rug wool, at the low end of the scale, to the wools which are used for hand knitting, in the middle to upper range. Soft and silky *Merino* wool is the finest grade available, a fact reflected in its relatively higher cost. *Lambswool,* from the first shearing of animals up to seven months old, is also very soft and fine. Both of these types are well suited for use in baby clothes and in sweaters to be worn close to the skin.

Wool is sometimes reprocessed, but what's called *virgin wool* has never been used before, except by the sheep. Nearly all knitting yarns are virgin wool. Reprocessed wool is occasionally available for knitting, but it is harsher than and not as strong as virgin wool. Nylon is usually added to reprocessed wool to give it strength.

Wool can be spun by two methods, *worsted* and *woolen.* Worsted yarn is made from the longest strands of combed fleece, and is especially smooth and strong. Woolen yarn is spun from a mixture of long and short fibers; it is warmer and has greater texture, but is not as strong.

Mohair is the long-stapled hair of the Angora goat (what we call *angora* fiber comes from rabbits) and is graded by the age of the animal and quality of the fiber. *Kid* mohair, from young animals, is finer than fiber produced by adult goats.

While mohair is similar to wool in its warmth, resilience, lightness, and durability, it has more sheen and is slightly stronger. It takes dyes more brilliantly, so it's usually available in a wide range of vibrant colors. It is often brushed, and frequently blended with wool and nylon. (Brushed mohair should not be used for infants' garments; children can choke on the fine hairs.) Mohair is a good choice for big, heavy garments—like coats and jackets—since it can be spun into a high-bulk yarn, one that is warm but relatively lightweight.

Alpaca comes from members of the South American camel family who live at high altitudes in the Andes Mountains. Alpacas produce long-stapled hair which is shorn every other year. *Suri* alpaca resembles mohair, while *huayaco* alpaca is closer to wool in texture. Alpaca fiber is soft and silky. It drapes better than wool because it has less crimp—and also, as a result, less resilience. It is fairly warm and dense, but not appropriate for large garments because it is a heavy fiber and would stretch out of shape easily. Alpaca comes in a wide range of natural colors, including a true black, but the limited quantities make it expensive.

Cashmere is the soft, downy under-coat of the Kashmir goat. The down is gathered after the spring shedding, or can be harvested by combing. Cashmere is extremely fine and soft to the touch, but it is also very warm. The fiber is not as strong as wool, and therefore not as hard-wearing. Since the Kashmir goat is smaller than the Angora goat and yields only one-quarter pound of down per year, cash-mere yarn is more expensive than either wool or mohair. Cashmere is often com-bined with wool—the combination is not as soft as pure cashmere, but it is less expensive and stronger.

Camel, like cashmere, refers to the down of the animal and not the guard hairs. The fine fibers from the Bactrian camel are gathered after shedding. They are soft and lightweight, but have good insulative qualities so fabrics made from them are warm. Camel down can be blended with wool, for added strength and durability. The name camel has become synonymous with the color of the fibers, which ranges from light tan to dark brown.

Angora is the hair of the Angora rab-bit. The fibers are very soft, fine, silky, and warm. Fabrics made from angora drape well. Angora is expensive, because each animal produces a relatively small amount of fiber, so it is most often found in blends. Angora yarns are usually avail-able in a wide range of natural and dyed colors. They are not appropriate for use in infants' garments, because the fine hairs can cause choking.

Commercially processed angora has a furlike appearance and the yarns fre-quently shed small amounts of fiber. If you refrigerate your yarn before knitting, you can cut down on the fly-away fuzzies. While handspun yarn made from shorn (cut) angora also sheds, handspun yarn from hand-plucked fibers doesn't have this tendency.

Silk is a filament excreted by the silkworm, a caterpillar, when it builds its cocoon. The quality and appearance of silk are directly related to the species of silkworm, its diet, and the fiber-har-vesting procedures.

Cultivated silkworms which are fed solely on mulberry leaves produce the finest silk available. This *Bombyx mori* silk is smoother, softer, whiter, and more lustrous than the tan *tussah* silk of the undomesticated Indian silkworm.

The finest silk is harvested by unwind-ing the cocoons, a procedure which re-quires great time and skill. Strands from several cocoons are wound together onto a reel to form a skein of the highest qual-ity silk—*reeled silk*. When the strand breaks, the remnant of the cocoon is combed to separate the longer, more lustrous fibers (which are spun into *combed silk*) from the shorter, textured ones. These irregular, sometimes knotted, fibers (known as noils) can be spun into a yarn that lacks the sheen associated with silk, but instead has a dry, cottony look. *Noil silk* is often used in textured or tweedlike yarns.

Silk is lightweight but warm, relatively strong, elastic, and crease-resistant. It is an excellent choice for designs which re-quire good draping qualities. The fiber sizzles when ignited and is self-extinguish-ing when removed from the flame.

As a group, **PLANT FIBERS** are not as elastic as animal fibers. This means yarns made from plant fibers won't resume their original shape after being stretched as quickly as will yarns made from animal fibers. For the knitter, this means you will want to work ribbing in a yarn of this type on needles three sizes smaller than those used for the body of a sweater. If the ribbing still stretches too much and doesn't spring back, loosely weave in elastic thread on the back side of the rib-bing, working a strand into every other row.

Cotton is the downy coating of seeds from cotton plants. The quality of cotton varies; fibers are graded by length, uni-formity, and fineness. The best quality, or longest staple length, comes from Egyptian and Sea Island cotton, followed by American (medium staple) and Indian (short staple) cotton.

Cotton is absorbent. It draws moisture away from the body and allows the wearer to feel cool. It blends well with other fibers, which can contribute addi-tional elasticity, handling ease, warmth, and/or texture. Blends with more than 60 percent cotton will feel like cotton, although their characteristics will be slightly modified by the fibers which have been blended in. *Mercerization* adds strength and luster to cotton yarns, and increases their ability to absorb dyes.

Since cotton by itself is not very elastic, heavy cotton garments may stretch out of shape. However, cotton is extremely durable and launders well—although if you're working with one of the poorer grades of cotton, test your swatch for possible shrinkage and take this into account when charting your garment.

Linen is the least elastic of the natural fibers. It is made from the stalks of flax plants. The highest quality linen yarns are called line; these are made from the longest fiber strands and are smooth and strong. Yarns made from shorter, broken fibers are called tow; they look and feel hairier. Linen for knitting is usually found blended with other fibers which make it easier to handle.

Linen is lustrous, cool, strong, and hard-wearing. It drapes well. Test your swatch for shrinkage, as you would for cotton. You'll discover that repeated washing of linen actually softens and improves the fabric.

Ramie comes from an Asiatic plant which is a member of the nettle family. It is softer than linen, finer, more lustrous, and very white. It is also absorbent and strong, with excellent mildew resistance. Both economic factors and new processing methods have made it more readily available in recent years.

Rayon fits somewhere between the plant and synthetic categories, but behaves more like a plant fiber so we'll tuck it in at this point. Rayon is made by pressing cellulose derived from wood pulp through very small holes and solidifying the result into filaments. These filaments are sometimes used as is, but are more often chopped into shorter lengths and spun into yarn. Rayon is considered the first "man-made" fiber, and is often used as a less expensive substitute for silk because of its sheen. With different processing, it can mimic wool. Rayon is often found in blends.

Rayon is strong, cool to the touch, has a fluid drape, and takes dyes very well. Like other fibers which originate from plant materials, it is not very elastic. It can stretch out of shape, especially when wet.

Acetate is also made from cellulose. It is processed from wood pulp or very short cotton fibers. It is lustrous, drapes well, takes dyes in brilliant colors, and shows up in blends. In a burn test, acetate behaves more like a synthetic fiber than rayon does. When ignited, it melts and burns quickly, and keeps burning after the flame is removed. It also disintegrates in acetone, or nail polish remover.

The SYNTHETIC FIBERS which will be spun into yarns are produced by pushing chemical solutions, most of which are petroleum-based, through perforated disks. This makes filaments, and the size of the perforations in the disk determines the thickness. These continuous strands are cut into shorter lengths before they are spun into yarn. Synthetic fibers are often blended with natural fibers, to strengthen them and to lessen the cost of the finished yarn.

Synthetics are hard-wearing, easy to care for, and moth-resistant. However, they lack the insulative qualities of animal fibers. As a group, synthetics are heat-sensitive and should never be exposed to the direct heat of an iron. When ignited, synthetics melt and drip, instead of burning with a flame.

The quality of synthetic yarns improves with each technological advance in their production methods. Synthetics are lighter and softer than they used to be, and have greater anti-static qualities.

Because they are inexpensive and easy to care for, they are popular choices for children's garments—though natural fibers still have greater fire-resisting abilities.

Acrylic is the major synthetic fiber, and appears in many forms. It can resemble wool or cotton, or be textured by brushing or through a special spinning process. It is strong, hard-wearing, and washes easily. It is warmer than other synthetics, but wool still tops the list for insulating qualities. Since acrylic fiber is very heat-sensitive, you'll need to be careful when you block or launder it, or it will lose its crimp and stretch permanently. You'll find all-acrylic yarns, as well as blends which include wool, mohair, or other natural fibers.

Nylon was the first completely synthetic fiber (rayon is made from reprocessed cellulose, a natural substance). Nylon fibers are often blended with wool or cotton, or a thin nylon binder thread is spun with plies of other fibers, to increase a yarn's strength. Nylon does not absorb moisture and is not good for insulation; this means that it can be cold in winter, but hot and clammy in the summer. On the other hand, it dries quickly and that can be a plus.

Polyester, a strong, resilient fiber, resists moisture, doesn't insulate well, and tends to pill. Despite these drawbacks, it is used (as nylon is) to add strength to yarns made primarily of natural fibers. The fiber is extremely heat-sensitive, and can be damaged by heat applied in blocking or laundering. Glitter yarns often have a polyester base, and, therefore, must be handled with care.

The **Cleaning Care** a finished garment will require is determined by your selection of yarn. The yarn label can help you figure out whether you're about to knit a *prima donna* garment which will demand special attention (and perhaps be worth every bit of it) or a workhorse which can tolerate daily use, as well as machine washing and drying.

As a rule, it's better to wash a knit garment than to dry clean it. Dry cleaning fluids are harsh and can never be completely rinsed out; the residual chemicals can yellow a garment. Dry cleaning can also remove the natural oils from animal fibers, reducing their insulative qualities. People who have dry cleaned their knitwear as a matter of course are often amazed by the new life and loft of the same garments after they have been washed.

Washing requires a little more time and care, but the results are worth the effort. Try out your intended laundering method on your swatch to see how it responds. Is the yarn colorfast? Does the fabric shrink or stretch? Is the fabric's hand—its softness, drape, and general feel—the same after washing? If you're satisfied with the results of your trial run, always use that method for the finished garment. If you're giving the sweater away, include cleaning instructions.

Let's examine how the different fiber types should generally be handled.

Animal fibers, including silk, can be hand washed in cool to lukewarm water (cold for angora) with a mild soap. Avoid detergents, as well as commercial products aimed at wool, which contain whiteners or bleach. Squeeze the fabric gently; do not wring it out or rub it. Wools in particular can felt and pill if they are rubbed together with any sort of vigor (some wools felt faster than others). Rinse the fabric well, then drain it and squeeze it gently to remove as much water as possible. Gently lay the garment out on a towel; roll the towel and the garment up together, and press the roll firmly to force the water from the garment into the towel.

If you're careful, most animal fibers (except cashmere, which is even more delicate than the finest wools) can also be machine washed. Fill the tub with cool water, then add the soap and mix it in thoroughly. Put in the sweater and run the machine on a gentle or knitwear cycle. You'll find that the spin cycle removes a lot of excess moisture, and you may even want to use a spin-only treatment on sweaters you wash by hand. It's often more effective at getting water out than the towel method.

When your garment is clean and you've removed as much water as possible, lay the sweater flat to dry on an air-permeable surface, away from direct sunlight. Towels are often recommended as a drying surface, but since air can't circulate underneath, garments take a long time to dry; if you live in a humid climate they can even mildew. Sweater-drying racks work well (find them at yarn shops, department stores, and through mail order), as do nonrusting window screens. You can also make your own racks with canvas stretcher frames (available at art supply stores) and rustproof fiberglass screening (from a hardware store). Make sure that the tacks or staples you use are

DRYING RACK

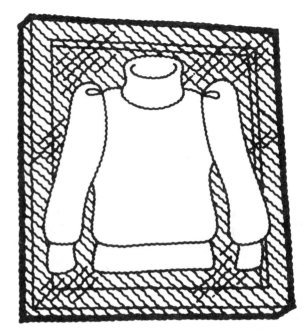

also rustproof, or else attach the screening at the back of the frame. Place your rack so air can circulate from underneath—over the bathtub works well.

Plant fibers can be hand or machine washed, in cool to warm water, following the guidelines given for animal fibers. With plant fibers you can safely use some detergents. However, when washing cotton avoid detergents which contain chlorine, because they may yellow the fabric.

Many fabrics made of plant fibers can also be machine dried, but check your swatch for heat shrinkage before you commit an entire garment to this treatment. Most plant fibers benefit from a short spin in the dryer, which will tighten the areas which stretch during wearing—especially the ribbing. But whether you let your sweater go in the dryer for just a quick half-drying or whether you fully dry it there depends on what your swatch tells you.

Begin with a test which dries the fabric completely. Carefully measure your swatch before you begin. Wash, dry thoroughly on medium heat (wash-and-wear setting), then recheck your measurements. If no shrinkage has occurred, you can safely machine wash and dry your sweater. If you do discover shrinkage, it will usually affect the length more than the width. There are two ways to deal with shrinkage when you plan your garment.

First, you can make your calculations to include a shrinkage allowance. Count the number of rows and stitches in your laundered swatch and use these to determine the width (in stitches) and length (in rows) of your garment. Know that the finishing process for the sweater will involve machine washing and machine drying, and that the fabric will achieve its final size after laundering. Then you will be free to clean it by machine washing and drying for the life of the garment.

Second, you can make another swatch and put it in the dryer only until it is *damp dry,* thus avoiding the serious shrinkage. Then lay it flat and let it finish drying on its own. When it's fully dry, remeasure the swatch. If it's the same size as when you started, you can arrange to launder the sweater by this method.

Synthetics can be hand or machine washed in warm water, in a manner similar to that used for animal fibers. A mild detergent may be used. Machine dry the fabric carefully, on the wash-and-wear setting. Hot dryers can damage synthetics; the "sweater which grew" was probably an acrylic knit left too long at a hot setting.

How a Yarn is Made has a lot to do with what your fabric will look like. Yarns can be smooth and one-color, or heavily textured and multicolored, or any place in between. As you choose yarns, you'll need to decide if the main visual interest of your fabric will be the stitch pattern or the yarn. If pattern and yarn compete, neither will win.

Complex stitch patterns usually show their details best when worked in relatively plain yarns. If you're spending the time to work cables and laces, the full effect may be lost if you choose a highly textured yarn.

On the other hand, plain stitches and simple patterns, such as stockinette, reverse stockinette, seed, and garter stitch, often display textured yarns to their best advantage. The abundance of textured yarns available today helps designers create unique, high-fashion looks, even with a simple stockinette fabric.

Yarns come in many *finishes and textures.* All fibers are first spun into strands commonly known as singles. These most basic of yarns can vary widely in thickness and amount of twist. A tightly twisted singles yarn will be stronger and more durable than its loosely twisted counterpart, but when worked in stockinette will tend to bias—a rectangle will turn into a rhombus (see page 40 for more on biasing). This distortion, which cannot be blocked out, can be controlled if you select patterns with combinations of knit and purl stitches. Singles with less twist produce a softer fabric, but it will be less durable and may pill easily.

A singles yarn can have textural interest if it is spun with thick and thin spots. The thicker sections, called slubs, can be closely spaced, to produce a fairly uniform nubby fabric, or spread out, for a more uneven look. If your yarn has very thick slubs, your choice of stitch patterns will be limited because the yarn will provide the primary texture in the fabric.

When two or more singles are twisted together, a plied yarn results. Plying usually softens, but often also strengthens, the yarn. As with singles, the amount of twist can vary from tight to loose, but biasing problems fade.

Two-ply yarns show more texture when knit than do yarns with larger numbers of plies. Generally, the tighter the twist, the greater the texture in the fabric. When two strands of different sizes are plied together, a yarn with a spiral twist is made and the fabric made from this yarn will be even more heavily textured than a plain two-ply. When a smooth strand and a slubbed strand are plied, the yarn's texture increases still further; the slub areas show the spiral effect most clearly.

If you want your stitch pattern to be dominant, yarns with three or more plies are often your best choice. They are rounder and smoother than two-ply yarns, and the patterns will show up to full advantage. In addition, these yarns are durable and abrasion-resistant.

A new dimension of visual and tactile fun begins when we consider novelty yarns. Novelties have dramatic textures; stitch patterns get pushed into a low second place. Stockinette and garter stitch are the mainstay structures, because the yarn itself speaks loudly.

You can produce a frothy, woolly fabric by using an evenly spaced loop yarn, of mohair or one of the lustrous wools, or a bouclé, ratinée, or gimp spun from any of a number of fiber types. In heavier weights, these yarns are excellent for coats and jackets, because they are bulky but not too heavy. In finer versions, they make lovely sweaters and dresses—and you have more stitch options. Spun from rayon, cotton, or silk, these novelties will have the drape we expect from these fibers so you can design in gathers and pleats as the thickness of the fabric allows.

Knops are the "bumps" or "cocoons" on some yarns. Yarn designers use knops to add both texture and color interest. If the color varies along a yarn, each knop can showcase the color of its section. The knit result is a flecked fabric.

Where a textured yarn has extremes of thickness, as in a knop yarn, you'll find that the greatest amount of texture will occur on the purl side of a stitch—on the reverse side of stockinette fabric, or on the purl rows of garter stitch. If you prefer the knit surface and want as much texture to show as possible, you can pull the knops or thick spots through to that side with a crochet hook.

The mention of *brushed* yarn brings mohair quickly to mind, but other fibers are also used for brushed effects—the long, lustrous types of wool, acrylics, and alpaca are possibilities. This type of yarn is airy, warm, elegant, and well suited to use in dressy garments. If you work cables, lace, or color patterns in brushed yarn the fabric will be softer and less well defined than when these patterns are knit in a smooth yarn. Brushed yarns aren't great for infants' and toddlers' clothes; the fuzzy fibers can cause sneezes, and sometimes choking, in little people.

Snarl yarns bring something like the brushed look to softer, shorter fibers. When the snarls are long, the fabric will be hairy and spiky. When the snarls are short, the fabric will look like terrycloth. Because of the strong yarn texture, stitch-pattern options are limited to the basics.

Chenille, a pile yarn with a velvety appearance, creates a very elegant fabric—but can be tricky to knit. Since unworking stitches wears out the pile, the yarn doesn't forgive mistakes. The pile also prevents the yarn from sliding smoothly within the knit fabric. If you work on too large a needle, the yarn can loosen and form loops on the sweater. For this reason, check the manufacturer's label for a recommended gauge and plan your sweater accordingly.

Shop shelves contain limitless possibilities in novelty yarns. Look for *metallics* and *ribbons*. Be adventurous. Strips of leather, suede, string, cloth, or feathers can get your imagination going and be worked into your sweaters.

Yarn **Colors** occur in solid, heathered, tweedy, variegated, and marled forms, and in combinations of these possibilities. Fibers can be dyed before they are spun, after they've been made into yarn—or even in the finished fabric state.

For clear, even, *solid colors,* white single-fiber yarns are spun and then dyed. The resulting colors are especially vivid in the brighter hues.

If fiber is dyed before it is spun, and then two or more hues are blended to achieve a final color, the resulting yarn is described as *heathered*. Heathered colors are softer than solid colors, with a greater feeling of depth. The fibers can be thoroughly blended, for an even appearance, or mixed less completely, so the original colors retain more of their identity and the yarn looks tweedy.

True *tweeds* result from a combination of these two coloring processes. Solid-dyed yarn is cut into snips, then blended with dyed fiber, and spun into a yarn which has distinct color flecks on a background of a single heathery hue. If you want lots of color from one strand of yarn, tweeds are one answer.

A *variegated* yarn changes color along its strand. The appearance of the knit fabric depends on the spacing of the color changes.

Variegated yarns made from dyed fiber can have yards of each color, so the resulting fabric can have wide stripes. Flashes of other colors can be introduced randomly along a strand, to produce unique color accents in the fabric.

If spun yarn is dyed in several colors, the length of each color area is limited. If the color changes every 1/2" to 2", the knit fabric will look like tortoise-shell (these are called *chine* yarns). Yarns with longer sections of color will usually striate (form horizontal short stripes) when knit. The color effect produced by yarns of this type will vary with the width of the fabric being made; in wider pieces, the colors can align and produce a piebald (patchy or spotty) effect. If you want to avoid this, knit with two balls of the yarn, working alternate rows from alternate balls (the technique is the same as for one-row stripes, page 8).

Marled yarns are plied yarns in which the strands are of different colors. One type of marled yarn is known as "ragg" and frequently used to make rugged sweaters and socks. Marled yarns can also be more delicate. The individual strands can be colored by any of the methods we've mentioned—solid-dyed, heathered, tweed, or variegated. The fabric made with a marled yarn has a sense of depth and subtle movement; this is more pronounced when the contrast between the colors in the plies is strong. The overall impression of color in the garment depends on how the eye blends the hues of the plies, and varies with the viewer's distance from the fabric.

Solid-dyed and heathered yarns offer the greatest potential for use with stitch patterns. Tweeds and simpler marls, because of their greater visual complexity, may overwhelm some patterns but generally can be used in a wide range of pattern stitches. If you're using a variegated yarn, it's often best to keep the stitch pattern simple and let the yarn carry the day.

With so many exciting yarns within easy reach, sooner or later you will want to face the challenge of using two or more types of yarn in the same garment. There are two distinct methods of **Combining Yarns**. You can work several yarns together as one throughout the fabric, or you can work the different yarns separately within the garment.

Before you decide how you will use your yarns together, explore the individual yarns first, particularly the way each is affected by laundering. If incompatibility is an issue, it will show up in the washtub. Does one of the yarns shrink, felt, or bleed color? If the problems are drastic, try another combination. If they are minor and related to cleaning, you can care for your finished garment as if it were made entirely of the more delicate yarn.

SEVERAL YARNS WORKED AS ONE. Yarn manufacturers create *compound yarns* by twisting together two or more finished yarns. They do this to create special effects: for example, a knopped, variegated yarn combined with a yarn-dyed brushed mohair produces a fuzzy tweed fabric, and a fiber-dyed variegated yarn joined to a brushed wool will give a soft fabric with subtle background striping. The possibilities are unlimited.

You, too, can venture closer to total control by making your own compound yarns. Select the component yarns with an eye toward achieving a unique color or texture, and treat the several strands as one when you knit.

You can work the yarns from separate balls, or you can ply them together before you knit. If you knit from separate balls,

your fabric will have a mottled look—this may be just fine for your design. A more uniform coloring results if you ply the yarns together before you cast on. Taking the time to ply will also eliminate the frustrating tangles that can occur when you've got several balls of yarn in action. Some shops—especially those which cater to machine knitters—have a tool called a *yarn twister,* which joins the yarns and winds them together into a single unit. If you are, or have a friend who is, a hand-spinner, commercial yarns can be plied on a spinning wheel.

Do you need to predict what your gauge will be when you'll be working yarns together? Do you want an idea of what size needles to use? These questions surface quickly when you begin to consider compound yarns.

A partial, rule-of-thumb answer to the first question is travelling along the knitters' grapevine. It works well when you'll be combining two yarns of similar thicknesses—for example, when each has a recommended gauge of 6 stitches per inch. To estimate the combined gauge, add the suggested gauges of the two yarns together, then divide the sum by three:

$$6 + 6 = 12 \div 3 = 4 \text{ stitches/inch}$$

If you're combining yarns of different thicknesses, the only sure method of predicting gauge is by knitting swatches. Make as many as necessary, until you're satisfied. Our chart will help you roughly estimate the gauge you might get, and will give you sizes of needles to start trying, but remember that the compound yarn—and its gauge!—are your creations. Feel free to make different choices if the results aren't pleasing.

COMPOUND YARN/NEEDLE CHART

Recommended Gauge of Thicker Yarn (stitches/inch)	Recommended Gauge of Thinner Yarn (stitches/inch)	Increase Size of Needle Recommended for Thicker Yarn By: (number of sizes)
3	7	1
3	6	2
3	5	3
3	4	4
3	3	4
4	7	1
4	6	2
4	5	3
4	4	4
5	7	2
5	6	3
5	5	4
6	7	3
6	6	4
7	7	4

How to use this chart: Note the manufacturer's recommended *gauge* and *needle size* from the skein wrapper for the *thicker* of your two yarns (first column). Check the recommended gauge from the skein wrapper for the *thinner* yarn. Find the matching row, and increase the needle size recommended for the thicker yarn by the number of sizes listed in the third column.

For instance, if your thicker yarn should gauge at 3 stitches per inch on size 9 needles, and you are combining it with a thinner yarn which works up at 7 stitches per inch, work your first swatch on needles one size larger—size 10. If you are not satisfied with the result, use larger or smaller needles until you like the fabric.

WORKING YARNS SEPARATELY. Various colors and textures can also be worked into a fabric through stripes, color slip-stitch patterns and mosaic knitting, tapestry designs, and stranded-color work. Successful use of each of these methods requires that you pay attention to gauge and plan ahead. Swatches and forethought are worth their weight in gold.

Yarns with radical gauge differences can be worked in one- or two-row color *slip-stitch patterns* and one- or two-row *stripes* without major adjustments. The heavier yarn will hold the finer one to its looser gauge. If you want deeper stripes and the gauges are quite different, you'll need to increase (for the finer yarn) or decrease (for the thicker yarn) the number of stitches in the row, in order to keep the fabric width consistent. For deeper stripes with yarns which work to only slightly different gauges, you may be able to get by with changing the needle size at the same time you change yarns (using a larger needle with the finer yarn, or a smaller one with the heavier yarn).

Other color designs require yarns of equal thickness, since they will be knit with the same needle across the row. For *tapestry designs, mosaic knitting,* or color patterns like *Fair Isle* or other stranded knitting, select equivalently sized yarns in the colors you need. A discrepancy in yarn size could ruin your garment.

For *tapestry or intarsia* work, you will need to be stricter with your yarns, even if they knit to the same gauge. Consider the weight and drape of each yarn.

Is it compatible with its potential neighbors? Or will differences in density cause distortions in the way the garment hangs? A large section of cotton or rayon on a fine mohair field could sag and pull the fabric out of shape. Interestingly enough, you can avoid this if you (1) reverse the positions of the fibers, (2) divide the pattern or design into smaller sections, or (3) choose fibers in similar weights as well as gauges.

You'll encounter problems of this sort if the right and left sides of your sweater are knit of yarns in different weights. You can work your way around this one by (1) balancing the fabric more evenly with vertical stripes, or, again, (2) changing fibers.

If you want to use two weights of yarn in a sweater and minimize distortion, try using the heavier fabric at the yoke. Although there will be differences in the ways the yarns drape, the shoulder and/or armhole seams will carry the weight of the heavier fabric and reduce the problem.

Selecting **Yarns for Children's Garments** requires consideration of everything we've talked about in relation to yarn, with some additional requirements.

Easy-care fibers may not be important to the child, but they probably will matter to the parent. Synthetics are quick to launder, of course, but don't rule out natural fibers. Many blends give the benefits of natural fibers along with the washability of synthetics. Some all-wool yarns, called "superwash," are now chemically treated so they can be machine washed and dried without felting.

COMBINING YARNS BY WORKING THEM SEPARATELY

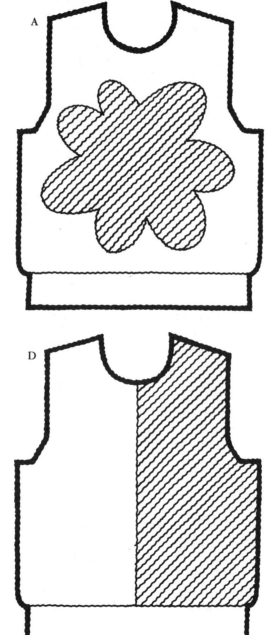

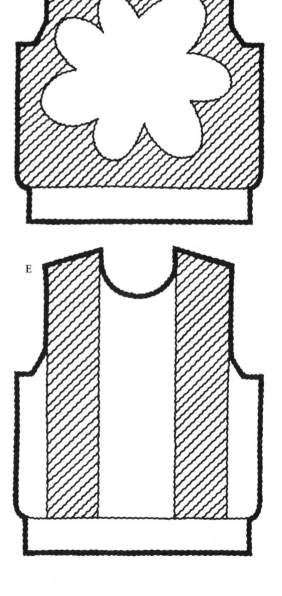

A large section of cotton or rayon on a fine mohair field could sag and pull the fabric out of shape (a). This can be avoided if the positions of the fibers are reversed (b), or if the pattern or design is divided into smaller sections (c), or if fibers of similar weights and characteristics are chosen.

A comparable problem is presented if the right and left sides of the sweater are of different-weight yarns (d). Here your options include balancing the fabric more evenly with vertical stripes (e), or changing fibers entirely. This problem is not as significant if the heavier fabric is used at the yoke of the garment (f). In this case, the shoulder or armhole seams will tend to support the fabric's weight.

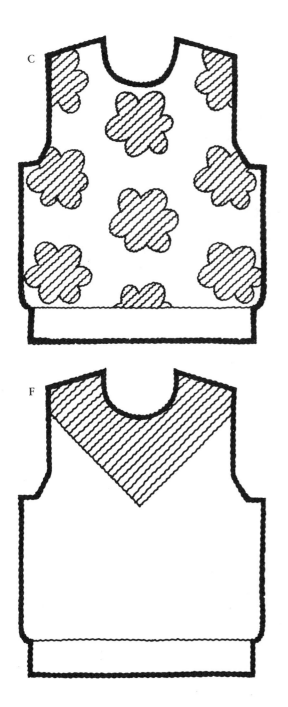

C

F

Stay away from brushed fibers for infants and toddlers. As soft, cuddly, and ideal as they may seem, the loose fibers can be breathed in or swallowed and young ones don't have the adult reflexes to help them avoid sneezing or choking.

Consider yarn thickness in relation to the child's size. Bulky or highly textured yarns can overwhelm an infant—but might make a good bunting. Fine yarns permit detailed garment shapes, stitch patterns, and color work; you may need lots of stitches across the front of a size 4 pullover in order to put a dinosaur there.

Children are attracted to bright colors. If possible, ask the child you'll be knitting for about favorite colors, or bring the child with you when you shop for yarn. These little considerations will make the sweater or jacket very special, because the child is a participant in its creation.

Multicolor patterns can help hide stains. If you're getting your color effects by stranding yarn across the back, though, be sure to weave the loose yarn into the fabric often. Long strands can be inconvenient, and sometimes dangerous, to little fingers when the sweater is put on or removed.

Color Theory

The pleasure of working with color increases with your knowledge and understanding. When you select yarns, you'll find yourself frequently asking, "Do these colors work?" Keeping in mind that taste in colors is extremely personal, some classic guidelines about color use can help you answer this question more quickly and with greater confidence.

One exciting challenge we face when designing knitwear is in taking a group of yarns and working them into a harmonious arrangement. Even more important than getting a set of colors to make sense in the world of color theory is knowing that the intended wearer of the sweater will be happy. We've mentioned taking kids with you when you shop for yarn; adults like to be in on these decisions, too. Find out about the prospective recipient's preferences, and consider including the person in your shopping trip. You may find yourself knitting with colors you wouldn't have considered, and being pleasantly surprised both by the results and by how frequently the finished sweater is worn.

We can only offer a brief introduction to color concepts, but you can take off from here.

Colors can be placed in a logical order on a circular grid, called the **Color Wheel**. This can help us by defining relationships between colors.

The first descriptive words in the language of color are the names of the **Hues**, or color families. These are arranged in the color wheel with each hue grading into the next. The first spokes of the wheel are the *primary hues* of red, blue, and yellow. If you blend any two primaries, you get the *secondary hues,* which are orange, green, and violet. The *intermediary (or tertiary) hues* are made by mixing a primary with an adjacent secondary color. The resulting hues bear the names of their components: for example, red-violet, blue-green, or yellow-orange.

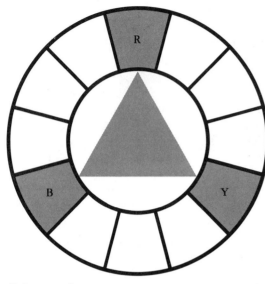

Primary colors

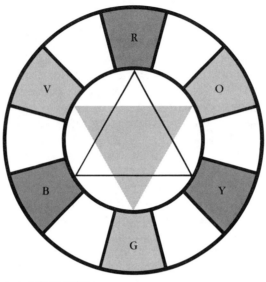

Secondary colors

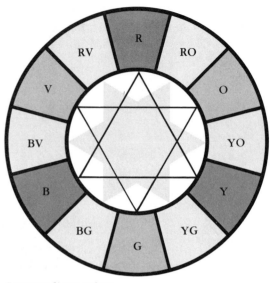

Intermediary colors

Before we get into more words which describe colors, we can establish an overview of some ways in which colors interact. You can choose a color scheme for a design based on ideas like the following:

Monochromatic designs are limited to a single hue, with its shades, tints, and saturations.

Analogous designs use three or four hues which are next to each other on the color wheel.

Complementary designs are composed of two hues which lie opposite each other on the color wheel.

Split complementary designs contain three hues: a given hue, and the two colors on either side of its complement.

Triadic designs also contain three colors, all of which are equidistant from each other on the color wheel; lines drawn to connect the three colors form an equilateral triangle.

Tetradic designs involve four colors; lines drawn to connect these colors on the color wheel form a square or rectangle.

Polychromatic designs contain many hues.

To simply hear a hue's name brings an image to mind, and defines its family for us. We learn what *orange, blue,* and *green* are when we are children—but there are lots of different oranges, blues,

and greens in this world. Everyone knows what orange is; but when you need to discuss a *particular* orange, you need more descriptive color words.

Any individual color can be described by its family name, and we can also say whether it is light or dark. This is a measure of its **Value**, or its *degree of lightness or darkness*. Colors change in value when hues are mixed with white, producing a *tint* of the original color, or with black, producing a *shade* of the original color. The *value scale* for a specific hue extends from pure white, through tints of the hue to the pure hue.

The scale continues to grade through shades of the hue to black. The value scale for red extends from pure white through the tints of red to pure red. The scale continues to grade through shades of red to black.

We can also talk about color in terms of how bright it is. This is also called its **Intensity**, or the measure of its *saturation*. As brightness decreases, a color is *desaturated*. This occurs when a hue is modified by the addition of any color which makes it less bright—in practice, when any shade of gray or some of the hue's complement is mixed in.

Getting straight on the difference between value and intensity takes a while—they sound pretty similar. But while tints and shades (value changes) are made by mixing in either black or white, a color's intensity is decreased when *both* black and white (or the complement) are added.

There is a difference in where the scales measuring value and intensity start and end. A value scale begins with white, moves through the colors, and ends with black. An intensity scale begins with the pure hue in its most brilliant form and ends in gray. Thus red, desaturated by a dark gray, will grade from bright red to garnet to maroon to charcoal. Since there are an infinite number of colors, you can take a color through both value and intensity scales simultaneously: each of these intensities of red could also be altered by a value change. For example, you could add white to the garnet to produce old rose.

The *strength* of a color, or its ability to advance and dominate a design, is based on both value and intensity. Pure hues, arranged on a value scale, range from yellow at the light end to violet at the dark end. The light colors will appear to advance, and the dark colors to recede. The pure hues, arranged on an intensity scale, follow the same course: yellow is the most intense (or vivid) hue, and violet is the least intense (yellow prevails, while violet retires). Because yellow is both the lightest and brightest hue, very small amounts of yellow tend to grab our attention. To keep yellow from stealing the show, you can learn to monitor the amount you use, its value, its intensity, or all three. You don't have to use bright yellow; try a less intense yellow (like ecru), or a gold, or a bronze.

Exploring Color. The more you use color, the more confident you will feel about your choices. We urge you to play. Here are some ideas to help you develop your color sense.

1. Somewhere in your kitchen cupboards lurks a box of food coloring. Take it out, and mix colors, drop by drop, in water. What happens when you add blue to orange?
2. Pick up a child's box of watercolors at the drug store. Start mixing your own colors in this form. What happens when you add white or black to each color?
3. Pull out your yarn collection and arrange the balls and skeins according to the color wheel. Group yarns by hue, by value, by intensity, and, finally, by combinations which you find appealing. Make a record of your efforts on file cards, using snips of the yarns.
4. If you would like to experiment with fiber, begin to work with dyes. Get the dyepots brewing, then apply intense colors to gray fleece or yarn and see how the color's brilliance is toned down.
5. If you are a spinner, buy some colored batts and blend colors on your cards. Mix two hues thoroughly so you create a third color; or stop short of complete blending and get a tweedy effect.
6. Above all, have fun! Color is your toy; it exists to be enjoyed.

Color in Knitting has its own unique dimensions. It's all very well to mix paints and food coloring, and to understand relationships on the color wheel. But yarn isn't liquid color, and the knit fabric is not smooth paper. A rayon yarn of a given color will look different than a wool yarn in the same color, and a slub yarn will give a different color impression when knit than a smooth yarn from the same dyebath.

As we follow our color discussion into the yarn shop, we'll discover more general principles. Remember, though, that your own instincts—or even simple curiosity—and the willingness to make samples will take you farther toward color confidence than all the theory in the world. Color isn't a set of laws; it's a game.

What can we do with just one color? Most knitters begin their color work with a *monochromatic scheme*. There's lots of variety for the knitter even here. You can increase the visual interest in a monochromatic design by combining bright and dull fibers, smooth and textured yarns, or using the variations in light reflection produced by textured stitch patterns.

The fiber content of a yarn and the texture with which it is spun influence our perception of its color. Shiny fibers, like silk and rayon, reflect light so the color on these yarns appears brighter and lighter than a matte fiber in the same hue. Those matte fibers, like wool or unmercerized cotton, appear to absorb light; they look darker than their lustrous counterparts. This ability to reflect or absorb light is present in both the individual fibers and in the structure of the yarn. A worsted-spun singles wool has a smoother, more light-reflective surface than a textured wool bouclé of the same color.

You can heighten this sense of contrast in a monochromatic color scheme by placing a design worked from a smooth, shiny yarn against a background knit with a textured, matte yarn.

Your choice of stitch pattern also affects how light will be reflected from your fabric, and consequently how the color(s) will appear. The role of pattern stitches in this interaction is displayed most clearly by fishermen's knits. Arans, for instance, show off the smooth knit stitches of cables against a background of textured purl stitches. The cables appear lighter than the background, although they are knit from the same yarn. Guernseys reverse the contrast: the more textured purls become the pattern against the smoother knit background.

You can expand the potential in a monochromatic design by adding the *full range of values* to your palette. When you're using dark, light, and medium values of a single color, you need to be sensitive to the interactions between the lights and darks. This will help you get the most important elements of your design to stand out—or, if you'd rather, maintain a subtle balance between design areas.

When used in equal proportions, a light color will dominate its dark partner. As a result, the dark areas will appear to recede—to be the "background."

On the other hand, if you isolate a shape on a background of opposite value (place a dark object on a light ground, or vice versa), the shape will appear to advance and become dominant—regardless of whether it is lighter or darker than its surroundings. This effect can be strengthened or minimized, depending on how much contrast you have between the values of the two areas. When there's a lot of contrast, the shape will appear to advance strongly; it may even look like it's floating off the surface. If you like this idea, use high contrast. Put a lemon yellow on a navy background. If you'd rather keep your design more visually integrated, choose two values that are closer together—try black and gray, instead of black and white, or place a dull gold shape on that navy surface.

The size of your shape will influence your choice of its color. Generally, if you want a small shape to show up it needs to be worked in high contrast to its background. Small details remain distinct when the contrast is high; if you work details in close values, they will need to be large or they'll blend together when viewed from a distance.

It's also true that a shape knitted in a light color will appear larger than a shape of the same size worked in a dark color. Therefore, if you want two shapes to look like they're the same size, but you want to make one light-colored and one dark-colored, the darker one will need to be slightly larger. We've all learned this principle in clothing selection: black diminishes, and white increases the perceived size.

We've discussed the interaction between value and the appearance of shapes. The same principles are true for intensity. Brighter, more intense colors advance, appear larger, and can have the illusion of floating.

All these aspects of a hue can become part of your experiments with monochromatic designs.

The simplest expansion of a color scheme to include three or four hues moves us into *analogous* color harmony. Many designers move beyond monochromatic designs by exploring adjacent colors. Analogous combinations are comfortable; it's easy to achieve pleasing results with them.

You've still got all the possibilities discussed under monochromatic schemes. You can play with value and intensity, size and shape of design elements, texture of fiber and of yarn and of stitch pattern. *Plus* increased color options!

When you begin to explore analogous color schemes, you may also need to consider the *strength* of your colors for the first time. A line can be drawn on the color wheel to separate the hues with greater color strength (the lighter, more intense hues) from those with less color strength (the darker and less intense hues). The stronger colors range from yellow through red, while the colors from green through violet are less assertive.

Knowing which members of your analogous scheme are strongest will affect how you use them. If you are working with green, yellow-green, and yellow, yellow is the strongest hue. You'll need to watch the quantities of yellow you use—unless you want it to blast all the other colors out of the game. Even if you weaken the yellow by changing its value—say, from pure yellow to a pale tint—it's strong enough to dominate the field if used in equal quantities with the green and yellow-green. If you want the yellow to dominate and the green and yellow-green to be accents, then go ahead! But if you prefer a different balance, familiarity with this principle will help prevent surprises.

Any group of analogous hues can be modified to make an infinite number of impressions. Consider the feel of a design worked in tints and lightened shades of pure green, yellow-green, and yellow. It brings spring to mind, with its clear, crisp, sunlit colors. You could increase this sensation by using shiny yarns. On the other hand, compare this to the feel of the same design worked in shades of a less intense green, yellow-green, and yellow. When these three hues are desaturated and darkened, the color scheme feels more subdued. This effect can be heightened through the use of textured yarns. (For fun, you could add a bit of textured yarn to the basically light, shiny scheme, or a glint of rayon or silk to the somber combination—a dash of the opposite can add depth to the cloth.) Neither of these designs is ''better'' or ''more beautiful'' than the other. They're just different—and both analogous!

When you're ready to try your wings on a more challenging flight, try working with *complementary* colors. Some of the most visually satisfying and longest-lasting designs are based on complements. The most common complementary pairs are red and green, orange and blue, and yellow and violet. Although you're working with only two colors, they're opposite on the color wheel. That complicates your job, but you'll approach it with all the color tools we've discussed and explored so far.

Used at full intensity, complements placed next to each other are startlingly vivid. For example, red and green intensify each other, creating a feeling of tension—especially at the edges of the shapes, where the two hues meet and are in most obvious contrast. You can tone down this effect without sacrificing the power of the combination by altering the colors' values. If you darken the green to a forest green, the eye relaxes, yet remains interested.

You could also change the intensity of one or both hues. See what happens by returning to your paintbox, food coloring, or dyepot. Remember that one way to desaturate (change the intensity of) a hue is to add some of its complement. Slowly add one complementary hue to another—say, violet to yellow. Get to know the colors that result from the blending of two complements. Lovely neutrals appear: browns and greenish grays (at full desaturation), or rusts, golds, soft greens, and navies (when a mixture contains more of the starting hue).

When we examine the most common complementary pairs, we see that each pair contains one color which is stronger than its partner. Red is stronger than green; orange is stronger than blue; yellow is stronger than violet. The stronger color can be brought into balance if you use it in a smaller area. As an example, let's take our red and forest green again. If you work this combination in stripes of four rows each, the red will dominate, even if you use green for all the borders and finishes. Red is simply stronger. If instead you work one-row stripes of red and four-row stripes of green, you will have a green sweater with red accents. In design terms, the red will still be a strong element in the garment, but it will be in balance with the forest green.

You can also get complementary pairs to work together by asking neutrals to negotiate a settlement. By separating the two hues with black, white, gray, or a compatible brown, you can control the mutually intensifying effect of the complements—again without loss of excitement.

When you consider using neutrals, remember the value and intensity guidelines we've already covered. Each neutral will have a different effect on your total composition. On a white background, units of color look smaller, less intense, and more likely to float off. Black draws the colored units into a coherent whole, intensifies the colors, and makes the shapes seem larger. Grays and neutral browns create a softer mood, by toning things down. If you work with grayed or brownish neutrals and also alter your complements (by graying them, or desaturating them), your garment will have a very unified look.

Complementary colors can also add zip to color schemes which aren't based on them. Spark an analogous color scheme with a small amount of the complement of one of the hues. This is like adding some shiny yarn to a predominantly matte composition—only here you'd add a hint of red, for example, to the green/yellow-green/yellow group we discussed earlier. (Other complementary sparks for this combination would be red-violet or violet.) If we move our analogous combination one step around the color wheel, so it includes blue-green, green, and yellow-green, we can still use a touch of red, or we can play with red-orange or red-violet.

Split complementary color schemes are very close to this idea, but with a different emphasis. In the latest example of blue-green, green, and yellow-green, sparked with red, you simply drop the green from your palette and work with blue-green, yellow-green, and red. Play

with all the ways of working with color and pull these hues into a pleasing design.

When you've got a pile of yarn that doesn't make sense according to the schemes listed above, or if you want to enlarge your sense of the possibilities, look for *triadic* or *tetradic* color harmonies. Once you've selected the main color for a garment, these relationships can help you find compatible accent colors. Finding these harmonies is easiest if you have a color wheel, as well as an equilateral triangle, a rectangle, and a square which you can superimpose on it. If you put one point of your geometric guide (the triangle, rectangle, or square) on the basic color, you can see what other hues might work well with it.

Yarn First or Color Scheme First?

Do you make color decisions and then find yarn to fit them, or do you visit a yarn shop, fall in love with a color, and then try to invent appropriate partners? In practice, you'll find yourself working back and forth between these approaches.

You might, for example, establish ahead of time the hue families you want to draw from. When you start shopping for yarns, keep in mind the factors which make color effects in knitting unique: the textures of fibers, yarn structures, and stitches.

Polychromatic designs can be the most fun, and they usually have their start in your scrap basket. When you stare at that helter-skelter heap of dissimilar textures and colors, order and cohesion seem impossible. But they can emerge.

Begin by grouping the yarns—by thickness, by color family, by value and intensity within each family—and see what pattern(s) emerge.

Next, establish a dominant color—this will often depend on which color you have in greatest abundance. Then think about what relationships can be found between that color and the others in the piles. If your colors are grayed, a natural gray can be added to pull things together.

The technique of maintaining an overall color tone in a piece—being sure that all colors are similar in value—can help create a feeling of unity. Being able to see only value, without being influenced by the hue, is a useful planning skill which takes practice. Group balls of yarn and squint at them. You'll be better able to eliminate your sense of the hues and to see just the values. Pull out any yarn that appears too dark or light, and you will unify the value of the group.

Open your eyes to check for intensity. The colors that stand out are more intense. You can add a dash of intense color to a grayed collection, for that interesting spark of contrast we've discussed in terms of texture and color families. When you plan your design, watch the placement of these contrasts: put them where they'll enhance your design or the wearer. Put the spark near the face, if the color is flattering, or in a diagonal line or a central panel (both of which have slimming effects). Let your eye guide you, and play around until you know you can trust your judgment.

PULLING IT ALL TOGETHER

Getting the Design to Work with the Figure

The person you're knitting for has a unique shape. Most of us have parts of our bodies that we're comfortable with and don't mind having emphasized. Other parts we'd rather ignore. To be completely successful, your sweater design needs to take the wearer's physique into account. If you're knitting for someone else, ask if there's any problem which should be disguised and plan your garment accordingly. Pay careful attention to all the little details of design—garment shape, pattern, texture, color—with the figure in mind.

Some figure "faults" can be minimized by your choice of garment style, or by the selective use of yarns, or of color or stitch patterns. When we introduce charting, we'll take particular figures into account, with suggestions for styles which flatter one shape more than another. Here we'll consider color, texture, and the more general design decisions which contribute to making garments flattering.

We've all heard and read how color and pattern in clothing affect appearance. We know that bright, bold colors call attention, while soft, dark shades and earth tones help us blend into the background. This doesn't mean that an extra-large garment must always be olive green, navy, or black, or that smaller individuals should always dress in fire-engine red. If you take time to select the right hue and to balance your design, you can wear your favorite colors, whatever they are, in one or another of their manifestations. If purple is your passion, you may be wise to choose a muted, pastel version of plum, or to search out a more vibrant, rosy incarnation. The essence of good design is freedom—not anarchy.

We've learned that horizontal stripes make a person look shorter and wider, while vertical stripes make a body taller and thinner. Although this effect is most obvious when worked out in strongly contrasted colors, it also occurs when stripes are knit in yarns of different textures, or in varying stitch patterns.

Consider overall body size when you select your yarn or stitch. A bulky knit or heavy texture can make a person look heavier. They can also overwhelm a small woman's or child's figure. On the other hand, practicality may override looks if warmth is the primary consideration in a particular garment.

Avoid "fussiness" around areas you want to conceal. Bobbles around the yoke of a sweater for a full-busted woman may draw undesired attention. A bold, colorful pattern around the body of a jacket for a man who is rounder than he wishes can do the same.

Fitting

Many fitting problems common in store-bought garments can be avoided in custom knits. Accurate measurements are the key to perfect fit. Not all of us are a "standard" size—have you ever met anyone who really was? Two women, both size 10s, can have very different measurements in crucial areas, such as armhole depth or shoulder width. If those same size 10s become size 14s, their shoulder-width measurements will remain the same, but they'll find that commercial size-14 clothing is wider across both the body and the shoulders. Routine measurement-taking will resolve these difficulties.

More complex fitting challenges arise when a body is not symmetrical. For example, many women have one shoulder which slopes more steeply than the other, after years of carrying heavy packages and handbags. Never hesitate to take the same measurements on both right and left sides—or on both front and back. You may need to chart each side differently to get a garment which fits perfectly.

In the case of the sloping shoulder, measure the raglan and armhole depth on both right and left sides of the body. If you find a discrepancy, there are two solutions at your command: you can knit a garment with a steeper slope on one side, and adjust the sleeve caps accordingly, or work to the shallower of the two slopes and visually correct the difference with a shoulder pad.

As another example, age tends to lean the upper body toward the front, causing various degrees of what we call stooped shoulders. Again, measure the armhole and raglan depths at both the front and back. If you find a difference you have two remedies at hand: you may decrease the front armhole depth, or you may increase the amount of fabric across the back by working short rows.

Short rows (see "How Tos") are a handy trick which allows you to add extra fabric at specific points, while keeping the seamed edges at their original measurements. Bust darts are a perfect example of how short rows can be used. Extra fabric is added at the center front, but the side edges of both front and back body sections remain the same length. If you added extra fabric just by knitting an extra-long front, you'd have to ease in the excess along the side seams when you assembled the sweater. This is easier to avoid than to accomplish; if you were working with very fine yarns you could make a dart, but most hand-knitting yarns produce a fabric which gets dauntingly thick when folded triple.

Potential fitting problems and their solutions are discussed in greater detail under "Taking Measurements."

Refining the Idea

Are you ready to launch into your sweater yet? Maybe—at least you're close. We've explored many of the areas which a designer must consider. Now it's time to put that knowledge to work.

If your sweater will be simple, perhaps based on a single overall stitch pattern, you can:

1. Knit your swatch to establish the gauge (pages 4–5),
2. Take the necessary body measurements (pages 33–35),
3. Determine ease (pages 36–38), and
4. Proceed directly to the charting.

If you're working with a number of decorative elements, your idea may still need to be refined. A simple line drawing can help you visualize your sweater, and plan what you'll need to consider when you chart.

Once your idea is down on paper, check out both the overall effect and the individual details. You'll probably discover a minor modification or two that will make a major improvement in your design.

Pay careful attention to where design elements are located in relation to shaping. For instance, will a panel of cables, lace, or color pattern be chopped in half when you decrease for the armholes? Can you incorporate a panel into the yoke shaping (take a look at raglan styling)? Does the neckline relate to the center panels, or to other stitch or fabric designs? Are the pockets placed where they make both practical and visual sense?

Are the design elements of the right sizes, and are they in the right places?

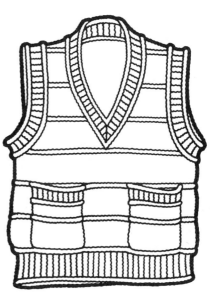

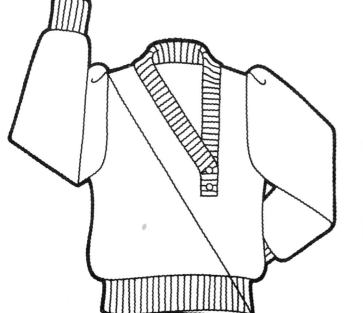

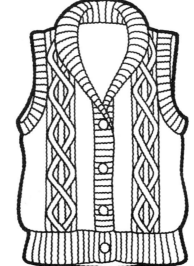

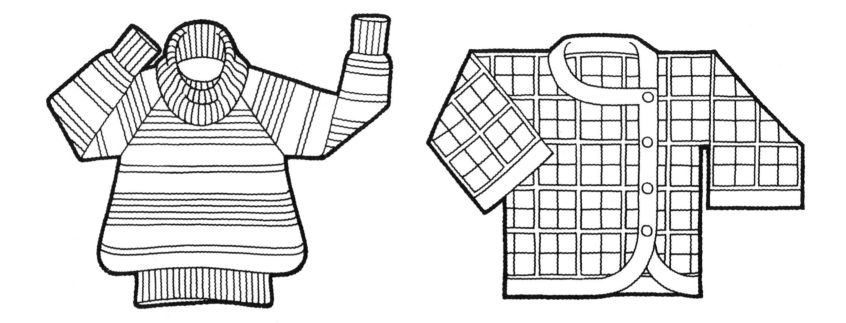

Would your fabric be more exciting if your stripes were wider? Should your picture be larger . . . or smaller? Can part of a picture be carried to the back, or to the sleeves?

Does the sweater have a single area of interest, perhaps a special yarn, stitch pattern, picture, or shape? Is the overall effect too busy—are you trying too hard to be creative? Will you want to feature unique buttons, feathers, sequins, or beads? Is one element of the styling critical—pleats or gathers within the body, a special sleeve cap, or a unique neck finish? Is an asymmetrical panel or opening obviously off-center, or does it just look like a mistake?

Determine the focal point, and then treat everything else as an extra. Do the extras add to or detract from your main idea? It may be time to eliminate some thoughts and save them for another project.

Many sweaters, especially mass-produced ones, seem to have been designed to be viewed only from the front: all the decoration is on the front of the body, and the back and sleeves are plain. Have you considered the three-dimensional nature of knitting? Don't forget that your garment will be seen and admired from all directions when it is worn.

Above all, remember that this process of refinement will continue as you chart and knit your sweater. Some design problems may not even be apparent until those stages. And some decisions you make at this time may change as the work progresses and your sweater takes shape.

Do you have a pretty good idea of what you'd like to make? Then you're ready for stage two, the charting.

The Charting Preliminaries

Once you have developed a visual concept for your sweater, you will need to gather the information necessary for the actual pattern drafting and knitting. This information includes:

- body measurements,
- desired ease allowances,
- stitch and row gauge, and
- yarn requirements.

Some of these will be familiar—we discussed test swatches and gauge calculations on pages 4–5, and have talked about yarn requirements on pages 5–9—although we'll go into greater depth on those topics here.

TAKING MEASUREMENTS

The Tape Measure in Action

Accurate measurements are the key to good fit. It is virtually impossible to do a good job of taking one's own measurements. If the sweater will be for you, ask a friend to do the measuring in accordance with our guidelines—a handy measurement form is on page 389. If the sweater is for someone who's not within reach of your tape measure, see if accurate measurements can be sent to you. If measurement-taking isn't feasible—perhaps the sweater is planned as a surprise—we've included standard measurement charts in the Appendix. If you work from them, be sure to take any special fitting problems into account and adjust the numbers accordingly.

All of our measurements will be in inches. The sample measurements in this book will be used to help you follow our step-by-step guidelines. *Don't use these sample measurements for your charting*—they're for demonstration purposes only. They will help you see how the knitting directions evolve, and how the charting process works. The only important measurements are those of the person for whom you are designing a garment.

Measurements should be taken over normal foundation garments and, at most, a lightweight garment over those. Start with a piece of string; we'll refer to this from now on as the *Measurement String*. This string will be an important reference point for some of the measurements. It is represented by the dotted line on the diagram. Have the person being measured raise both arms; tie the string snugly around the upper body at the underarms. The string will lie an inch or two below the point where the arms join the body. It should fit comfortably when the arms are raised and lowered. Make sure that the string lies straight across the front and doesn't sag in back.

TAKING MEASUREMENTS

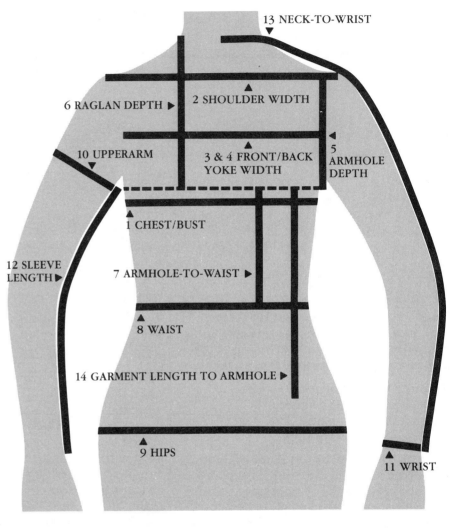

13 NECK-TO-WRIST

6 RAGLAN DEPTH ▶

2 SHOULDER WIDTH

10 UPPERARM

3 & 4 FRONT/BACK YOKE WIDTH

5 ARMHOLE DEPTH

1 CHEST/BUST

12 SLEEVE LENGTH ▶

7 ARMHOLE-TO-WAIST ▶

8 WAIST

14 GARMENT LENGTH TO ARMHOLE ▶

9 HIPS

11 WRIST

▬ ▬ ▬ ▬ ▬ MEASUREMENT STRING

	Sample Numbers		Sample Numbers

1. **Chest/Bust** — 33"
Around the fullest part of the bust or chest with the tape measure straight across the back. The chest should be fully expanded, so breathe deeply.

2. **Shoulder Width** — 13½"
Straight across the back, from the outside tip of one shoulder bone to the other.

3. **Front Yoke Width** — 12"
Straight across the front, halfway between the shoulders and string, measured from directly above the underarms.

4. **Back Yoke Width** — 12"
Straight across the back, halfway between the shoulders and the string, measured from directly above the underarms.

5. **Armhole Depth** — 8¼"
In back, from the top of the shoulder bone straight down to the string. Wear shoulder pads when taking this measurement if your garment will include them.

6. **Raglan Depth** — 9¼"
In back, from the base of the neck **straight** down to the string.

7. **Armhole-to-Waist** — 9"
From the string to the waist, with the arm slightly raised.

8. **Waist** — 24½"
At the natural indentation, eased by placing one finger between the waist and the tape measure.

9. **Hips** — 34"
Around the widest part.

10. **Upperarm** — 10½"
Around the fullest part.

11. **Wrist** — 5¾"
Around the wristbone.
- If the wrist is small and the knuckles are large, hold the hands flat and measure around the knuckles of the palm. Compare this measurement to the wrist measurement plus 1". Use the larger of the two numbers in your calculations.

12. **Sleeve Length** — 17½"
With the arm slightly away from the body and the elbow slightly bent, measure from the string straight down the inside of the arm to the wristbone.
- If you are planning shorter sleeves, measure to that point only.

13. **Neck-to-Wrist Measurement** — 26½"
From the center of the neck at the back, across the top of a shoulder, down the outside of the arm, over a slightly bent elbow to the wrist.
- This is used for charting some specific types of sweaters, like Ts and dolmans. If you are planning shorter sleeves, measure to that point only.

14. **Garment Length to Armhole** — varies
At the center back, from the string down to the desired bottom edge of the garment.
- A typical sweater ends between 3" and 5" below the waist. A jacket or coat should be long enough to cover the clothing worn underneath.

Potential Fitting Problems

If you suspect a fitting problem, don't hesitate to take the same measurements on both front and back, or left and right sides. Compare them to see where the numbers differ. If a discrepancy occurs, you may decide to alter your design to de-emphasize it, or adjust your charting procedures to compensate. Let's look at some common figure features.

A person with a **Steep Shoulder Slope** has a Raglan Depth Measurement which is substantially larger (1½" or more) than the Armhole Depth Measurement (measured without shoulder pads).

This discrepancy is best dealt with through careful choice of garment style and perhaps the addition of shoulder pads. If you plan to use shoulder pads, wear them when taking the Armhole Depth Measurement for your sweater. Avoid styles which emphasize the shoulder slope (Round Yokes, Raglans, and Dolmans). Try a Saddle-Shoulder style, which will usually make the shoulders appear more square. Or consider a sleeve cap which visually adds height (like the gathered cap).

A person with **Square Shoulders** has a Raglan Depth Measurement which is nearly the same as the Armhole Depth Measurement (not more than 1" difference).

Again, this is best handled through de-emphasis. Consider Round Yokes, Raglans, T shapes, and Dolmans. Select simply styled sleeve caps, like the Set-in and Semi-raglan. Avoid Saddle-Shoulder styles, as well as other design elements at the shoulders (like button bands or epaulets).

A person with **Wide Shoulders** has a Shoulder Width Measurement which is fairly close to the body width of the sweater. In other words, there isn't much fabric to decrease for the armhole shaping. Many people with wide shoulders complain of excess fabric at the front yoke of a garment.

A good choice for this person is a shaped-yoke style. The extra fabric will be subtracted at the underarm, but the armhole shaping tapers out to accommodate the shoulder width.

Styles similar to those appropriate for people with square shoulders are also recommended. If the wide-shouldered person really wants gathered sleeve caps, subtract an inch or two from the Shoulder Width Measurement before drafting the sweater, so the cap will fit higher and not exaggerate the impression of shoulder width.

There are several design solutions which can help the person with a **Large Bust**, all of which involve adding extra fabric at the front of the garment.

You can knit an Enlarged Sweater Front. To plan this, take the Bust Measurement in two stages. Measure across the bust at the front, from side seam to side seam. Then take the back portion of the Bust/Chest Measurement, from side seam to side seam. Divide the garment ease (pages 36–38) between the front and back body sections. (If the front measurement is more than 6″ larger than the back, borrow a bit from the front and add it to the back.) Work front and back sections to their separate measurements.

You can also use Bust Darts, which are explained fully in the body section. Bust darts will give a more tailored fit, but can

cause problems with color designs or complex stitch patterns. Work out the details of your pattern before you start to work the short rows for the darts.

Avoid a tight fit, which will emphasize the bust. Looser styles like Dolmans and Ts are good selections.

If your person has a **Large Midriff**, or needs **Maternity Wear**, you've got the same concerns as with the large bust, but a different location for your shaping. Be sure the garment is long enough to cover the entire tummy.

Consider working an Enlarged Sweater Front, taking your measurement across the tummy instead of the chest.

Also look at the guidelines for Bust Darts, but work the short rows around the widest part of the body instead of at the chest. Work each "tummy dart" so that its total width is approximately one-third of the front body section. For example, if the body front is 18″ wide, each dart should be about 6″ wide.

Another option is the Reverse Tapered Body. You can work a reverse taper on both front and back. Or plan a Reverse Tapered Front and a Classic Back—you should have the same number of stitches on each section when you reach the armhole bind-off.

Wide Hips can be thought of as an asset or a problem, depending upon your point of view or upon the fashion of the moment.

If you're planning a classic sweater style, use your hip measurement for charting the body width. If this leaves you with too much fabric at the bust, taper inward (see the Reverse Tapered Body).

Wide hips frequently contribute to an hourglass figure, which you may want to emphasize. If so, look into the Double

Tapered Body, or consider a Cinched-Waist Garment.

If the shoulders are very narrow in relation to the hips, consider using a sleeve cap that extends the shoulder line. Your choices would include the gathered, pleated, box, and designer's choice caps. In most cases, you'll want to avoid ending the sweater at the hipline.

DETERMINING EASE AND OTHER ADJUSTMENTS

Ease

If you knit a garment to someone's precise measurements, it will fit like a leotard or swimsuit. Ease is the amount of extra fabric necessary for a stylish and comfortable fit in non-exercise clothing. In a world which contains both skintight slinky sweaters and oversized T-shirts, it quickly becomes obvious that the desirable amount of ease is partly a matter of taste. How much ease you add or subtract at various measurement points depends on how tight or loose you want the garment to be, the garment's purpose, and the type of yarn you're using. An easy and accurate way to determine how much ease you'd like is to measure a similar garment which fits comfortably. If you don't have one, some general principles can be applied.

The first set of figures relates to **Ease for Adult-Size Garments**. Notice that some of the guidelines are negative (–) while others are positive (+). Add or subtract the suggested amounts from the *specific* body measurements you are using.

EASE FOR ADULT GARMENTS

Chest/Bust Measurement (Body Ease)
Skintight fit . . . . – 2″ to 0″
Tight-fitting sweater, meant to be
worn over a lightweight
undergarment . . . . 0″ to + 1″
Average ease, for a sweater of
moderate fit . . . . + 2″ to + 3″
Outerwear: sweater, vest, or jacket
meant to be worn over other
clothing . . . . + 4″ to + 6″
Oversized jacket or coat . . . . + 6″ to + 8″

Remember that a tight fit accentuates a full
figure; add extra body ease. For very large
sizes, however, take into account the elasticity of the knitted fabric. A wide piece of knitting may expand enough to compensate for
some of the needed ease.

Hip Measurement
For ribbing, if hip measurement is used
as basis . . . . 0″ to + 1″
For additional ease, follow the chest/bust
guidelines.

Waist Measurement
For waist ribbing or snugly fitting
tapered garments . . . . 0″ to + 1″

Shoulder Width Measurement
For the average sweater, the exact
measurement is used . . . . 0″
Outerwear: sweater, vest, or jacket meant
to be worn over other clothing . . . . . . + ½″
Coat . . . . + ½″ to + ¾″

If you prefer a gathered, pleated, box,

or other sleeve cap finish to fit higher
on the shoulders . . . . – 1″ to – 2″

*Armhole Depth Measurement/Raglan
Depth Measurement*
For the average sweater, the exact
measurement is used . . . . 0″
Outerwear: sweater, vest, or
jacket to be worn over other
clothing . . . . + ½″ to + ¾″
Coat . . . . + 1½″ to + 2″

Wrist Measurement
For ribbing or other snugly fitting
sleeve cuff finishes . . . . + 1″

Upperarm Measurement
Depending on desired fullness, use a
percentage of Body Ease . . . . 50% to 100%
of Body Ease
For special sleeve cap finishes, such
as gathered, pleated, and so forth,
where greater fullness is
required . . . . + 4″ to + 6″

*Sleeve Length Measurement/Garment Length
to Armhole*
For the average sweater, the exact
measurement is used . . . . 0″
Outerwear: subtract the same amount
that you add to the armhole
measurement . . . . – ½″ to – 2″
Blousing, if desired . . . . + 1″ to + 3″

Blousing requires a snug fit at the wrist
(or waist). Also, remember that a soft, draping fabric can accommodate more fullness
than a thick, bulky fabric.

The adult guidelines can be easily adjusted to help you determine **Ease for
Infants' and Children's Garments**. A
child's body is smaller overall, and a
child's head is larger in relation to its
body than an adult's. When charting a
garment for a child, you will need to use
these ease guidelines, and to make sure
the neckline is generous enough to let the
head through without a struggle. (Refer-
ences to neckline measurements will
make sense when you reach the appropriate point in charting.) The remainder
of charting, since it is based on body
measurements, is exactly the same as for
an adult's sweater.

Although a sweater for a youngster is
usually quick to knit, a child can also
grow out of it quickly . . . if you get
distracted by other projects, perhaps
before it's completed! Take into account
some simple styling ideas that could
increase a sweater's length of time in the
child's wardrobe.

Make fold-over cuffs or ribbing, which
can later be turned down to lengthen the
sleeves. Add a little extra ease to the
body, sleeves, and armhole depth, and
the child will have growing room. A yoke
which doesn't rely on the Shoulder Width
Measurement (a T-Shape, a Round Yoke,
or a Raglan, instead of a style with Set-in
Sleeves) will fit longer.

Knitting for kids is fun. And if you can
interpret a drawing in yarn, or encourage
the child to specify some of the details,
you'll find it's particularly rewarding.

Infants' sweaters fit fairly snugly, in
part because they have traditionally been
knit with fine yarns. Unless you work a
very deep or very wide pullover neckline

(like a boatneck), we highly recommend an additional neck opening. This can be at the back, the front, or along one or both shoulders. Adapt the adult guidelines for ease as follows:

1. Body Ease, Shoulder Width, Armhole Depth, Wrist, and Upperarm: Use half of the ease specified for adults.
2. Neckline Width: Allow half of the body stitches. Note that we're talking about the body stitches, not the yoke stitches.
3. Neckline Depth: Use 1" for a high neckline with minimal neckline finishing, 2" to 2½" for a crewneck, 3" to 4" for bulky yarns.
4. Shoulder Shaping: Shoulder seams on infants' clothing are very short. Bind off straight across, or on two levels at most.

Children from 2 to 6 require a slightly looser fit, but a less dramatic opening for their heads.

1. Body Ease, Shoulder Width, Armhole Depth, Wrist, and Upperarm: Use three-quarters of the ease specified for adults.
2. Neckline Width: For a garment with a supplementary neckline opening (like a placket), use slightly more than one-third of the number of stitches in the yoke. For a pullover without a supplementary neckline opening, use one-half of the number of stitches in the yoke plus the width of the neckband from each shoulder (see page 114 for how to do this).

Children from 7 to 12 are getting pretty grown up, although there are still minor modifications to be made.

1. Body Ease, Shoulder Width, Armhole Depth, Wrist, and Upperarm: Use ease specified for adults.
2. Neckline Width: For a garment with a supplementary neckline opening, use one-third of the number of stitches in the yoke. For a pullover, use one-third of the number of stitches in the yoke plus the width of the neckband from each shoulder (see page 114 for how to do this).
3. Neckline Depth: For round or square necklines, use adult guidelines minus ½". For a V neckline, begin a minimum of ½" below the armhole bind-off.

Seam Allowances

Seam (or selvedge) stitches are an often-overlooked part of charting. When garment sections are assembled, one stitch at each seamed edge disappears to the inside. If your gauge has many stitches to the inch, these "lost" stitches will not make much difference in the size of the finished garment. However, if you are knitting with only two stitches per inch, side seams could reduce the circumference of your sweater by 2". This could make the difference between a sweater which fits, and one which doesn't!

Learn to think about the assembly process for each sweater before you begin to chart. If two sections will be joined, you will need to include seam stitches at the appropriate edges in your calculations.

Whether and where you need to add seam stitches will depend on whether your sweater is worked in a circular format, a flat format, or with a combination of both methods. Circular knitting eliminates seams—therefore, no seam stitches are needed. Flat knitting requires seams, so add a seam allowance of one stitch per edge on the body, yoke, and sleeve sections. When combining methods, add seam stitches to the flat-knit portions and eliminate them on the circular-knit areas.

Sometimes you may need to add seam stitches at the neckline. If a collar or part of a collar will be sewn to the side edges of a V or Square Neckline, cast on an extra stitch or two after the start of the neckline shaping. This will avoid the loss of a yoke and/or collar stitch when the pieces are joined.

Our graphs are not drawn with seam stitches, but our written guidelines indicate where to add them when working flat.

THE TEST SWATCH REVISITED

Basic information on test swatches and gauge measurement is covered on page 4, but swatches are your source of all kinds of additional information which you will need as you plan your sweaters.

Four simple equations are the foundation for all charting and are worth remembering. The first two, directly derived from the swatch, represent the basic premise of charting—the conversion of a measurement into the number of stitches or rows needed to knit a fabric of that dimension.

1. Stitch gauge × number of inches = number of stitches in fabric *width*
2. Row gauge × number of inches = number of rows in fabric *length*

The second two—actually the opposite sides of the same coin—are used less frequently, but are called for at times in the charting guidelines.

3. Number of *stitches* ÷ stitch gauge = fabric *width* in inches
4. Number of *rows* ÷ row gauge = fabric *length* in inches

If your sweater will have a simple overall stitch pattern, like stockinette, a simple swatch is all you need to be able to determine your gauge. But your garment may be more complex, and your swatch, or swatches, may need to reflect that complexity.

More than One Swatch

If you plan to change yarns or stitch patterns within your work, or if the principal pattern stitch you will use is intricate, you will need to make several swatches.

For a sweater which will include changes of yarns or patterns, make a swatch for each change. If the gauges are different, you may need to plan increases or decreases at the changeover points, or use different sizes of needles, to accommodate the shifts.

When your dominant stitch pattern is complex, you will not be able to use its stitch gauge to accurately figure the number of stitches for ribbing or border areas. There are two ways to handle this problem, either of which requires an extra swatch.

The first option is the one to choose if your borders will be finished in either of the two standard ribbings (a 1/1 or a 2/2 rib). Make a stockinette swatch using the needles you would select if the entire sweater were to be knit in stockinette stitch. The stitch gauge of this swatch is then used to calculate the number of stitches needed for all the borders of the garment. Using a needle two or three sizes smaller than the ones used in making the swatch, cast on and work your border. You may need to increase or decrease stitches as you begin to work the body or sleeve, but you will be sure that the ribbing fits.

If your borders are worked in a stitch pattern other than ribbing, you can work a swatch in the desired stitch pattern on the smaller needles you plan to use for that part of your sweater. Use the gauge of this swatch to determine how many stitches to cast on for the border. Use your pattern-stitch gauge to calculate the body stitches, and, if necessary, increase or decrease to this number on the first row of the body.

Pattern Repeat Gauge

If you are designing a sweater with a repeat pattern, it may be simpler to measure the gauge of a single *repeat* than to count the stitches. This is certainly true if the stitch pattern is one where it's difficult to distinguish (and therefore count) the individual stitches; examples include complex laces and cables.

You can get stitch and row gauge numbers for an intricate stitch pattern by measuring the width and depth of one repeat, although if a repeat is less than 1″ wide, you may want to measure several repeats. Since the number of stitches and rows within a repeat are known (for example, a pattern 12 stitches wide which requires 6 rows to complete), you can work a swatch approximately 4″ square with full repeats in both directions. Carefully measure one or more repeats in both width and length, then figure, using the repeat multiples, how many stitches and rows you have in the measurement. Divide the number of stitches and rows by the number of inches of the width and length of the repeats to find out how many stitches and rows per inch you are getting in your pattern stitch. See the formula below, and do not round off any fractions—use them in your further calculations.

Pattern Repeat Gauge

STEP 1

Number of stitches (or rows) in repeat ÷ number of inches measured = number of stitches (or rows) per inch for gauge

Example: 12 stitches ÷ 1.5" = 8 stitches per inch
 6 stitches ÷ 0.875" = 6.86 stitches per inch

　　Use the stitch gauge to determine the number of stitches in both the body and yoke areas of your sweater. Dividing the number of stitches in each of these sections by the number of stitches in one repeat will tell you how many repeats of the pattern will fit in that section. Keep in mind that when the garment is worn the seams between yoke and sleeves are more visible than the side seams, and avoid partial repeats at the armhole edges by making small adjustments if necessary.

Aran Sweater Test Swatches

Special test swatches will be necessary if various stitch patterns will cover the entire width of your sweater. The outstanding example of this type of design is the Aran sweater (see "Knitting Ethnic" in appendix).

　　In this situation, a test swatch should be at least *half the width of the planned design,* from the center to a side edge. Make one test swatch for the body and a separate one for the sleeves. As a general rule, intricate patterns like those found in Arans require 15 to 25 percent more stitches than fabric worked in stockinette.

　　Here's how to plan an Aran-style garment.

1. Obtain rough estimates of required numbers of stitches in body and sleeve.

　　a. Knit a swatch in *stockinette* and measure the stitch gauge. Base the number of stitches in the ribbing or border on this swatch.

　　b. Determine the width of the sweater back in inches.

　　c. Multiply this width by the stockinette gauge.

　　d. Multiply that result by 115 percent (Step c × 1.15) and by 125 percent (Step c × 1.25). This part of your sweater will probably require somewhere between these two numbers of stitches.

　　e, f, g. Repeat Steps b, c, and d for the width of the upper sleeve.

2. Design preliminary layout of stitch patterns.

　　Use the two rough numbers calculated in Steps 1d and 1f to plan the cable patterns for your back and sleeve, then work a swatch as described above

for each of these garment sections. If your swatch represents one-half the back patterning, for example, it should produce fabric that is one-half the desired width of your sweater back. You may need to add or subtract a cable pattern to meet your exact measurement requirements. You can also add stockinette, seed, or garter stitch at the side edges to increase the fabric width.

　　Plan the entire sweater carefully, using the swatches as guides. Pay attention to the effect of garment shaping on the cables; yokes are a particular area of concern. If you are charting a standard yoke to be used with set-in sleeve caps, will only a portion of a cable remain at the edge after armhole shaping is complete? Measure your swatch to find out, and adjust the positions of the cables (or change them completely) to avoid a problem. If you're making a raglan sweater, will the cable patterns match where the yoke and sleeve-cap edges come together? If not, work the raglan decreases several stitches in from the edge, and carry a stockinette band or a small cable along the tapered edges, to separate the different patterns.

Biasing

There may be times when your swatch is not rectangular, but instead drapes or hangs diagonally. There are three possible culprits that could be causing this problem, which is called *biasing:* the stitch pattern, the yarn, or the method of working the stitches.

　　The first step to take in determining if the biasing can be corrected is to block your swatch, by either the steam or the wet-wrap method (see "How Tos"), and let it sit for a day. If the biasing is still evident, up the ante by using the immersion method of blocking. Again let the dry swatch sit for a day, to see if it will hold its shape. If it reverts to its skewed shape, your sweater will not hang correctly even after blocking.

If you are using a pattern stitch which contains a diagonal line formed by working decreases which slant in one direction, you may be able to correct the biasing by alternating the directions of the decrease stitches. You will lose the smooth line of decrease progressions, but could eliminate the bias. If this does not seem workable, you can choose a different stitch altogether.

If the problem stems from the yarn's twist, experiment with patterns worked in combinations of knit and purl stitches (see examples on page 6). Is your swatch still crooked? Exchange the yarn for a different type, if you can. Unless you're intrigued by the challenge of finding a way to convert the bias to your advantage, going farther with this yarn will not be worth the time and effort because the finished sweater will never hang correctly.

Examine the fabric to find out if the biasing is a result of your knitting method. If there are twisted stitches in the fabric, you may either be wrapping the yarn incorrectly as you knit and/or purl, or working into the backs of the stitches inadvertently. In this case, you may want to have an expert knitter watch you work and help you learn how to correct the problem.

Swatches and the Sweater-in-Progress

Swatches do not become useless after your sweater begins to take shape. You'll want to measure your work as the sweater progresses. Be aware that your ribbing will affect the gauge, and wait until you have about 4″ of fabric above the ribbing before you check your gauge.

You may find you're working more tightly or loosely than the test swatch indicates. Adjust your needle size, if necessary, to maintain the established gauge.

Above all, *take a new measurement before any major garment shaping occurs.* An obvious time to remeasure is just before the armhole shaping.

YARN REQUIREMENTS
How Much Yarn?

There are four basic ways to determine how much yarn you will need for a particular sweater, but with all the options a word of caution is advised: buy more yarn than you think will be necessary. For sources of guidance you can:

1. Ask the salesperson,
2. Read similar printed patterns for the yarn selected,
3. Check the yarn label,
4. Knit up one skein and calculate the amount of fabric produced.

The salesperson's experience, in having sold the yarn for use with printed patterns, can help you estimate how much you will need. A description of your sweater and an approximation of its size may be all that's needed. Using this method requires some trust in the salesperson's level of expertise.

You can leaf through printed patterns in the yarn of your choice, and note the amount of yarn needed for a sweater in the size closest to that of your planned garment. If patterns in the same yarn are not available, refer to patterns worked at the same stitch gauge as your selected yarn. In this case, the yardage of the yarn becomes a significant factor in your estimation—are there about the same number of yards per ounce in both yarns?

Comparable yardage is perhaps more important than skein weight in making conversions. Two knitting worsteds may appear similar, but if one is slightly thicker it will have fewer yards per ounce than its thinner cousin. Determine the total yardage needed for your sweater by multiplying the number of skeins required in the pattern by the number of yards in a single skein of that yarn. If yardage information is not listed on the label or given in the pattern, yarn shops often have books or yarn-company literature which provide these numbers.

Some yarn companies have information on their labels which indicates how many balls are needed for a medium-sized basic pullover. You can use this as a guide, but keep in mind that your design may require more or less than this amount, depending on its size, style, and stitch pattern(s).

Fast knitters can buy one skein and knit it up. This has the advantage of providing yarn requirements which are specific to your chosen yarn *and* your stitch patterns. However, don't wait too long before purchasing the remainder of your yarn, or the shop may be out of your dye lot. Ask if the store will hold a certain number of skeins for you, for a specific period of time.*

There are several ways to use this first skein. You can break off a specific length of yarn—perhaps ten yards—and knit a swatch, then see how many square inches it produces and calculate the total number of yards you will need. Or knit a swatch, figure how many square inches are in it, and weigh the swatch on a diet or postal scale—this will give you the total weight of yarn you will need.

Better yet, make a normal-sized gauge swatch and then begin to knit the back of your garment, using the whole skein. Calculate how many square inches of fabric the skein produces (remember to include the swatch in these calculations), then figure out how many square inches of fabric your garment will require (see formula). Divide the garment total by the knitted total to find out how many skeins you will need.

---

*Most yarn shops will accept returns or exchanges of unopened skeins, as long as you come back within a reasonable period of time, and retain your sales slip. If you are concerned about this, ask the salesperson for the store's policy before purchasing the yarn.

YARN REQUIREMENTS

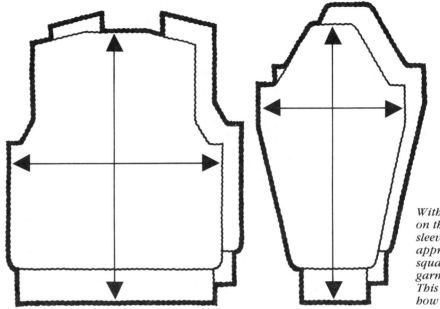

With four measurements, two on the body and two on the sleeve, you can calculate the approximate number of square inches of fabric in the garment you are planning. This will help you determine how much yarn you need.

To Find the Number of Square Inches of Fabric in Your Garment

STEP 1
Width of sweater back (at widest point) × (Garment Length to Underarm *plus* Raglan Armhole Depth) = unadjusted area of sweater back, in square inches

STEP 2
Width of sleeve (at widest point) × [Sleeve Length (to underarm) *plus* estimated height of sleeve cap] = unadjusted area of one sleeve, in square inches

STEP 3
(Step 1 + Step 2) × 2 = unadjusted area of whole sweater, in square inches

STEP 4
Step 3 – 10% of Step 3 = adjusted area of whole sweater, in square inches

Use your judgment in calculating Step 4. On a Classic Sweater, 10 percent is usually subtracted to compensate for body, sleeve, and neckline shaping. But keep in mind how much body and sleeve shaping your sweater requires. If you are charting a T-Shaped Sweater with Box Sleeves, you won't need to subtract anything.

Also consider your neck finish in arriving at a final number. A crochet finish or a 1″ ribbed band requires very little yarn, while a Cowl or Shawl Collar requires extra. For a cowl or shawl collar, you will need to add square inches to Step 4.

plus-cap is generally longer.) If you find that more than one-fourth of your yarn has been used to knit the back, it may be time to locate more yarn or rethink your design.

First steps first! Stop knitting the moment you discover you're running short. There's no sense in wasting stitches if "unknitting" is in your future.

Next, phone the shop and see if any skeins are still available in your dye lot. It may be worth trying other stores in your area that carry the same brand. However, if it's been a while since you bought the original yarn, chances are you'll be out of luck.

Can you, however, buy the same brand and color in a different dye lot? Sometimes new yarn can be blended in, by alternating one row of the new and one row of the original dye lot. This will be least noticeable if done on the sleeves (but not the sleeve caps, which will be joined to the body sections). Treat both sleeves identically.

If you can't come up with a reasonable match, it's time to redesign. That's not as bad as it sounds—you have lots of options available. Can you shorten the sleeves, or make a more tapered style of sleeve? Would it be possible to work the sleeves and/or front of the sweater in a simpler or more open pattern stitch?

Can your front neckline be more open? A deep V requires less yarn than high round shaping. Will a different collar or neck finish use less yarn?

How about incorporating a contrasting color or texture of yarn into the sweater as a design element? Perhaps the contrast can occur in horizontal bands on

To Use Your Swatch to Figure Yarn Requirements

STEP 5
Length of swatch × width of swatch = area of swatch, in square inches

STEP 6
[(Step 4 ÷ Step 5) × weight of swatch or yards used in swatch] ÷ weight of one skein or yards per skein = amount of yarn required for sweater (in skeins or yards)

Too Much Yarn

If you wind up with too much yarn and can't (or don't want to) exchange it, begin your resource drawer. As you experiment more with designing, you'll discover that unused yarn is never wasted. An extra skein can often be used to knit a matching cap, or saved to be combined with other yarns in a future sweater. A drawer or basket full of leftovers is an excellent place to locate yarn for a contrasting stripe or trim.

Not Enough Yarn

What happens if, in spite of all your planning, you run short of yarn before you reach the last stitch? This even happens to knitters who follow patterns and purchase the recommended number of skeins. Don't feel alone.

A possible yarn shortage can usually be anticipated before the garment is nearing completion. We recommend that you always knit the back section first. The amount of yarn required for a classic back is fairly close to that needed for a long sleeve. (The back is wider, but a sleeve-

the yoke or sleeves, or in vertical panels on both sleeves and front, or in the ribbing, front edge bindings, and collar.

Can the sleeves be knit entirely in a different color or fiber? You can make this look like your original intention by working the new yarn into the front and back, in duplicate stitch or other embroidery techniques.

If you're *really* running short, can you rework the yoke on the sweater's back and front, and make a vest?

An understanding of design and charting will give you many options not readily recognized by knitters who strictly follow patterns. But along with the title *designer* comes the subtitle *problem solver.*

You'll learn not to think of a yarn shortage (or any other stumbling block) as a disaster, but as a challenge. Be sure you don't rip out all your hard work and relegate the yarn to a bottom drawer until all the possibilities have been fully explored (we'll bet you'll have a lot of fun, and an empty bottom drawer). This particular sweater may not turn out exactly as you first planned, but the lessons learned are valuable, especially as they build your confidence. And the solution may be even better than your original design!

CHARTING TOOLS

You can design sweaters with only a tape measure, pencil, and paper, but a few additional items can make the process much easier. As you already know, charting involves numbers: a pocket calculator is a valuable first addition to your charting tools.

Pocket Calculators

Calculators are available with many different functions and in various price ranges. Math for charting is simple, so an inexpensive solar- or battery-operated calculator is all you'll need. It should add, subtract, multiply, and divide; a square root key ($\sqrt{}$) is handy for charting sleeve caps.

Calculators have one drawback. Knitters usually think in terms of fractions ($1/2''$) and calculators use decimals (.50). We've provided a chart to help you convert back and forth. As an example, $3 1/4''$ will be keyed into a calculator as 3.25, and $6 5/8''$ will be punched in as 6.625.

To convert decimals back into fractions, work with the closest number on the chart. If your calculator reads 4.43, use 4.5 or $4 1/2''$; if it reads 7.91, use 7.875 or $7 7/8''$.

CONVERTING FRACTIONS TO DECIMALS (AND VICE VERSA)

Fraction	Decimal
$1/8''$	.125
$1/4''$	.25
$3/8''$	.375
$1/2''$	.5
$5/8''$	.625
$3/4''$	.75
$7/8''$	.875

Standard Graph Paper

Another important tool for a knitwear designer is graph paper. The numbers arrived at in charting can easily be converted into a graphed pattern—no artistic background is necessary! Graphs are easy to follow when you are knitting, enable you to make design decisions where several possibilities exist, and will help you gain the courage to experiment beyond our guidelines.

Graphed patterns will show you the basic shape of a garment section, even before the first stitch is cast on. They will help you determine where increases and decreases work best, how necklines look, where pockets should be placed, and where stitch or color patterns will occur in relation to garment shaping. Changes can be made easily—after all, it's a lot simpler to erase a few lines on paper than it is to rip out several inches of knitting.

Standard, or square, graph paper is suitable for most charting, and is available where stationery supplies are sold. Add a pencil, a ruler, and the mathematical calculations for your sweater, and you're on your way.

Treat each square on the paper as one stitch, and each row of squares as one row of knitting. If the graph paper isn't large enough for a complete pattern, tape two sheets together. Or chart only half of the body or sleeve—unless the design varies on the right and left sides, half the drawing is all you'll need.

Graph paper is also useful for creating color designs, knit/purl patterns, laces, and cables. Borrow symbols from printed patterns or books, or make up your own; the only one who needs to understand the pattern is you.

Knitting Graph Paper

Although the boxes on standard graph paper are square, a knit stitch is not. A knit stitch forms a rectangle—it is wider than it is high. For this reason, a stockinette stitch sweater charted on square graph paper will appear long in relation to its width. For use as a pattern, that's just fine.

There are, however, instances where the use of knitting graph paper can help in the design process. The boxes on knitting graph paper are drawn to resemble the proportions of stockinette stitch, which has an approximate ratio of 5 stitches to 6 or 7 rows.

Take a look at the graphs of the snowflakes. The top one was charted on square graph paper, the bottom one on knitting graph paper. The proportions of the bottom drawing are much closer to those of actual knitting. While this doesn't affect the beauty of geometric designs, the differences should be considered when you plan picture knitting. Compare the identically charted cats. If the pattern on the left were followed in stockinette, the knitted cat would resemble its squat neighbor.

We have included a sheet of knitting graph paper in the Appendix. It has a ratio of 5 stitches to 6 rows.* Use it when you want a graph that reflects the knitted proportions of the proposed garment, or if you're charting a picture.

*In worsted-weight yarn worked at a "normal" tension, you'll get 5 stitches and 6–7 rows per inch; in other weights of yarn, the ratio remains the same although the number of stitches per inch changes.

WORKING WITH GRAPH PAPER

The snowflakes on top were charted on square graph paper; those on the bottom were on knitting graph paper. The proportions of the bottom drawing are much closer to those of actual knitting.

The cat on the left was drawn on square graph paper instead of knitting graph paper. The illustration on the right shows how this cat would look if knitted in stockinette from the squared graph.

PICTURE KNITTING
Charting a Picture

Yes, charting a picture! You can design picture knits even if you don't think you can draw. Knitting lends itself to big, bold graphics. Simplicity is the key to good sweater art. Children are great sources for pictures, because they keep their drawings simple and simple drawings are easy to copy. Large areas of color are easy to knit, since only a few yarns must be handled simultaneously. Small details can be knitted in or added later in duplicate stitch or embroidery.

Keep your eyes open for pictures of animals, flowers, boats, and even landscapes. Choose a favorite cartoon character for a child's pullover, or have a child draw something special for grandpa's cardigan. The possibilities are endless.

Before you can translate the picture into knitted stitches, you'll need to make a pattern of the sweater on knitting graph paper. Graph all sections of the sweater on which the picture might appear—back, front (including neckline shaping), and/or sleeves.

Next, decide how tall or wide you want the picture to be in relation to your graphed pattern, and where the picture will be placed. You'll need to enlarge or reduce your picture to that size. This can be done at a full-service photocopying shop or through a photographic process called photostating. A local printer or graphic designer should be able to tell you where you can have a photostat made. Or scale the drawing yourself—it isn't hard.

When your picture is the right size, trace it lightly in position onto the graphed sweater pattern. A sunny window or a light box can help out here.

You're almost done! All that's left is to translate your picture into knitting stitches. Like the picture of the cat, your drawing probably has curves and you'll need to turn those into stepped lines. Staying as close to the outline of the drawing as possible, redo your lines following the squared edges of the rectangles on the graph. If your original drawing only covers a portion of the box, you'll need to decide whether that stitch will be part of the drawing or part of the background. Final decisions can be made after the entire picture is complete—or even just before that stitch is actually knitted.

If your picture is on more than one body section—front and back, perhaps—

PLACING A DRAWING ON A GARMENT

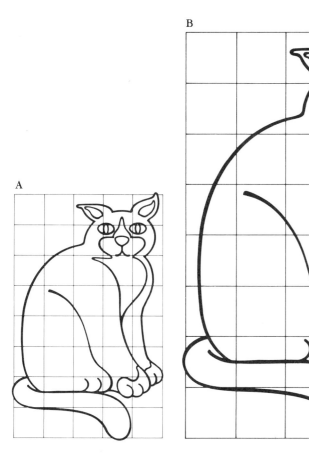

Begin with a drawing of the figure you want to knit (a). Scale the drawing up to the size at which you want it to appear (b). Superimpose the drawing on the chart of the garment piece and redo the lines, following the rectangular grid of the graph (c).

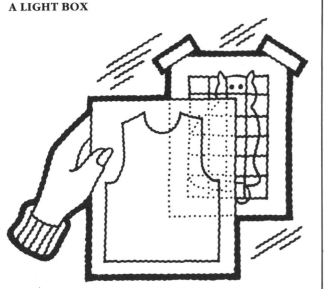

Whether your source of light is a professional artist's light box or a sunny window, illuminating paper from the back makes it much easier to make tracings.

make sure that the picture will line up correctly at the shoulders and side seams after the sweater is assembled. Remember that the edge stitches may be seam stitches which will not appear on the finished sweater.

That's it! Now you can reproduce your masterpiece in yarn.

Scaling a Drawing to Size

Using a pencil and ruler, divide your picture in half horizontally, then into quarters, and so forth. These lines can be any convenient distance apart—you don't want them so close together that you can't see what you're doing, or so far apart that the sections of drawing between the lines are very complex. Next, draw vertical lines the same distance apart as the horizontal lines. Your picture is now within a *square grid.*

Make a second grid, at the size the picture should be in relation to your graphed sweater pattern. Be sure that this grid has the same number of squares as the first grid, both horizontally and vertically. You can draw the new grid directly onto the sweater pattern, if you're sure of the picture's position.

Now, transfer the picture from the original grid onto the second grid, one square at a time. If you concentrate only on the corresponding squares you'll find this isn't hard to do. Even if you're not very precise, you'll have a good rough sketch and can refine the lines when you're finished.

A Light Box

A light box is a tool used by professional designers and illustrators, and it might interest you if you plan to make lots of picture knits. It's a wooden or metal box with a light inside and a glass surface on top. When two sheets of thin- to medium-weight paper are placed on the glass, the image on the bottom sheet shows through the top sheet and can be easily traced. It's a lot like using tracing paper, but both sheets of paper can be heavier.

If the bottom sheet is the grid drawing or photocopy of your picture, and the top sheet is the graphed sweater pattern, you can shift the pattern until you like the placement before you trace the picture into position.

The idea of the light box can be duplicated at no expense if you tape your grid or photocopy to a window on a sunny day, and place your sweater pattern on top. Light will shine through both sheets and you can position your picture correctly for tracing.

Charting Your Pattern

Once you've determined your measurements, ease, and gauge, you're ready to start charting. Sweaters come in many styles, and we've included a wide selection for you to choose from. The accompanying graphs show you the basic silhouettes at a glance.

Charting is the bridge between the style and the knitted fabric. Narrowly defined, charting is knowing when and how to widen or narrow the knitted fabric. This is done by the familiar techniques of increasing, decreasing, casting on, binding off, and working short rows.

Before you dive into charting the style of your dreams, it's very important that you read and understand our guidelines for a Classic Sweater. This style has a Classic Body, Set-In Armhole shaping, and Standard Shoulder shaping; the sleeves are Tapered and are finished with a Set-In Cap. It would be a good idea to mark these pages with bookmarks or paperclips: 59, 197, and 199. Our guidelines for these shapes include many details which we will refer to often as we chart other styles. When we do, we will abbreviate them: **CB** for the classic body, and **TS** for the tapered sleeve. We will also give you the number of the specific step we are referring to.

There are two ways to chart a sweater, *all-at-once* and *as-you-go*. If you have a very firm idea of how you would like the finished sweater to look, chart each portion right at the start: body, armhole shaping, neckline, and sleeves. You can simply write down the numbers you get from our formulas, or you can draw an outline of your sweater and use symbols of your own choosing to indicate the rate at which various areas will be shaped. If you really want to see how the shapes will look, you can graph your entire sweater—or just specific parts. Naturally, changes can be made as your knitting progresses.

The as-you-go method gives more flexibility to the design process. If any questions remain in your mind about the finished sweater—pullover vs. cardigan, round vs. V neckline, and so forth—chart and knit the back of the garment first. You will need to make some initial choices about body style and armhole shaping, but seeing a completed back may help you reach decisions for the front.

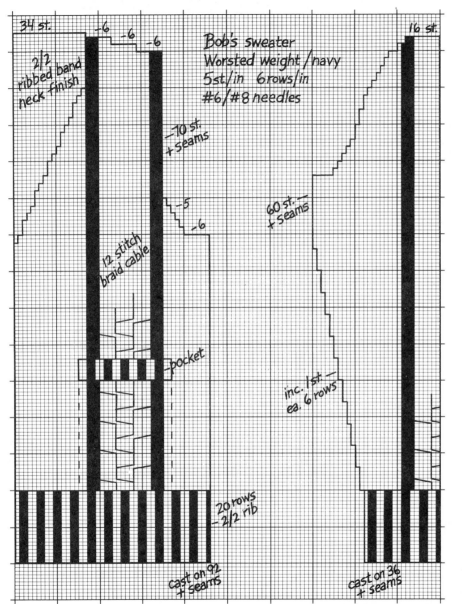

34 st.

−6 −6 −6

16 st.

2/2 ribbed band neck finish

Bob's sweater
Worsted weight /navy
5 st/in 6 rows/in
#6/#8 needles

−10 st.
+ seams

12 stitch braid cable.

−5
−6

60 st.
+ seams

pocket

inc. 1st.
ea. 6 rows

20 rows
2/2 rib

cast on 92
+ seams

cast on 36
+ seams

*When you have charted your pattern, you will
have a record of your plan which is much
easier to work from than a printed pattern.*

There's another reason for starting with the back which has to do with fit. If, after the back is finished, you feel the sweater needs more ease, you can add it to the front (see Enlarged Sweater Front). If you are an as-you-go designer, make sure that you have enough yarn to accommodate your choices.

When you understand the basics of sweater design, you will be free to discover how adaptable knitting is, and how this provides you with limitless design possibilities. To make your learning process easier, we have tried to be conservative in our guidelines. As your confidence grows, you'll find yourself diverging from our printed words and experimenting with your own ideas.

CHARTING ARITHMETIC

There's no way around it: charting involves numbers. But don't let that scare you, the process is actually very straightforward. All we'll be using is basic gradeschool arithmetic, and your handy pocket calculator will help make charting fast and easy.

Very often, the numbers you arrive at will need to be modified. The most common instance of this is changing a fraction to the nearest whole number. At other times, you may want to take greater liberties with the numbers to make them work to your benefit. A drawing of the sweater's shape on knitter's graph paper can help you see where to make creative modifications in your math. You may, for instance, decide to start a V Neckline or a Raglan Armhole a few rows early, so the spacing of decreases comes out even. You might also adjust the width of the body by a few stitches to accommodate a stitch pattern.

Knitting is a very forgiving medium, and no one will ever be the wiser.

BASIC CHARTING FORMULAS

Charting is a way of determining when and how to change the number of stitches on your needle to achieve a desired garment shape.

Our guidelines will tell you when a specific technique is required, and will help you determine the total number of stitches and/or rows involved. But sometimes you will also need to figure out the *spacing* of those increases or decreases across the width or along the length of the fabric.

We've worked out three basic formulas to help you achieve smooth spacing for different situations. Because they're in constant demand, we'll outline them here. We call them the *gathers formula,* the *taper formula,* and the *slope formula.* In our guidelines we will let you know when a formula may help, and refer you to the correct one. You may want to glance at the formulas now, but their uses will become clearer as you begin charting your sweater.

Gathers

When several increases or decreases are worked across a single row, they create gathers or blousing—as in a Blouson Body or a Lantern Sleeve. Gathers are for increasing or decreasing fullness across a row, above a ribbing (in body or sleeve), or to adjust for a difference in gauge (when changing yarns or stitch patterns).

Gathers Formula

STEP 1
Write down, and label with *a* and *b*, as noted:
a. The number of stitches on the needle.
b. The number of stitches you want to increase or decrease, plus 1.
Example: If you have 63 stitches on your needle and want to increase 5 stitches across a row, a = 63; b = 5 + 1 = 6

STEP 2
a ÷ b = unadjusted number of stitches between increases or decreases
■ If the result consists of a whole number and a fraction, go to Step 3.
■ If your result is a whole number (with no fraction), you can stop your calculations here and proceed as follows:
M1 Increase: Work one increase *after* each group of (number in Step 2) stitches, except for the last group.
Knit into Front and Back: Work an increase *in* the last stitch in every group of (number in Step 2) stitches, except the last one at the end of the row.
Decrease: Work one decrease *after* each group of (Step 2 − 2) stitches, except for the last group.
Example: 63 ÷ 6 = 10.5

STEP 3
Write down two numbers: the *whole number in Step 2* and the *next higher whole number.*
Example: 10 (whole number) and 11 (next higher whole number)

STEP 4
a − (b × *whole number*) = number of groups of stitches which will contain the *next higher whole number* of stitches
Example: 63 − (6 × 10, or 60) = 3; therefore, 3 groups of stitches will contain 11 stitches.

STEP 5

b – (Step 4) = number of groups which will contain the *whole number* of stitches
Example: 6 – 3 = 3; therefore, 3 groups of stitches will contain 10 stitches.

STEP 6

Using the *higher whole number* of stitches in the first group, form any regular pattern (for example, alternating) with the remaining groups of stitches.
Example: Work 11 (inc #1) 10 (inc #2) 11 (inc #3) 10 (inc #4) 11 (inc #5) 10.
<u>**M1 Increase:**</u> See Step 2 for basic method; in this example, *K11, M1, K10, M1* and end with K10.
<u>**Knit into Front and Back:**</u> See Step 2 for basic method; in this example, *K10, inc in the 11th st, K9, inc in the 10th st* and end with K10.
<u>**Decrease:**</u> See Step 2 for basic method; in this example, *K9 (which is 11 – 2), dec, K8 (which is 10 – 2), dec* and end with K10.

Markers can be placed between the groups of stitches to eliminate the need for counting as you knit. This is helpful if you are both shaping the piece *and* establishing, or maintaining, a stitch pattern across this row.

The markers will indicate where to increase or decrease; the stitch pattern will determine whether the shaping maneuver is worked as a knit or a purl.

Tapers

A taper is made by increasing or decreasing a number of stitches over a number of rows larger than the number of stitches. *Tapers are used primarily for increasing or decreasing at the side edges of sleeves and Tapered Bodies, Raglan Armholes, Shawl Collars, V Necklines, and some sleeve caps.* Either single or double increases and decreases can be worked, and this gradual shaping is usually done at or near the edges of the fabric.

The Taper Formula will help you determine which rows will be shaping rows, and how to smoothly distribute the increases or decreases along the edge. We recommend that the shaping be worked on the right side of the fabric only, and therefore we will be working with an *even number* of rows in each section. For instance, if your charting calls for four increases on each edge over twelve rows, your unadjusted arithmetic will show one increase every third row—an odd number, which will place every other increase on a wrong-side row. We suggest that two of the increases be worked on every second row, and two on every fourth row—even-numbered (right-side) rows.

Note that in this formula you are working with increases or decreases *per edge*.

Taper Formula

STEP 1

Write down, and label with *a* and *b,* as noted:

a. The total number of rows over which you will make your increases or decreases; make this an even number.

b. The number of stitches you want to increase or decrease at *each edge.* (This equals half the total number of stitches to be increased or decreased.)

Example: a = 88 rows, b = 17 stitches per edge

STEP 2

a ÷ b = unadjusted rate of increase or decrease

It's best to work all increases or decreases on the same side of the fabric—on right-side rows. If your unadjusted rate of shaping contains an odd number or a fraction, you will need to make some adjustments.

■ If your result is a whole, even number, you can stop your calculations here. Work a single increase or decrease at each edge every (number in Step 2) rows, b times.

■ If your result is *1 plus a fraction,* skip to Step 6.

■ If your result is an even number and a fraction, go to Step 3/even.

■ If your result is an odd number, or an odd number and a fraction, go to Step 3/odd.

Example: 88 ÷ 17 = 5.18

In this example, we have an odd number and a fraction. If we shaped the fabric every fifth row, the increases and decreases would fall alternately on right-side and wrong-side rows. We would complete 17 decreases in 85 rows, and have 3 rows left to work for the desired length of fabric. Ideally, we'd like our shaping to occur on right-side rows; we need to figure out how to work all the increases or decreases on even-numbered rows. So we continue.

STEP 3/even

Write down the *even number* and the *next higher even number.*

See note on Step 3/odd.

STEP 3/odd

Write down the *next lower even number* and the *next higher even number.*

Example (for 5.18 from Step 2): 4 (next lower even number) and 6 (next higher even number)

Some of the increases or decreases will be worked every 4 rows, while some will be worked every 6 rows. Next we'll find out how many increases or decreases will be worked at each of these two intervals.

STEP 4

[(b × higher even number) − a] ÷ 2 = number of single increases or decreases on each edge, to be worked every (*lower even number*) rows

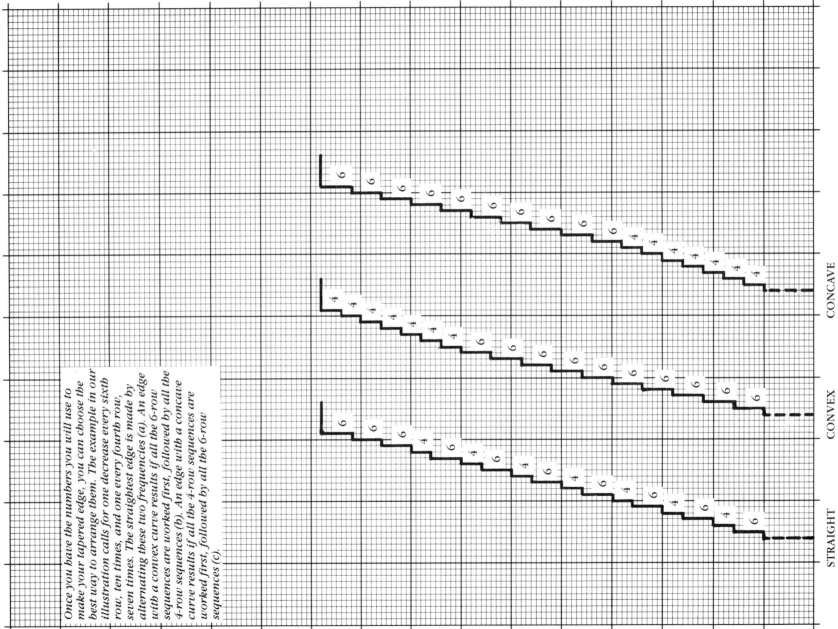

TAPERS

Once you have the numbers you will use to make your tapered edge, you can choose the best way to arrange them. The example in our illustration calls for one decrease every sixth row, ten times, and one every fourth row, seven times. The straightest edge is made by alternating these two frequencies (a). An edge with a convex curve results if all the 6-row sequences are worked first, followed by all the 4-row sequences are worked first, followed by all the 6-row sequences (c).

CONCAVE

CONVEX

STRAIGHT

Example: [(17 × 6 = 102) − 88] = 14 ÷ 2 = 7; therefore, work 1 increase or decrease per edge every 4 rows, 7 times.

STEP 5
b − Step 4 = number of single increases or decreases per edge, to be worked every (*higher even number*) rows
Example: 17 − 7 = 10; therefore, work 1 increase or decrease per edge every 6 rows, 10 times.
Summary of Steps 4 and 5: Seven of the increases or decreases will be worked "every 4 rows," and 10 of them will be worked "every 6 rows." This gives us our total of 17. There are three ways we can arrange the pattern of shaping rows, and each will affect the way the edge of the garment curves.
1. The straightest edge is made by alternating 4-row and 6-row sequences. Because we have 7 of one type and 10 of the other, we would need to work extra 6-row sections as we went. For example, 6 rows, *6 rows, 4 rows*, repeat between asterisks 6 additional times, 6 rows, 6 rows (a total of seven 4-row intervals and ten 6-row intervals).
2. An edge with a convex curve will result if all the 6-row sequences are worked first and then all the 4-row sequences follow. For example, shape knitting every 6 rows 10 times, then shape knitting every 4 rows 7 times.
3. An edge with a concave curve will result if all the 4-row sequences are worked first, followed by the 6-row sequences.

■ If the result in Step 3 was *1 plus a fraction,* you will need to combine single and double increases or decreases in order to have your fabric reach the desired width over the planned number of rows. Steps 6 through 8 take this possibility in hand. In the case of increases, you will combine single increases with two-stitch cast-ons; in the case of decreases, you will combine single decreases with either double decreases or two-stitch bind-offs. Shapings will occur every 2 rows throughout the taper.

STEP 6
a ÷ 2 = number of shaping rows per edge in the taper
Example: If we take our previous example where a = 88 rows, but we plan to decrease a larger number of stitches (b = 56, for example), in this calculation 88 ÷ 2 = 44 shaping rows per edge.

STEP 7
b − Step 6 = number of two-stitch increases or decreases to be worked at each edge
Example: 56 − 44 = 12 two-stitch increases or decreases per edge on every other row (this places the shapings all on right-side rows).

STEP 8
Step 6 − Step 7 = number of single increases or decreases to be worked at each edge
Example: 44 − 12 = 32 single increases or decreases to be worked per edge on every other row.
Whatever the results of your calculations, you can double-check them by graphing the shapes of your sweater pieces on graph paper.

Slopes

Slopes occur when a large number of stitches are added or subtracted over a relatively small number of rows, creating a more extreme diagonal than is produced by the taper. *Slopes are used for the cast-on or bind-off sequences across the width of the shoulders, for shallow necklines, and for dolman shaping.* The shaping stitches are cast on or bound off, usually at each edge of the fabric, on every other row—the shoulder and arm shaping of a Vertically Knit Dolman is a good example. In some cases, however, the shaping is worked with short rows, as in bust darts.

In a slope, you'll bind off a large number of stitches over relatively few rows. Slopes result when the number of stitches to be increased or decreased is greater than, or equal to, the number of rows over which they are shaped. The stitches will almost always be cast on or bound off (the exceptions are short-row shaping and full-fashioned back shoulder shaping). They will be worked at the beginning of *every other row* at a given edge.

The Slope Formula will help you calculate the number of stitches to cast on or bind off *per edge* on every other row.

Slope Formula

STEP 1

Write down, and label with *a* and *b,* as noted:
a. The total number of rows over which cast-ons or bind-offs will be worked; make this an even number. Divide it by 2 and begin your calculations with the result.
b. The number of stitches to be cast on or bound off at each edge. (This equals half the total number of stitches to be cast on or bound off.)
Example: a = 56 ÷ 2 = 28; b = 60

STEP 2

b ÷ a = unadjusted rate of cast-ons/bind-offs
■ If the result is a whole number, you can stop your calculations here. Cast on or bind off (Step 2) stitches every other row a times at each edge.
■ If the result in Step 2 contains a fraction, go to Step 3.
Example: 60 ÷ 28 = 2.14

STEP 3

Write down the *whole number* in the result and the *next higher whole number.*
Example: 2 (whole number) and 3 (next higher whole number)

STEP 4

(a × *next higher whole number*) − b = number of cast-ons/bind-offs that will consist of the *whole number* of stitches
Example: (28 × 3 = 84) − 60 = 24; therefore, 24 cast-ons/bind-offs will consist of 2 stitches; cast on or bind off 2 stitches per edge on every other row, 24 times.

STEP 5

a − Step 4 = number of cast-ons/bind-offs that will consist of the *higher whole number* of stitches
Example: 28 − 24 = 4; therefore, 4 cast-ons/bind-offs will consist of 3 stitches; cast on or bind off 3 stitches per edge on every other row, 4 times.

BODY AND YOKE SHAPING

Classic Body with Set-In Armhole Shaping, and Standard Shoulder Shaping, labeled CB

This is the basic design combination used for most traditional sweaters—cardigans and pullovers, sporty and dressy styles, lightweight summer blouses and heavy winter jackets. Spend some time becoming familiar with this basic shape; a thorough understanding of its charting is essential to the material that follows. We'll go into more detail here than on other shapes, so we can provide helpful hints and troubleshoot potential pitfalls along the way.

A Classic Sweater is ideal for your first charting project. In spite of its traditional structure, the design possibilities are endless. This style can be long or short, can have a hem, fancy border, or ribbing at the bottom, and can have as much ease as you want. You can select a plain or complex yarn—and simple or intricate stitches.

The front and back sections are charted identically, except for the neckline. In most cases, only the front section requires neckline shaping. If the back of the neck is shaped, it usually is contoured less than the front. Necklines are covered in detail in the next chapter.

The formulas are much easier and faster to work through than you might think at first glance. As you saw in the three basic formulas for gathers, tapers, and slopes, our instructions consist of a series of steps which give you numbers to knit from. We're also teaching you the process of charting, so each formula contains details to help you make decisions under many different circumstances.

In the fundamental sections on the Classic Body and the Tapered Sleeve, we've put a mark (*) next to the steps which result in actual numbers necessary for knitting. The other steps are preliminary ones, but essential to the charting process. As your experience grows, you will find that you automatically condense these steps and that charting becomes very simple.

Ready? Take out your measurements and a gauge swatch, and try the first formula—the Classic Body.

About the Formulas

Each step-by-step formula includes a mathematical example: calculations for a sample sweater. The resulting garment shapes are shown in the accompanying graphs.

The following information applies to all our formulas:

1. All body and garment measurements are in inches.
2. The *body measurements* used in our examples are the "sample measurements" shown on page 35.
3. The *garment ease* in our examples is based on an "average"-size sweater. See page 37 for information on figuring your own ease.
4. The *gauges* used in our examples are as follows: 5 stitches = 1″ and 6 rows = 1″.
5. *Seam stitches* are not included in the formulas or shown on the accompanying graphs, but you will be told when they should be added. See page 38 for information on seam stitches.
6. To translate inches into fractions (or vice versa) when using your calculator, see the chart on page 44.

It is important to use *your own numbers* when charting your garment.

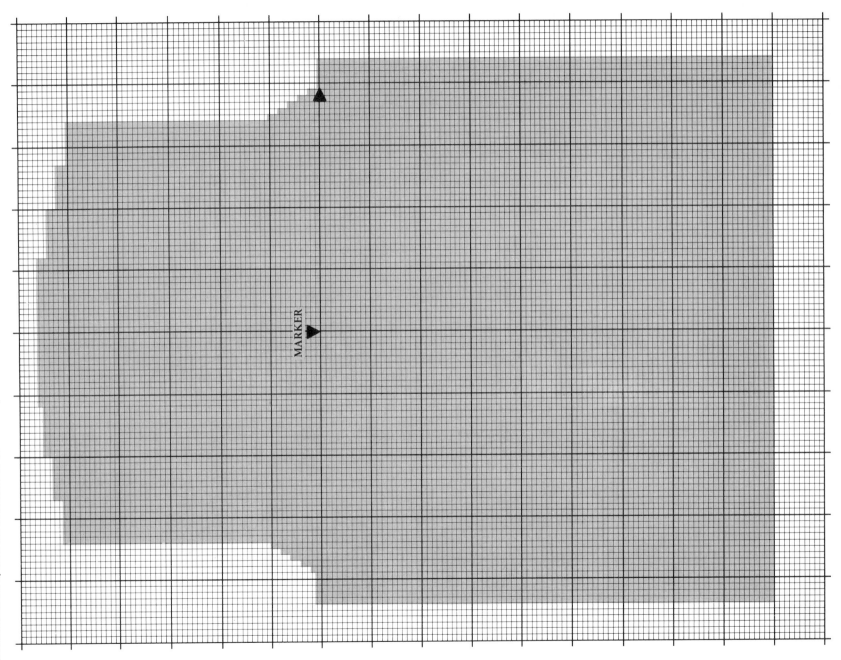

MARKER

Learn to play with the dimensions of color by working swatches. The neutral gray here is a unifying factor, but the diamond patterns explore different ideas of color harmony.

- ■ *1.* Monochromatic *color scheme, with variations in* value.
- ■ *2.* Monochromatic *color scheme, with variations in* intensity.
- ■ *3.* Analogous *color scheme.*
- ■ *4.* Complementary *color scheme, with muted hues.*
- ■ *5.* Triadic *color scheme.*

The child's classic V-neck vest demonstrates a polychromatic *use of color, although the movement between colors reflects the supporting use of other color harmony principles. This vest was designed by Jody Michelson-Hubbell and his mother, Carmen Michelson, who also knit it. Worked in sportweight yarn, it has a slip-stitch pattern. There is a piped finish on the ribbing.*

Sometimes you'll want to select a plain yarn and put your designing thoughts into the shape and texture. The yellow pullover, *knit in worsted-weight yarn, has a square neckline and a designer's choice cap. The patterns are lace stitches. The* natural pullover *has a classic body, crew neckline (high round neckline), and tapered sleeves with set-in caps. The cable patterns recall the design traditions of Aran sweaters. Note in particular the way the ribbing aligns with the bases of the cables. The* brown vest, *worked in heavy yarn, has a vertical ribbed shawl collar, horizontal inset pockets, and cable patterning. All three sweaters designed and made by Mary-Ann Davis.*

The mouse *is on the back of the sweater shown at left. There's a cat on the front of this sweater, shown in black-and-white in our section on charting pictures. The lavender-heather cardigan, of worsted-weight wool, has a picked-up shawl collar and front bands, inset pockets, and gathered sleeve caps. The stitch pattern is a brocade (a combination of knit and purl stitches). The olive pullover, in cotton yarn, has basic T styling and a crew neckline. The patterns derive from classic Guernsey sweaters. The first two sweaters designed and knit by Mary-Ann Davis, the third by Katie Swanson.*

The blue tweed pullover, *in medium-weight yarn, has a classic body along with a three-quarter-length lantern sleeve and gathered sleeve caps. A double-thickness shawl collar finishes the round neckline. All ribbings are cabled. The* pullover vest, *in medium-weight cotton yarn, has a tapered body, a square neckline, and cap sleeves. The rolled finishes complement the use of color and texture within the body of the vest, achieved through slip-stitch patterning and purled rows. The* bright rose pullover *is a recreation of the knitter's second sweater, which she made at the age of 14. Knit of worsted-weight cotton yarn, it has a classic body and a crew neckline, with set-in tapered sleeves. The pattern is a simple basket-weave brocade stitch. All three sweaters designed and knit by Carmen Michelson.*

The blue cardigan vest has a vertically worked band and picked-up cap sleeves. The dark yarn works well with the very deeply textured but relatively simple cable patterns. The light rose pullover, worked in worsted-weight yarn, has a round yoke. The cables are carried from the body onto the yoke, and decreases are worked into the design. Once again, cables move smoothly from the ribbing area into the main pattern. The multicolored oversized pullover has a classic body, set-in sleeves, and a doubled band on the crew neckline. The Fair Isle–influenced designs allowed the knitter to gracefully incorporate leftover yarns. The first two sweaters designed and knit by Mary-Ann Davis, the third by Jackie Truelove.

The camelhair cardigan, *in fingering-weight yarn, features a vertical finish on the front, set-in sleeve caps, and unique button placement. The lace stitch is used as an all-over pattern. The* mohair cardigan, *in worsted-weight yarn, is based on modified T styling. The stripes in the finishes coordinate with the slip-stitch pattern used for the body. The* boatneck pullover *has a blouson body, lantern sleeves, and gathered sleeve caps. A cable pattern and a lace pattern are combined in the fabric, and the lace area is shaped. Sweaters designed and knit, left to right, by Jackie Truelove, Katie Swanson, and Mary-Ann Davis.*

The gray-and-white pullover *has a horizontal shawl collar, tapered sleeves, and set-in caps. The anchor pattern on the white stripe, which carries over to the sleeves, is worked in purl stitches on a stockinette background. The dark raised ridges are also purled.* The tapestry-knit pullover *features angora squares on an angora-blend tweed background. The classic body is finished with modified lantern sleeves, gathered sleeve caps, and a standard collar. The standard collar is shown here as it was worked—it's a split, extra-long ribbed finish. When worn, it will open out and lie flat.* The *tiny pullover is a simple infant's garment made of handspun wool. It has a self-finished square neckline, worked in seed stitch to match the sleeve and bottom finishes. Sweaters designed and knit, left to right, by Mary-Ann Davis, Katie Swanson, and Carmen Michelson.*

This sample sweater is described in detail, with the steps we went through to achieve the design. By working with graph paper, we were able to refine both shape and use of pattern stitches to fit our vision. You can make your sweater as simple or as complex as you choose. In order to demonstrate the power of this process, we made a fairly intricate cardigan with a tapered body and a wide vertical shawl collar, tapered sleeves, and box caps. We started out with one stitch pattern in addition to the border, and decided while knitting to add a second at the yoke and the tops of the sleeves. By Jean Scorgie.

Classic Body

CB/STEP 1
Chest Measurement + Ease = total circumference of body
Example: 33" + 2" = 35"   *35"*

CB/STEP 2
Step 1 ÷ 2 = width of garment back or front
Example: 35" ÷ 2 = 17.5   *17¹/₂"*

*CB/STEP 3
Step 2 × stitch gauge = number of stitches to cast on
Example: 17.5" × 5 = 87.5 stitches   *88 stitches*
- For flat knitting, add 2 stitches for seams. You will knit front and back separately.
- For circular knitting, double the number in Step 3 and do not add the seam stitches.
  You will knit the front and back simultaneously.

  Border Notes
  1. In general, use needles two or three sizes smaller for your border, rib, or hem
     than you use for the body.
  2. If the body pattern gauge is different than the gauge of stockinette, work a
     stockinette swatch and use its gauge to determine the number of stitches to use
     for the ribbing or border. On the first row after the border, increase or decrease
     to obtain the appropriate number of stitches for the pattern gauge.
  3. Plan the border or ribbing so that the pattern will remain in sequence at the side
     edges. For example, on a 1/1 rib be sure that a knit stitch will be next to a purl
     stitch at the seam. If you are working flat with an even number of stitches in each
     piece, begin the rows of both front and back with a K and end with a P. If there is
     an odd number of stitches in each piece, begin and end the first piece with K and
     begin and end the second piece with P.

*CB/STEP 4
Work even on (number in Step 3) stitches for desired Garment Length to Armhole shaping in
inches *or* in numbers of rows. In most cases you can measure your fabric with a tape measure
or ruler. If, however, you are charting a picture or need to know the exact placement of a
design, you'll need to know the actual number of rows.
Example: Desired Length to Underarm = 15"
Garment Length to Armhole × row gauge = number of rows for garment body
Example: 15" × 6 = 90   *15" or 90 rows*

- The desired Length to Underarm will include the border stitch or ribbing, if it is worked along with the body. If the border will be picked up later, subtract it from this length. (If the row gauge of the border or ribbing is different from that of the body, subtract the depth of the border from this length, using inches, and calculate the number of rows to be knitted for the border separately.) If the sweater has a hem, measure from the hem's turning row.
- If the garment is long or made of heavyweight yarn—for example, a jacket or coat—work 1–2″ short of the desired body length and let the garment hang for 24 hours before you take a measurement. The fabric may lengthen under its own weight.
- This is a good time to *re-check your gauge.* If you are knitting more tightly or loosely than on your original swatch, you may want to change needles or to re-chart the yoke based on your new gauge. A bit more or less ease probably won't matter on the body of your sweater, but proper fit is important at the yoke.

Yoke and Set-In Armhole Shaping

CB/STEP 5
Shoulder Width Measurement × stitch gauge = number of stitches for yoke
Example: 13.5″ × 5 = 67.5 stitches   *68 stitches*
- If Step 3 is an even number, make Step 5 even. If Step 3 is an odd number, make Step 5 odd. When knitting, you will need to add 2 stitches for seams.

CB/STEP 6
Step 3 − Step 5 = total number of stitches for armhole shaping
Example: 88 − 68 = 20   *20 stitches*

CB/STEP 7
Step 6 ÷ 2 = total number of shaping stitches per armhole
Example: 20 ÷ 2 = 10   *10 stitches*

*CB/STEP 8
Step 7 ÷ 2 = number of stitches to bind off at each armhole edge
This is the one-row underarm bind-off which begins the shaping of the armhole.
- If the result includes a fraction, round off to the next higher number.
Since this figure represents the number of stitches to bind off at each armhole *edge,* you will use it differently for circular knitting than for flat knitting. In circular knitting, you will subtract 1 seam stitch from this number, then double the result to determine how many stitches to bind off at the underarm. The yoke sections will be worked flat; seam stitches will be available because they were not bound off. In flat knitting, you will bind off the Step 8 number of stitches at each side of the back and of the front.

Knitter's Trick

Markers can make life simpler. A yarn marker (a 6″ scrap of contrasting yarn, knit right along with the stitch) inserted toward the center of the yoke on the *first bind-off row* makes it easier to measure the finished depth of the yoke (in Step 10) or the position where you want to start shaping the front neckline. In the *last bound-off stitch,* place a yarn marker or a safety pin. You will use this as a reference point when you measure the armhole curve and chart the sleeve cap.

Example: 10 ÷ 2 = 5   *5 stitches*

*CB/STEP 9

Step 7 – Step 8 = number of stitches to single-decrease per armhole edge
This is the single-decrease series which curves up from the underarm bind-off, completing the shaping of the armhole.
Decrease one stitch at each armhole edge on every other row, on the right side of the fabric only.

Example: 10 – 5 = 5   *5 stitches*

*CB/STEP 10

Work even on remaining (number in Step 5) stitches until Depth of Armhole is reached, measuring in inches or rows

Example: Desired Armhole Depth = 8¹/₄″. Measure directly, placing the end of your tape measure or ruler at the bind-off row or at the yarn marker mentioned in Step 8, or figure the number of rows (see Step 4 for applications of each method).
Armhole Depth Measurement × row gauge = number of rows in yoke
Example: 8.25″ × 6 = 49.5 rows   *8¹/₄″ or 50 rows*

If you are working in a relatively fine yarn, you may want to consider the Alternate Set-In Armhole shaping method (page 80).

Standard Shoulder Shaping and Back Neckline Bind-Off

This basic sweater is charted for a neckline width which includes one-third of the yoke stitches (the other two-thirds is equally divided between the shoulders). The width of the neckline can vary for reasons which are explained in the neckline section.

CB/STEP 11

Step 5 ÷ 3 = number of stitches per shoulder
If the result is a whole number and a fraction, use the whole number only; do not increase to the next higher number. Use any extra stitches within the neckline.

Example: 68 ÷ 3 = 22.6   *22 stitches*

*CB/STEP 12
Step 5 – (Step 11 × 2) = number of stitches for neckline
Example: 68 – (22 × 2 = 44) = 24   *24 stitches*

CB/STEP 13
Raglan Depth Measurement – Armhole Depth Measurement = height of shoulder slope
Example: 9.25" – 8.25" = 1"   *1" shoulder slope*

CB/STEP 14
Step 13 × row gauge = total number of rows for shoulder shaping
Example: 1" × 6 = 6   *6 rows*

CB/STEP 15
Step 14 ÷ 2 = number of bind-off levels per shoulder
A bind-off level consists of two rows. You should have a minimum of two bind-off levels (four rows) per shoulder. (Some infants' wear may complete binding off on one level.)
Example: 6 ÷ 2 = 3   *3 levels*

*CB/STEP 16
Step 11 ÷ Step 15 = number of stitches per level to bind off on each shoulder
These stitches can be bound off on every other row (using the bias bind-off), or left on a stitch holder to be grafted or closed with a knitted seam. (See "How-Tos" for techniques.)
■ If the shoulder stitches do not divide into even groups, bind off the smaller amount(s) first.
Example: 22 ÷ 3 = 7.3   *7, 7, and 8 stitches*

CB/STEP 17
For *back neckline,* bind off remaining (number in Step 12) stitches, or place them on a stitch holder.
For *front neckline,* chart according to guidelines given in the neckline section, depending on the type of neckline you have chosen.

If we translate our Classic Body instructions so they read like a printed pattern, they will appear like this:

Back: Using smaller needles, cast on 88 stitches (*Step 3*). Work in ribbing for 3". Change to larger needles and work even in pattern stitch until piece measures 15", ending with a wrong-side row (*Step 4*).

Shape armholes: At the beginning of the next 2 rows, bind off 5 stitches (*Step 8*). Decrease 1 stitch at each end of needle every other row 5 times (*Step 9*). Work even on remaining 68 stitches (*Step 5*) until piece measures 8¼" (*Step 10*).

Shape shoulders: At the beginning of each of the next 4 rows, bind off 7 stitches; at the beginning of the next 2 rows bind off 8 stitches (*Step 16*). Bind off remaining 24 neckline stitches (*Step 12*) or place on stitch holder.

Front: Work the same as back, except for neckline shaping.

VARIATION. Shoulder shaping does not have to occur at the very top of the sweater body. For a design variation, work your normal shoulder shaping 1–3″ before you reach the Armhole Depth Measurement. Use short rows (see "How Tos"), instead of binding off the stitches. Then continue across all of the stitches, working in a different stitch pattern (perhaps garter stitch, or seed stitch), until you reach the Armhole Depth Measurement. You will have a balanced pattern band across the shoulders, which will not be interrupted at the shoulder seams.

Enlarged Sweater Front

In some cases, you may want to knit the front of your sweater so it is larger than the back. Perhaps you'd like more body ease than you originally thought, or perhaps the sweater is for a person who needs additional leeway in the midsection. Whatever the reason, it's simple to add an extra inch or two to the front of a garment.

In our example, we will increase the front body width by 1″. The additional stitches will be decreased out in the armhole shaping, so the Yoke and Shoulder Widths will remain the same as on the back. Because of the additional stitches, the armhole in front will be slightly larger than in the back. When you chart a sleeve cap for this type of sweater, determine the Curve Measurement by adding the front and back armhole curves together and then dividing the result in half (see "Set-In Sleeve Caps").

SHOULDER SHAPING VARIATION

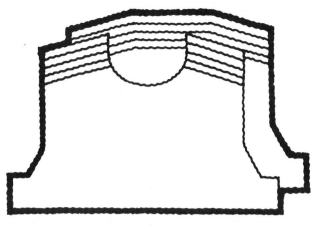

Working your shoulder shaping rows between 1 and 3″ below the armhole depth measurement will give you a balanced pattern band across the shoulders.

Enlarged Sweater Front

STEP 1
Additional sweater width × stitch gauge = number of extra stitches to cast on for front
Make this an even number.
Example: 1″ × 5 = 5   *6 stitches*

STEP 2
Step 1 + number of stitches for Classic Back (CB/Step 3) = total number of stitches to cast on for enlarged front
■ If you are working flat, add two stitches for seams.
Example: 6 + 88 = 96   *96 stitches*

STEP 3
Work even to armhole shaping. Bind off the same number of stitches per armhole as for Set-In Armhole shaping of the back.
This is the underarm bind-off which begins the shaping of each armhole.
Example: *5 stitches*

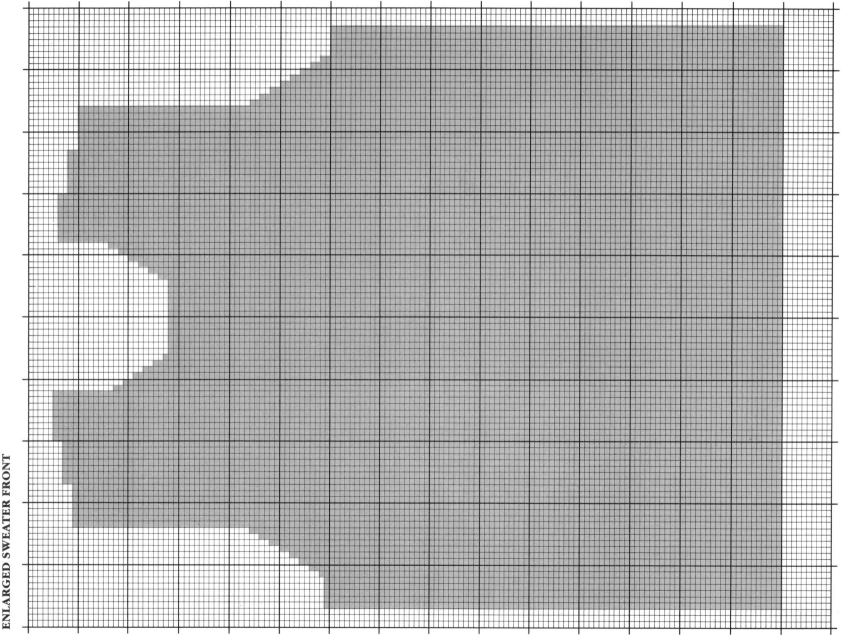

This modification gives extra ease in the sweater front.

STEP 4

Number of single decreases per Set-In Armhole (CB/Step 9) + (Step 1 ÷ 2) = number of stitches to single-decrease per armhole
Example: 5 + (6 ÷ 2 = 3) = 8　　　　　　　　　　　　　　　　　　　　*8 stitches*

STEP 5

Work even on remaining stitches, shaping the front neckline as you choose. Shape shoulders exactly as you did on the sweater back.

Blouson Body

A Blouson Sweater fits snugly at the waist, and increases dramatically after the ribbing. The waist measurement can include up to an inch of ease. If the sweater will be worn over a skirt or slacks, measure the waist over the garment's waistband.

The design effect of the sweater depends on having enough fabric between waist and underarms to "blouse," or drape. When you work the body of a waist-length Blouson add at least 2" of fabric between waist and underarms to allow for garment movement when the arms are raised. You may want to think of this as starting the ribbing at least 2" below the waist indention, although when the sweater is worn this extra fabric will fall above, rather than below, the waist.

Blousons are often waist-length, but the style can also be charted to begin at or below the hips. This creates a comfortable loose-fitting garment flattering to many body types. For a longer Blouson, cast on the equivalent of half the hip measurement plus optional ease and work the ribbing or border. Increase to the desired amount of fullness after you complete the border.

Blouson Body

STEP 1

(½ Waist Measurement + ½ optional Ease) × stitch gauge = number of stitches to cast on for ribbing
■ Add 2 seam stitches if you are working flat.
Example: If the Waist is 24" and ½" of Ease is planned,
(12 + .25 = 12.25) × 5 = 61.25　　　　　　　　　　　　　　　　　*62 stitches*

STEP 2

(½ Chest Measurement + ½ Ease) × stitch gauge = number of stitches for body
■ Add 2 seam stitches if you are working flat.
Example: If the Chest Measurement is 33" and 2" of Body Ease is planned,
(16.5 + 1 = 17.5) × 5 = 87.5　　　　　　　　　　　　　　　　　*88 stitches*

STEP 3

Step 2 − Step 1 = number of stitches to increase after ribbing
Example: 88 − 62 = 26　　　　　　　　　　　　　　　　　　　　*26 stitches*

STEP 4

Step 1 ÷ (Step 3 + 1) = stitch interval(s) at which to work increases
See Gathers Formula, Step 2, to work out pattern for increases.
Example: 62 ÷ (26 + 1) = 2.29　　　　　　　　　　　　*Every 2nd or 3rd stitch*

STEP 5

After completing increases, work even on (number in Step 2) stitches until it's time to shape the armholes. For greater blousing, add an extra inch or more of fabric length (beyond the minimum 2" leeway mentioned above) between the ribbing and armhole shaping.

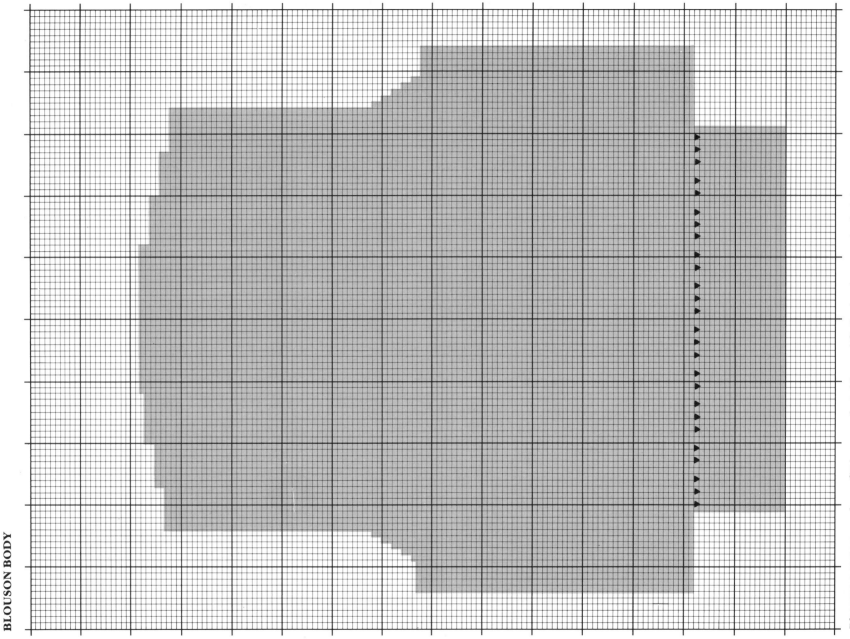

BLOUSON BODY

Blouson sweaters are loose-fitting, comfortable, and flattering to many body types.

66

Tapered Body

A waist-length Tapered Sweater fits snugly at the waist, then tapers along the side edges to within 3–4″ of the armhole shaping. A hip-length Tapered garment is suitable for a body type that is smaller in the hips and larger in the bust, or if for design purposes you want the sweater to fit more tightly at the hips and more loosely at the top.

A waist-length version can include up to 1″ of ease at the waist; if the sweater will be worn over a skirt or slacks, measure the waist over the waistband.

For a hip-length sweater, cast on the equivalent of half the hip measurement plus half the optional ease. You have the choice of tapering the garment from above the ribbing to the bust or chest area, or of working even to the waist and beginning the taper at the waist indention.

Our example shows a waist-length Tapered Body with ribbing. As in the Blouson shape, add at least 2″ of fabric between waist and underarms to allow for garment movement when the arms are raised. The ribbing can end at the waist, as our sample 3″ rib does, or above it. When the ribbing extends above the waist, subtract the extra amount in Step 4.

Steps 1 and 2 are the same as for the Blouson Body.

Tapered Body

STEP 1

(½ Waist Measurement + ½ optional Ease) × stitch gauge = number of stitches to cast on
- Add 2 stitches for seams if you are working flat.

Example: If the Waist is 24″ and ½″ of Ease is planned,
(12 + .25 = 12.25) × 5 = 61.25　　　　　　　　　　　　　　　　　　*62 stitches*

STEP 2

(½ Chest Measurement + ½ Ease) × stitch gauge = number of stitches for body
- If Step 1 is an even number, make Step 2 an even number.
- If Step 1 is an odd number, make Step 2 an odd number.
- Add 2 stitches for seams if you are working flat.

Example: If the Chest Measurement is 33″ and 2″ of Body Ease is planned,
(16.5 + 1 = 17.5) × 5 = 87.5　　　　　　　　　　　　　　　　　　*88 stitches*

STEP 3

(Step 2 − Step 1) ÷ 2 = number of stitches to increase at each side edge for taper
Example: (88 − 62 = 26) ÷ 2 = 13　　　　　　　　　　　　　　　　*13 stitches*

STEP 4

(Armhole-to-Waist Measurement − ribbing above waist, if any) − 3–4″ = number of inches over which increases will be made
Example: If the Armhole-to-Waist Measurement is 9″ and ribbing will not extend above waist, (9 − 0 = 9) − 3–4″ = 5–6″　　　　　　　　　　　　　　　*5–6″*

STEP 5

Step 4 × row gauge = number of rows over which increases will be made
Make this an even number.
Example: 5–6″ × 6 rows = 30–36 rows　　　　　　　　　　　　　*30–36 rows*

STEP 6

Step 5 ÷ Step 3 = rows on which to work increases
See Taper Formula to work out intervals.
Example: 30–36 rows ÷ 13 stitches = 2.3–2.7 rows　　　*Increase at 2-row and 4-row intervals*

STEP 7

After the taper is complete, work even for the remaining 3–4″, to the armhole shaping.

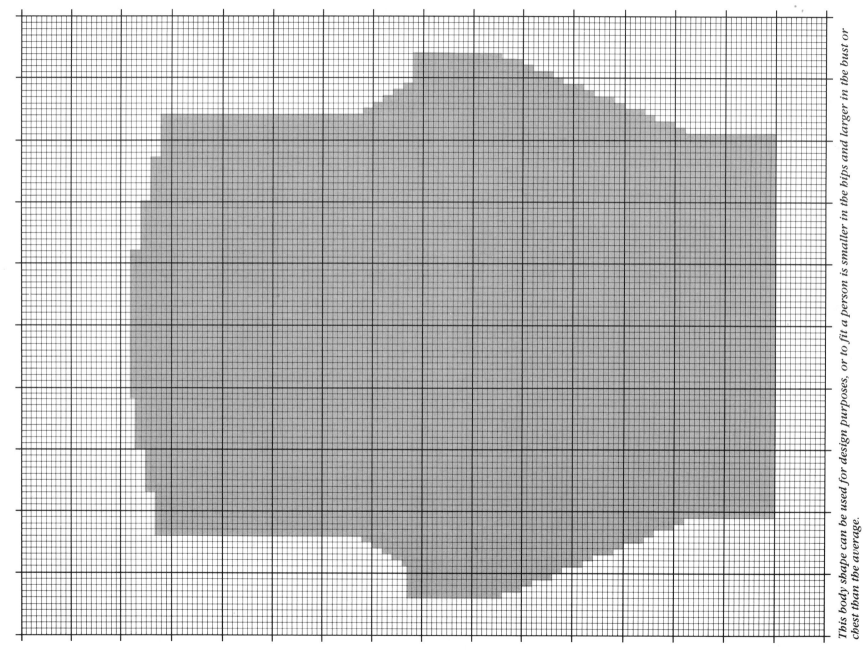

TAPERED BODY

This body shape can be used for design purposes, or to fit a person is smaller in the bips and larger in the bust or chest than the average.

Double-Tapered Body

A Double Taper is also known as an "hourglass" shape. Closely following the female curves, it tapers in along the side edges from the hips to the waist, and out from the waist to the bust. For a more graceful curve, an inch or two can be worked even at the waist indention.

An adult Hip-to-Waist Taper averages 5". For a custom fit, measure from the waist indention to the desired length or the widest part of the hips. The formula given below determines the Hip-to-Waist Taper.

The Tapered Body guidelines are used for the Waist-to-Bust Taper, which should again end 3–4" below the armhole shaping.

Reverse-Tapered Body

A Reverse-Tapered Body is wide at the bottom, and tapers in along the side edges to the armhole shaping. The greater the number of decreases, the more pronounced the taper will be.

For a waist-length garment, like the one in our example (which combines the Blouson with the Reverse-Tapered Body), cast on the equivalent of half the Waist Measurement (plus optional Ease) and work the ribbing. If the sweater will be worn over a skirt or slacks, measure the waist over the waistband. As in the Blouson and the other tapered shapes,

Doubled-Tapered Body

STEP 1
(¹/₂ Hip Measurement + ¹/₂ Ease) × stitch gauge = number of stitches to cast on
■ Add 2 stitches for seams if you are working flat.
Example: If the Hip Measurement is 34" and 2" of Body Ease is planned,
(17 + 1 = 18) × 5 = 90   *90 stitches*

STEP 2
Work even on (number in Step 1) stitches to the start of the Hip-to-Waist Taper.

STEP 3
(¹/₂ Waist Measurement + ¹/₂ Ease) × stitch gauge = number of stitches at waist
■ If Step 1 is an even number, make Step 3 an even number.
■ If Step 1 is an odd number, make Step 3 an odd number.
■ Add 2 stitches for seams if you are working flat.
Example: If the Waist is 25" and 1" of Ease is planned, and the sweater will be worked at
5 stitches/inch, (12.5 + .5 = 12.75) × 5 = 63.7   *64 stitches*

STEP 4
(Step 1 – Step 3) ÷ 2 = number of stitches to decrease at each side edge
Example: (90 – 64 = 26) ÷ 2 = 13   *13 stitches*

STEP 5
Length of taper × row gauge = number of rows over which decreases will be made
Make this an even number.
Example: 5" × 6 rows = 30   *30 rows*

STEP 6
Step 5 ÷ Step 4 = rows on which to work decreases
See Taper Formula to work out intervals.
Example: 30 rows ÷ 13 stitches = 2.3 rows   *Increase at 2-row and 4-row intervals*

STEP 7
If desired, work even for 1–2" at the waist before beginning the Waist-to-Bust Taper; see Tapered Body for these guidelines.

DOUBLE-TAPERED BODY

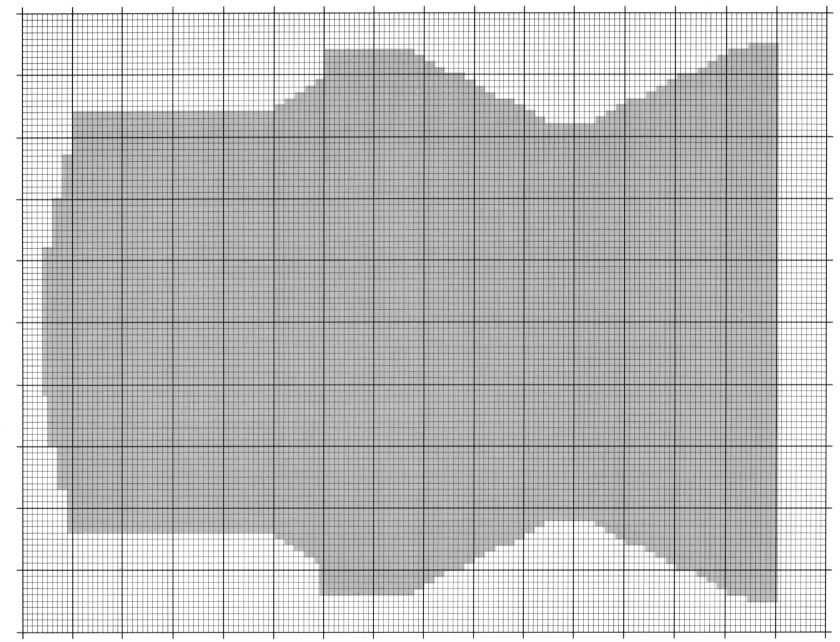

This "bourglass" shape tapers in from hips to waist, and out from waist to bust.

70

VARIATIONS OF THE REVERSE-TAPERED BODY

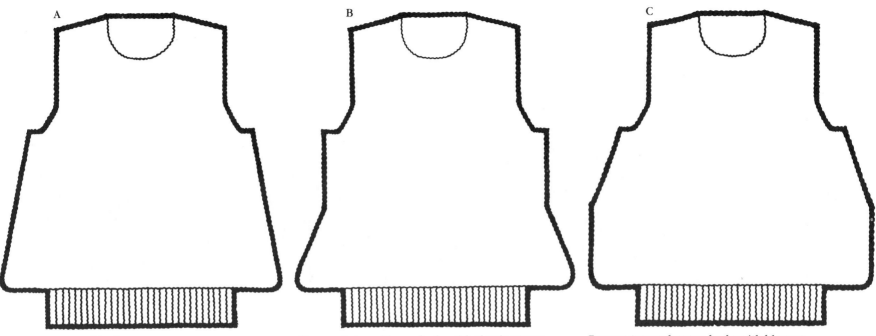

Reverse-tapered body

Reverse-tapered lower body with classic upper body

Reverse-tapered upper body with blouson lower body

add at least 2" of fabric between waist and underarms to allow for garment movement when the arms are raised.

A hip-length version of the Reverse-Tapered Body is a perfect way to ease the discrepancy between wide hips and a small bust or chest. Cast on the equivalent of half the Hip Measurement, plus Ease, and work the ribbing, border stitch, or hem. Then begin decreasing until you

have enough stitches left for half the Bust Measurement, plus Ease. It's not necessary to increase after the ribbing, although you may do so if you want additional fullness (see illustration a).

You can work many variations of the basic hip-length Reverse-Tapered Body; you can even combine it with a Classic or Blouson style. In the first of these, you complete your taper at the waist or in a

short space above the waist, then work even on the stitches required for half the Bust Measurement, plus Ease, until you reach the armhole shaping (illustration b). In the second, you work even on the larger amount of stitches to the waist, or above it, then taper fairly rapidly to the armhole shaping (illustration c). Both of these choices are excellent for maternity wear.

REVERSE-TAPERED BODY

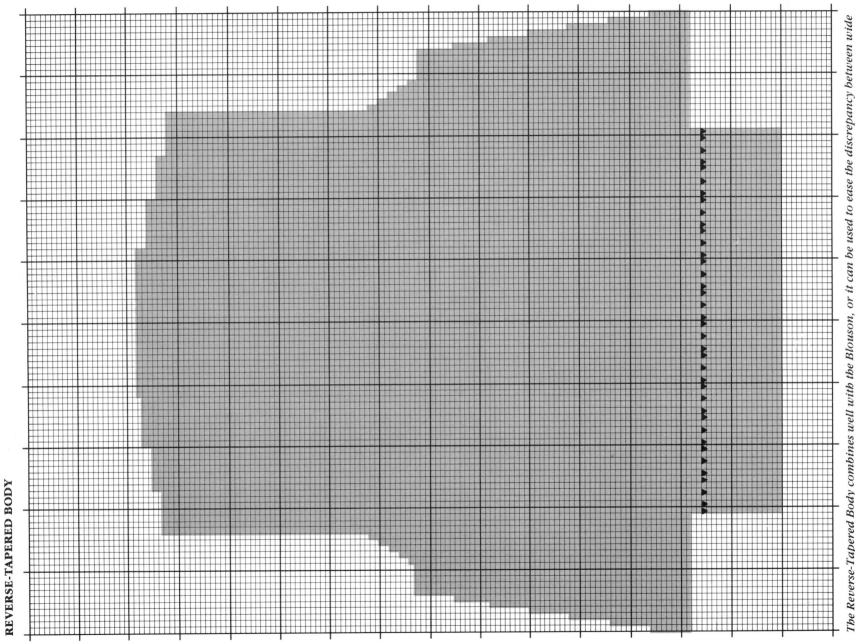

The Reverse-Tapered Body combines well with the Blouson, or it can be used to ease the discrepancy between wide hips and a small bust or chest.

Reverse-Tapered Body

STEP 1
($\frac{1}{2}$ Waist Measurement + $\frac{1}{2}$ optional Ease) × stitch gauge = number of stitches to cast on for ribbing
- Add 2 stitches for seams if you are working flat.

Example: If the Waist is 24" and $\frac{1}{2}$" of Ease is planned,
(12 + .25 = 12.25) × 5 = 61.25   *62 stitches*

STEP 2
($\frac{1}{2}$ Chest Measurement + $\frac{1}{2}$ Ease) × stitch gauge = number of stitches at upper body
- Add 2 seam stitches if you are working flat.

Example: If the Chest Measurement is 33" and 2" of Body Ease is planned,
(16.5 + 1 = 17.5) × 5 = 87.5   *88 stitches*

STEP 3
(Desired circumference at sweater bottom ÷ 2) × stitch gauge = number of stitches at beginning of taper
- If Step 2 is an even number, make Step 3 an even number.
- If Step 2 is an odd number, make Step 3 an odd number.
- Add 2 seam stitches if you are working flat.

Example: If the desired circumference at the sweater bottom is 40",
(40 ÷ 2 = 20) × 5 = 100   *100 stitches*

STEP 4
Step 3 – Step 1 = number of stitches to increase after ribbing
Example: 100 – 62 = 38   *38 stitches*

STEP 5
Step 1 ÷ Step 4 = stitch interval(s) at which to work increases
See Gathers Formula, Step 2, to work out pattern for increases.
Example: 62 ÷ 38 = 1.6   *Every 1 or 2 stitches*

STEP 6
(Step 3 – Step 2) ÷ 2 = number of stitches to decrease at each side edge
Example: (100 – 88 = 12) ÷ 2 = 6   *6 stitches*

CINCHED-WAIST BODY
A cinched waist formed by working on
smaller needles

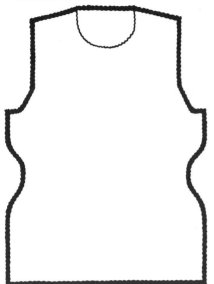

B cinched waist formed with ribbing

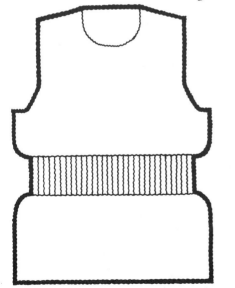

*A sweater can be made to fit the waist without
a great deal of effort.*

STEP 7
(Length of taper to armhole − 1″) × row gauge = number of rows over which decreases will
be made
Make this an even number.
End the taper 1″ or more below the armhole shaping (the formula is written for the 1″
minimum).
This length does not include the ribbing or border. For greater blousing, add an extra inch or
more of fabric length.
Example: (9 − 1 = 8) × 6 = 48   *48 rows*

STEP 8
Step 7 ÷ Step 6 = rows on which to work decreases
See Taper Formula to work out intervals.
Example: 48 ÷ 6 = 8   *Decrease at 8-row intervals*

STEP 9
After the taper is complete, work even for the remaining length to armhole shaping (usually 1″).

Cinched-Waist Body

A sweater can be pulled in at the waist
without tapers, darts, or a great deal of
effort. There are two ways to work a
sweater with a Cinched-In Waist.

Chart a Classic Body. Work even to 1″
short of the waistline, then decrease the
width of the sweater so it fits snugly. The
cinched-in section can be narrow (about
2″ deep) or wide (ending 1″ below the
point where the bust fullness begins).

CINCHED-WAIST BODY, VERSION 1. The
decrease in width is achieved by working
in the original body stitch pattern using
needles two or three sizes smaller than
those you are using for the rest of the garment. Be sure to make a test swatch to see
how this stitch pattern will be affected.

CINCHED-WAIST BODY, VERSION 2.
Here the fitted section is worked in ribbing, on needles two sizes smaller than
those you are using for the rest of the garment. If you want the ribbing to be snug,
decrease the number of stitches in the
first row of ribbing to match the Waist
Measurement (plus optional Ease), and increase back to the number of stitches
required for the body in the last row of
ribbing. On a snug-waisted sweater, you
may want additional blousing above the
waist; add an extra inch or more of fabric
length between the top of the ribbing and
the armhole shaping.

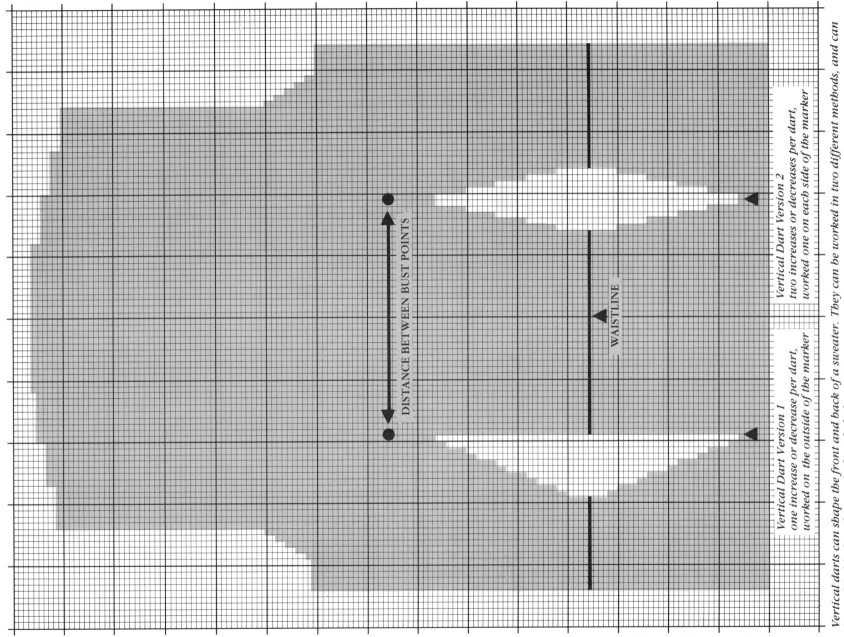

DART-TAPERED BODY

DISTANCE BETWEEN BUST POINTS

WAISTLINE

Vertical Dart Version 2
two increases or decreases per dart,
worked one on each side of the marker

Vertical Dart Version 1
one increase or decrease per dart,
worked on the outside of the marker

Vertical darts can shape the front and back of a sweater. They can be worked in two different methods, and can be used in hip-length or waist-length designs.

Dart-Tapered Body

A sweater can be shaped with front and back darts. Our graph illustration shows a Dart-Tapered Body decreasing in width from the hips to the waist and increasing from the waist to the bust. If your sweater is waist-length, you can use waist-to-bust darts alone.

You'll need two new measurements in order to determine the placement and length of the darts:

a. the distance between bust points, and
b. the distance from a bust point straight down to the waist.

The front Bust Darts should end about ½–1″ below the bust points. Above-waist darts on the back can extend the full length of the Bust-Point-to-Waist Measurement. The length for a hip-to-waist dart averages 5″.

At its widest point, each dart should eliminate between 1″ and 2″ of stitches. If you want more shaping than this, combine darts with side tapering.

Darts can be formed in two ways. On the left of the graph, we show Vertical Dart Version 1, with one increase or decrease per dart, worked on the outside of the marker. On the right of the graph, we show Vertical Dart Version 2, with two decreases or increases per dart, worked one on each side of the marker. Use one method or the other on your garment; don't use both on the same sweater. Note that the top and bottom points of the darts are in the same position on both examples.

Before beginning to work darts, change Vertical Dart Measurement *a* into a stitch count by multiplying it by your gauge. *Example: for a gauge of 5 stitches per inch and a Bust-Point Measurement of 7″, this would be 35 stitches.*

For Version 1 darts, place two markers on your needle, with this number of stitches in between them; the measured group of stitches should be centered on your fabric. *Example: if the fabric is 115 stitches wide, the center 35 stitches will be between the markers; the remaining 80 stitches will be in two groups of 40, outside the markers.* Decreases and/or increases will be made before the first marker and after the second marker.

For Version 2 darts which will be worked from the waist up only, take the number of stitches in Vertical Dart Measurement *a*, subtract the number of stitches to be increased on the inside of the markers, and you will get the number of stitches to be centered between the markers. *Example: 7″ × 5 stitches = 35 stitches – 10 stitches (5 stitches from each dart) = 25 stitches centered between markers.* Decreases and/or increases will be worked before and after each marker.

Bust Darts

You can improve the fit of a tight sweater, or of a sweater designed for a full-figured woman, by adding Bust Darts. Bust Darts are worked in short rows (see "How Tos"). Since not all stitch patterns allow short rows to be worked successfully, check out the pattern you will be using on a test swatch.

Two additional measurements will help you decide if bust darts will be helpful:

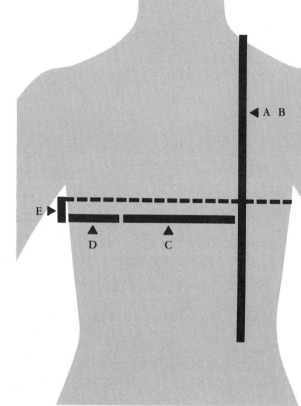

MEASUREMENTS FOR BUST DARTS

A shoulder-to-waist (front)
B shoulder-to-waist (back)
C distance between bust points
D distance between bust point and underarm
E side seam bust level to measurement string
----- measurement string

a. on the front of the body, measure from the shoulder to the waist, taking the tape straight down over the fullest part of the bust, and
b. on the back of the body, measure from the same point on the shoulder to the waist.

If Bust Dart Measurement *a* is larger than Measurement *b* by 1″ or more, consider bust darts.

The *depth of the dart* will equal the difference between Bust Dart Measurements *a* and *b*. Our example will be 1½″ deep.

You'll need a few new measurements in order to place the darts on the garment. Taking these measurements may be easier if you wear an old T-shirt and mark the bust points with marking pen. Measure:

c. the horizontal distance between bust points,

d. the horizontal distance between bust point and underarm, at the approximate location of a side seam, and

e. from that point on the seam straight up to the Measurement String you use for your basic measurements. If your garment will have a lowered armhole, as in a jacket or coat, subtract the amount added to the Armhole Depth from this measurement.

Bust Darts

STEP 1

Garment Body Length to Armhole − Measurement *e* = position of dart at side seam

STEP 2

½ width of garment front (CB/Step 2) − ½ Measurement *c* − (½″ to 1½″) = length of dart
A bust dart should end ½ to 1½″ short of the bust point, and this is taken into account when calculating how long it should be.
Example: If the garment front is 17½″ wide and the distance between bust points is 7⅝″ (7.625 or 7.63″), 8.75 − 3.8 = 4.95; if the dart will end 1½″ short of the bust point, 4.95 − 1.5 = 3.45   3½″ long

STEP 3

Step 2 × stitch gauge = number of stitches included in each dart
Example: 3.5 × 5 = 17.5   17 stitches

STEP 4

Depth of dart × row gauge = number of rows over which to shape dart
Make this an even number.
Example: 1.5″ × 6 = 9   10 rows

STEP 5

Step 3 ÷ (½ Step 4) = number of stitches to subtract for each short row (see Slope Formula)
Example: 17 ÷ 5 = 3.4   3 or 4 stitches

STEP 6

Complete the short rows. Work even for Measurement *e*, to the point where you will begin your choice of armhole shaping.

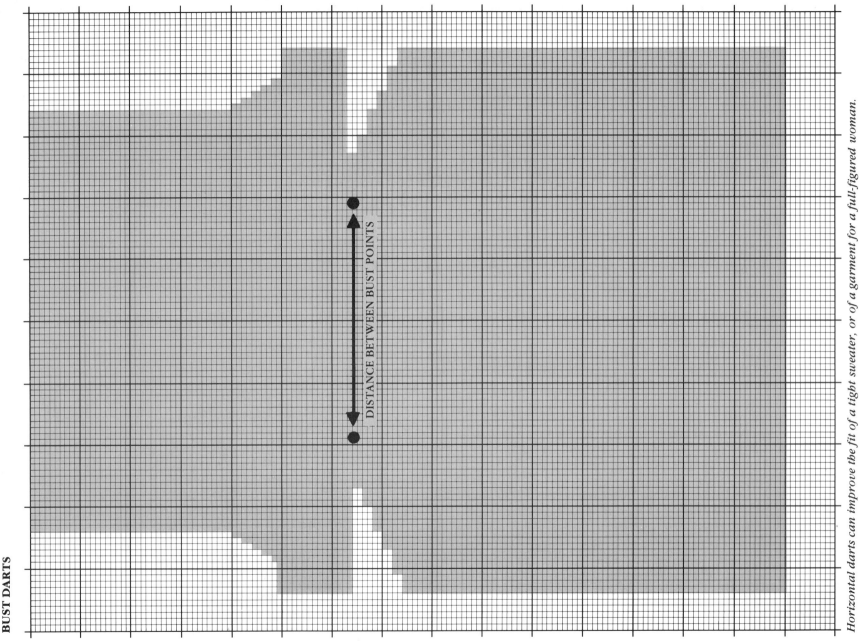

BUST DARTS

DISTANCE BETWEEN BUST POINTS

Horizontal darts can improve the fit of a tight sweater, or of a garment for a full-figured woman.

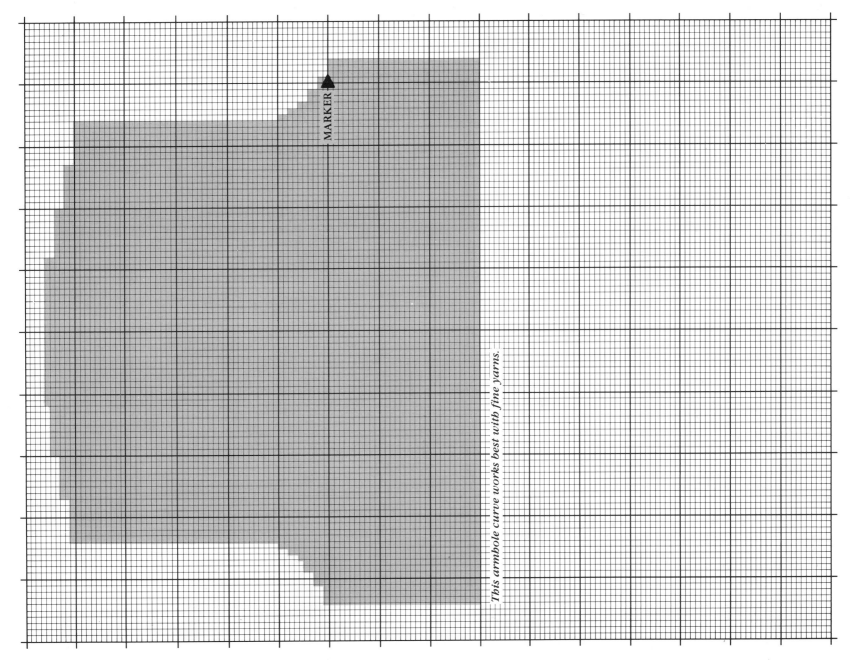

MARKER

This armhole curve works best with fine yarns.

Alternate Set-In Armhole Shaping

This alternate method of shaping Set-In Armholes is better for fine yarns with many armhole-shaping stitches than for bulky yarns, which have few shaping stitches. In this method, you divide the shaping stitches for each armhole (CB/Step 7) into thirds. Bind off the first third all at once at the beginning of the shaping, bind off the second third in two or three levels (as "stair steps"), and then decrease the remaining third at the rate of one stitch per edge on every other row (single decreases).

Try charting both versions on graph paper and decide for yourself which armhole curve you prefer. If you choose the alternate version for the armhole, use the same bind-off sequence when you begin to shape your sleeve caps.

Semi-Raglan Armhole Shaping

This shaping method is a variation of the Classic Set-In Armhole and is suitable for vests, and for use with the Semi-Raglan Sleeve Cap and most Set-In styles—Gathered, Pleated, Box, and Designer's Choice. However, it does not work well with the Standard Set-In Cap.

Shaping begins with the initial all-at-once bind-off (CB/Step 8). The change occurs in the way the single decreases are handled (CB/Step 9). These decreases are worked over half the armhole depth, resulting in a gradual taper.

Alternate Set-in Armhole Shaping

STEP 1

Number of shaping stitches per armhole (CB/Step 7) ÷ 3 = number of stitches to bind off per armhole
These are the stitches that are bound off all at once, as the armhole shaping begins.
Example: 10 ÷ 3 = 3.3   *3 stitches*

STEP 2

Same calculation as Step 1 = number of stitches to decrease in "stair steps" per armhole
■ This is the second group of stitches, and it must contain at least 4 stitches. If there are fewer than 4, use the Standard Set-In Armhole shaping (page 60).
Example: 10 ÷ 3 = 3.3   *4 stitches*

STEP 3

Step 2 ÷ number of "stair steps" (2 or 3) = number of stitches to bind off per "stair step"
Each "stair step" needs at least 2 stitches.
Example: With 2 "stair steps," 4 ÷ 2 = 2   *2 stitches*
■ If the number you get here contains a fraction, bind off the larger amount first.
Place a yarn marker or safety pin at the last bound-off stitch in this group. It will be a reference point for measuring the armhole curve when you chart the sleeve cap.
Example: If 9 stitches are to be bound off in 2 "stair steps," 9 ÷ 2 = 4.5. Bind off 5 stitches, then 4 stitches.

STEP 4

CB/Step 7 − (Step 1 + Step 2) = number of stitches to single-decrease per armhole
Example: 10 − (3 + 4 = 7) = 3   *3 stitches*

STEP 5

Work even on remaining stitches and shape the shoulders in the usual manner.

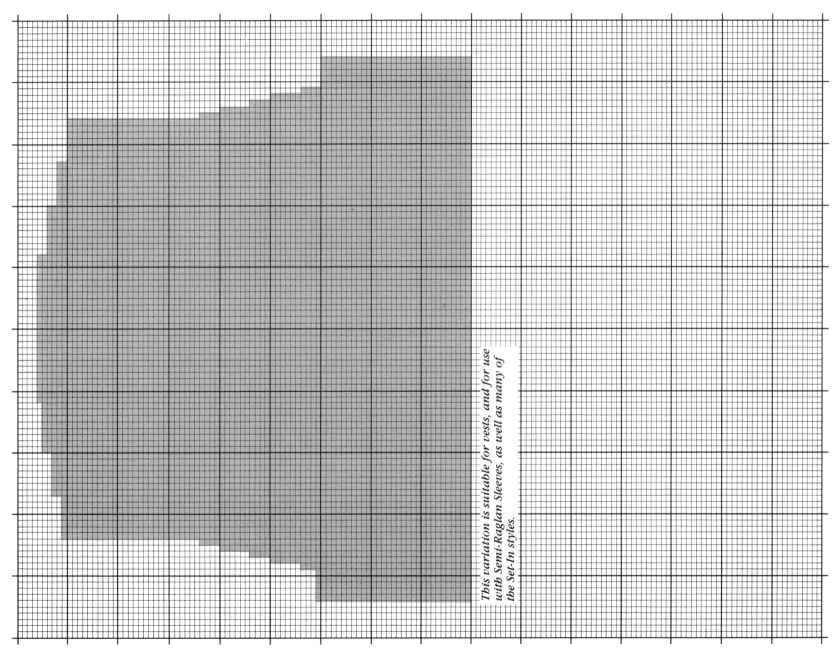

This variation is suitable for vests, and for use with Semi-Raglan Sleeves, as well as many of the Set-In styles.

For a decorative effect, you can work the decreases two or three stitches in from the edges on the yoke. Follow the same procedure on Semi-Raglan Caps, if you are using them; the decreases on Semi-Raglan Sleeve Caps are worked at the same rate as the decreases on the yoke, and align with the yoke decreases when the garment is assembled.

Shaped Yoke

Using *increases* while shaping the armholes—the Shaped Yoke—is a possibility if the *front and/or back Yoke Width Measurement* is substantially smaller than the *Shoulder Width Measurement*. If you are knitting for a broad-shouldered or round-shouldered person, consider shaping the front yoke, or possibly both the front and back yokes.

At the halfway point of the Armhole Depth, an outward taper is worked so that there is enough fabric for a good fit at the shoulders, and so the front and back shoulders will have the same number of stitches. If you shape both front and back yokes, you may find that the front and back armholes differ, depending on the measurements you are working from.

Below is the Shaped Yoke charting for a Standard Set-In Armhole, although the technique can be used with Alternate Set-In shaping as well.

Semi-Raglan Armhole Shaping

STEP 1
Begin to chart as you would for Set-In Armhole shaping, using CB/Step 5 through CB/Step 9, and jot down the numbers.

STEP 2
Bind off the number of stitches in CB/Step 8 at each armhole edge.
Example: *5 stitches*

STEP 3
$1/2$ Armhole Depth Measurement × row gauge = number of rows over which the remaining decreases will be made
Make this an even number.
Example: For an armhole depth measurement of 8.25", 4.12 × 6 = 24.7   *24 rows*

STEP 4
Step 3 ÷ number of single decreases per armhole (CB/Step 9) = rows on which to work the decreases
Use even-numbered rows, so decreases occur on the right side of the fabric. See the Taper Formula.
Example: 24 ÷ 5 = 4.8   *Decrease every 4th or 6th row*

STEP 5
Work even on the remaining stitches to the Armhole Depth Measurement. Shape the shoulders in the normal manner.

Shaped Yoke

STEP 1
Front *or* Back Yoke Measurement × stitch gauge = number of stitches for lower half of yoke
Example: 12" × 5 stitches/inch = 60   *60 stitches*
■ Add 2 seam stitches in your knitting, although you will continue the calculator work without these stitches.

STEP 2

[Number of stitches at upper body of sweater (CB/Step 3) − Step 1] ÷ 2 = total number of shaping stitches per armhole
Example: (88 − 60 = 28) ÷ 2 = 14   *14 stitches*

STEP 3

Step 2 ÷ 2 = number of stitches to bind off per armhole edge
Example: 14 ÷ 2 = 7   *7 stitches*

STEP 4

Step 2 − Step 3 = number of stitches to single-decrease at each armhole edge
Example: 14 − 7 = 7   *7 stitches*

STEP 5

Work even on remaining stitches for half the Armhole Depth Measurement, measured from the bind-off row.
Example: for an Armhole Depth of 8¹/₄″, work even for 4¹/₈″; 8.25 ÷ 2 = 4.125   *4¹/₈″*

STEP 6

(Shoulder Width Measurement × stitch gauge) − Step 1 = total number of stitches to single-increase at armhole edges
Make this an even number.
Example: (13.5″ × 5 = 67.5) − 60 = 7.5   *8 stitches*

STEP 7

Step 6 ÷ 2 = number of stitches to single-increase per armhole edge
Example: 8 ÷ 2 = 4   *4 stitches*

STEP 8

¹/₂ Armhole Depth Measurement × row gauge = number of rows over which increases will be made
Make this an even number.
Example: 4.12″ × 6 = 24.7   *24 rows*

STEP 9

Step 8 ÷ Step 7 = rows on which to work increases
Use even-numbered rows, so decreases occur on the right side of the fabric. See the Taper Formula.
Example: 24 ÷ 4 = 6   *Every 6th row*

STEP 10

After the last increase has been completed, work even to the Armhole Depth Measurement. Then shape the shoulders in the normal manner.

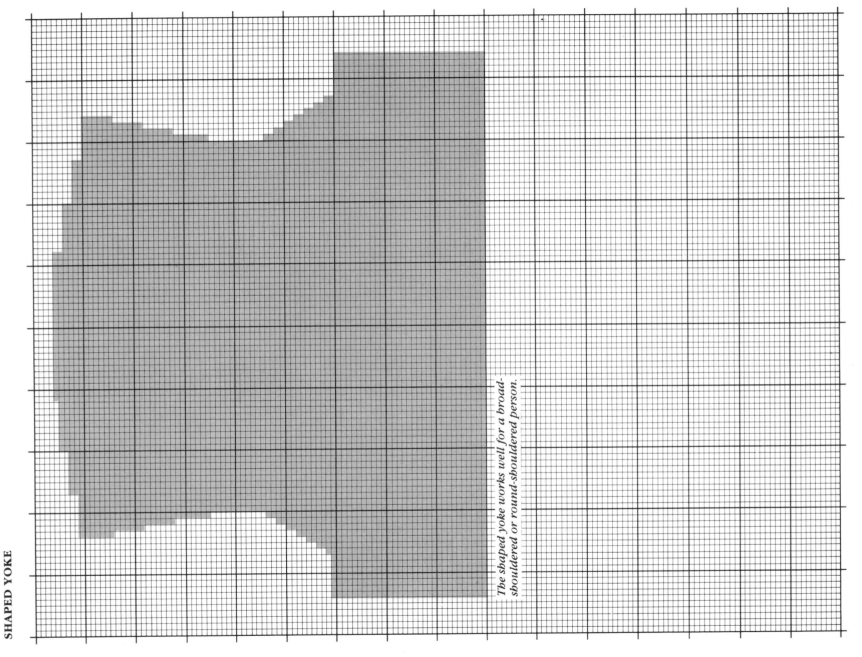

SHAPED YOKE

The shaped yoke works well for a broad-shouldered or round-shouldered person.

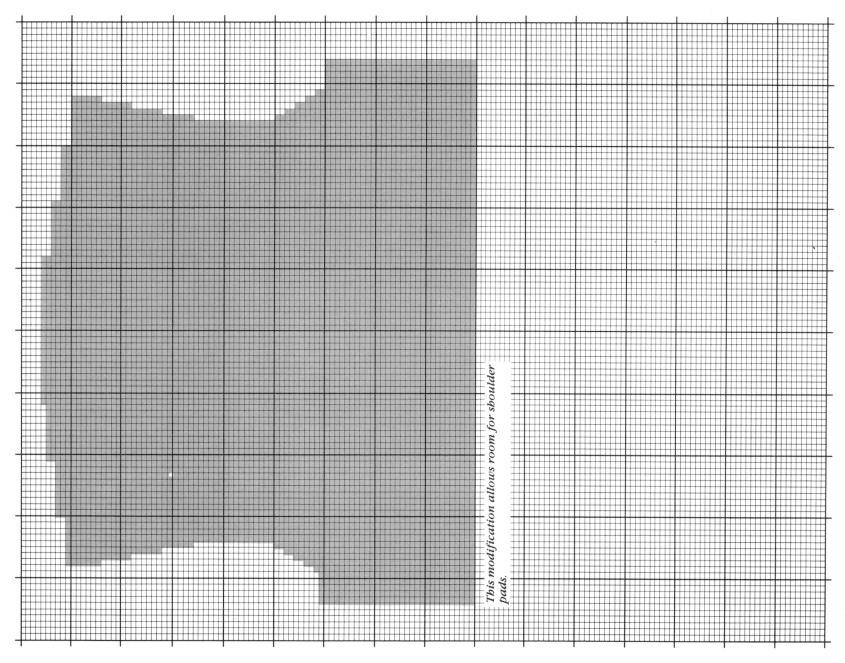

This modification allows room for shoulder pads.

Extended Shoulder Shaping

The popularity of shoulder pads in lightweight garments comes and goes in cycles. Whatever the fashion of the moment, shoulder pads always improve the fit of jackets and coats, and they are indispensable for the proper fit of a garment on a person with a steep shoulder slope.

If you plan to use shoulder pads, consider charting your garment with Extended Shoulder Shaping. Work as you normally would through Set-In or Semi-Raglan Armhole shaping. At the halfway point of the Armhole Depth Measurement, work evenly spaced single increases along each edge to extend each shoulder width by 1/2″ to 1″.

When charting the sleeve cap, the armhole curve is measured like any Set-In or Semi-Raglan Armhole.

Basic T Yoke

The ever-popular, incredibly adaptable Basic T is the easiest of all sweaters to chart. However, hidden behind its simple construction is a style which lends itself to a tremendous number of knitting variations.

At this point, we will chart a Basic T Yoke with sleeves knit separately. See the One-Piece T instructions for other charting possibilities.

Also known as a "drop-shoulder" sweater, a Basic T begins as a Classic Body, but omits armhole shaping. In-

Extended Shoulder Shaping

STEP 1
Chart the garment through Set-In Armhole shaping (CB/Step 5 to CB/Step 8) or Semi-Raglan Armhole shaping. Work to half the Armhole Depth Measurement, measured from the bind-off row.

STEP 2
(1/2″ to 1″) × stitch gauge = number of stitches to increase per edge
Example: .75 × 5 = 3.75   *4 stitches*

STEP 3
1/2 Armhole Depth Measurement × row gauge = number of rows over which increases will be made
Make this an even number.
Example: 4.12 × 6 = 24.7   *24 rows*

STEP 4
Step 3 ÷ Step 2 = number of rows on which to work increases
See Taper Formula to work out intervals.
Example: 24 ÷ 4 = 6   *Increase every 6th row*

STEP 5
Number of stitches per shoulder (CB/Step 11) + Step 2 = number of stitches per Extended Shoulder
Example: 22 + 4 = 26   *26 stitches*

STEP 6
Step 5 ÷ number of shoulder shaping bind-off levels (CB/Step 15) = number of stitches to bind off on every other row per shoulder
■ If the shoulder stitches do not divide evenly, bind off the smaller amount(s) first.
Example: 26 ÷ 3 = 8.6   *8, 9, and 9 stitches*

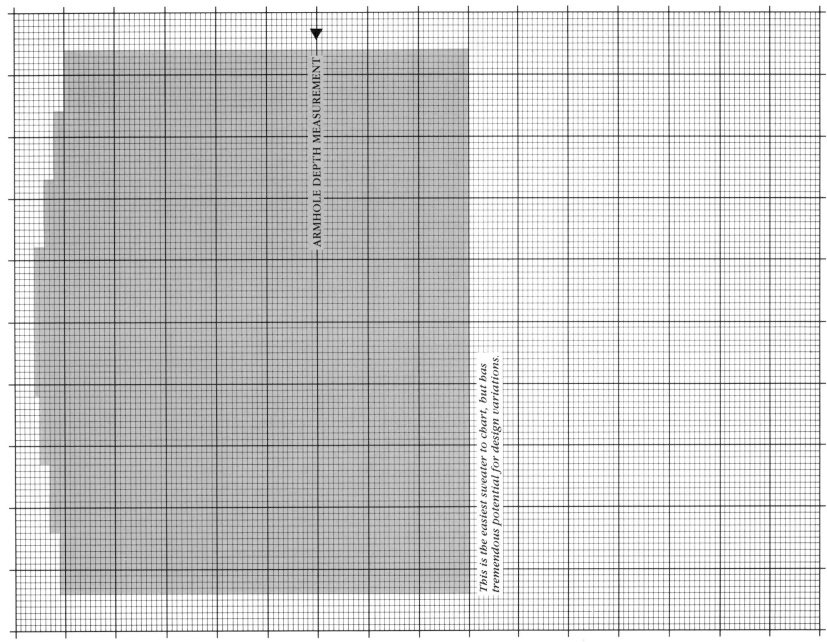

BASIC T YOKE

ARMHOLE DEPTH MEASUREMENT

This is the easiest sweater to chart, but has tremendous potential for design variations.

87

stead, it is worked straight all the way to the shoulders.

Sleeves can begin at the normal Armhole Depth. On the other hand, the armhole can be as deep as you'd like, even beginning at the waist. (As with any other yoke, add between 1/2" and 2" to your Armhole Depth Measurement if you are charting an outerwear sweater or coat.) Mark the Armhole Depth on your garment with a piece of yarn or a safety pin. The upper sleeves must be charted to correspond to this depth.

Shoulder shaping is optional. If you are making a Boatneck or very wide shaped neckline, bind off all of the shoulder stitches at one time, at the row on the yoke corresponding to the Raglan Depth Measurement. If you are planning a smaller neckline such as a Round or V Neck, shoulder shaping will make the garment fit better.

In its purest form (as a Boatneck, with no neck or shoulder shaping), a Basic T body is simply a square or rectangle and can easily be knit horizontally instead of vertically. This allows additional design possibilities for cables or other textured and multicolor patterns.

Use the Basic T Sleeve with this yoke.

Vertically Knit Basic T

STEP 1

[1/2 Chest Measurement + 1/2 Ease (CB/Step 2)] × stitch gauge = number of stitches to cast on
■ Add 2 stitches for seams if you are working flat.
Example: (16.5 + 1 = 17.5) × 5 = 87.5   *88 stitches*

STEP 2

Work even on Step 1 number of stitches to the Garment Length to Armhole. Place marker on fabric. Continue to work even to start of shoulder shaping (at Armhole Depth Measurement) or straight shoulder bind-off (at Raglan Depth Measurement).

Horizontally Knit Basic T

STEP 1

(Garment Length to Armhole + Raglan Depth Measurement = total garment length) × stitch gauge = number of stitches to cast on
■ Subtract ribbing or border if it is to be picked up later.
Example: 24 × 5 = 120   *120 stitches*

STEP 2

Work even on Step 1 number of stitches for 1/2 (Chest Measurement + Body Ease). Bind off.

Modified T Yoke

The Modified T Yoke is a simple variation of the Basic T. Between 1″ and 2″ of stitches are bound off per edge at the underarm; that amount will be added later to each sleeve to replace the eliminated stitches. We will bind off 1″ in our example.

Follow the Basic T guidelines for Armhole Depth and shoulder shaping. Use the Modified T Sleeve bind-off (page 247) with this yoke.

Saddle Shoulder Yoke (Standard and Modified)

A Standard Saddle Shoulder Sweater has a saddle band across the shoulders with a maximum width of 2″ for a child and 3″ for an adult. Your choice of necklines can vary, but the neckline shaping must be finished before the final shoulder bind-off level. Use a Standard Saddle Shoulder Sleeve Cap (page 233) for this style.

If you wish to have a wider saddle band (perhaps to carry a wide sleeve pattern design all the way to the neck), you will need to chart a Modified Saddle Shoulder Sleeve Cap. Part of the saddle band will, in effect, become part of the yoke in back, and perhaps include part of the neckline shaping in front. This is an advanced style best charted on graph paper, so read through the Modified Saddle Shoulder Sleeve Cap instructions (page 235) before you decide to use it.

Both Standard and Modified Yokes are charted in the same manner. They look identical to the yoke on our Classic Body, except they are shorter by half the width of the saddle band.

In our example, we will chart a yoke for a 2″-wide saddle band.

Modified T Yoke

STEP 1

½ [Chest Measurement + Body Ease (CB/Step 2)] × stitch gauge = number of stitches to cast on

Example: (16.5 + 1 = 17.5) × 5 = 87.5   *88 stitches*

■ Add two stitches for seams if you are working flat.

STEP 2

Work even on Step 1 number of stitches to desired length to armholes.

STEP 3

(1–2″ or desired width to bind off per armhole) × stitch gauge = number of stitches to bind off per armhole

Example: 1 × 5 = 5   *5 stitches*

STEP 4

Step 1 – (Step 3 × 2) = number of stitches remaining on needle for yoke

Example: 88 – (5 × 2 = 10) = 78   *78 stitches*

STEP 5

Work even on Step 4 number of stitches to shoulder shaping position (at Armhole Depth Measurement) or straight shoulder bind-off position (at Raglan Depth Measurement).

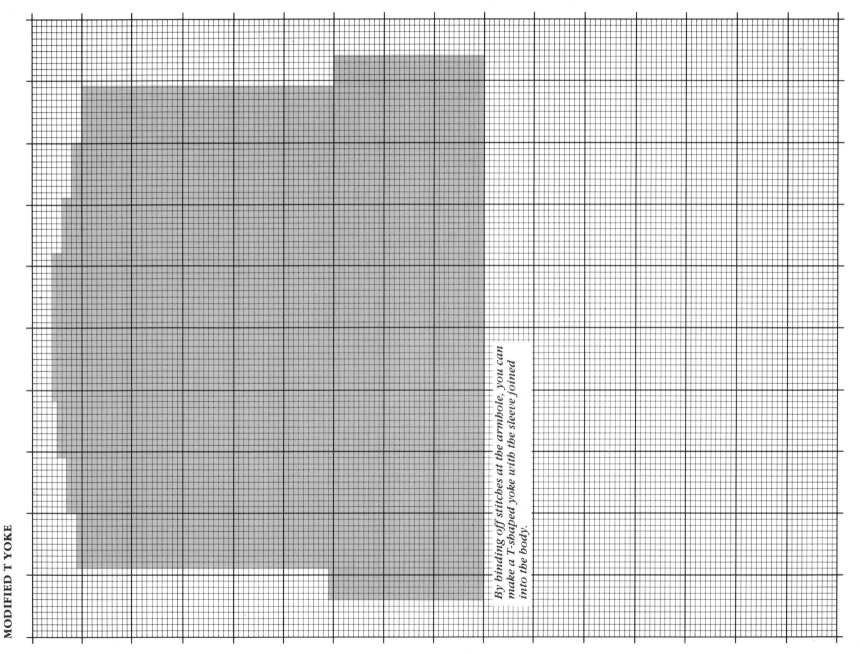

MODIFIED T YOKE

By binding off stitches at the armhole, you can make a T-shaped yoke with the sleeve joined into the body.

SADDLE SHOULDER YOKE (STANDARD AND MODIFIED)

ARMHOLE DEPTH MEASUREMENT

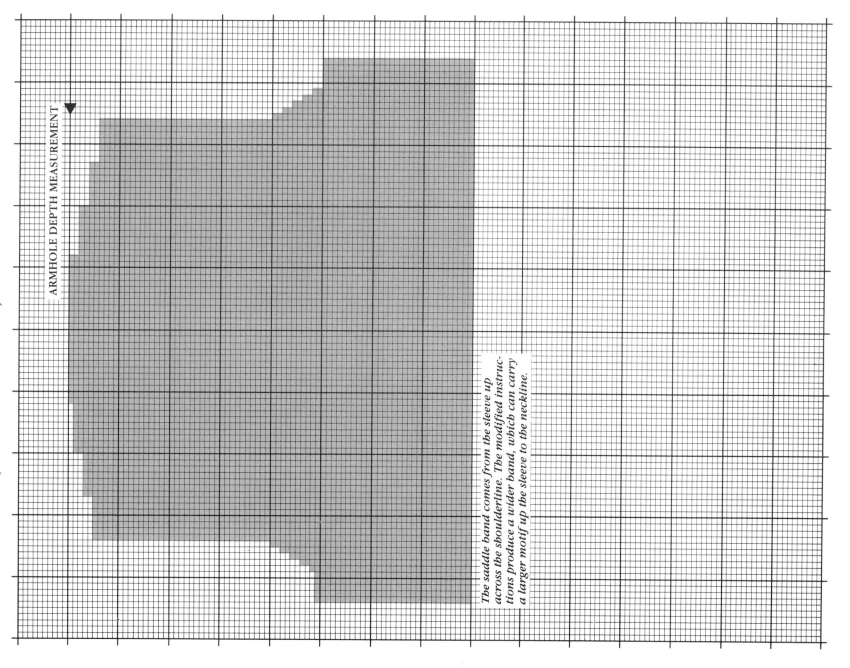

The saddle band comes from the sleeve up across the shoulderline. The modified instructions produce a wider band, which can carry a larger motif up the sleeve to the neckline.

STANDARD

MODIFIED

Saddle Shoulder Yoke

STEP 1
Chart sweater through Set-In Armhole shaping (CB/Step 1 through CB/Step 9).

STEP 2
Armhole Depth Measurement − (saddle band width ÷ 2) = adjusted armhole depth for Saddle Shoulder Yoke
Example: 8.25 − (2 ÷ 2 = 1) = 7.25   7¼"

STEP 3
Work even on remaining stitches until Step 2 measurement is reached.

STEP 4
Bind off shoulder shaping in same manner as for the Classic Body (CB/Step 16).
Example: 7, 7, and 8 stitches

Standard Raglan Yoke

The Standard Raglan Yoke is different from any yoke previously charted, in that the decreases for the armhole are determined by the width of the neckline rather than by the shoulder width. With the exception of neck shaping, both front and back yokes are charted alike.

The sleeve cap is shaped until a 1″ width of stitches remains at the top. These stitches will become part of the neckline when the garment is assembled.

You can work decreases for Raglan shaping at the edge of the fabric, but also consider working them in a decorative manner. Decreases can be an important and effective design element on the finished garment. Try different possibilities on a test swatch. Work the decreases two or more stitches in from the edge. Try slanting them toward the center of the fabric, then try slanting them toward the edges. Try working cable or lace pattern bands along the edges, positioning the decreases to fall at the point where the cable or lace band and yoke stitch pattern meet. Whether or not you insert decorative elements, however, make sure that the decreases along the two edges are paired—the two decreases in each pair should slant in opposite directions (see "How Tos").

You can choose any style sleeve, but it must be finished with a Standard Raglan Sleeve Cap.

In charting a Raglan garment, use the Raglan Depth Measurement in your calculations, rather than the Armhole Depth Measurement.

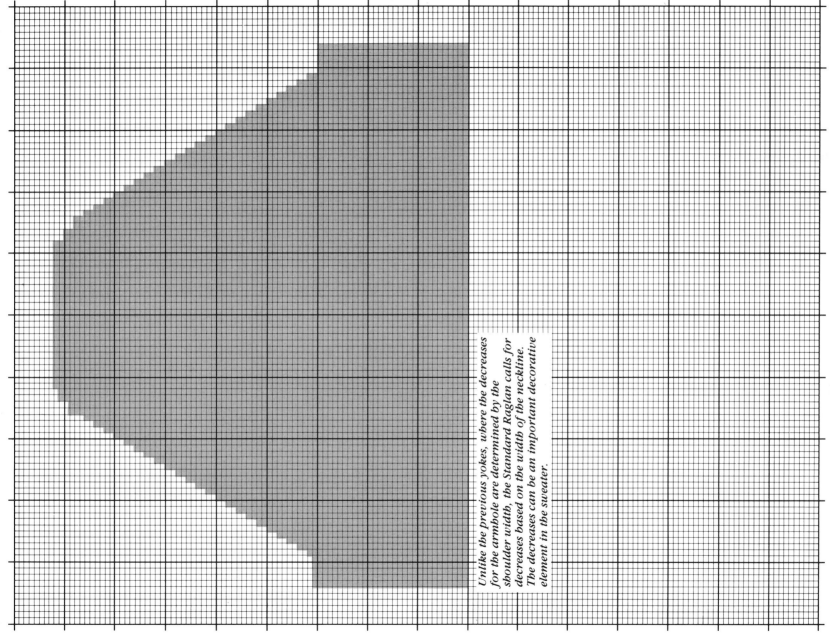

Unlike the previous yokes, where the decreases for the armhole are determined by the shoulder width, the Standard Raglan calls for decreases based on the width of the neckline. The decreases can be an important decorative element in the sweater.

RAGLAN SWEATER CONSTRUCTION

STANDARD

Standard Raglan Yoke

STEP 1
Chart Set-In Armhole shaping (CB/Step 5 through CB/Step 8) to determine the number of stitches to bind off at the armholes.
Example: *5 stitches*

STEP 2
Number of stitches at upper body of sweater (CB/Step 3) – (Step 1 × 2) = number of stitches at start of Raglan decreases
Example: 88 – (5 × 2 = 10) = 78   *78 stitches*

STEP 3
(Shoulder Width Measurement ÷ 3) × stitch gauge = number of stitches for neckline
Adjust, if desired, according to the guidelines under Necklines.
Example: (13.5 ÷ 3 = 4.5) × 5 = 22.5   *24 stitches*
■ If Step 2 is an even number, make Step 3 an even number. If Step 2 is an odd number, make Step 3 an odd number.

STEP 4
Step 2 – Step 3 = total number of Raglan decrease stitches
Make this an even number.
Example: 78 – 24 = 54   *54 stitches*
■ Add any extra stitch to the neckline (Step 3).

STEP 5
Step 4 ÷ 2 = number of decreases per edge
Example: 54 ÷ 2 = 27   *27 stitches*

STEP 6
Raglan Depth Measurement – ¹/₂″ = number of inches over which Raglan decreases will be worked
The ¹/₂″ equals half of the stitches at the top of the Standard Raglan Sleeve Cap.
Example: 9.25 – .50 = 8.75   *8³/₄″*

STEP 7
Step 6 × row gauge = number of rows over which Raglan decreases will be worked
Make this an even number.
Example: 8.75 × 6 = 52.5   *52 rows*

STEP 8

Step 7 ÷ Step 5 = rows on which to work decreases

See Taper Formula or Slope Formula to work out intervals.

- If your result is not an even number, decrease more slowly at the start of the shaping (over the greater number of rows) and faster toward the neckline (over the lesser number of rows). An exception to this guideline can occur if your Step 8 calculation results in a number less than 2. In this case, on some (right-side) rows you will need to decrease 2 stitches instead of 1 at each edge. To do this, you can use "stair steps" (binding off multiple stitches) or double decreases (see "How Tos"), either of which is a suitable method for decreasing two stitches in Raglans. If you feel that these decrease methods would be very obvious on your sweater at a location near the neckline, work them immediately after the armhole bind-off where they'll be less visible.

Example: 52 ÷ 27 = 1.9   *Every 2nd row*

RAGLAN SWEATER CONSTRUCTION

MODIFIED

Modified Raglan Yoke

If you want to chart a Raglan with more than 1″ of stitches remaining at the top of the sleeve cap (perhaps to accommodate a decorative pattern on the sleeve, continuing at its full width to the neckline), a Modified Raglan shaping will do the trick.

First, the back yoke is calculated with numbers, then the numbers are transferred into a graph-paper pattern. The pattern for the front yoke results from a combination of the back yoke graph and a graph of the front neckline. We recommend that you chart an entire front as a Classic Yoke and superimpose it over the graph of the back yoke. The end result will be a graph pattern to follow when knitting your Modified Raglan Front.

Note on our graph that the neckline is narrower on the back than on the front. Part of the Modified Raglan Sleeve Cap will become part of the back neckline.

In our example, we will have 3″ of stitches remaining as the finished width at the top of the sleeve cap. An average range would be 2″ to 5″. The neckline width determines the maximum finished width at the top of the cap; Step 4 will let you know if your finished width will need to be narrower than you originally intended.

MODIFIED RAGLAN YOKE

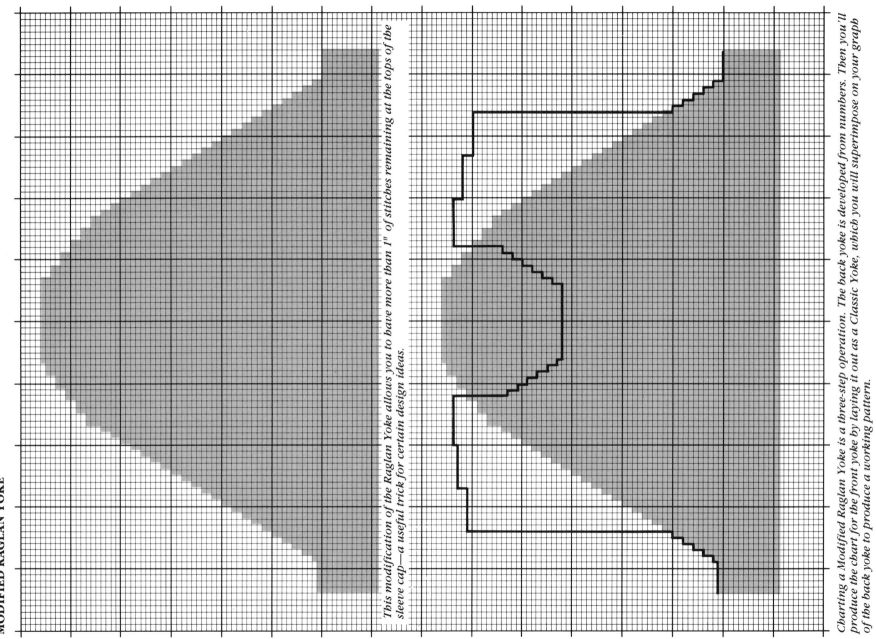

This modification of the Raglan Yoke allows you to have more than 1" of stitches remaining at the tops of the sleeve cap—a useful trick for certain design ideas.

Charting a Modified Raglan Yoke is a three-step operation. The back yoke is developed from numbers. Then you'll produce the chart for the front yoke by laying it out as a Classic Yoke, which you will superimpose on your graph of the back yoke to produce a working pattern.

Back Yoke

STEP 1
Chart Set-In Armhole shaping (CB/Step 5 through CB/Step 8) to determine the number of stitches to bind off at the armhole.
Example: ⠀⠀⠀*5 stitches*

STEP 2
Number of stitches for upper body (CB/Step 3) − (Step 1 × 2) = number of stitches at start of Raglan shaping
Example: 88 − (5 × 2 = 10) = 78 ⠀⠀⠀⠀⠀⠀⠀⠀⠀⠀⠀⠀⠀⠀⠀⠀⠀⠀⠀⠀⠀⠀⠀⠀⠀⠀⠀⠀*78 stitches*

STEP 3
(Shoulder Width Measurement ÷ 3) × stitch gauge = number of stitches for neckline
Adjust, if you wish, according to the guidelines under Necklines.
Example: (13.5 ÷ 3 = 4.5) × 5 = 22.5 ⠀⠀⠀⠀⠀⠀⠀⠀⠀⠀⠀⠀⠀⠀⠀⠀⠀⠀⠀⠀*24 stitches*
- If Step 2 is an even number, make Step 3 even. If Step 2 is an odd number, make Step 3 odd.

STEP 4
(Finished Width at top of sleeve cap in inches − 1″) × stitch gauge = number of stitches to subtract from back neckline
Make this an even number.
- If the result is greater than half the neckline stitches (Step 3), it will be necessary to plan a narrower Finished Width at the top of the sleeve cap.

Example: (3 − 1 = 2) × 5 = 10 ⠀⠀⠀⠀⠀⠀⠀⠀⠀⠀⠀⠀⠀⠀⠀⠀⠀⠀⠀⠀⠀⠀⠀⠀⠀*10 stitches*

STEP 5
Step 3 − Step 4 = number of neckline stitches for the Modified Raglan Back
Example: 24 − 10 = 14 ⠀⠀⠀⠀⠀⠀⠀⠀⠀⠀⠀⠀⠀⠀⠀⠀⠀⠀⠀⠀⠀⠀⠀⠀⠀⠀⠀⠀⠀⠀⠀⠀*14 stitches*

STEP 6
(Step 2 − Step 5) ÷ 2 = number of raglan decreases per edge
Example: (74 − 14 = 64) ÷ 2 = 32 ⠀⠀⠀⠀⠀⠀⠀⠀⠀⠀⠀⠀⠀⠀⠀⠀⠀⠀⠀⠀⠀⠀*32 stitches*

STEP 7
Raglan Depth Measurement × row gauge = number of rows over which raglan decreases will be worked
Make this an even number.
Example: 9.25 × 6 = 55.5 ⠀⠀⠀⠀⠀⠀⠀⠀⠀⠀⠀⠀⠀⠀⠀⠀⠀⠀⠀⠀⠀⠀⠀⠀⠀⠀⠀⠀⠀*56 rows*

ROUND YOKES

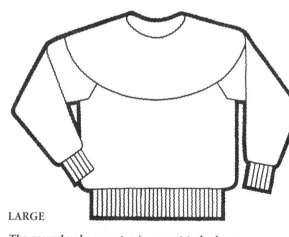

SMALL

LARGE

The round yoke sweater is meant to be loose-fitting, not tailored. It provides an unbroken yoke area, ideal for the display of color or texture patterns.

STEP 8

Step 7 ÷ Step 5 = rows on which to work decreases
See Taper Formula or Slope Formula to work out intervals.

■ If your result is not an even number, decrease more slowly at the start of the shaping (over the greater number of rows) and faster toward the neckline (over the lesser number of rows). An exception to this guideline can occur if your Step 8 calculation results in a number less than 2. In this case, on some (right-side) rows you will need to decrease 2 stitches instead of 1 at each edge. To do this, you can use "stair steps" (binding off multiple stitches) or double decreases (see "How Tos"), either of which is a suitable method for decreasing two stitches in Raglans. If you feel that these decrease methods would be very obvious on your sweater at a location near the neckline, work them immediately after the armhole bind-off where they'll be less visible.

Example: 56 ÷ 32 = 1.75   *Every 2 rows*

Front Yoke

STEP 9

Transfer Steps 1 through 8 of the Back Yoke onto a graph paper pattern.

STEP 10

Chart a Classic Yoke with front neckline shaping. Any standard neckline (Round, Square, V) is suitable. Use the same number of stitches for the neckline as you determined in Step 3.

STEP 11

Superimpose the Classic Front (Step 10) over the graph of the Back Yoke. The drawing which results from the intersection of lines will be your pattern of the Modified Raglan Front Yoke.

Round Yokes (Large and Small)

A Round Yoke is used to display a multicolor or textured stitch pattern on a background uninterrupted by seams. The front, back, and sleeves are worked separately through the armhole shaping, then are joined together on a circular needle for working the yoke.

A Round Yoke can be Large or Small, depending on the depth of your pattern and how close you'd like the pattern to be to the neckline.

This is not a tailored style. The fit is meant to be loose and comfortable. The neckline usually is finished as either a Turtleneck or a Crewneck, although other Round Neck finishes are possible.

For simplicity we have divided our Round Yoke guidelines into two parts.

Part One describes *Round Yoke shaping*, which is worked on the front (and on the back as an option) at the top of the body just before the sections are joined on a circular needle. Separate step-by-step guidelines are given for *Large* and *Small* Round Yokes. Part Two describes *Round Yoke decreasing*, which is done on the yoke after the four sections are joined. Decreasing guidelines apply to both Large and Small Round Yokes.

Round Yoke Shaping is worked on the front (and on the back as an option) immediately before the body and sleeve sections are joined.

Shaping for a Large Round Yoke begins at the armhole bind-off level.

Yoke shaping for a Small Round Yoke can begin at any point you like. Below this point, armhole shaping is charted directly from Standard Raglan calculations.

The front shaping depth for both Large and Small Yokes is identical: 2″ for an adult or teenager, 1½″ for a child, 1″ for a toddler. Optional back shaping should be half the front depth: 1″ for an adult, ¾″ for a child.

The shaping stitches are not bound off, but are worked as follows. With the front of the garment facing you, work across to the first level of shaping stitches (do not work them) and place them on a stitch holder. Join a new ball of yarn at the left front and work both left and right sides in short rows (see ''How Tos''); for a smooth look, slip the first stitch after turning.

After the shaping is complete, all of the stitches, including those on the stitch holder, will be placed on a circular needle.

Front, back, and sleeves must have the same number of rows at the armhole edges above the armhole bind-off level when the sections are joined. A Large Round Yoke Sweater will have the same number of decreases per armhole edge on the front, back, and sleeves. The armhole decrease rate on a Small Round Yoke, since it is charted from a Raglan, may be different on the body sections and sleeves. Just make sure that the front, back, and sleeves are worked to the same depth from the armhole bind-off before you join them and work the yoke.

The four sections are joined together on a circular needle in this order: left sleeve, front yoke, right sleeve, back yoke. The next step is Round Yoke decreasing.

Round Yoke Decreasing involves getting from the number of stitches on the circular needle to the number of stitches needed for the neckline, over the depth of the yoke.

As a general rule, approximately one-fourth of the total body and sleeve stitches are used for a tighter neckline finish such as a Turtleneck, and one-third for a more open style such as a Crewneck. Note that this is based on the stitch count prior to binding off at the armhole.

It's simple to double-check the Round Yoke Neckline circumference for your garment. Add the body circumference (Chest Measurement plus Body Ease) to the width at the Upperarms of both sleeves. Divide the result by 4 or by 3,

ROUND YOKE SHAPING

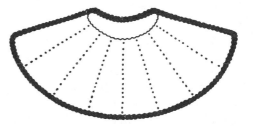

The top of the body is shaped just before the body and sleeve sections are joined on a circular needle.

ROUND YOKE DECREASING

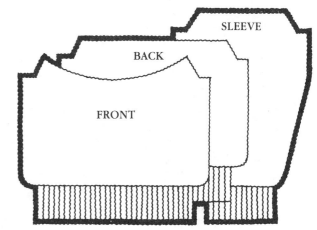

The yoke itself is shaped as all four sections are worked at the same time.

depending on your neckline type. (For children, divide by no more than 3 because they have proportionately larger heads.) Place a tape measure (or a marked string) around your neck and see if it fits comfortably at the calculated circumference. Remember that this is the neckline circumference and does not include the neck finish. Ribbing will tighten the neckline. Also remember that necklines on Round Yokes have a lot of elasticity and will stretch easily over the head since there are no bound-off stitches or shoulder seams. Make any adjustments you deem necessary.

The Round Yoke decreases will be worked over the Raglan Depth Measurement minus the shaping depth at the armhole edges. There are no hard-and-fast rules about the rate or method of decreasing. Generally, on a Small Round Yoke decreasing should begin immediately and continue fairly evenly to the neckline. A Large Round Yoke can be tapered fairly evenly along the full depth, or be worked even for up to half the depth before the decreases begin.

Much depends on your pattern. In most cases, some adjustments are necessary for the pattern and decreases to work together as a unit.

If you're planning a multicolored yoke, look at commercial Fair Isle patterns to see how the decreases are planned. Most of these patterns are in chart form, so they're very easy to understand at a glance. Work out your pattern on graph paper using traditional motifs or designs from your own imagination.

Decreases can also be made between or within cables. If you're not familiar with working cables, a Round Yoke is not the best place to begin. However, if you have a good understanding of them, try decreasing cables on test swatches. Often, decreases can be worked into the background stitches. If you're planning a cabled yoke, remember that cables require more stitches per inch than stockinette stitch; it may be necessary to increase the number of yoke stitches before beginning the cable pattern. A test swatch of several repeats over the entire yoke depth will be very important to your planning.

Another way to decrease the circumference of a Round Yoke is through changes in needle size. For ribbed yokes, a rule of thumb is to work one-third of the depth on the body-size needle, the

Large Round Yoke Shaping

STEP 1
Armhole Shaping: Chart front and back body sections and sleeves to armhole shaping level, and bind off the same number of stitches per armhole as for Set-In Armhole shaping (CB/Step 8). For all four sections, decrease one stitch per armhole edge on every other row for 2″. (On the front and back sections, this edge shaping will be carried out simultaneously with the shaping for the yoke at the center of the piece.)

STEP 2
Front Yoke Shaping: On the same level as the armhole bind-off, begin shaping the Front Yoke by working short rows (see "How Tos"). Divide the stitches on the needle by 3. Place the center third of stitches on a stitch holder for the first level of shaping. Decrease the remaining stitches (¹⁄₃ of the original on each side) over 2″ in depth. Work out a pleasing curve on graph paper if possible. You can use the Slope Formula to determine the *average* number of stitches to shape per row, but in actual practice first shape a greater number of stitches per row, then a progressively smaller number per row as you work upward.
Optional Back Yoke Shaping: After the armhole bind-off, continue working for 1″. Then begin shaping the back yoke in the following manner. Place approximately ¹⁄₂ of the stitches on the needle onto a stitch holder for the first level, and shape the remainder at ¹⁄₄ per side over 1″ in depth, using the same principles as for front yoke shaping.

STEP 3
Starting with the left sleeve, then the Front Yoke, place all four sections on a circular needle, ready to begin the Round Yoke decreasing.

next third on a needle two sizes smaller, and the remaining third on a needle two sizes smaller still (for example, needle sizes 10, 8, and 6). Decreases, if necessary, can be worked in the purl stitches. Of course this is subject to adjustment for specific patterns. Try it on a full-length test swatch to check out the gauge changes.

As your yoke decreases in size, change to a shorter circular needle or to double-pointed needles to avoid stretching the fabric.

If possible, try on the garment after the yoke is complete. Put the stitches on a long piece of yarn (at least twice the neckline circumference), sew underarm and side seams, and try the garment on. You may decide to work a few additional rows or make the neckline tighter.

As you can see, the options for a Round Yoke are many, and having the confidence to adjust the shaping is a must. Just remember what we said earlier: knitting is an adaptable and forgiving medium. That's part of the reason why so many design options exist, as well as being part of the fun of knitting!

Small Round Yoke Shaping

STEP 1
Armhole Shaping: Chart your choice of body and sleeves with Standard Raglan Yoke and Sleeve Cap decreases.

STEP 2
Front Yoke Shaping: At desired point above the armhole bind-off, begin shaping the front yoke by working short rows (see "How Tos"). Divide the stitches on the needle by 3. Place the center third of stitches on a stitch holder for the first level of shaping. Decrease the remaining stitches (one-third of the original on each side) over 2″ in depth. Work out a pleasing curve on graph paper if possible. You can use the Slope Formula to determine the *average* number of stitches to shape per row, but in actual practice first shape a greater number of stitches per row, then a progressively smaller number per row as you work upward.
Optional Back Yoke Shaping: Begin shaping the Back Yoke 1″ higher than the front, in the following manner. Place approximately one-half of the stitches on the needle onto a stitch holder for the first level, and shape the remainder at one-quarter per side over 1″ in depth, using the same principles as for Front Yoke shaping.

STEP 3
Starting with the left sleeve, then the Front Yoke, place all four sections on a circular needle, ready to begin the round yoke decreasing. Front, back, and sleeves must be worked to the same depth from the armhole bind-off before they are joined. Note that on our Small Yoke graph, the sleeves do not necessarily decrease at the same rate as the body sections since they are charted from a Raglan.

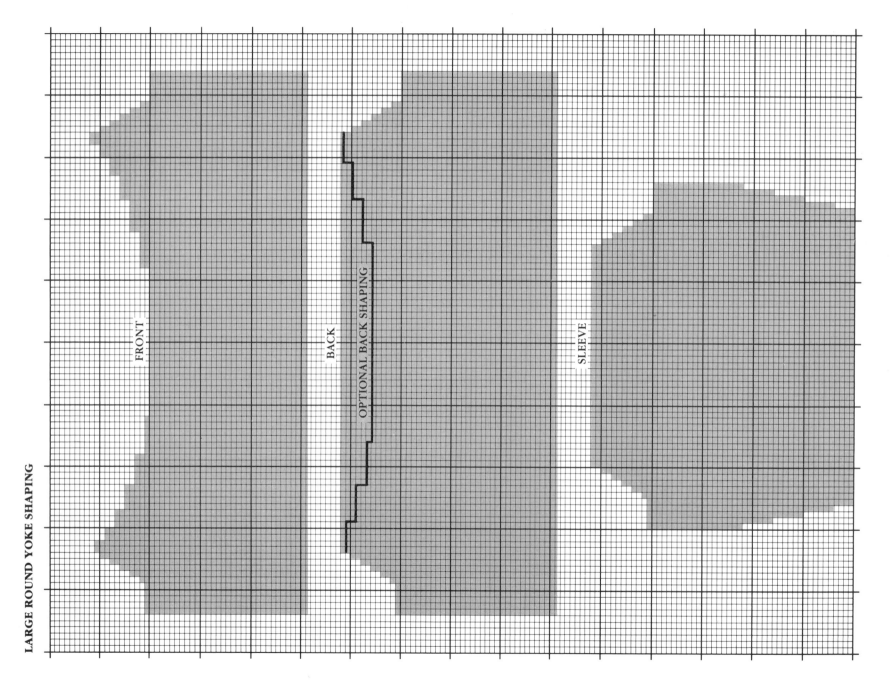

LARGE ROUND YOKE SHAPING

FRONT

BACK

OPTIONAL BACK SHAPING

SLEEVE

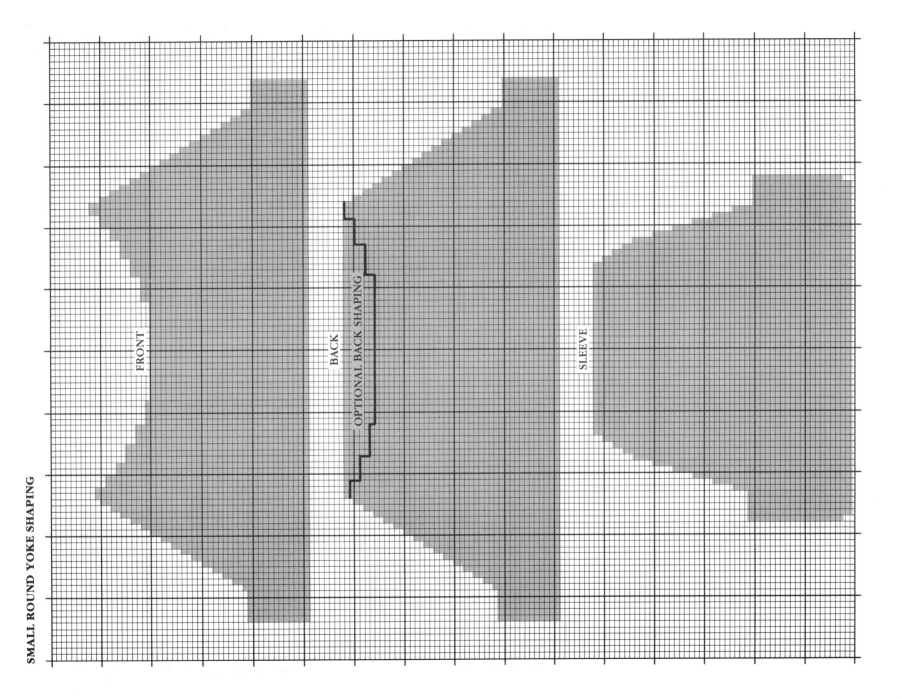

SMALL ROUND YOKE SHAPING

FRONT

BACK

OPTIONAL BACK SHAPING

SLEEVE

Round Yoke Decreasing

STEP 1

Total number of stitches on needle at start of Round Yoke − number of stitches required at neckline = total number of stitches to decrease

Our example shows our Large Round Yoke with a neckline size (number of stitches) suitable for a Crewneck (see discussion above).

Example: 208 − 72 = 136   *136 stitches*

STEP 2

Raglan Depth Measurement − depth of armhole shaping = depth of Round Yoke

On a Large Round Yoke the depth of the armhole shaping is 2" for an adult, 1½" for a child, 1" for a toddler. The armhole shaping depth on a Small Round Yoke is measured from your own individual garment.

Example: 9.25 − 2 = 7.25   *7¼"*

STEP 3

Step 2 × row gauge = number of rounds for Round Yoke

Example: 7.25 × 6 = 43.5   *44 rounds*

STEP 4

Work the decreases in any of the ways discussed above depending on your design motif or stitch pattern.

Full-Fashioned Shoulder Shaping

A very popular style in commercial knitwear, this method of shaping seldom is found in hand knit patterns. In it, the seams joining the front to the back are not at the shoulders, but are dropped to the back of the garment.

Front and back yokes are charted and worked differently.

The **Back Shoulder Shaping** begins 2" (1½" for a child) short of the Armhole Depth Measurement, and is worked for approximately 3" (2½" for a child). The slope is not worked in short rows or by binding off stitches, but by decreasing. The decreases are an important decorative part of the style. There may be two, three, or even four decreases per edge on a given row.

Each of the two possible methods for working the decreases gives a different look. The first method uses our cabled decrease for two or more stitches (see "How Tos"). The second method combines single and double decreases (see

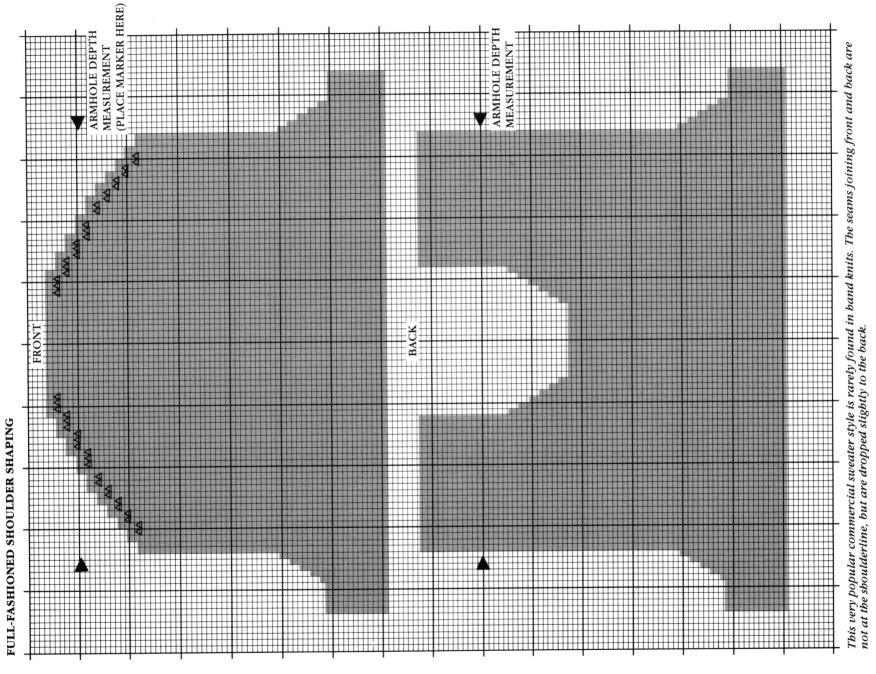

FULL-FASHIONED SHOULDER SHAPING

FRONT

BACK

ARMHOLE DEPTH
MEASUREMENT
(PLACE MARKER HERE)

ARMHOLE DEPTH
MEASUREMENT

This very popular commercial sweater style is rarely found in hand knits. The seams joining front and back are not at the shoulderline, but are dropped slightly to the back.

"How Tos"). For a decrease of only one stitch, work a single decrease; for a decrease of two stitches, work a double decrease; for a decrease of three stitches, work one single and one double decrease; for a decrease of four stitches, work two double decreases. (For additional information, see also "Decrease Placement for Full-Fashioned Shoulder Shaping," page 372.

The **Front** is worked 2″ (1½″ for a child) past the Armhole Depth Measurement, then the shoulder stitches are bound off even. Place yarn markers or safety pins at both edges at the normal Armhole Depth Measurement to help when charting and setting in the sleeve caps.

The neckline shaping is worked in the usual way, using one-third or a bit more of the yoke stitches. (This style is not suited to very wide necklines.)

For the **Sleeve Cap**, chart a Set-In Cap with 4″ (3″ for a child) finished width across the top. (This is twice the distance between the marker and shoulder seam on the front yoke.) Measure the armhole curve to the marker for the Armhole Curve Measurement.

Back

STEP 1
Chart and work Standard Set-In or Alternate Set-In Armhole shaping.

STEP 2
Armhole Depth Measurement − (2″ for an adult or 1½″ for a child) = length of yoke to start of shoulder slope
Example: 8.25 − 2 = 6.25   *6¼″*

STEP 3
[2″ for an adult or 1½″ for a child + shoulder slope (CB/Step 13)] × row gauge = number of rows for shoulder taper
Example: (2 + 1 = 3) × 6 = 18   *18 rows*

STEP 4
Step 3 ÷ 2 = number of rows on which to work decreases
Example: 18 ÷ 2 = 9   *9 rows*

STEP 5
Number of stitches per shoulder (CB/Step 11) ÷ Step 4 = number of stitches to decrease per row per edge
■ If the stitches do not divide into even groups, work the smaller number of stitch decreases first. The total decreases per edge will be the same number as the stitches per shoulder.
Example: 22 ÷ 9 = 2.4   *2, 2, 2, 2, 2, 3, 3, 3, and 3 stitches*

Front

STEP 1
Chart and work Standard Set-In or Alternate Set-In Armhole shaping.

STEP 2
Armhole Depth Measurement + (2″ for an adult or 1½″ for a child) = total length of front yoke
Place a yarn marker or safety pin at each edge at the Armhole Depth Measurement.
Example: 8.25 + 2 = 10.25   *10¼″*

STEP 3
Bind off even.

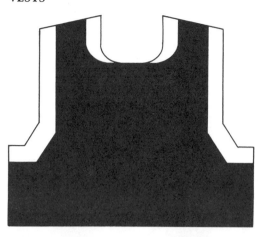

Set-In and Semi-Raglan Vest Shapings (solid areas) as compared to standard sweater yokes (outlined areas).

Vest Armhole Shaping

A traditionally styled vest is charted like any regular yoke with Set-In or Semi-Raglan Armhole shaping minus the depth of the Bands around the armholes. The Bands will be picked up and worked after the body sections are assembled; when the Bands are complete, the Vest Yoke will be as wide and as deep as any standard sweater yoke.

The knitted depth of an average Vest Band is ³/₄″ to 1″. We will use 1″ in our example.

Most pullover vest necklines are finished with Bands of the same knitted depth as charted for the armholes. Since the vest is a garment worn over other clothing, the Band should lie flat on the shoulders and not against the collar of the garment underneath. This means that the depth of the Neckline Band should be subtracted from the width of each shoulder.

For a Cardigan Vest with Neckline Band finish, Shawl Collar, or Lapel Collar, follow the guidelines under "Cardigans."

Armhole and neckline adjustments result in a Vest Yoke with substantially fewer stitches at each shoulder than a sweater with sleeves. As a result, shoulder shaping on a vest has one level less than on a normal sweater.

Vest Armhole Shaping

STEP 1
Garment Length to Armhole Measurement − Band depth = length to Vest Armhole shaping
- If the vest will be worn over a heavy sweater, you may want to lower the armholes. Subtract ½″ to 1″ from the Step 1 result, but *be sure to add the same amount to the Armhole Depth Measurement.*
Example: 15 − 1 = 14   *14″*

STEP 2
Armhole Depth Measurement + Band depth = adjusted armhole depth for vest
Example: 8.25 + 1 = 9.25   *9¼″*

STEP 3
Band depth × stitch gauge = number of stitches for Band depth
Example: 1 × 5 = 5   *5 stitches*

STEP 4
Chart CB/Step 5 through CB/Step 9 as you would for a Set-In Armhole Yoke, and jot down the numbers.

STEP 5
Number of stitches to bind off per armhole (CB/Step 8) + Step 3 = number of stitches to bind off per vest armhole
Example: 5 + 5 = 10   *10 stitches*

STEP 6
Version 1: Set-In Armhole Type Shaping
On every other row, single decrease the same number of stitches per armhole as calculated for Set-In Armhole shaping (CB/Step 9).
Example: *5 stitches*
Version 2: Semi-Raglan Type Armhole Shaping
a. (½ Armhole Depth Measurement + band depth) × row gauge = number of rows over which decreases will be made
   Make this an even number.
Example: (4.12 + 1 = 5.12) × 6 = 30.72   *30 rows*
b. Step 6a ÷ number of single decreases per armhole (CB/Step 9) = rows on which to work decreases
   See Taper Formula to work out intervals.
Example: 30 ÷ 5 = 6   *Decrease at 6-row intervals*

STEP 7
Work even on remaining stitches to *adjusted* Armhole Depth Measurement (Step 2).

STEP 8
Number of stitches for Classic Yoke (CB/Step 5) – (Step 3 × 2) = number of stitches for Vest Yoke
Example: 68 – (5 × 2 = 10) = 58   *58 stitches*

STEP 9
Number of stitches for neckline (CB/Step 12) + (Step 3 × 2) = number of stitches for Vest Neckline
Example: 24 + (5 × 2 = 10) = 34   *34 stitches*

STEP 10
(Step 8 – Step 9) ÷ 2 = number of stitches per vest shoulder
Example: (58 – 34 = 24) ÷ 2 = 12   *12 stitches*

STEP 11
Number of standard bind-off levels (CB/Step 15) – 1 = number of bind-off levels for vest shoulder shaping
Example: 3 – 1 = 2   *2 levels*

STEP 12
Step 10 ÷ Step 11 = number of stitches to bind off on every other row per shoulder
■ If the shoulder stitches do not divide evenly, bind off the smaller amount(s) first.
Example: 12 ÷ 2 = 6   *6 stitches*

STEP 13
Join front and back sections at the shoulders and sides. Pick up stitches around the armholes and work in border stitch pattern to the depth of the band. Complete neckline with Band or other neck finish.

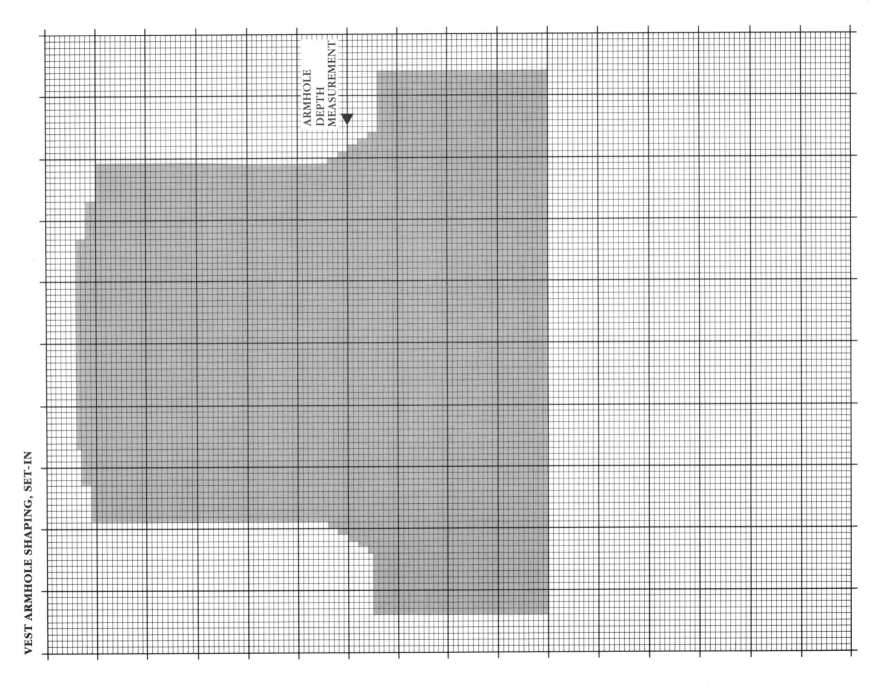

ARMHOLE
DEPTH
MEASUREMENT

VEST ARMHOLE SHAPING, SET-IN

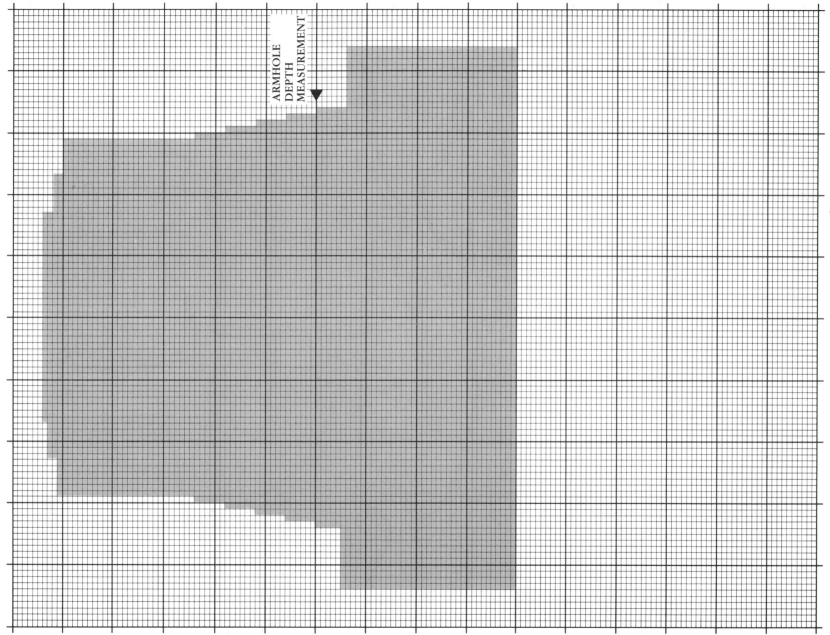

ARMHOLE
DEPTH
MEASUREMENT

VEST ARMHOLE SHAPING, SEMI-RAGLAN

VARIATIONS FOR SUMMER TOPS

Summer Tops

Tank tops, halters, and rib ticklers in lightweight yarns are popular items for summer wear.

Ease is usually kept to a minimum or subtracted from the body measurements—these garments are meant to fit snugly. Many are worked entirely in ribbing to follow the body's curves. Armhole shaping can be based on Set-In, Alternate Set-In, Semi-Raglan, or Raglan techniques, depending upon the style to be charted.

Measurements must be taken over the bra if one is to be worn under the top. Pay careful attention to the bra straps—measure their location when the wearer is standing straight up as well as when she is hunching her shoulders forward, to make sure they won't show when the top is worn. Also be sure that the bra doesn't show at lowered armholes or neckline.

If the top has narrow straps, eliminate shoulder shaping and bind off straight across. Measure the Armhole Depth to the location of the straps at the shoulder—the new measurement will probably fall somewhere between the Armhole Depth Measurement and the Raglan Depth Measurement.

If the top is strapless or has a minimal yoke, take a circumference measurement under the arms, at the spot where you've tied the measurement string. The garment should fit snugly at this point in order to stay up, and you may want to decrease above the bust or work a tight ribbing stitch through this area.

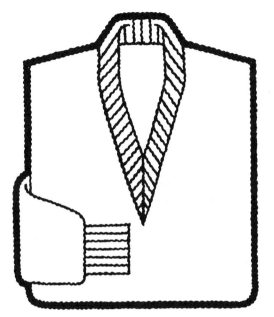

Shaping a V neckline over one-third of the yoke stitches makes a neckline which fits close to the body.

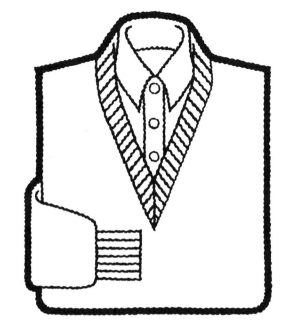

Subtracting additional stitches from the shoulders forms a wider neckline, suitable for outerwear or for sweaters which will be worn over other garments.

NECKLINES

Necklines, or *neck shaping,* should not be confused with neck finishes. A neckline is the foundation upon which a neck finish is worked. For example, a Round Neckline can have a Turtleneck or Crewneck finish. In this chapter we will discuss how necklines are charted. Finishing options will be covered in a later chapter.

Although basic neckline shapes are few, a great deal of variety can exist within each shape. A Round, V, or Square Neckline can be deep or shallow, narrow or wide, or anything in between.

General Information

Neckline Width. Our examples are charted using one-third of the Shoulder Width Measurement for the neckline (and one-third per shoulder). This is the minimum neckline width for an adult garment. Infants and children, due to their larger proportion of head size to body, require a larger neckline (see "Ease for Infants' and Children's Garments").

Very often, fashion or necessity will dictate that the neckline be wider. For example, additional stitches must be subtracted from the shoulders and added to the neckline width for highneck pullovers which need to stretch over the head, for outer garments which should not lie too closely against the neck, or for fashionably wide necklines. In the case of the ribbed Band, a popular finish for a Round or V Neckline, the depth of the Band is subtracted from each shoulder when charting outerwear.

When widening the neckline, be sure to subtract an equal number of stitches from all shoulder sections, both front and back. It is very important that each shoulder contain the same number of stitches. Do not just subtract these stitches from the last level of shoulder shaping. Recalculate the shoulder bind-off (CB/Step 16) using the actual number of stitches, so that a smooth slope is maintained. On wide necklines, it may be wise to eliminate one or more of the shoulder shaping levels; on very wide necklines, shoulder shaping may be eliminated altogether.

Neckline Depth, like neckline width, will depend upon the choice of neck finish and the way you prefer that finish to fit. Some finishes, such as a Crochet Edge or Narrow Band, will affect the charted neckline opening very little, if at all. Others, such as a Wide Band or Shawl Collar, will fill in the opening substantially, requiring adjustments to neckline size.

Our neckline depth guidelines are based on the Armhole Depth Measurement (not Raglan Depth Measurement). A yarn marker placed at the center of the front yoke on the armhole bind-off row (CB/Step 8) is handy for measuring the depth of the yoke to the start of the neck shaping.

NECKLINE DEPTH

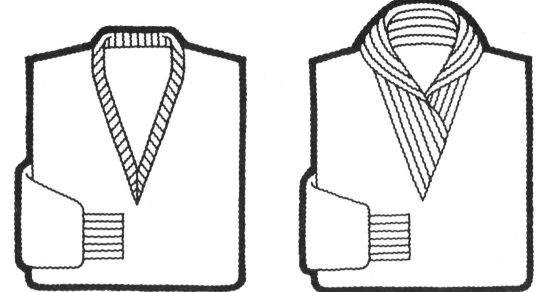

A narrow finish will require only minor adjustments to the charted neckline opening. Other finishes, like a Wide Band or Shawl Collar, affect the size of the neckline.

While exceptions do exist, neck shaping generally occurs only at the front. If any neckline shaping is done at the back, it is usually minimal (see ''Optional Back Neckline Shaping''). However, more extreme shaping at the back may be desirable on wide, deep necklines. If you do want a deeper back neckline, it should be no more than half of the depth of the front shaping.

Duplicating a Neckline. If you have a favorite sweater with a neckline you'd like to duplicate, put it on and tie on the measurement string (see ''Taking Measurements''). Measure from the string to the bottom of the neckline (not including the finish). The result is the depth

of the yoke from the armhole bind-off (CB/Step 8) to the start of the neckline shaping.

Next, take the sweater off, lay it flat, and measure the neckline width at its widest part. You now have the measurements necessary for charting a similar shaping.

Seam Stitches. If the neck finish will be joined to the neckline with a seam, be sure to add a seam stitch at each edge so that stitches from the neckline will not be ''lost'' when the pieces are joined. This is especially important on V and Square Necklines with sewn collars and bands.

Sewn finishes on Round Necklines and picked-up finishes on all types of necklines do not require the addition of seam stitches.

Neckline Variations. "Families" of basic neckline shapes, for which we give you complete instructions, include Round, V, Square, and Boatneck.

Once basic neckline shapes are understood, experimentation becomes possible. Several such variations are illustrated here. Shapings can be combined (a, b, c). The sweater can have different shapings at the front and back, and perhaps be worn either way (d, e, f). Or the neckline can be asymmetrical (g, h, i). Such variations are best charted on graph paper.

Stitch Holder versus Bind-off. For Round and Square Necklines, Blunt Vs, and back necklines, you will need to decide whether to leave the first row of shaping stitches on a stitch holder or bind them off.

The choice is one of *elasticity* versus *stability*. Bound-off stitches do not have as much elasticity as stitches which are placed on a holder to be worked later. Necklines which must stretch over the head (Turtlenecks and Crewnecks, for example) require elasticity, so the natural choice is to place the stitches on a holder. Wide necklines or necklines with an opening (such as Cardigans or Keyhole finishes) can have greater stability, so you may choose to bind the stitches off. Bulky yarns which knit into heavier fabric also require the greater stability of the bind-off more than do fine yarns. If you decide to bind off, remember to bind off loosely.

Working Neckline Finishes. Most neckline finishes are worked in the round, after the front and back sections of the garment are assembled at the shoulders. This eliminates the need for a seam in the neckband, ribbing, or collar.

NECKLINE VARIATIONS

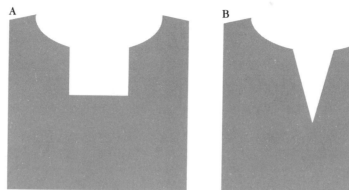
A

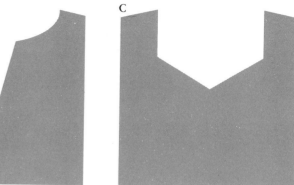
B

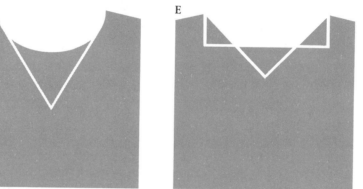
C

Neckline combinations

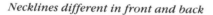
D

E

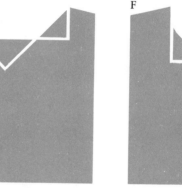
E

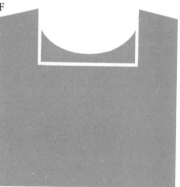
F

Necklines different in front and back

G

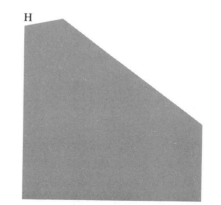
H

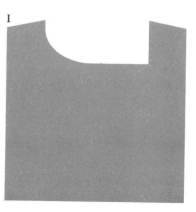
I

Asymmetrical necklines

BASIC NECKLINE SHAPES

ROUND

V

SQUARE

Round Neckline

This classic shape is probably the most popular one in the knitter's repertoire. Our Round Neckline is charted with one-third of the Shoulder Width Measurement (or yoke stitches). Round Necklines used with Round Yokes are charted somewhat differently, however (see pages 99–100). Your garment style and neck finish will determine whether your neckline should be based on this basic measurement, or should be wider.

Your chosen finish also will strongly influence the neckline depth. The following guidelines are not cast in concrete, but simply offer a conservative starting point for designing. Many finishes can be successfully accomplished within a great deal of leeway.

A **High Round Neckline** begins 2″ below the first level of shoulder shaping (or 2″ short of the Armhole Depth Measurement). If this neckline is charted over one-third of the yoke stitches in a pullover, a supplementary neck opening will be necessary so the garment will fit over the head. The opening can be at the shoulders, front, or back of the garment, and can be open or finished with buttons or a zipper. If no additional opening is planned (a Turtleneck, for example), subtract ½″ to 1″ from *each* shoulder and add it to the neckline width. This neckline style is suitable for Turtlenecks, jewel neck finishes, and finishes with Keyholes, Plackets, or other openings, including Cardigan styles.

A **Medium Round Neckline** begins 3″ below the shoulder shaping (that is, 3″ short of the Armhole Depth Measurement). The minimum width is one-third of the yoke stitches. No additional opening is required.

A **Low Round Neckline** begins 4″ to 6″ below the shoulder shaping.

For round necklines, bind off (or place on a holder) one-half of the neckline stitches for the first shaping level. The remaining stitches are decreased one stitch per neckline edge on every other row.

Round Neckline

STEP 1

Armhole Depth Measurement − neckline depth = number of inches from armhole bind-off to start of neckline shaping
Example: 8.25 − 3 = 5.25

5¼″

STEP 2

Neckline stitches (CB/Step 12) ÷ 2 = number of stitches to bind off or place on a stitch holder
■ If the number of neckline stitches is even, make Step 2 even. If it is odd, make Step 2 odd.
Example: 24 ÷ 2 = 12

12 stitches

STEP 3

[Number of neckline stitches (CB/Step 12) − Step 2] ÷ 2 = number of stitches to decrease per neckline edge
Decrease one stitch per neckline edge on every other row, on the right side of the garment only.
Example: (24 − 12 = 12) ÷ 2 = 6

6 stitches

STEP 4

Work even on remaining stitches to the Armhole Depth Measurement, and shape shoulders.

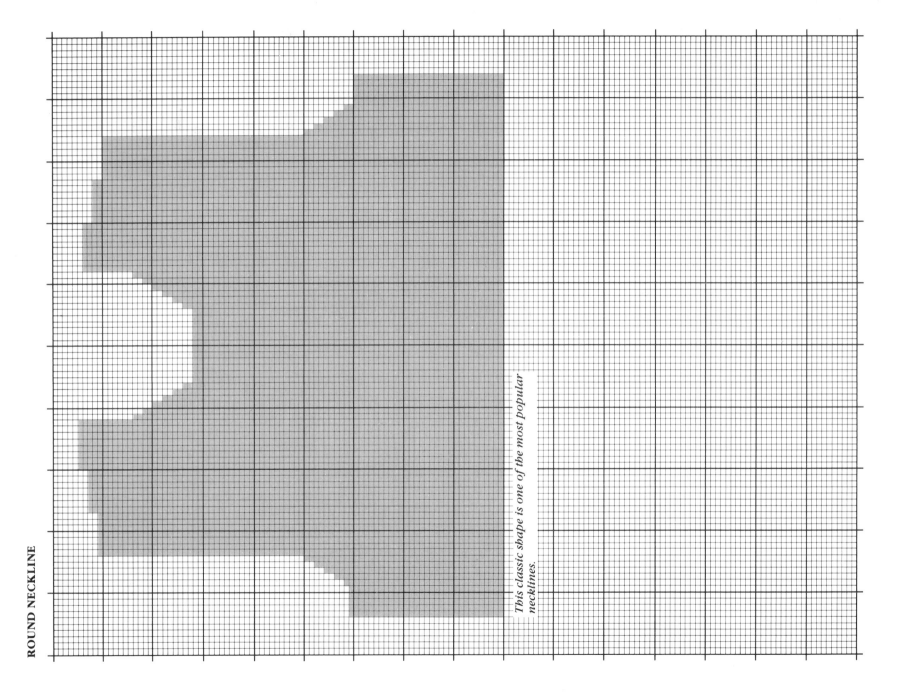

ROUND NECKLINE

This classic shape is one of the most popular necklines.

118

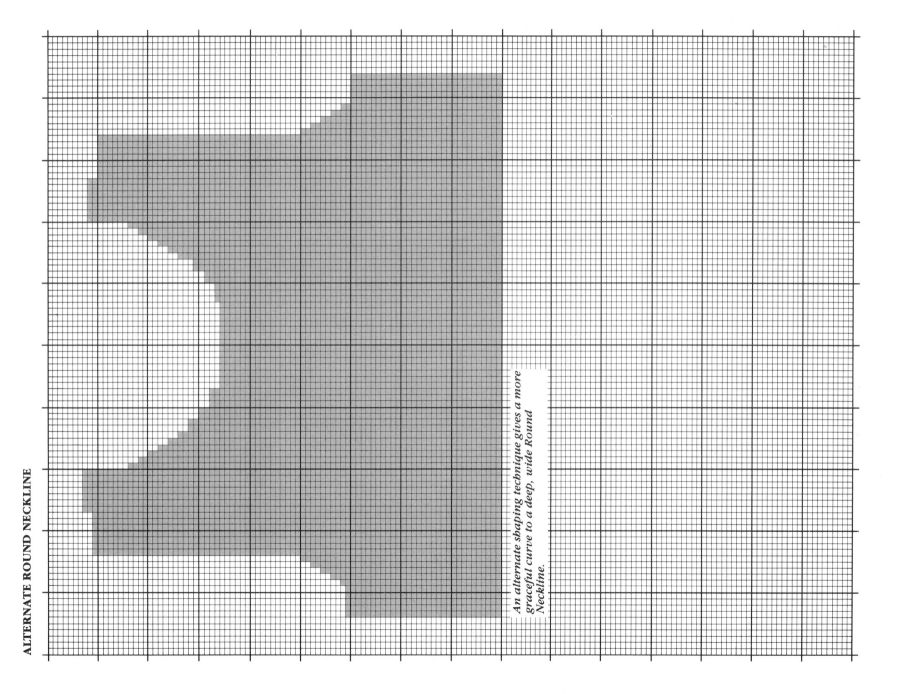

An alternate shaping technique gives a more graceful curve to a deep, wide Round Neckline.

Alternate Round Neckline

For a more graceful curve on deep, wide Round Necklines, consider this alternate shaping. To decide between the two neckline shapes, chart both versions on graph paper and see which curve you prefer for your sweater. Work the Alternate Round Neckline as follows:

Alternate Round Neckline

STEP 1
Bind off or place on a stitch holder one-third of the neckline stitches.

STEP 2
Decrease one-third of the neckline stitches in 2- or 3-stitch "stair steps," half at each neckline edge.
- If you are combining 2- and 3-stitch decreases, bind off the 3-stitch decreases first.

STEP 3
Decrease one-third of the neckline stitches in single decreases, half at each neckline edge.
- If your neckline stitches don't divide evenly, don't hesitate to borrow a stitch or two from one group to add to another.

Traditional V Neckline

The Traditional V Neckline tapers to a point. Width and depth will vary with your selection of finish and the way you want that finish to look. As a general rule, the narrower the width of the neckline, the deeper the neckline should be.

The most popular V finish is a 1″ ribbed Narrow Band, worked on a narrow neckline width. One-third of the yoke stitches are sufficient for the neckline width if the garment will be worn against the body. If the Band is deeper than 1″, subtract the difference from each shoulder, and add it to the neckline width. On outer garments and vests, subtract the full depth of the Band from each shoulder and add it to the neckline.

On an average-size pullover, shaping usually begins on the same level as the armhole bind-off. For larger sizes, start the neckline taper after the armhole shaping is complete, to avoid making too large an opening. On children's sweaters, begin about 1″ below the armhole bind-off so that the sweater can fit over the head. The V taper on a cardigan may begin several inches below the armhole bind-off (even as low as the waist) depending upon how you'd like it to look.

The V taper usually is worked with paired single decreases, one on each neck edge. Try working each decrease a stitch or two in from the edge; this will give you a smooth edge on which to pick up the finish. On wide necklines, single decreases may not be sufficient for the

V-NECKLINE VARIATIONS

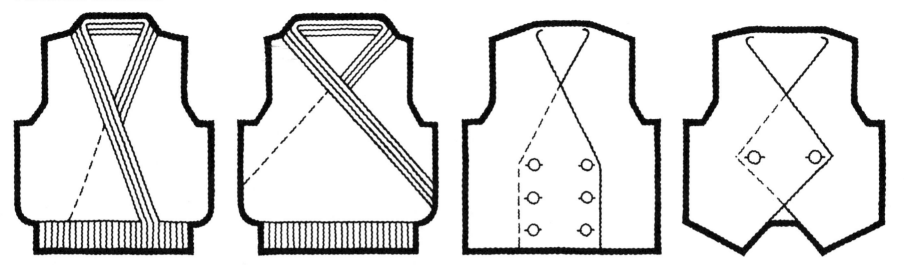

taper. If this is the case, bind off the taper in ''stair step'' decreases, two or more stitches at a time.

On narrower necklines, the V taper ends 1¹/₂″ to 2″ below the first level of shoulder shaping, so that the neckline will lie evenly along the sides of the neck. The taper on wide necklines can continue to the shoulder shaping.

If your neckline has an odd number of stitches, decrease only one stitch (the center stitch) on the first shaping level. If you are planning a Decreased Band finish (page 283), leave the center stitch on a holder instead of binding it off.

In our example, we are charting a Traditional Narrow V Neckline. Shaping begins on the same level as the armhole bind-off.

Traditional V Neckline

STEP 1

Armhole Depth Measurement − neckline depth = number of inches from armhole bind-off to start of neckline shaping
Example: 8.25 − 8.25 = 0   *0″*

STEP 2

Neckline stitches (CB/Step 12) ÷ 2 = number of stitches to single decrease per side edge
■ If your neckline has an odd number of stitches, the center stitch will be bound off or placed on a holder on the first shaping row.
Example: 24 ÷ 2 = 12   *12 stitches*

STEP 3

Neckline depth − 1¹/₂″ to 2″ = number of inches over which decreases will be made
■ If the neckline is wide, the taper can be worked over the entire neckline depth.
Example: 8.25 − 1.5 = 6.75 or
           8.25 − 2 = 6.25   *6¹/₄″ to 6³/₄″*

STEP 4

Step 3 × row gauge = number of rows over which decreases will be made
Make this an even number.
Example: 6.25 × 6 = 37.5 or 6.75 × 6 = 40.5

STEP 5

Use the Taper Formula to determine positions of decreases.

Blunt V Neckline

This variation of the Traditional V Neckline is used for some collar and band finishes. For it, instead of a single stitch or two at the center front, 1″ or more of stitches (up to one-third of the neckline width) are bound off or placed on a stitch holder at the beginning of the taper.

Charting is similar to the Traditional V, but the taper will be a bit steeper since there are fewer stitches to decrease per edge.

Blunt V Neckline

STEP 1

Armhole depth measurement − neckline depth = number of inches from armhole bind-off to start of neckline shaping
Example: 8.25 − 8.25 = 0   *0″*

STEP 2

Width of blunt edge in inches × stitch gauge = number of stitches to bind off on first shaping level
Example: 2 × 5 = 10   *10 stitches*

STEP 3

[Neckline stitches (CB/Step 12) − Step 1] ÷ 2 = number of stitches to single decrease per side edge
Example: (24 − 10 = 14) ÷ 2 = 7   *7 stitches*

STEP 4

Follow steps 3 through 5 of the Traditional V Neckline.

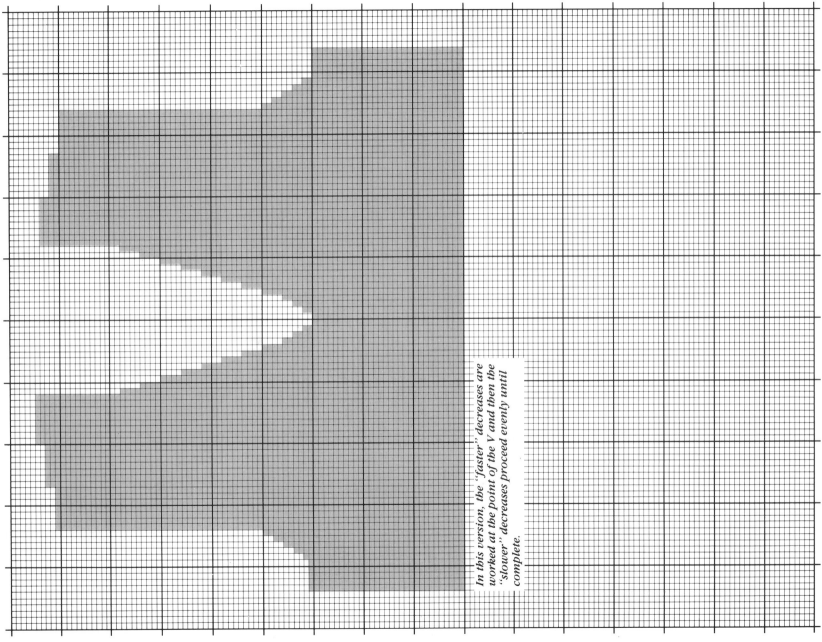

In this version, the "faster" decreases are worked at the point of the V and then the "slower" decreases proceed evenly until complete.

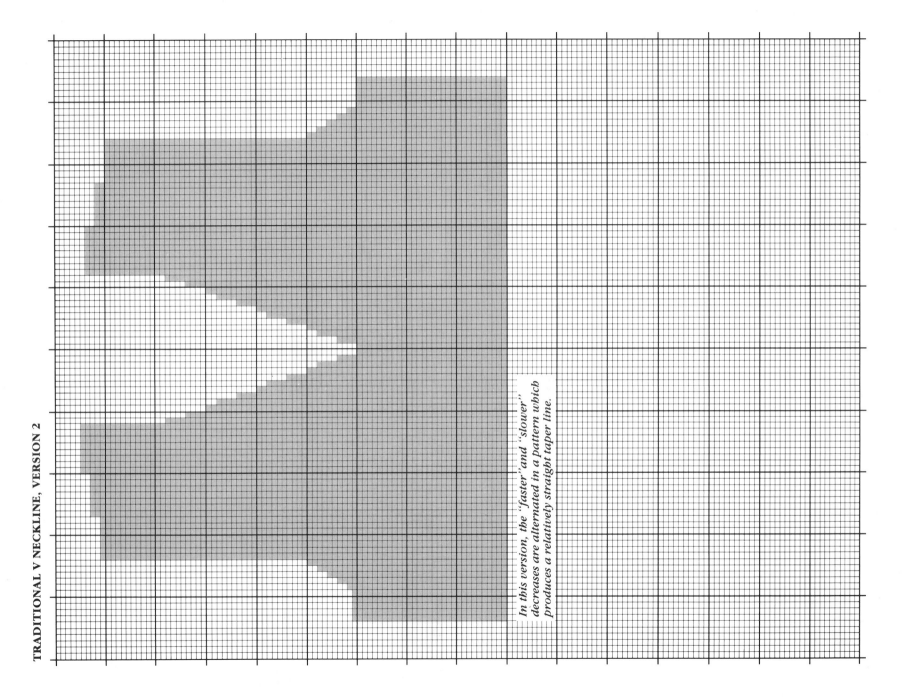

TRADITIONAL V NECKLINE, VERSION 2

In this version, the "faster" and "slower" decreases are alternated in a pattern which produces a relatively straight taper line.

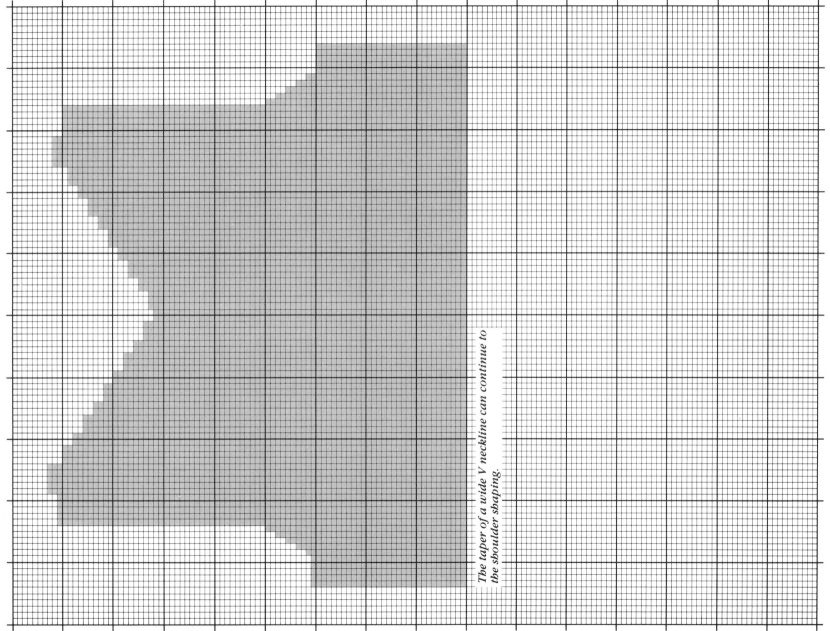

The taper of a wide V neckline can continue to the shoulder shaping.

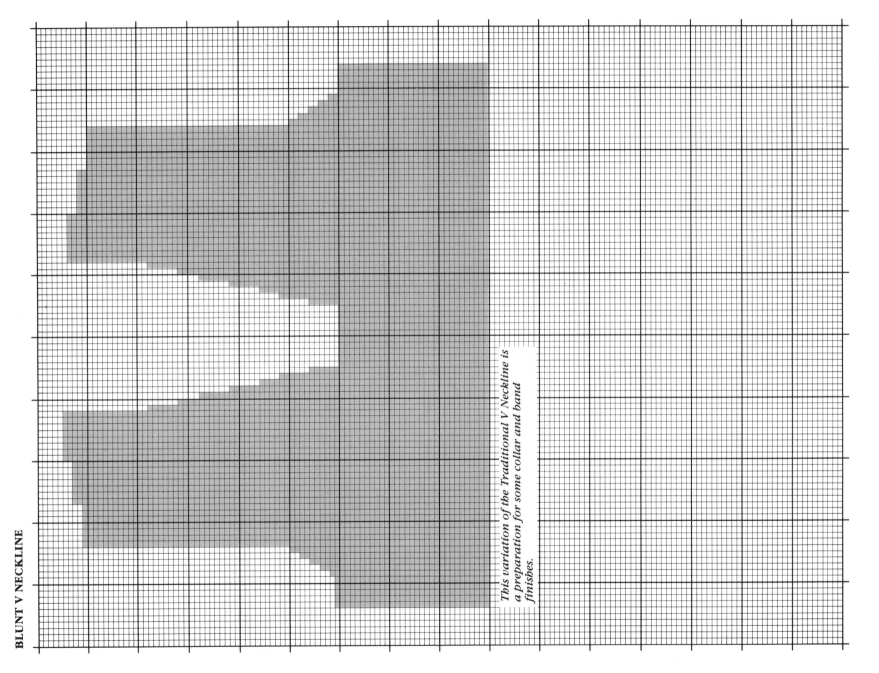

BLUNT V NECKLINE

This variation of the Traditional V Neckline is a preparation for some collar and band finishes.

Square Neckline

The Square Neckline is the easiest of all to chart. At the desired depth, bind off or place on a holder all of the neckline stitches, and work even on the remaining stitches to the start of the shoulder shaping.

A **Shallow Square Neckline** can begin 2″ below the shoulder shaping. If no additional neckline opening is planned, subtract ¹/₂″ to 1″ from each shoulder and add it to the neckline width.

Medium Square Necklines—3″ to 6″ deep—can be charted at one-third of the Shoulder Width Measurement, although additional width can be added to the neckline for outerwear or styling.

Deep Square Necklines can begin at the armhole bind-off or slightly above it. This depth is necessary for finishes which fill a good portion of the opening—for example, Shawl Collars.

Wide necklines may be tapered slightly (¹/₂″ to 1″ per edge), to avoid gaping at the corners. On wide necklines, some or all of the shoulder shaping levels may be eliminated.

Square Neckline

STEP 1
Armhole Depth Measurement − neckline depth = number of inches from armhole bind-off to start of neckline shaping
Example: 8.25 − 3 = 5.25   5¹/₄″

STEP 2
Bind off, or place on a stitch holder, all of the neckline stitches. A slight taper may be charted for wide necklines.

STEP 3
Work even on remaining stitches to the Armhole Depth Measurement, and shape shoulders.

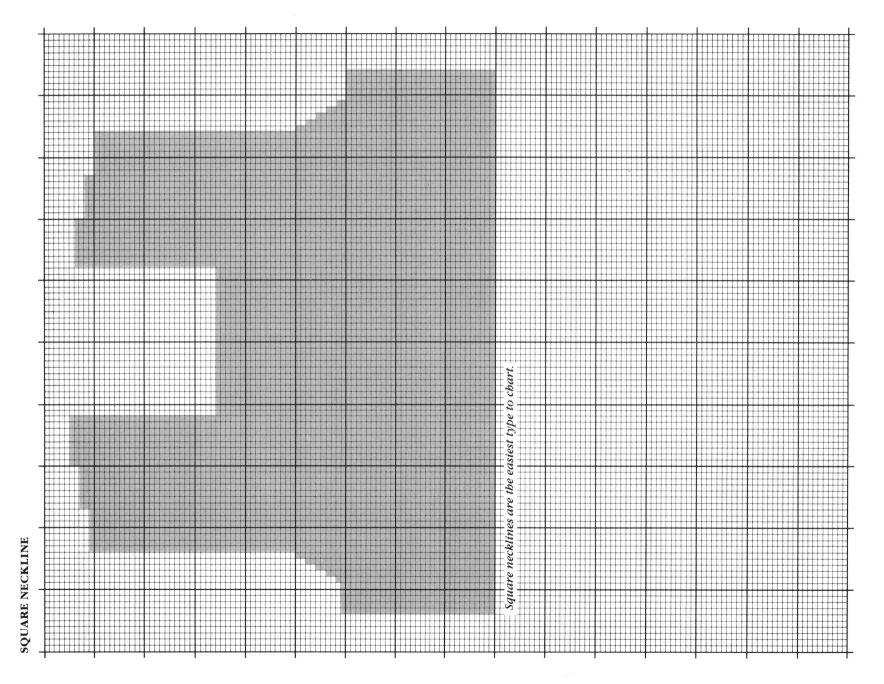

SQUARE NECKLINE

Square necklines are the easiest type to chart.

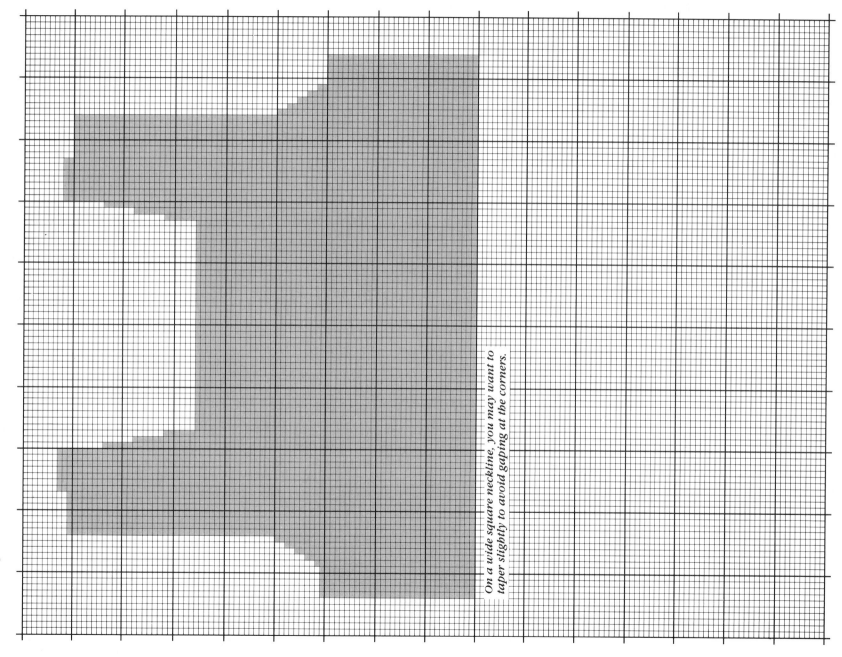

On a wide square neckline, you may want to taper slightly to avoid gaping at the corners.

BOATNECKS

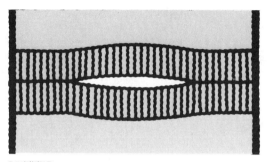

BUTTED

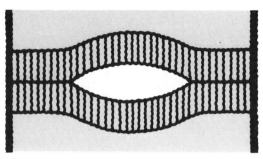

SHAPED

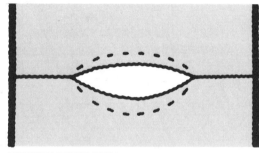

BUTTED WITH HEM

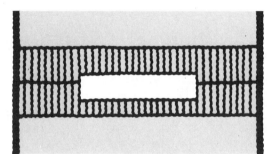

SQUARE

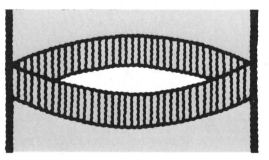

OVERLAPPED

Boatnecks

When planning a Boat Neckline, you can choose among several shaping variations. In all versions, both front and back necklines are charted alike, and their width is equal to half of the Shoulder Width Measurement.

Boatnecks have no shoulder shaping, so you will be charting the yoke with the Raglan Depth Measurement.

If you wish, you can pick up stitches and work a finish such as Crochet Edge or Piping around the neckline after the garment is assembled. Or you can self-finish a Boatneck with a border stitch such as a ribbing, or (for a Butted Boatneck) with a hem. Be sure to include the depth of any knitted self-finish within the total yoke depth.

The **Butted Boatneck** is the simplest Boat Neckline variation.

Work even on the yoke stitches to the Raglan Depth Measurement. Bind off all of the stitches on the needle. Sew the front to the back at the shoulders, leaving at least one-half of the Shoulder Width Measurement for the neck opening. If you prefer, the shoulder stitches may be grafted together rather than sewn (see "How Tos").

The neckline can be stabilized with ribbing or another border stitch pattern worked to a depth of ½″ or more. This depth would be included within the Raglan Depth Measurement.

A self-finished neckline in an unstable pattern stitch can be turned under and hemmed. Make a 1″ to 2″ hem at the center front, ½″ to 1″ at the center back.

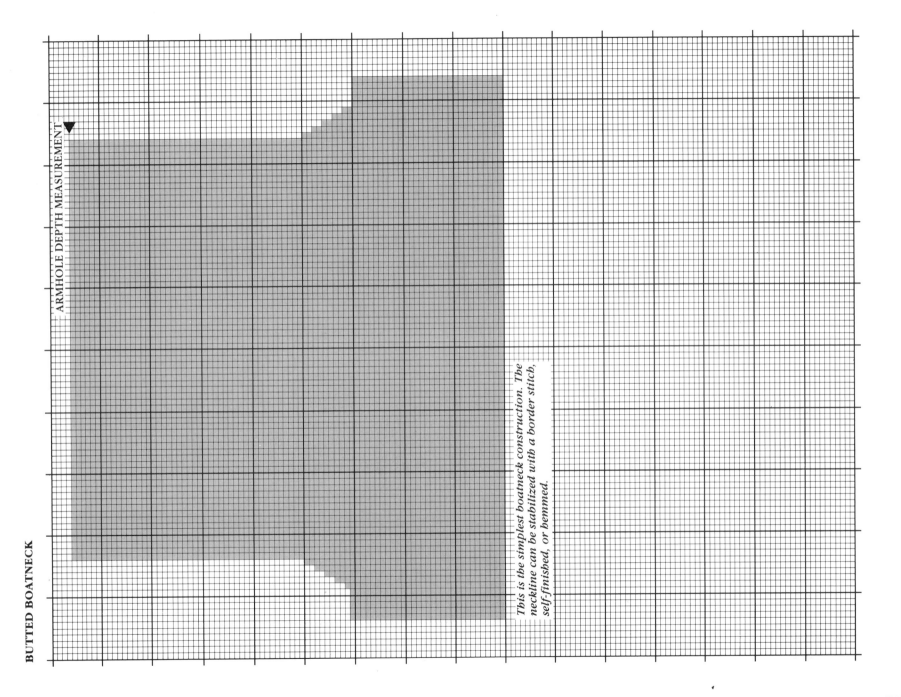

BUTTED BOATNECK

ARMHOLE DEPTH MEASUREMENT

This is the simplest boatneck construction. The neckline can be stabilized with a border stitch, self-finished, or hemmed.

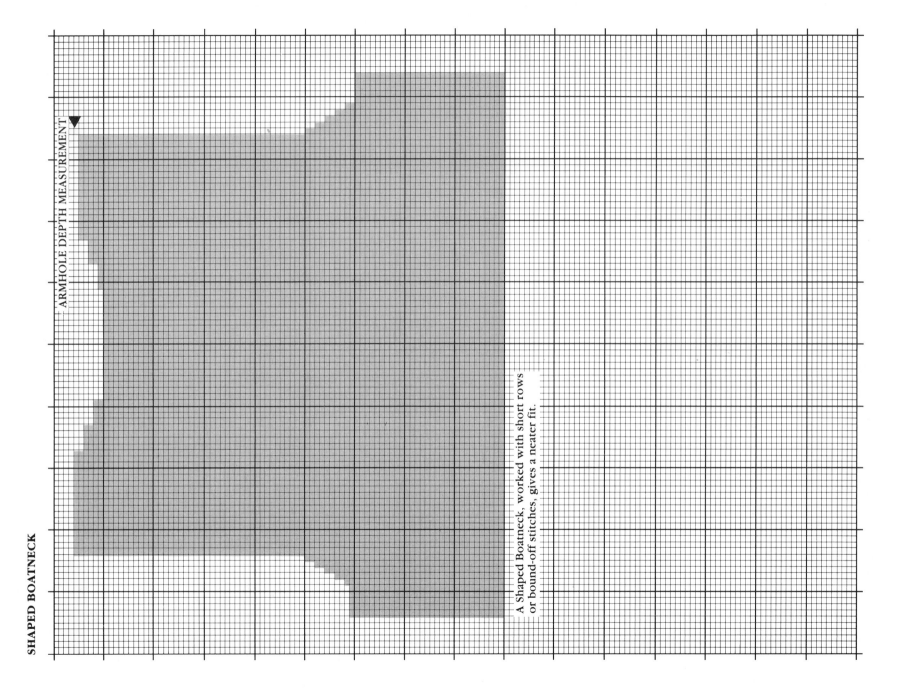

ARMHOLE DEPTH MEASUREMENT

SHAPED BOATNECK

A Shaped Boatneck, worked with short rows or bound-off stitches, gives a neater fit.

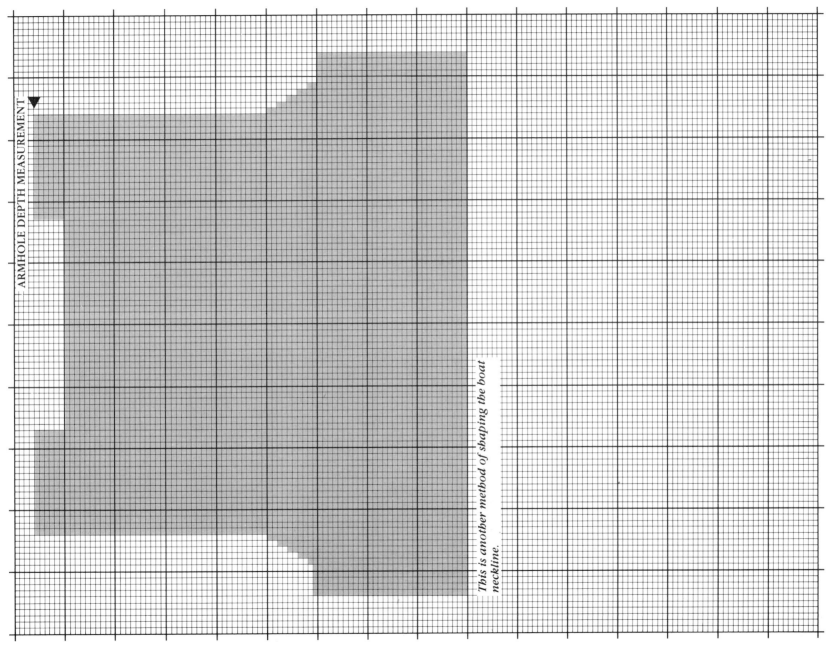

ARMHOLE DEPTH MEASUREMENT

SQUARE BOATNECK

This is another method of shaping the boat neckline.

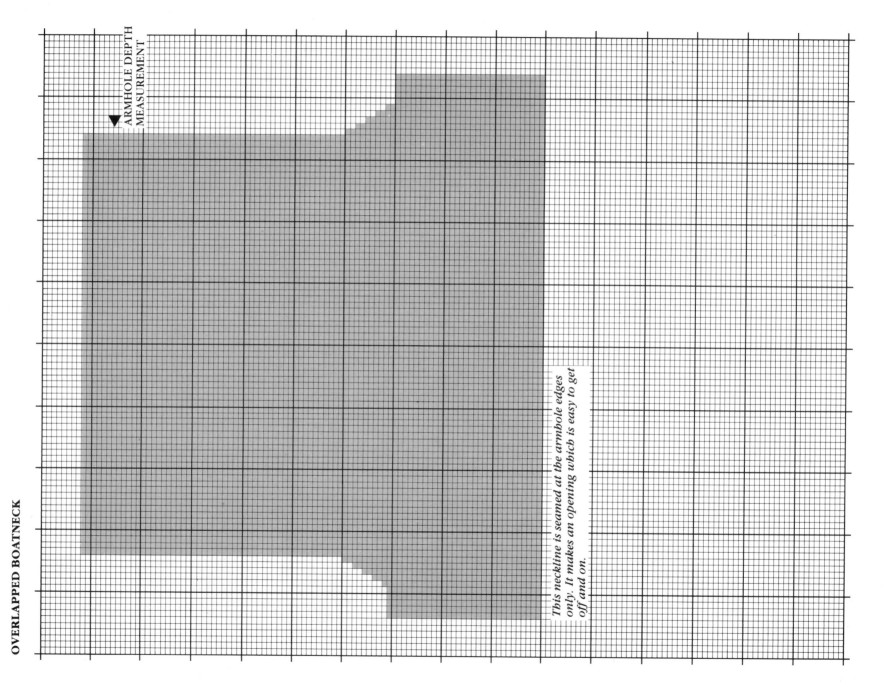

ARMHOLE DEPTH
MEASUREMENT

OVERLAPPED BOATNECK

This neckline is seamed at the armhole edges only. It makes an opening which is easy to get off and on.

Taper the hems toward the shoulders. The hem depth is in addition to the Raglan Depth Measurement.

Shaped Boatneck. For a neater fit, a Boatneck can be slightly shaped. The shaping depth is 1" on both front and back.

If the neckline will have a picked-up finish, the shaping should begin 1" before reaching the Raglan Depth Measurement. The shaping stitches may be bound off or left on a holder.

If the neckline will be self-finished with a ribbing or border, work the shaping with short rows (see "How Tos") just before the border stitch pattern.

On Self-Finished Boatnecks where the body stitch pattern continues to the top, begin working short rows 1" before the Raglan Depth Measurement is reached. Work one final row across all of the yoke stitches as you bind off.

Square Boatneck. For this shape, bind off the equivalent of half the Shoulder Width Measurement at the center of the yoke before reaching the Raglan Depth Measurement. The shaped depth should be approximately 1" on the front, 1/2" on the back. Work even on remaining stitches to the Raglan Depth Measurement, and bind off. Join front to back at the shoulders by sewing or grafting (see "How Tos").

Overlapped Boatneck. For this neckline, first determine the amount of overlap you want at the shoulders: from one to several inches. Then work both front and back to the Raglan Depth measurement plus half the amount of the overlap. For example, if the overlap is 2",

work even to the Raglan Depth Measurement plus 1".

Bind off all stitches, overlap at the shoulders, and stitch the overlap together at the armhole edges. The overlap can be toward the front or toward the back.

Boatnecks

STEP 1
Number of yoke stitches (CB/Step 5) ÷ 2 = number of neckline stitches
Example: 68 ÷ 2 = 34   *34 stitches*

STEP 2
Row gauge ÷ 2 = number of neckline shaping levels for a 1" shaping depth
Example: 6 ÷ 2 = 3   *3 rows*

STEP 3
Number of neckline stitches ÷ 2 = number of stitches to bind off (or shape by short rows) on the first shaping level
■ The remaining neckline stitches must be divisible by 2. If necessary, add an extra stitch to the first shaping level to make this so.
Example: 34 ÷ 2 = 17   *Bind off 18 stitches*

STEP 4
Number of neckline stitches − Step 3 = neckline stitches remaining on knitting needles
Example: 34 − 18 = 16   *16 stitches*

STEP 5
(Step 4 ÷ 2) ÷ remaining neckline shaping levels = number of stitches to bind off on every other row per neckline edge
■ If your remaining stitches are not evenly divisible, bind off the larger amount(s) first.
Example: (16 ÷ 2 = 8) ÷ 2 = 4   *4 stitches*

Draped Neckline

This neckline is an advanced style suitable for fine- to medium-weight yarns with a draping quality. The stitches of the front neckline are increased to create extra fabric which drapes into soft folds at the neckline. No increasing is done on the back.

Markers, which indicate where to work the increases, are essential for knitting a Draped Neckline. At the start of the neckline shaping, they are placed at the center front. As the yoke is worked, they are gradually moved outward, in the shape of a V, while stitches are added between them.

To know when to increase and when to move the markers, you will need to chart two tapers. On graph paper, chart an inner taper, for the moving of the markers, and an outer taper, for the increases. The inner taper "contains" the draped section of the front, which is gradually built up by stitch increases. The combination of a detailed graph and the use of markers makes the working of this complex neckline much easier.

The Draped Neckline can be used on any body style except the Modified Saddle Shoulder and the Modified Raglan.

We've divided our guidelines into two parts: charting and knitting.

Charting the Draped Neckline

STEP 1
Number of yoke stitches (CB/Step 5) ÷ (2 or 3) = number of stitches in back neckline
Chart the back of the garment through the Armhole Depth. Allow between one-third and one-half of the Shoulder Width Measurement for the back neckline. Our example is calculated based on one-third of the shoulder width.
- Note that when the Draped Neckline is based on one-third of the shoulder width, an opening may be needed in the back neckline to allow room for the head.

Example: 68 ÷ 3 = 22.7   *24 stitches*

STEP 2
Number of stitches in back neckline ÷ stitch gauge = width of back neckline
Example: 24 ÷ 5 = 4.8 $4^3/_4''$

STEP 3
There is no set maximum for the width of the front neckline. This is a decision based on the amount of drape desired and how low the neckline will be when the sweater is worn. The minimum width of the front neckline can be established in one of three ways, as follows.
a. Back neckline width × 2 = front neckline width
Example: 4.75 × 2 = 9.5 $9^1/_2''$
b. Head circumference – back neckline width = minimum front neckline width
- If the back neckline is one-third the width of the shoulders and no additional opening is desired, use this method.

Example: $20^3/_4$ – $4^3/_4$ = 16   16''
c. To *visually* determine the front neckline width and finished depth, measure as follows.
   With the person wearing a close-fitting shirt, such as a T-shirt, measure the back neckline width across the back of the neck and mark this width with pins. Drape a measuring tape

or string, from pin to pin, to the desired depth on the front. This length is the width of the front neckline. (This method of measuring can also be used to double-check the depth of the drape on front necklines calculated from the head circumference measurement.)

STEP 4

(Head circumference – front neckline width – back neckline width) ÷ 2 = depth of vertical opening at the back neckline
■ This step is not necessary if neckline is calculated as Step 3c above.
Example: (20.75 – 9.5 – 4.75 = 6.5) ÷ 2 = 3.25   *3¼"*

STEP 5

Front neckline width × stitch gauge = number of stitches in front neckline
Example: 16 × 5 = 80   *80 stitches*

STEP 6

Step 5 – Step 1 = number of stitches to increase in the front neckline shaping
Make this an even number.
Example: 80 – 24 = 56   *56 stitches*

STEP 7

Depth of shaping × row gauge = number of rows over which to work the neckline shaping
The depth of the shaping is measured down from the start of the shoulder shaping. This must be equal to or greater than the number of stitch increases calculated in Step 6. Thus, in order to find the *minimum* depth, multiply the number of Step 6 stitch increases by the row gauge. This is the highest point at which you can begin the shaping. The lowest point at which to start the increases of the front neckline shaping is the waist.
Example: 10 × 6 = 60   *60 rows*

STEP 8

Step 7 ÷ (Step 1 ÷ 2) = number of rows between shapings of the inner taper
Make this an even number.
See Taper Formula for help in working out exact sequence. The inner taper indicates the rows on which to move the markers outward by one stitch at each edge. The taper should end at the start of the shoulder shaping, or just below it.
Example: 60 ÷ (24 ÷ 2 = 12) = 5   *Every 4 or 6 rows*

STEP 9

Step 7 ÷ (Step 6 ÷ 2) = number of rows between the increases of the outer taper
Make this an even number.
See Taper Formula for help in working out exact sequence. The outer taper indicates the rows on which to increase. On the graph, the outer taper will extend into the shoulder area—or off your garment's chart in the case of a Raglan—but in the knitting of the garment the stitches actually are increased at the inside of the inner taper.
Example: 60 ÷ (56 ÷ 2 = 28) = 2.14   *Every 2 or 4 rows*

FINISHING OPTIONS FOR A DRAPED NECKLINE

A

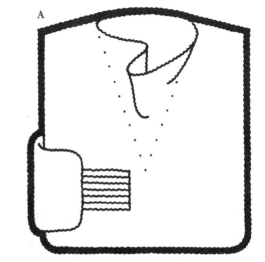

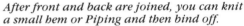

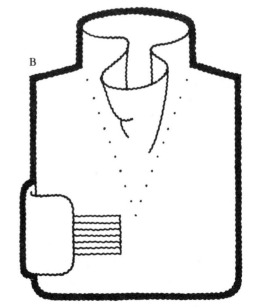

After front and back are joined, you can knit a small hem or Piping and then bind off.

B

After front and back are joined, you can work even for several inches, and then bind off or work a hem.

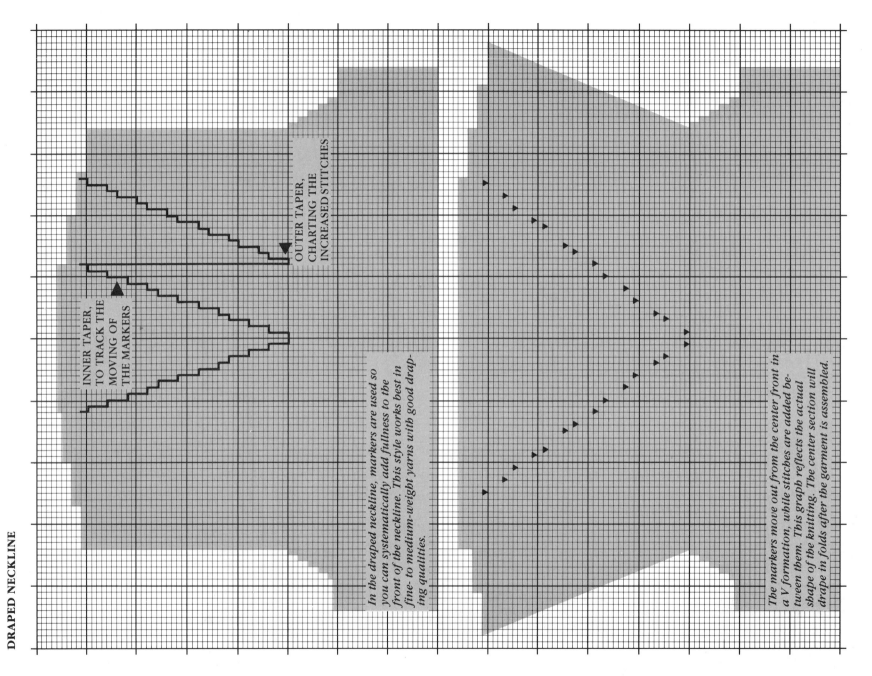

DRAPED NECKLINE

INNER TAPER,
TO TRACK THE
MOVING OF
THE MARKERS

OUTER TAPER,
CHARTING THE
INCREASED STITCHES

In the draped neckline, markers are used so you can systematically add fullness to the front of the neckline. This style works best in fine- to medium-weight yarns with good draping qualities.

The markers move out from the center front in a V formation, while stitches are added between them. This graph reflects the actual shape of the knitting. The center section will drape in folds after the garment is assembled.

138

Knitting the Draped Neckline

STEP 1
Decide on the type of increases to use. We recommend the M1 Increase (see "How Tos") as the cleanest, most invisible type.

STEP 2
Place the markers in the row below the first row of the neckline shaping as follows.
a. If the garment has an odd number of stitches, work to the center stitch, place a marker, work the center stitch, place a second marker, and finish the row.
b. If the garment has an even number of stitches, work to one stitch before the center, place a marker, work the two center stitches, place a second marker, and finish the row.

STEP 3
Read the graph to work the shapings, as follows:
a. **On the rows where only the inner taper indicates a shaping,** move the markers out in this manner. Work to one stitch before the first marker, place a new marker on the right needle, work the next stitch, remove the old marker, work to the next marker and remove it, work the next stitch, place a new marker on the needle, and finish the row.
b. **On the rows where only the outer taper indicates a shaping,** increase inside of the markers in this manner. Work to the first marker, slip the marker, increase, work to the next marker, increase, slip the marker, and finish the row.
c. **On the rows where both tapers indicate a shaping,** move the marker out and increase at each edge, in this manner. Work to one stitch before the first marker, place a new marker on the right needle and increase, work the next stitch, remove the marker, work to the next marker and remove it, work the next stitch, increase, place a marker on the needle, and finish the row.
d. **Mark off the work rows on the graph** as you knit the neckline, to make keeping track of the shapings easier.

STEP 4
Work the front through the shoulder shaping. The shaping of the front neckline should be completed at, or within a few rows of, the Armhole Depth Measurement. At this point, the number of stitches to the outside of the markers should equal the number of stitches in the shoulder shaping of the back. Place the neckline stitches on a holder.

STEP 5
Join the front and back at the shoulders.

CONSTRUCTING THE DRAPED NECKLINE

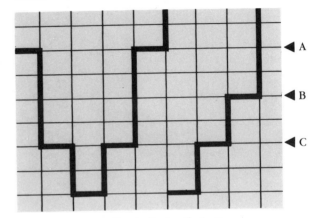

A The inner taper line indicates that you should move each marker outward by one stitch.
B The outer taper line indicates that you should work an increase to the inside of each marker.
C If both types of taper line appear on the same row, when you reach each marker you should move it outward by one stitch, then work an increase to the inside of that marker.

STEP 6

Place the front and back neckline stitches on a circular needle and finish as follows.

a. Work a small hem or Piping. Bind off.

   or

b. Work even for 2″ or more. If your pattern stitch is stable, bind off. If not, add a ½″ to 1″ hem.

Optional Back Neckline Shaping

If you would like some slight shaping of the back neckline, it can be worked at the same time as the shoulder shaping, over the same number of levels as the shoulder shaping (CB/Step 15).

Half of the neckline stitches are shaped on the first level. The remaining stitches then are divided between the remaining levels. These stitches can be bound off or worked in short rows (see "How Tos") and placed on a stitch holder.

Work the garment to the Armhole Depth Measurement and chart the shoulder shaping, then use the position of the shoulder shaping to chart the back neckline. Our example has three shaping levels.

Optional Back Neckline Shaping

STEP 1

Neckline stitches (CB/Step 12) ÷ 2 = number of stitches to bind off on first shaping level
- If CB/Step 12 is an even number, make Step 1 even. If it is odd, make Step 1 odd.

Example: 24 ÷ 2 = 12   *12 stitches*

STEP 2

[Neckline stitches (CB/Step 12) − Step 1] ÷ 2 = remaining neckline stitches to shape per edge
Example: (24 − 12 = 12) ÷ 2 = 6   *6 stitches*

STEP 3

Step 2 ÷ remaining shaping levels = number of stitches to bind off on every other row of neckline edge
- If Step 2 is not evenly divisible, bind off the larger amount(s) first.

Example: 6 ÷ 2 = 3   *3 stitches*

CARDIGANS

Simply put, a cardigan sweater is charted by slicing a pullover front right down the middle. In fact, if the cardigan will have a zipper, that's all you need to do. A little more work will be required if the cardigan will have buttons and buttonholes, to plan for the overlapping of the front finishes.

Front finishes are necessary to stabilize the cardigan's opening, but can also be important decorative additions to your sweater. Either a border stitch Band or a Facing can be used to finish front edges. Simple bands are worked in a stable stitch pattern, such as ribbing, seed stitch, or garter stitch. Finishes with facings (which are basically the same as hems) can be worked in a continuation of the body's pattern stitch, in a pattern stitch compatible with the body's stitch pattern, or in stockinette.

Styling

Cardigans can be charted to any length—waist length, hip length, even knee length or longer, at which point the garment becomes a coat. Cardigans can be adapted to any body or yoke shaping, including Round Yokes, Saddle Shoulders, and Raglans. Our examples are charted from a Classic Body.

Several special styles exist within the general "cardigan" category. Those included in this section are the Bolero Jacket, the Chanel Jacket, the Lapel Jacket, and several variations of the Shawl Collar Cardigan.

When you are comfortable with basic cardigan shaping, think about knitting a more complex style, such as a double-breasted garment or one with a side closure. To begin, chart a pullover front, then determine where the opening will be in relation to the neckline and neckline finish. Observe that on side closures you may be working different shapings on the right and left sides; they will not necessarily be mirror images.

Buttonholes

To determine the placement of buttonholes, chart their positions on graph paper before you begin to knit. Buttonholes should be evenly spaced, or spaced in an obvious patterned sequence. Be sure to take into account any buttonholes located within the neck finish.

Buttonholes should not be placed at the top or bottom edge of the front finish. Leave a minimum of $1/2''$ at both edges. Also leave a minimum of two stitches at the side edges of a Vertical Band or a Facing. For a V-Neck Cardigan, locate the top button at the first taper decrease, or within $1/2''$ below it.

Whether knitting vertical or horizontal buttonholes, make sure that all are worked on the correct side of the fabric (see "How Tos"). Maintaining an even number of rows between the buttonholes will ensure that this occurs, as long as the first buttonhole is placed correctly.

Men's garments traditionally close from left to right, with the buttonholes on the left front (from the wearer's point of view). Women's garments reverse this, closing from right to left, with buttonholes on the right front.

CARDIGAN VARIATIONS

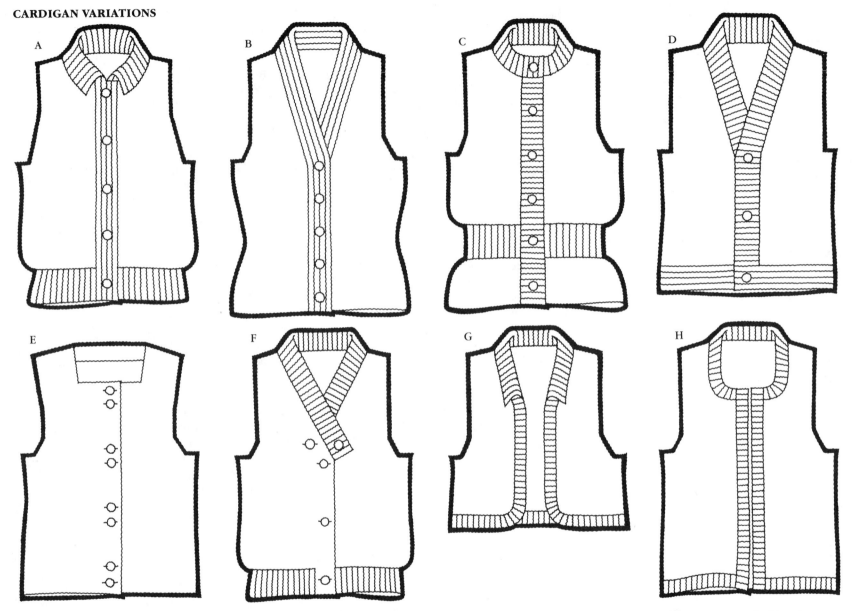

A Cardigan with bands, round neckline, and collar

B Cardigan with vertical bands on front edges and hem at bottom edge

C Cardigan with ribbed cinched waist, horizontal bands on front edges, and picked-up band at neckline

D Cardigan with horizontal bands at bottom edge and along front edges

E Cardigan with faced square neckline, faced front edges, and hemmed bottom edge

F Cardigan with vertically worked border across a portion of the bottom, front facings, and picked-up band at neckline

G Bolero jacket with ribbed bands and collar

H Chanel jacket with medium round neckline, vertical ribbing at lower edge neckline, and picked-up horizontal bands on front edges

CARDIGAN VARIATIONS

I *Double-breasted cardigan with faced front edges, vertical band at lower edge, and ribbed collar*

J *Double-breasted cardigan with facings*

K *Asymmetrical cardigan with vertical band at lower edge, and horizontal band picked up along front edge and around neckline*

L *Asymmetrical cardigan with hemmed lower edge, faced front edges, and ribbed collar*

M *Cardigan with deep V neckline, vertical ribbing at lower edge, and vertical shawl collar*

N *Cardigan with horizontal shawl collar and ribbings*

O *Cardigan with vertical notched shawl collar and ribbings*

P *Cardigan with lapel collar, horizontal band at lower edge, and vertical band on front edges*

Cardigan Necklines

Charting necklines for cardigans is not as straightforward as it is for pullovers. On pullovers, neckline shaping is calculated from the exact number of front neckline stitches—no more, no less. On cardigans, you will need to consider the stitches of the Bands and Facings, and adjust the shaping of the neckline accordingly.

The illustrations show several considerations. The center fronts of the sweaters are indicated by arrows. On a cardigan with a Round Neckline that is finished with a Band down the center front (a), the Band should be no wider than the first neckline shaping row (the bind-off row). In other words, limit the Band's width to one-half of the back neckline stitches on a Standard Round Neckline, or to one-third of the back neckline stitches when using the Alternate Round Neckline shaping. Limiting the width of the Band in this manner prevents it from extending into the curved portion of the neckline.

Because the front bands of a cardigan completely overlap, each side of the finished cardigan is wider than half of a pullover by a measurement equal to half the width of the Band. This is taken into account as follows, when starting to shape a Round Neckline. If the Band is worked along with the body (as in Cardigan Version 1), a number of stitches equivalent to one-half of those in the Band are added to the bound-off stitches at the start of the neckline shaping. If the Band is worked separately (as in Cardigan Version 5), stitches equal to one-half the Band are subtracted from the number of bound-off stitches. On the Round Neckline of a cardigan with a narrow Facing, $1\frac{1}{2}$ times the overlap, plus a turning-ridge stitch, are added to the initial neckline bind-off (as in Cardigan Version 10). However, if the Facing is wide (b) and extends into the curved portion of the neckline, it will be necessary to work an equivalent shaping on the Facing (as in Cardigan Version 14).

Cardigans with V Necklines also require additional planning when calculating the taper. When a V-Necked Cardigan is finished with a Band (c), you will need to take the Band stitches into account when calculating the number of stitches for the neckline taper (Cardigan Version 3). The decreases of the neckline taper are worked on the body

CARDIGAN NECKLINES AND FRONT FINISHES

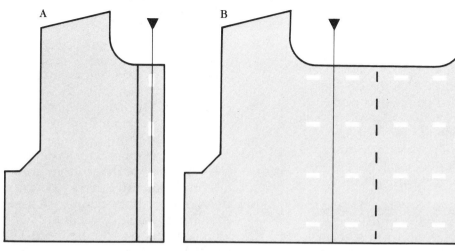

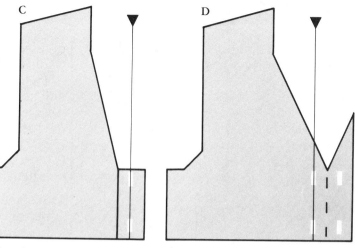

A On a cardigan with a Round Neckline that is finished with a Band down the center front, the Band should be no wider than the first neckline shaping row (the bind-off stitches).

B On a cardigan with a Round Neckline and a wide facing which extends into the curved portion of the neckline, the facing needs to be shaped to match the garment front.

C When a V-Necked Cardigan is finished with a band, you will need to take the Band stitches into account when you design the neckline taper.

D On a V-Necked Cardigan with a faced front edge, the taper needs to extend into the overlap width and the facing may need to be shaped.

stitches, at the inside of the Band. On a Faced V-Neck Cardigan, where the decreases are worked at the turning ridge (d), you will need to take the overlap width into account (as in Cardigan Version 11). If the upper neckline is not faced, the V shaping must be worked on the Facing of the lower front edge, where the overlap occurs (as in Cardigan Version 15).

Check "Necklines" for guidelines on neckline width and depth. On outerwear, a minimum of ½" to 1" (or the width of the band) should be subtracted from each shoulder and added to the neckline opening.

Remember to keep the same number of stitches per shoulder on the front sections as on the back. Bands and Facings are not included in the shoulder shaping. Charting the yoke on graph paper will provide a pattern to follow and make knitting your cardigan a lot easier.

Many of our Neckline finishes are suitable for cardigans. Even those usually worked in the round (such as Turtlenecks and Crewnecks) can be adapted easily for cardigans by working them in rows. Complete guidelines for the popular Shawl and Lapel Collars are included at the end of "Cardigans."

CHARTING A CARDIGAN

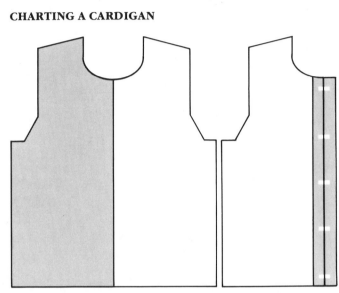

The charting for a cardigan begins with a basic pullover. The cardigan back is identical to the pullover back. Begin to plan the cardigan front by charting a pullover, including the neckline. Then you will adjust these numbers to take the front band and the overlap into account.

Charting a Cardigan

Cardigans come in many styles, but charting for all of them begins with a basic pullover (Classic Body). A cardigan back is identical to a pullover back; just be sure to include sufficient ease if the cardigan will be an outer garment. Chart neckline shaping for a pullover front, and you will have the measurements necessary for a cardigan front. From these measurements, though, two additional numbers need to be calculated for cardigans, as follows.

1. Starting Number of Stitches: Divide the pullover front in half vertically and you have the Starting Number of stitches for the body and neckline of a cardigan front. In other words, *one-half of the number of stitches for a pullover front is the starting number of stitches for a cardigan front.*

   To this Starting Number you will either add or subtract stitches (depending on the type of finish you choose for the front edges), in order to determine the number of stitches to cast on and the number of stitches for neckline shaping. The number of stitches to be added or subtracted is calculated from the width of the front overlap or the width of the Band or Facing.

2. Number of Front Overlap Stitches: The minimum width of a front overlap is double the width of the buttons. For example, 1″ buttons would require that a band or facing be at least 2″ wide.

   There is also a maximum width for a front overlap or band on a Round Neck Cardigan. The band should not extend into the neckline shaping decreases, that is, it should be no wider than the first neckline shaping or bind-off row—one-half of the front neckline stitches on a Standard Round Neckline, one-third of the front neckline stitches on an Alternate Round Neckline. After the band or overlap width has been determined, multiply it by the stitch gauge of the body to obtain the *number of Front Overlap Width stitches.*

   With these two numbers—the *Starting Number* of stitches for a cardigan front, and the *number of Front Overlap (or Band) Width Stitches*—you will be ready to start charting your favorite cardigan style.

   Charting affects only the center front of the garment. The side, armhole, and shoulder shapings remain the same as on the back. For a cardigan with a traditional center closure, it is only necessary to chart one front section.

CARDIGANS

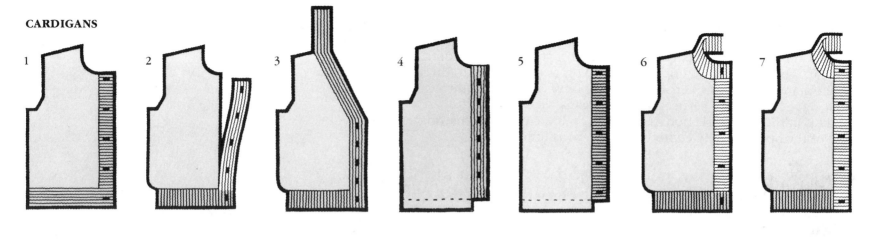

1 Cardigan with vertical band which is worked together with the front section

2 Cardigan with vertical band which is worked separately and attached to garment after assembly

3 Cardigan with V Neckline and vertical band

4 Cardigan with vertical front band, worked together with body, and bottom hem

5 Cardigan with horizontal front band, worked separately, and bottom hem

6 Cardigan with horizontal front bands and border along bottom edge

7 Cardigan with horizontal front bands which extend from bottom edge to top of neckband

8 V-Neckline variation of Version 7

9 Cardigan with picked-up finish on all outer edges and mitered corners (horizontal bands)

10 Cardigan with faced front and a vertically worked border across most of the bottom

11 V-Necked Cardigan with faced front and a border across entire bottom edge

12 Cardigan with faced front and hemmed bottom

13 V-Neckline Cardigan with faced front and hemmed bottom

14 Cardigan with wide front facing and vertically worked border across a portion of the bottom

15 V-Necked Cardigan with front facing, vertically worked border across a portion of the bottom, and unfaced neckline

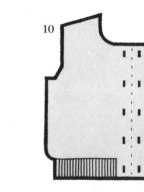

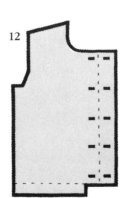

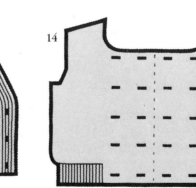

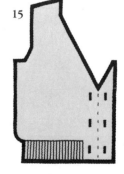

Our illustrations show many possibilities, not only for the front finish, but also for the bottom and neckline edges. Mix and match, where applicable, for your own special look. Cardigan Versions 1 through 4 are charted for Vertical Bands (bands knit in the same direction as the stitches of the body, usually continuing the border pattern used at the bottom edge of the sweater). Cardigan Versions 5 through 9 have Horizontal Bands (bands knit at right angles to the stitches of the body). Versions 10 through 15 are cardigans with Facings.

Basic cardigan charting calculations are as follows.

Cardigan

STEP 1
Number of body stitches for pullover back (CB/Step 3) ÷ 2 = Starting Number of stitches for cardigan front
Example: 88 ÷ 2 = 44   *44 stitches*

STEP 2
Front Overlap Width in inches × stitch gauge = number of Front Overlap Width stitches
Example: 2 × 5 = 10   *10 stitches*

STEP 3
a. Step 1 + ½ Step 2 = number of stitches to cast on for one side of cardigan front if band and body are knit together
Example: 44 + (10 ÷ 2) = 49   *49 stitches*
b. Step 1 − (½ Step 2) = number of stitches to cast on for one side of cardigan front if band and body are knit separately
Example: 44 − (10 ÷ 2) = 39   *39 stitches*

Front Finishes

Vertical Bands. Center-front Vertical Bands usually are a continuation of the border pattern used at the sweater's bottom edge. They can be knit along with the fronts (Cardigan Version 1), or worked separately and attached to the garment after it is assembled (Cardigan Version 2).

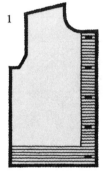

1

Cardigan with vertical band which is worked together with the front section

Cardigan Version 1

In this version, the front finish, a Vertical Band, is worked together with the front section. Seed-stitch or garter-stitch bands are suitable for this style.

STEP 1
Starting Number of stitches + ½ the number of Front Overlap stitches = number of stitches to cast on

STEP 2
Work the bottom border to the desired depth.

STEP 3
Work the band pattern stitch at the center front edge over the total number of Front Overlap Width stitches. Work the remaining stitches in the body pattern stitch.

STEP 4
Starting number of stitches in the neckline bind-off (CB/Step 17 and "Necklines") + ½ the number of Overlap Width stitches = adjusted number of stitches in the neckline bind-off

STEP 5
Work through the shoulder shaping and finish off.

STEP 6
Work the other front in the same manner, reversing the shapings.

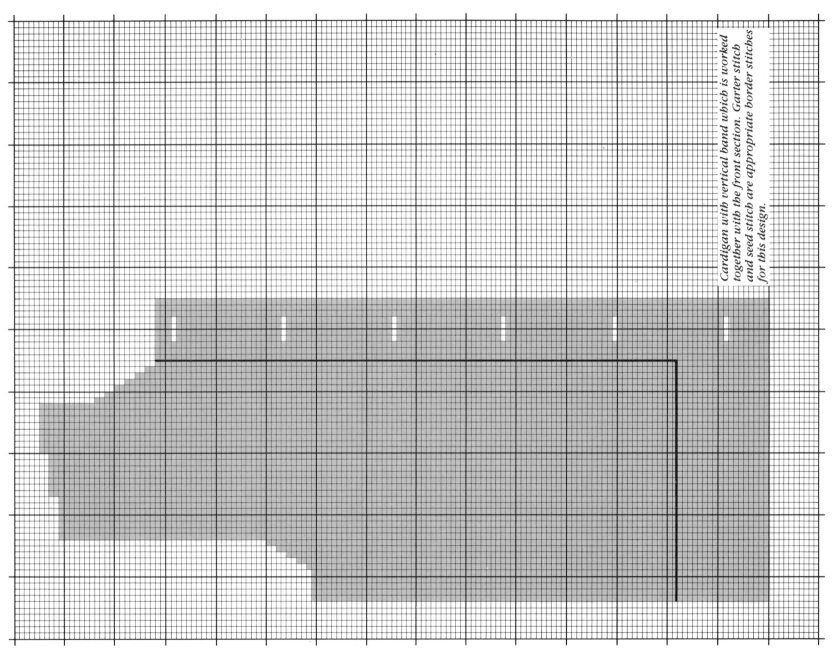

CARDIGAN VERSION 1

Cardigan with vertical band which is worked together with the front section. Garter stitch and seed stitch are appropriate border stitches for this design.

150

Cardigan Version 2

This version incorporates Vertical Bands which are worked separately. Its primary use is for ribbed bands, which tend to stretch out of shape if worked on the larger needles of the body.

STEP 1
Starting Number of stitches + ½ the number of Overlap Width stitches = number of stitches to cast on

STEP 2
On the border size needles, work the depth of the bottom ribbing. Place all the stitches for the band (equal to the total number for the Overlap Width) on a stitch holder to be worked later.

STEP 3
Change to larger needles, casting on one additional stitch at the band edge for a seam. Work the front section to the neckline.

STEP 4
Starting number of stitches in the neckline bind-off (CB/Step 17 and "Necklines") – ½ the number of Overlap Width stitches = adjusted number of stitches in the neckline bind-off

STEP 5
Work through the shoulder shaping.

STEP 6
On border size needles, pick up the stitches on the holder. Add one stitch for a seam at the body edge. Work in ribbing to 1″ less than the length of the front edge of the body. Stretch the band to fit when sewing it to the body.

STEP 7
Work the other front in the same manner, reversing the shaping.
Note: Ribbed bands also can be worked as for Cardigan Version 1 by the following method. Work the bands on smaller (border size) double-pointed needles while the body is worked on the larger needles. In other words, use four knitting needles in each row—two body size needles and two double-pointed border size needles.

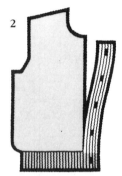

Cardigan with vertical band which is worked separately and attached to garment after assembly

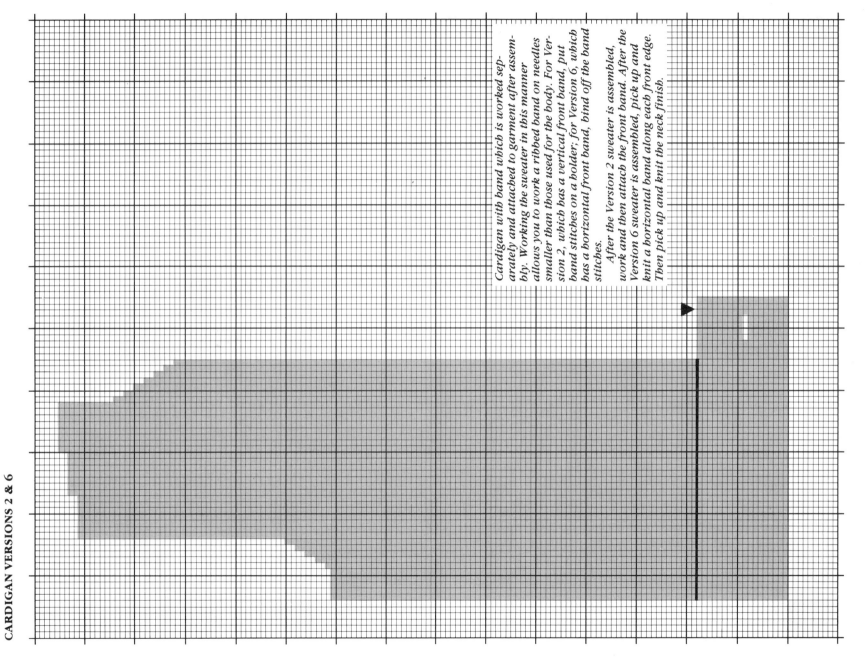

CARDIGAN VERSIONS 2 & 6

Cardigan with band which is worked separately and attached to garment after assembly. Working the sweater in this manner allows you to work a ribbed band on needles smaller than those used for the body. For Version 2, which has a vertical front band, put band stitches on a holder; for Version 6, which has a horizontal front band, bind off the band stitches.

After the Version 2 sweater is assembled, work and then attach the front band. After the Version 6 sweater is assembled, pick up and knit a horizontal band along each front edge. Then pick up and knit the neck finish.

Cardigan Version 3

This version incorporates a Vertical Band with a V Neckline. If the bands are in seed stitch or garter stitch, work them at the same time as the body (see Version 1). If the bands are in ribbing, place the band stitches on a holder after the bottom ribbing is complete, and work them separately (see Version 2). The back neckline finish is a continuation of the front bands.

STEP 1
Follow the cardigan guidelines of your choice (Version 1 or Version 2), and work the cardigan front to the start of the V taper.

STEP 2
Adjust the neckline stitches.
a. **For Version 1**
   Starting number of stitches in the neckline (CB/Step 12) − $\frac{1}{2}$ the number of Overlap Width stitches = adjusted number of neckline stitches for the calculation of the V Neckline taper
b. **For Version 2**
   Starting number of stitches in the neckline (CB/Step 12) − $\frac{1}{2}$ the Overlap Width stitches + the seam stitch = adjusted number of neckline stitches for the calculation of the V Neckline taper

STEP 3
Calculate the neckline taper (see "Traditional V Neckline"), using the adjusted number of neckline stitches.

STEP 4
Work the decreases.
a. **For Version 1**
   The decreases for the V taper are worked on the body, at the inside of the band stitches. Work the decreases immediately after the band, or, if a more obvious decrease line is desired, a few stitches in from it.
b. **For Version 2**
   Work the decreases at least one stitch in from the edge.

STEP 5
Finish the cardigan front.
a. **For Version 1**
   Work the front through the shoulder shaping.

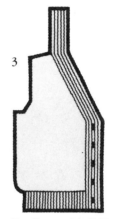

3

Cardigan with V Neckline and vertical band

b. **For Version 2**

Work the body stitches through the shoulder shaping. Pick up the band stitches from the holder. Add one stitch for a seam at the body edge. Work band to 1″ less than the length of the front edge. Place the band stitches on a holder and sew the band to the front, stretching it to fit. Return the band stitches to the needle.

STEP 6
Continue on the band stitches for one-half the width of the back neckline. Place the stitches on a holder.

STEP 7
Work the other front in the same manner, reversing the shapings and pairing the decreases (see "How Tos").

STEP 8
Join the fronts and back at the shoulders.

STEP 9
Graft the band stitches (on the holders) together (see "How Tos"), and sew the band to the back neckline.

Cardigan Version 4

This version combines a hem at the bottom with a Vertical Front Band worked with the body. The depth of the hem is up to you, but the standard is 1″. Plan ahead on this cardigan: a hem must also be worked on the back of the garment.

STEP 1
Starting Number of stitches − ½ the number of Overlap Width stitches = number of stitches to cast on

STEP 2
Work even for 1″ or the depth of the hem. Work a horizontal turning ridge (see "How Tos").

STEP 3
At center front, cast on the total number of stitches for the Overlap Width. Work the band in seed stitch or garter stitch, together with the body.
- A ribbed band should be worked separately and stitched into place. If this is your choice, follow the Cardigan Version 6 guidelines, then knit and sew on a ribbed Vertical Band rather than picking up stitches for a Horizontal Band.

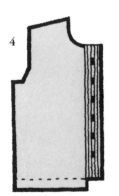

Cardigan with vertical front band, worked together with body, and bottom hem

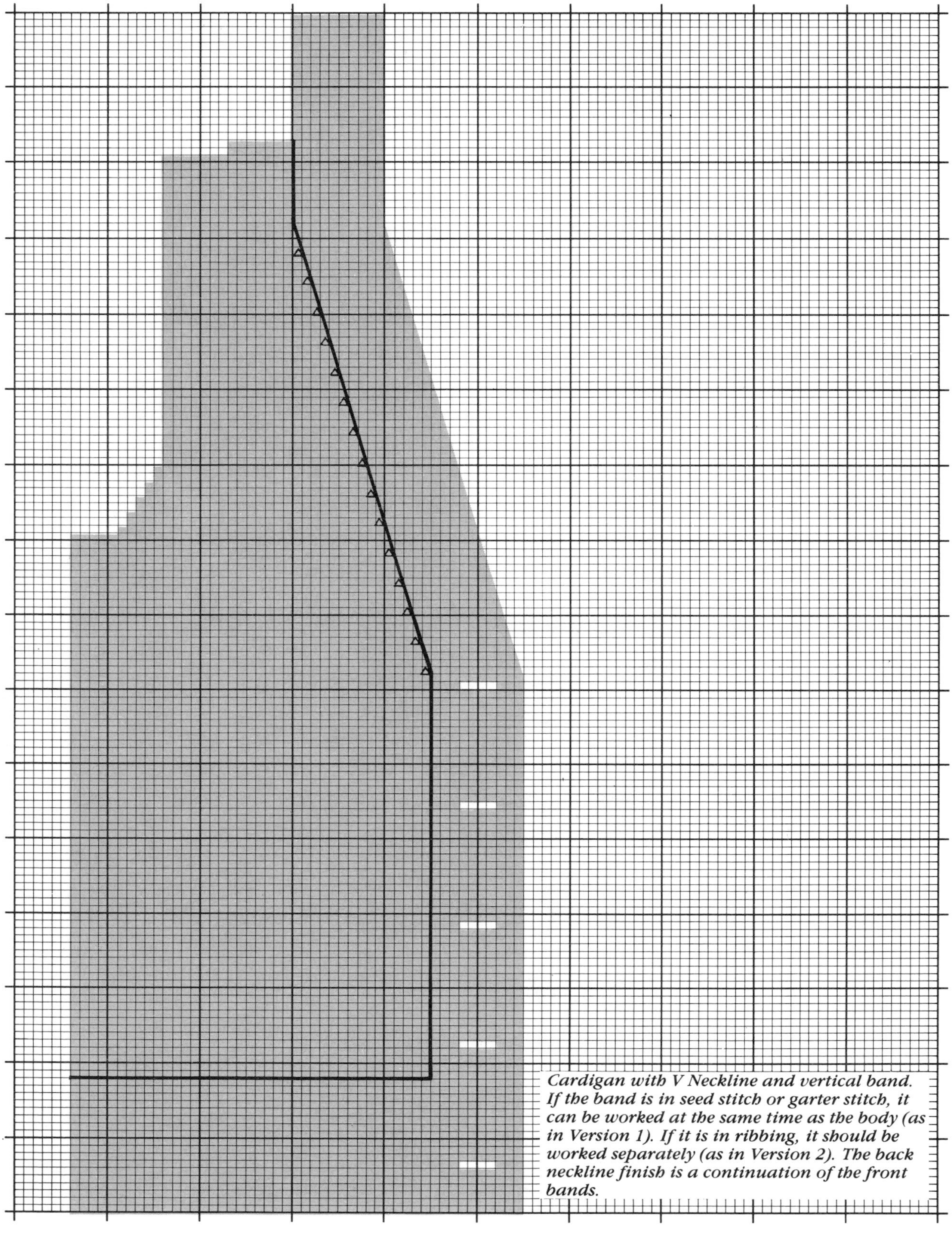

CARDIGAN VERSION 3

Cardigan with V Neckline and vertical band. If the band is in seed stitch or garter stitch, it can be worked at the same time as the body (as in Version 1). If it is in ribbing, it should be worked separately (as in Version 2). The back neckline finish is a continuation of the front bands.

155

STEP 4

Work the front through the shoulder shaping, adjusting the neckline shaping as in Cardigan Version 1, Step 4.

STEP 5

Work the other front in the same way, reversing the shaping.

STEP 6

Assemble the garment. Fold the hem to the inside and stitch in place.

Horizontal Bands. A Horizontal Band is picked up directly from the sweater edge, on the border size needles, after the garment is assembled, and is worked perpendicular to the stitches in the body of the sweater.

When a band is worked in this manner, its width is determined by numbers of rows rather than of stitches. In the case of Horizontal Bands, we will refer to band depth rather than band width—a 2"-wide Vertical Band is equal to a 2"-deep Horizontal Band.

Pick up the stitches for the band with the right side of the fabric facing you. A simple guideline for picking up stitches is to pick up three stitches for every four rows (vertical pick-up) and one stitch for each stitch (horizontal pick-up). This works well for solid fabrics of a gauge equal to the stockinette gauge of the yarn.

A more accurate method is to mark the edge every inch, and pick up the number of stitches in the stockinette stitch gauge of the yarn in each inch (see "How Tos").

Always be sure to pick up equal numbers of stitches along both front edges (or any other matching edges). Also make sure that the number of stitches picked up across the back neckline (or the bottom edge, in Version 9) will work with your stitch pattern. For example, 1/1 ribbing requires an odd number of stitches across the back neck for the pattern to be centered; 2/2 ribbing requires an even number of stitches, with the two center stitches being both knits or both purls.

Any stitch pattern suitable for a border will work for all Horizontal Band versions.

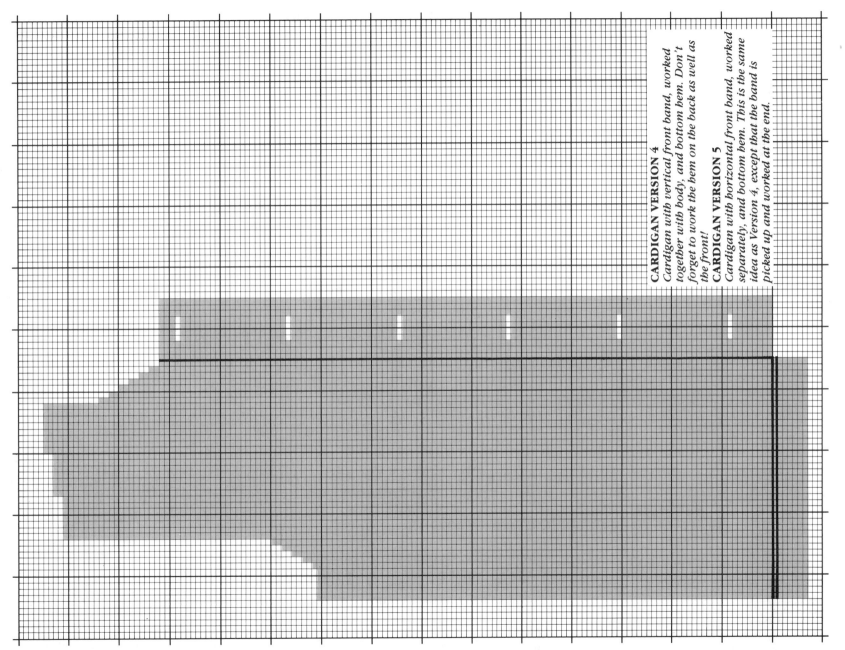

CARDIGAN VERSIONS 4 & 5

CARDIGAN VERSION 4
Cardigan with vertical front band, worked together with body, and bottom hem. Don't forget to work the hem on the back as well as the front!

CARDIGAN VERSION 5
Cardigan with horizontal front band, worked separately, and bottom hem. This is the same idea as Version 4, except that the band is picked up and worked at the end.

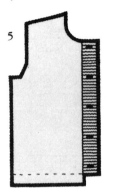

Cardigan with horizontal front band, worked separately, and bottom hem

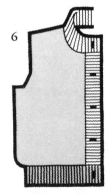

Cardigan with horizontal front bands and border along bottom edge

Cardigan Version 5

This version combines a hem at the bottom with a front Horizontal Band, picked up and worked separately from the body. A standard hem is 1″ deep, but this may vary. Note that the sweater back will also need a hem.

STEP 1
Starting Number of stitches − ½ the number of Overlap Width stitches = the number of stitches to cast on

STEP 2
Work even for 1″ or the depth of the hem. Work a horizontal turning ridge (see "How Tos").

STEP 3
Knit the body on the same number of stitches through the shoulder shaping, adjusting the neckline shaping as in Cardigan Version 2, Step 4.

STEP 4
Work the other front in the same manner, reversing the shapings.

STEP 5
Pick up the stitches for the bands along the front edges. Work for the band depth and bind off.

STEP 6
Assemble the garment. Fold the hem to the inside and stitch in place.

Cardigan Version 6

For this version, a border is worked along the entire bottom edge of the sweater. Horizontal Bands extend along the center front edges from the top of the bottom border to the neck shaping. The neck finish is picked up after the front bands are complete and encircles the entire neckline, including the top edges of the front bands.

STEP 1
Starting Number of stitches + ½ the number of Overlap Width stitches = number of stitches to cast on

STEP 2
Work in ribbing or other border stitch pattern for the depth of the bottom border.

STEP 3
At front center, bind off the total number of Overlap Width stitches.

STEP 4
Work the front on the remaining stitches through the shoulder shaping, adjusting the neckline shaping as in Cardigan Version 2, Step 4.

STEP 5
Work the other front in the same way, reversing the shapings.

STEP 6
Join the fronts to the back at the shoulders.

STEP 7
For each of the front sections, pick up front band stitches along the front edge, from the top of the bottom border to the neckline shaping. Cast on a seam stitch at the bottom edge. Work for the band depth, and bind off. Sew Horizontal Band to bottom vertical border.

STEP 8
Pick up stitches around the neckline circumference, including the tops of the front bands. Work to desired depth and bind off, or use any other Round Neckline finish.

Cardigan Version 7

In this version, the front Horizontal Bands extend from the bottom edge to the top of the neckband.

STEP 1
Starting Number of stitches − $\frac{1}{2}$ the number of Overlap Width stitches = number of stitches to cast on

STEP 2
Work in ribbing or other border stitch pattern for the depth of the bottom border.

STEP 3
Work the front to the shoulder shaping, adjusting the neckline shaping as in Cardigan Version 2, Step 4.

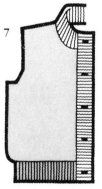

7

Cardigan with horizontal front bands which extend from bottom edge to top of neckband

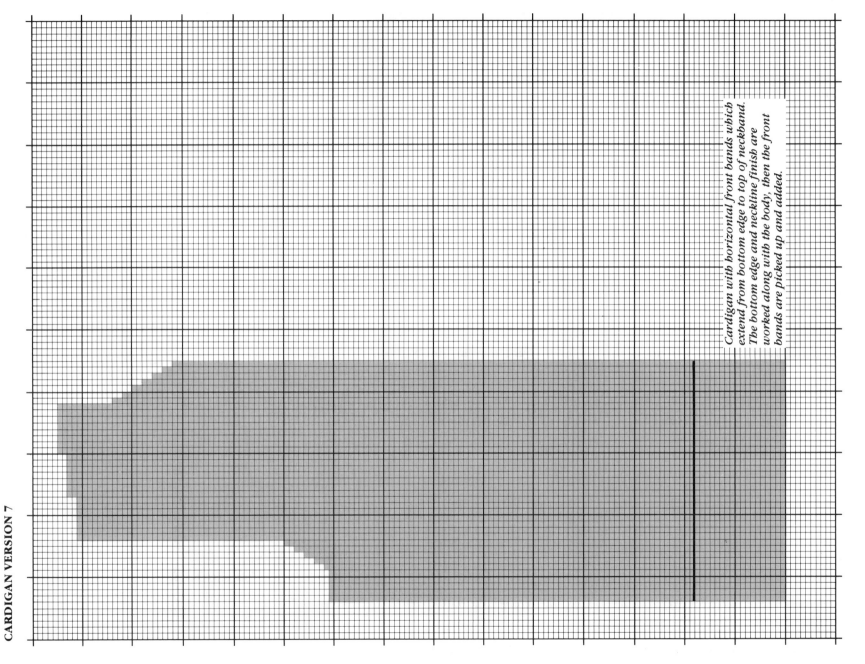

CARDIGAN VERSION 7

Cardigan with horizontal front bands which extend from bottom edge to top of neckband. The bottom edge and neckline finish are worked along with the body, then the front bands are picked up and added.

STEP 4
Work the other front in the same manner, reversing the shaping.

STEP 5
Join the fronts to the back at the shoulders.

STEP 6
Pick up stitches around the neckline edge. Work the neck finish to the desired depth and bind off.

STEP 7
Pick up stitches for the front band, from the bottom edge to the top edge of the neckband. Work for the band depth and bind off.

Cardigan Version 8

Version 8 is identical to Version 7, except that this cardigan has a V Neckline. The finish is picked up around the entire opening and worked at one time.

STEP 1
Work Steps 1 and 2 of Cardigan Version 7.

STEP 2
Work to the start of the neckline shaping.

STEP 3
Starting number of stitches in the neckline (CB/Step 12) − ½ the number of Overlap Width stitches = adjusted number of neckline stitches for the calculation of the V Neckline taper

STEP 4
Calculate the neckline taper, using the adjusted number of neckline stitches (see "Traditional V Neckline"). Work the decreases at least one stitch in from the front edge.

STEP 5
Work the two fronts to the shoulder shaping.

STEP 6
Join the fronts and back at the shoulders.

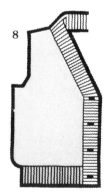

8

V-Neckline variation of Version 7

STEP 7
With a long circular needle, pick up stitches along the right front edge, across the back neckline, and along the left front edge. Work the finish to the desired depth, and bind off.

Cardigan Version 9

In this version, all of the outer edges have a picked-up finish, worked after the garment is complete. All the corners are mitered.

STEP 1
Starting Number of stitches $-$ $\frac{1}{2}$ the number of Overlap Width stitches $=$ number of stitches to cast on

STEP 2
Work the front to the shoulder shaping, *excluding the depth of the bottom border from the garment length* and adjusting the neckline shaping as in Cardigan Version 2, Step 4.

STEP 3
Work the other front, reversing the shapings.

STEP 4
Assemble the entire cardigan.

STEP 5
Mark each corner to be mitered. Starting at the right front side seam, pick up stitches on a long circular needle across the right front bottom edge, along the right front edge, around the neckline, along the left front edge, and across the left front and the back bottom edge, ending at the first stitch you picked up. Place a marker to indicate the end of the round.
For 1/1 ribbing, you will need an odd number of stitches between the corner markers. 2/2 ribbing needs to be centered on an even number of stitches between each marker. Be sure that equivalent edges have the same numbers of stitches.

STEP 6
Work in the round for the depth of the finish, increasing two stitches at each corner every other round.

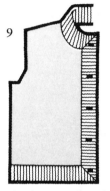

Cardigan with picked-up finish on all outer edges and mitered corners (horizontal bands)

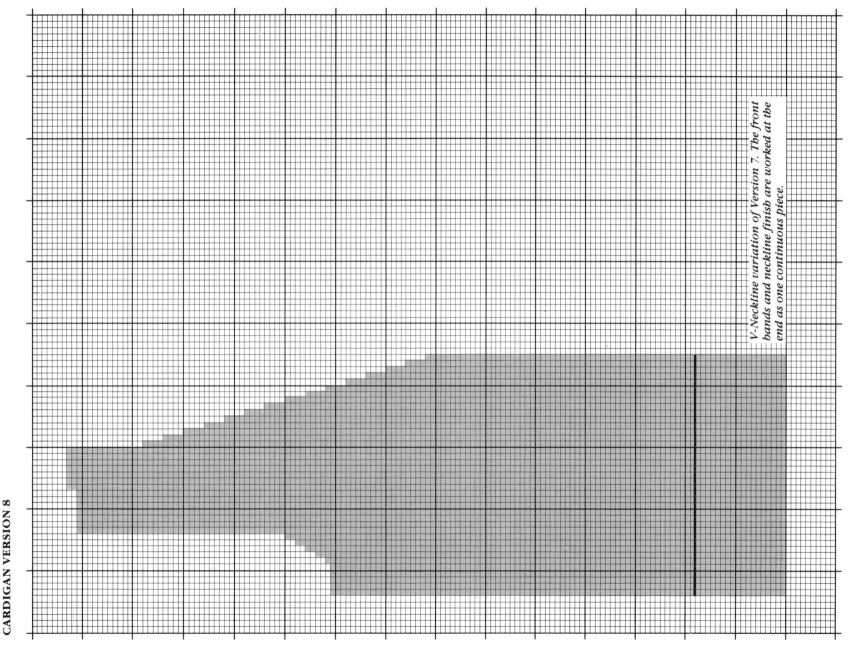

CARDIGAN VERSION 8

V-Neckline variation of Version 7. The front bands and neckline finish are worked at the end as one continuous piece.

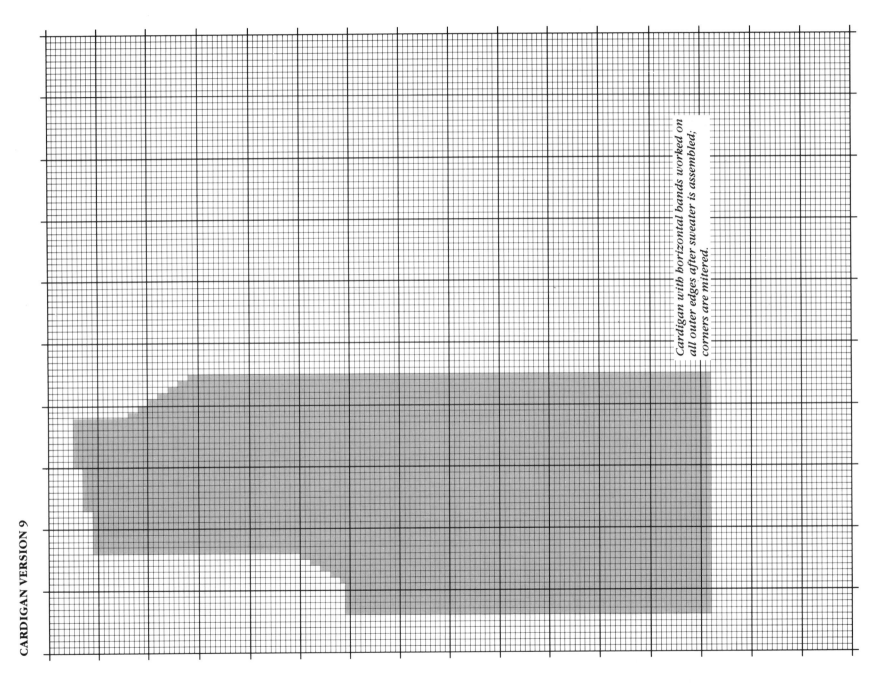

CARDIGAN VERSION 9

Cardigan with horizontal bands worked on all outer edges after sweater is assembled; corners are mitered.

Faced Finishes. When the front band is worked in stockinette stitch or the pattern stitch of the body is worked to the front edge of a cardigan, a facing is needed to stabilize the edge.

When charting a front finish with a facing, you will need to add the following to the Starting Number of body stitches:

1. One-half the number of Overlap Width stitches,

2. One stitch for a vertical turning ridge (see "How Tos"),

3. The total number of Overlap Width stitches.

The last group of stitches is for the facing. After the facing is completed, it is folded to the inside along the turning ridge, then stitched into place (like a vertical hem).

If buttonholes are included in your design, remember to work them into both the garment front and the facing.

Cardigan Version 10

This version consists of a faced cardigan front with a vertically worked border across a portion of the bottom.

If you want to separate the front overlap section from the rest of the body, work a purl stitch between the "Starting" body stitches and the stitches of the overlap and facing.

STEP 1
Starting Number of stitches + (the number of Overlap Width stitches × 1½) + 1 turning-ridge stitch = number of stitches to cast on

STEP 2
(Number of Overlap Width stitches × 2) + 1 turning-ridge stitch = number of stitches in the faced edge (both thicknesses)

STEP 3
Work the faced edge in stockinette or in the same pattern stitch as the body. Work the remaining cast-on stitches in ribbing (or any other border pattern) for the desired depth of the bottom border.

STEP 4
Work the front to the neckline shaping.

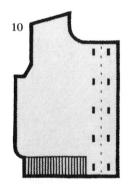

10

Cardigan with faced front and a vertically worked border across most of the bottom

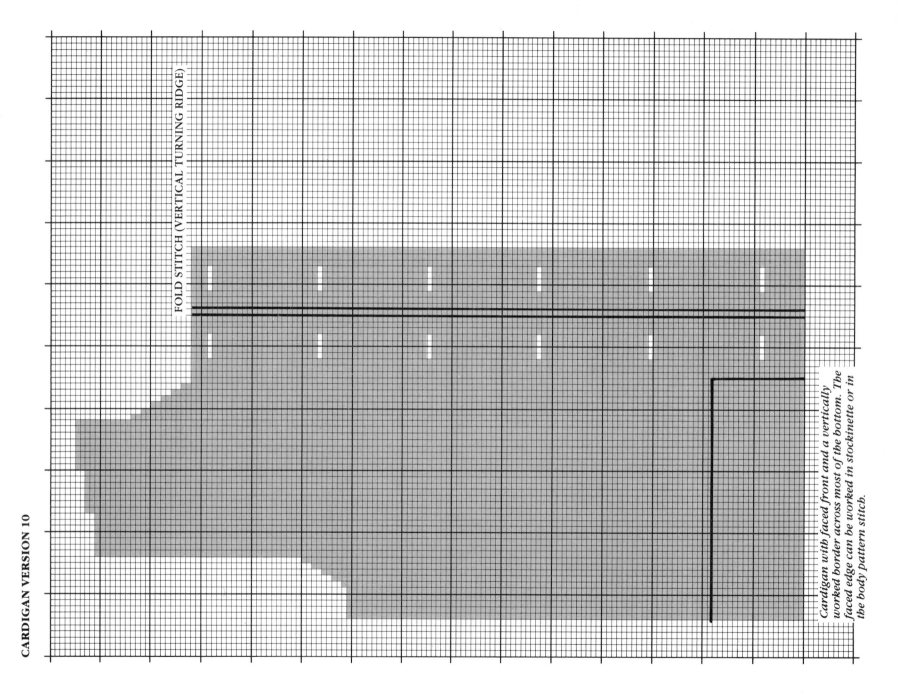

CARDIGAN VERSION 10

FOLD STITCH (VERTICAL TURNING RIDGE)

Cardigan with faced front and a vertically worked border across most of the bottom. The faced edge can be worked in stockinette or in the body pattern stitch.

STEP 5

Starting number of stitches in the neckline bind-off (CB/Step 17 and "Necklines") + (number of Overlap Width stitches × 1½) + 1 turning-ridge stitch = adjusted number of stitches for the neckline bind-off

STEP 6

Work the remainder of the front through the shoulder shaping.

STEP 7

Work the other front, reversing the shapings.

STEP 8

Assemble the garment. Turn the facings to the inside of the front edge and stitch in place.

Cardigan Version 11

This is a faced V-Neckline Cardigan with a border along the entire bottom edge of the sweater. There is no visual separation of the body stitches and the stitches of the front overlap. The neckline decreases are worked along the front edge of the V, just inside the vertical turning ridge. A faced cardigan worked entirely in the pattern stitch of the body will include a facing for the back neckline finish as well as for the front edges.

Back
STEP 1

Knit the back (including bottom border) through the shoulder shaping. With the back neckline stitches still on the needle, work a horizontal turning ridge (see "How Tos").

STEP 2

At each side of these back neckline stitches, cast on the total number of Overlap Width stitches.

STEP 3

Work for a minimum depth of 1″, tapering the edges inward if desired, then bind off. Match the depth of the back facing to the width of the front overlap.

Front
STEP 1

Starting Number of stitches + ½ the number of Overlap Width stitches = number of stitches to cast on

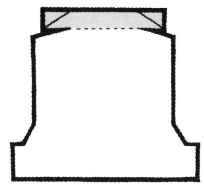

A To make a facing for the back neckline, cast on and work extra fabric after you complete the shoulder shaping (see Version 11 Back, Steps 2 and 3).

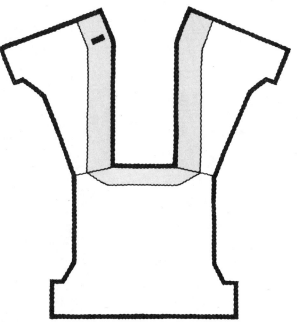

B When you assemble the garment, join the shoulders and facing edges, then stitch the facing in place (see Version 11 Front, Steps 8 and 9).

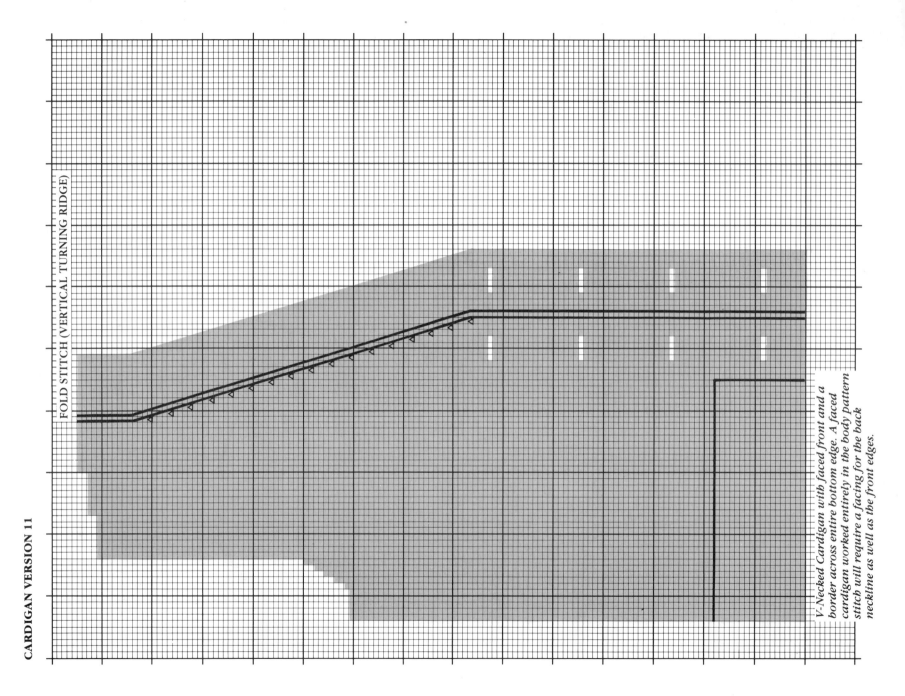

CARDIGAN VERSION 11

FOLD STITCH (VERTICAL TURNING RIDGE)

V-Necked Cardigan with faced front and a border across entire bottom edge. A faced cardigan worked entirely in the body pattern stitch will require a facing for the back neckline as well as the front edges.

STEP 2

Work even in a border stitch for the desired depth of the border.

STEP 3

At front edge, cast on the facing stitches: one vertical turning-ridge stitch plus the total number of Overlap Width stitches.

STEP 4

Work even in the stitch pattern of the body to the start of the neckline shaping.

STEP 5

Starting number of neckline stitches (CB/Step 12) + ½ the number of Overlap Width stitches = adjusted number of neckline stitches for the calculation of the V Neckline taper

STEP 6

Calculate the neckline taper with the adjusted number of neckline stitches (see "Traditional V Neckline"). Work through the neckline and shoulder shaping, decreasing on the front edges of the V, just inside the vertical turning ridge.

STEP 7

Work the other front, reversing the shapings.

STEP 8

Join the fronts to the back at the shoulders and the facings.

STEP 9

Turn the facings to the inside and stitch in place.

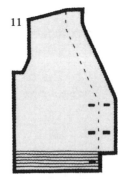

V-Necked Cardigan with faced front and a border across entire bottom edge

Cardigan Version 12

This version is a faced cardigan with a bottom hem. When knitting the back of the sweater, construct a hem by including Step 2, below.

STEP 1

Starting Number of stitches − ½ the number of Overlap Width stitches = number of stitches to cast on

STEP 2

Work even for 1″ or the desired depth of the hem. Work a horizontal turning ridge (see "How Tos").

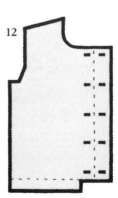

Cardigan with faced front and hemmed bottom

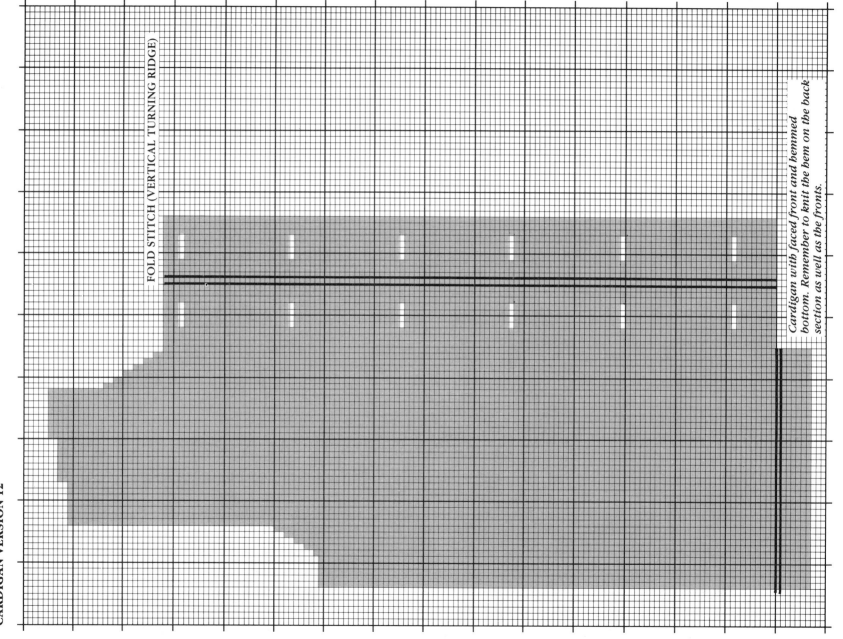

CARDIGAN VERSION 12

FOLD STITCH (VERTICAL TURNING RIDGE)

Cardigan with faced front and hemmed bottom. Remember to knit the hem on the back section as well as the fronts.

STEP 3
At the front edge, cast on twice the total Overlap Width stitches plus one vertical turning ridge stitch. These are the stitches of the front overlap and its facing.

STEP 4
Work through the shoulder shaping, adjusting the front neckline shaping as in Cardigan Version 10, Step 3.

STEP 5
Work the other front, reversing the shapings.

STEP 6
Finish all the garment pieces and assemble the cardigan.

STEP 7
Turn the facings and the hem to the inside and stitch in place.

Cardigan Version 13

This version has a hem, a faced front band, and a V Neckline. The back neckline band and facing are a continuation of the front finish.

Both the front band and the facing can be worked in the same stitch pattern. Alternatively, the band can be worked in a stitch pattern compatible with the pattern stitch of the body, and the facing in stockinette. Be aware of the possibility of gauge discrepancies between the band pattern stitch and the stockinette of the facing, and adjust the number of stitches of each section of the front finish accordingly.

The neckline decrease method most closely resembles Cardigan Version 3, with the decreases worked just inside the band, on the body of the garment.

STEP 1
Work Steps 1 through 3 of Cardigan Version 12.

STEP 2
Work to the beginning of the neckline shaping.

STEP 3
Starting number of neckline stitches (CB/Step 12) − ½ the number of Overlap Width stitches = adjusted number of neckline stitches for the calculation of the V Neckline taper

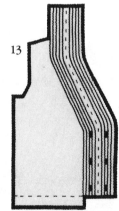

13

V-Neckline Cardigan with faced front and hemmed bottom

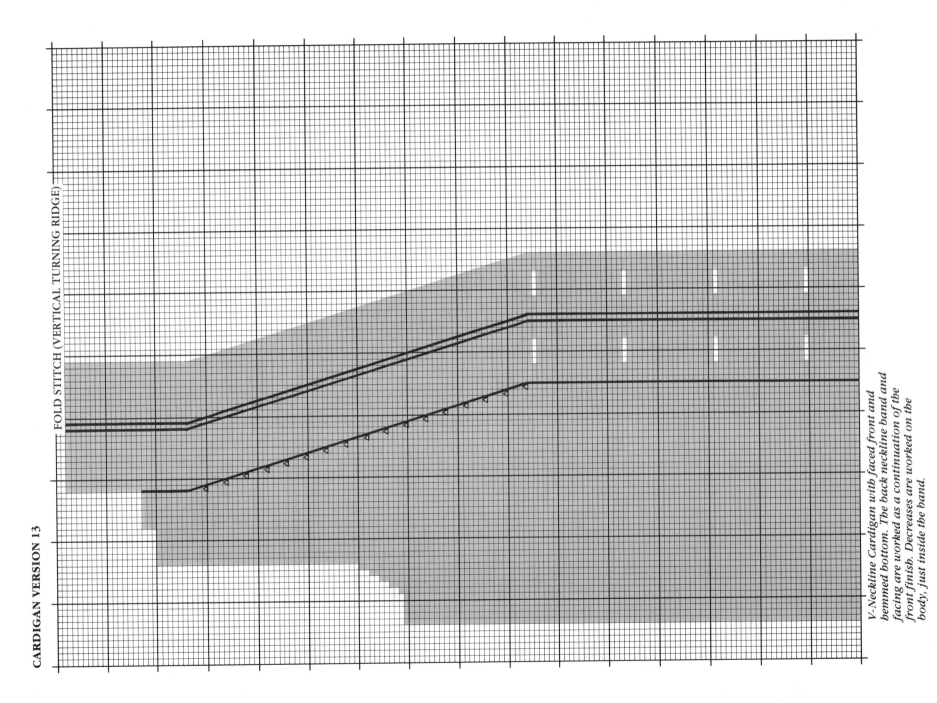

CARDIGAN VERSION 13

FOLD STITCH (VERTICAL TURNING RIDGE)

V-Neckline Cardigan with faced front and hemmed bottom. The back neckline band and facing are worked as a continuation of the front finish. Decreases are worked on the body, just inside the band.

STEP 4
Calculate the neckline taper with the adjusted number of neckline stitches (see "Traditional V Neckline"). Work the decreases inside the front band, on the body stitches.

STEP 5
Work through the shoulder shaping, keeping the stitches of the front band and facing on the needle.

STEP 6
Continue even on the stitches of the front band and facing for one-half the width of the back neckline. Place the stitches on a holder.

STEP 7
Work the other front, reversing the shapings.

STEP 8
Join the fronts and back at the shoulders.

STEP 9
Graft the stitches of the front finishes (see "How Tos"). Sew the inside edge of the finish to the neckline.

STEP 10
Turn the facing and the hem to the inside and stitch in place.

Cardigan Versions 14 and 15

In these cardigans, the front edges have facings while the V Necklines do not. Shape the facings as mirror images of the front neckline, working in reverse from the turning-ridge stitch position.

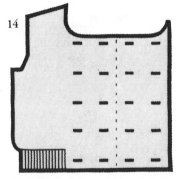

Cardigan with wide front facing and vertically worked border across a portion of the bottom

V-Necked Cardigan with front facing, vertically worked border across a portion of the bottom, and unfaced neckline

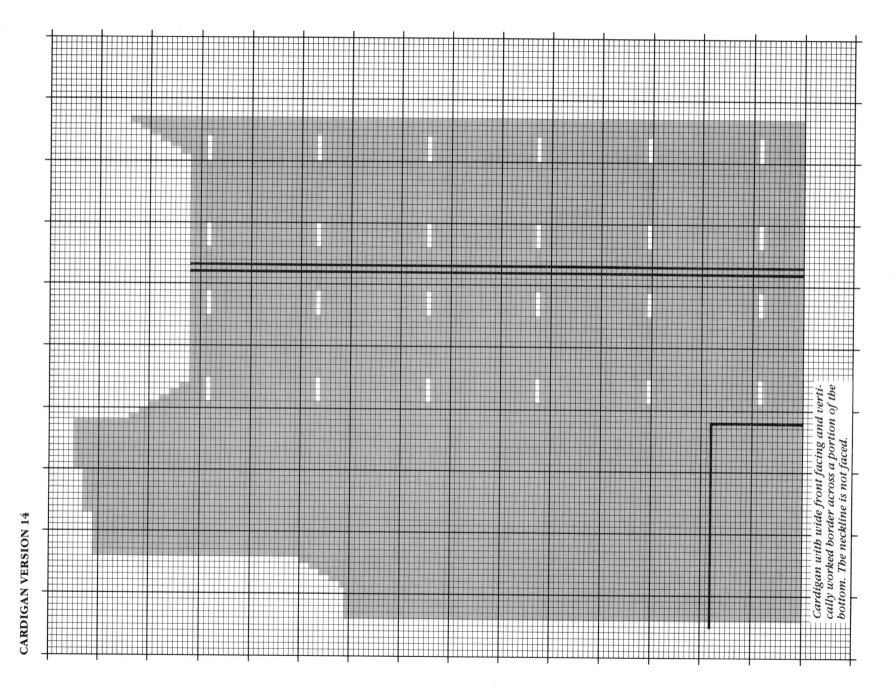

CARDIGAN VERSION 14

Cardigan with wide front facing and vertically worked border across a portion of the bottom. The neckline is not faced.

174

CARDIGAN VERSION 15

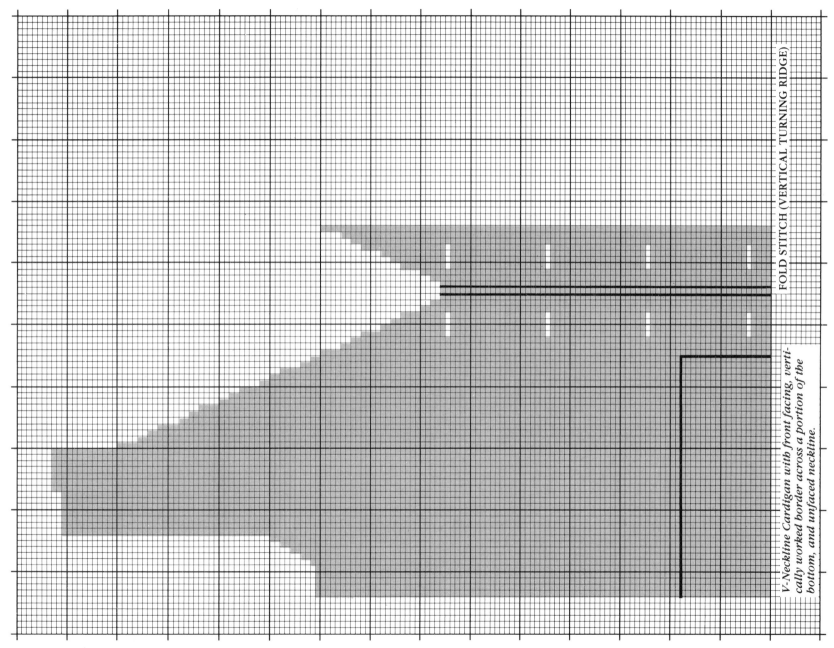

FOLD STITCH (VERTICAL TURNING RIDGE)

V-Neckline Cardigan with front facing, vertically worked border across a portion of the bottom, and unfaced neckline.

Non-Overlapping Cardigan Styles

The Bolero Jacket and the Chanel Jacket are two styles that do not overlap at center front. The Bolero is the shorter of the two, and sometimes has rounded front bottom edges.

Both styles can be finished with Vertical or Horizontal Bands, or with Facings. Since there are no buttonholes, the front finishes can be narrower than the standard for the classic cardigan. See the previous cardigan guidelines for ideas on finishes. If you do want to include closures on a sweater in one of these styles, toggle buttons are an option.

The **Bolero Jacket** begins at, or above, the waist, and frequently is made with rounded edges at the bottom of the front opening. The fronts may meet at the center, but can have up to 4″ of separation. Neckline options include most variations of the Round, Square, and V shapings.

Bolero Jacket

STEP 1
Decide on the separation width (if any) between the two front sections of the Bolero.

STEP 2
Starting Number of stitches − ½ (Step 1 × stitch gauge) = number of stitches in each front section
- If the front bottom will not be curved, cast on this number of stitches, work even to the neckline shaping, and proceed to Step 6.

STEP 3
If the front bottom will be curved, use the Curve Guide (see "How Tos") to determine the number of stitches in the curve.

STEP 4
Step 2 number of stitches − number of stitches in the front curve = number of stitches to cast on

STEP 5
Work the curve at the center front edge. Continue on the total number of body stitches to the neckline.

STEP 6
Starting number of neckline stitches (CB/Step 12) − ½ (Step 1 × stitch gauge) = adjusted number of neckline stitches

STEP 7
Work through the shoulder shaping.

A **Chanel Jacket** has no collar, is boxy in style, and has fronts which just meet at the center. The garment length can vary, ending anywhere between the waist and mid-hip.

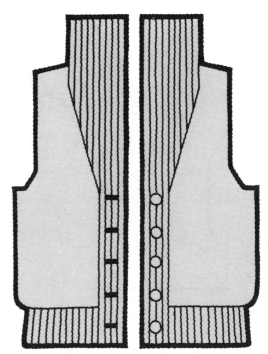

Chanel Jacket

STEP 1
Starting Number of stitches = number of stitches to cast on

STEP 2
Front edge variations include the following.

a. **Vertical Band Finish:** If the finish is worked along with the body, no stitches need to be added or subtracted. If the finish is worked separately, follow the guidelines for a Horizontal Band.

b. **Horizontal Band Finish:** Subtract a number of stitches equivalent to the band width from the Starting Number of stitches and the neckline bind-off. Add the Horizontal Band after working the body, as in Cardigan Version 7 above.

c. **Faced Finish:** Add one vertical turning-ridge stitch plus the stitches for the width of the facing to the Starting Number of stitches and to the neckline bind-off.

The collar is an extension of the front bands. The right and left front sections are worked as mirror images, except for placement of buttons and buttonholes.

Cardigans with Shawl Collars

The Shawl Collar is a finishing option for a V-Neck Cardigan. It can be worked in several ways, all of which have common elements.

The depth of the neckline opening is based on the placement of the top button. This placement is pretty much up to you—it can vary from just above the arm-hole shaping to below the waist.

The Front Overlap Width, or band width, is determined as for any cardigan. The amount of overlap will affect the width of the collar. The greater the overlap, the wider the collar will be when rolled back. (Conversely, if you want a wide collar, choose a greater overlap.)

The V taper follows the normal guidelines, starting $1/2''$ to $1''$ above the top buttonhole. The shaping should end $1\frac{1}{2}''$ to $2''$ below the beginning of the shoulder shaping (see "Traditional V Neckline").

For a close-fitting Shawl Collar, chart the V of the neckline over one-third of the yoke width. For a more open collar, widen the neckline by $1''$ to $2''$.

CONSTRUCTION OF SHAWL COLLAR CARDIGAN

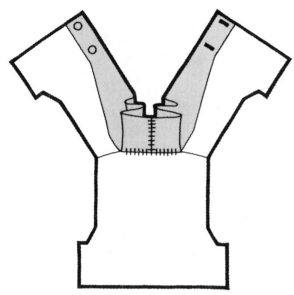

Stitch sections of collar together, then stitch collar to back of neckline.

The stitch pattern of the collar should be reversible, since both sides of the fabric will show when the collar is rolled. Seed stitch, double seed stitch, ribbings, and garter stitch are some of the possible choices.

The **Standard Vertical Shawl Collar** cardigan has a vertical finish, knit at the same time as the front of the garment, in a reversible border stitch. The stitches of the neckline shaping are not decreased, but simply moved to the front band by changing the pattern stitch from that of the body to that of the band. The widened front band becomes the shawl collar.

Standard Vertical Shawl Collar

STEP 1
Work Steps 1 through 3 of Cardigan Version 1.

STEP 2
$1/2$ starting number of stitches in the neckline (CB/Step 12) − $1/2$ the number of Front Overlap Width stitches = adjusted number of neckline stitches for the calculation of the V Neckline taper

STEP 3
Place a marker between the stitches of the body and the stitches of the band.

STEP 4
Following the graph of the neckline taper (see ''Traditional V Neckline''), move the marker one stitch toward the shoulder every time the taper indicates a decrease. As you knit, the number of stitches on your needles will remain the same, but the band will widen to become the Shawl Collar, and the number of body stitches will decrease to the number of stitches of the back shoulder shaping.

STEP 5
Work through the shoulder shaping.

STEP 6
Continue knitting the stitches of the collar for one-half the width of the back neckline. Place the stitches on a holder or bind them off.

STEP 7
Work the other front in the same manner, reversing the shapings.

STEP 8
Join the fronts and back at the shoulders.

STEP 9
Graft (see "How Tos") or sew the two sides of the collar together, and sew the collar to the back neckline.

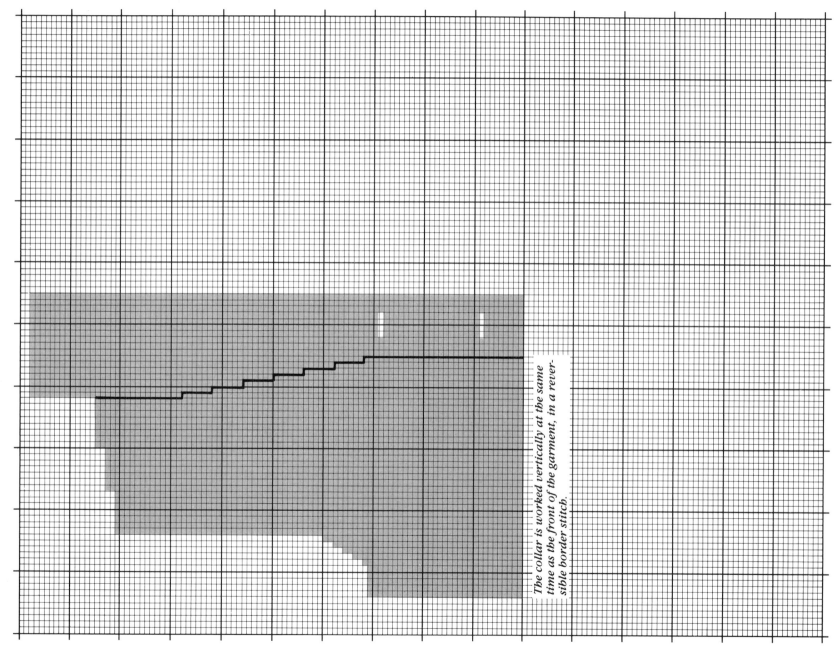

The collar is worked vertically at the same time as the front of the garment, in a reversible border stitch.

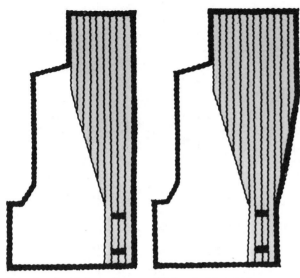

Standard: stitches of the neckline shaping are moved to the front band instead of being decreased.

Wide: shaping proceeds in the same way as for the standard collar, and increases are also made along the front edge.

For a cardigan with a **Wide Vertical Shawl Collar**, you can increase the standard width of a Shawl Collar 1″ or more by working evenly spaced increases near the inside or outside edge of the collar at the same time as you widen the collar at the inside edge by changing the stitch pattern.

Wide Vertical Shawl Collar

STEP 1
Follow the Standard Vertical Shawl Collar guidelines through Step 3.

STEP 2
Chart a second taper (see Taper Formula) using the number of stitches equal to the additional width desired (width × stitch gauge). This taper can be fairly shallow (several inches deep) or as deep as the original taper.

STEP 3
Follow both charted tapers when working the collar. The original taper indicates on what row to move the marker out by one stitch and change the stitch pattern. The second taper indicates on what row to work an increase.
- If there is only one shaping indicated for a row, work the appropriate one.
- If both shapings occur in the same row, work both.

STEP 4
Work the increases on the collar, right at the marker (a), or a stitch or two in from the outer edge (b).

STEP 5
For a wider roll to the collar, work a slope with short rows (see "How Tos") from the back neck edge of the collar to the outer edge (c). Begin the slope after the collar is equal to one-half the width of the back neckline (Step 6 of the Standard Vertical Shawl Collar cardigan). The slope can be from one to several inches deep. The wider the collar, the higher the slope should be.

WIDE SHAWL COLLAR CARDIGAN

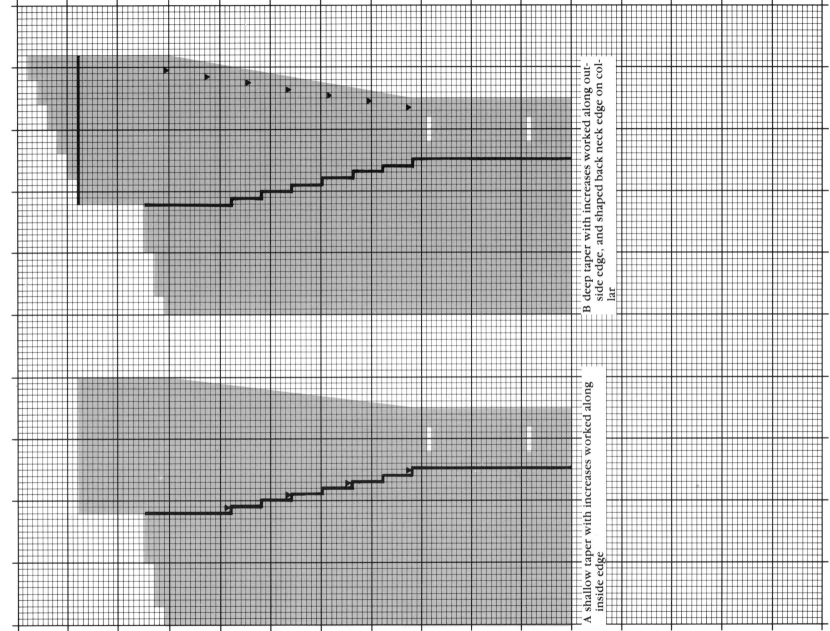

A shallow taper with increases worked along inside edge

B deep taper with increases worked along outside edge, and shaped back neck edge on collar

WIDE SHAWL COLLAR

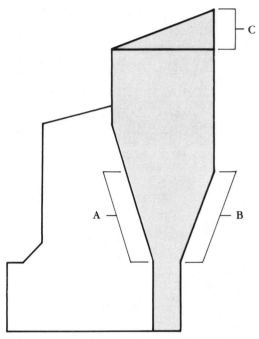

A Increases can be worked along the taper; each time (or every other time) you widen the band by one stitch, work an increase between the yoke and the band as well.

B Increases can also be worked along the outside edge.

C For a wider roll to the collar, work a taper with short rows from the back neck to the outer edge.

A **Separate Vertical Shawl Collar** can be made and later added to the body if you wish; for instance, if two different needle sizes are to be used for body and collar. The separate section is charted using the stitch gauge of the border stitch, and is sewn in place after the fronts and back are assembled at the shoulders.

Separate Vertical Shawl Collar

STEP 1
Follow the guidelines for Cardigan Version 3 through Step 5 using the Version 2 options, knitting the band only up to the point where the neckline taper begins.

STEP 2
Chart the Shawl Collar portion of the front band, as follows.
a. Number of stitches decreased in the neckline taper of the front (Cardigan Version 3, Step 2) ÷ stitch gauge for the front = number of inches for taper width
b. Step 2a × stitch gauge of the band = number of increases for Shawl Collar
■ If a wider Shawl Collar is desired, add to the increases the number of stitches equivalent to the extra width
c. Length of neckline taper × row gauge of the band = number of rows in collar taper
d. Step 2c ÷ Step 2b = number of rows between the increases on the Shawl Collar (see Taper Formula)

STEP 3
Work the Shawl Collar increases.

STEP 4
Continue working on the collar stitches for the length of the remaining front neckline edge (above the decreases), plus one-half the width of the back neckline. Place the stitches on a holder, or bind off.

STEP 5
Make a second border piece, the mirror image of the first.

STEP 6
Sew each border to its front, stretching it to fit when sewing the band portion.

STEP 7
Join the fronts and back at the shoulders.

STEP 8
Graft (see "How Tos") or sew the two halves of the collar together, then sew the complete piece to the back neckline.

Horizontal Shawl Collar

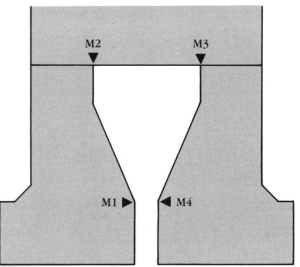

The collar finish is picked up and worked after the sweater is assembled. Markers help you place the collar correctly.

STEP 1
Chart and knit the fronts according to the guidelines for Cardigan Version 8.

STEP 2
Pick up stitches along the front of the cardigan, starting at the bottom right (from the wearer's point of view). As you do this, place a marker (M1) at the beginning (bottom) of the V taper, a second one (M2) at the beginning of the back neckline, a third (M3) at the other end of the back neckline, and a fourth (M4) at the bottom of the V taper on the left side of the front. Break off the yarn.

STEP 3
Count and record the total number of stitches in the two front V sections (that is, the number of stitches between M1 and M2, plus the number between M3 and M4). Be sure that the same number of stitches is included in each section.
Example: 30 + 30 = 60   *60 stitches*

STEP 4
Number of stitches decreased in the neckline taper of a front (Cardigan Version 8, Step 4) ÷ stitch gauge of the front = depth of collar V taper in inches
■ If you are planning a Wide Shawl Collar, add the desired extra width in inches to the inches calculated in this step, and use that larger number for the remaining calculations.
Example: 6 ÷ 5 = 1.2   *1.2"*

STEP 5
Step 4 × row gauge of the finish = depth of neckline shaping in rows
Make this an even number.
Example: 1.2 × 6 = 7.2   *8 rows*

STEP 6
Step 3 ÷ Step 5 = number of additional stitches to be worked in each row for Step 5 number of rows
Example: 60 ÷ 8 = 7.5   *7 or 8 stitches*
Chart the larger number of stitches first, using the Slope Formula to determine the exact sequence. In this example, 8 additional stitches are worked in the first 4 rows, then 7 additional stitches in each of the remaining 4 rows.

For the **Horizontal Shawl Collar** cardigan, the collar finish is picked up and worked after the sweater has been assembled at the shoulders. The collar shaping is worked in short rows (see "How Tos").

Since the collar and bands are worked horizontally, note that we use the term *depth* rather than *width* when referring to the V shaping in Steps 4 and 5.

STEP 7

Slip the stitches between the starting point and M2 onto the right needle. Join the yarn, and start knitting at M2. Work the back neckline stitches, turn the work, and work the back neckline stitches plus the first group of Step 6 stitches. (For information on knitting short rows, see "How Tos.") Turn the work. Continue to add another group of Step 6 stitches at the end of each row until all of the stitches of the front V have been worked. Turn the work, and knit to the end of the needle twice (using all of the collar and band stitches).

STEP 8

Work even on all stitches for the depth of the band, working the buttonholes on the appropriate front. Bind off all stitches.

The **Notched Shawl Collar** cardigan variation has the look of a Lapel Jacket but is constructed somewhat differently.

The top and bottom of the notch can be the same or different widths, depending on your choice.

Notched Shawl Collar

STEP 1

Determine the collar width above and below the notch. 1″ to 3″ is the standard range.

STEP 2

Chart and work a Vertical Shawl Collar cardigan to the length desired for the placement of the notch, and bind off a number of stitches equivalent to its bottom width.

STEP 3

On the next row, cast on a number of stitches equivalent to the top width of the notch. If the collar above the notch is quite wide, you may want to taper the neckline seam edge to make the collar narrower at the back neckline.

STEP 4

Finish the cardigan according to your design.

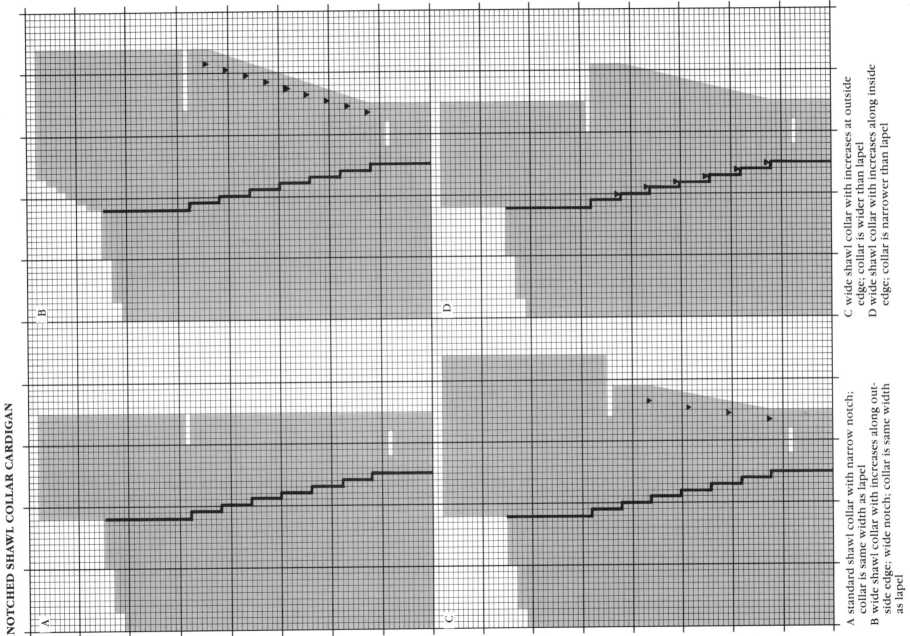

NOTCHED SHAWL COLLAR CARDIGAN

A standard shawl collar with narrow notch; collar is same width as lapel

B wide shawl collar with increases along outside edge; wide notch; collar is same width as lapel

C wide shawl collar with increases at outside edge; collar is wider than lapel

D wide shawl collar with increases along inside edge; collar is narrower than lapel

185

LAPEL COLLAR CARDIGAN

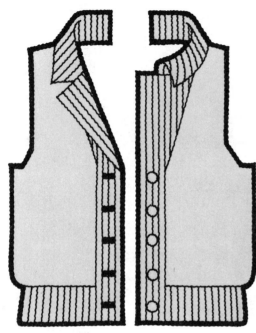

If you close a "typical" lapel collar jacket at the neckline, you'll see it's simply a collar on a round neckline.

CONSTRUCTION OF LAPEL COLLAR CARDIGAN

Collar stitches are picked up from a to b. Increase the collar width by the same number of stitches as were decreased at each side of the front neckline (c).

The **Lapel Jacket** technically is categorized as a Round Neckline garment. However, this style is included here because, like a Shawl Collar, it is worn open at the front, with the edges of the front rolled back onto the yoke.

Many of the guidelines for the Shawl Collar apply. Placement of the top button determines the depth of the opening at the front; the width of the overlap helps determine the width of the lapel; and stitch patterns need to be reversible. The roll of the lapels forms a V, and the stitch pattern of the front finish can be widened in the same manner as the Shawl Collar.

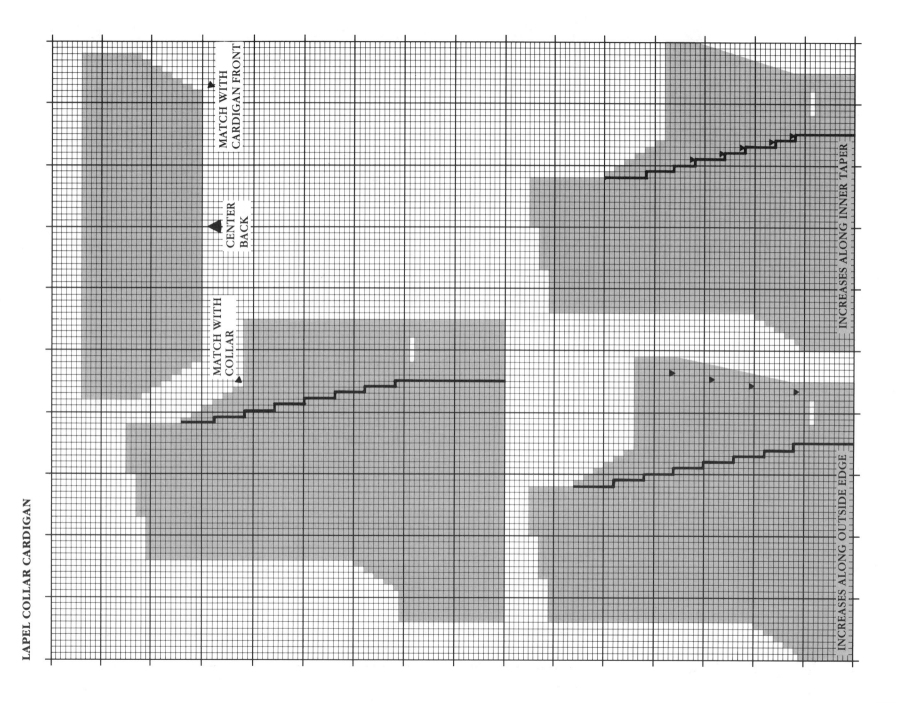

LAPEL COLLAR CARDIGAN

MATCH WITH CARDIGAN FRONT

CENTER BACK

MATCH WITH COLLAR

INCREASES ALONG INNER TAPER

INCREASES ALONG OUTSIDE EDGE

Lapel Jacket

STEP 1
Chart and graph a cardigan with a Round Neckline.

STEP 2
Chart, and add to the graph, a V taper based on the number of stitches of the Round Neckline. The depth of the taper is determined by the placement of the top button (see "Cardigan Buttonholes"). The shaping of this taper should end at the last of the Round Neckline decreases. Follow this V taper when widening the band pattern stitches as in the Vertical Shawl Collar.
- If you wish to increase the width of the lapel, follow the guidelines for the Wide Vertical Shawl Collar.

STEP 3
Work the back of the jacket. Bind off the neckline stitches to add stability at the back of the neck.

STEP 4
Work both fronts, and join the fronts to the back at the shoulders.

STEP 5
With the *wrong side* of the garment facing you, pick up stitches for the collar as follows.
1. On the left front, at the last neckline decrease (a), pick up stitches to the left shoulder, across the back neckline, and from the right shoulder to the last neckline decrease of the right front (b).
2. Turn your work, and, working in rows, increase the width of the collar by the same number of stitches as were decreased on each side of the front neckline (c). This can be done by casting on a stitch at the beginning of each row, or by increasing at both ends of the row on every other row. For example, the graph shows 6 stitches decreased on each side of the neckline, so you would increase 6 stitches per edge on the collar.

STEP 6
After the increases are complete, work even to the desired collar measurement, and bind off.
- Alternatively, the collar could be worked separately and sewn to the neckline edge.

STEP 7
Join the increased section of the collar to the decreased section of the neckline edge, with the selvedge of the seam on the right side of the garment.

SLEEVES AND SLEEVE CAPS

After charting the body of your sweater, you are ready to make another design choice—the style to use for sleeve and sleeve cap.

Some sleeve cap choices are obvious. A Raglan Cap is always used with a Raglan Yoke, a Saddle Band with a Saddle Yoke, and a T bind-off with a T Yoke. Sleeve cap options are much more numerous for yokes with Set-In Armhole shaping, as you will see in the following pages.

In most cases your choice of sleeve shape is wide open. Sleeves can be narrow or full, and can taper in, taper out, blouse out, or continue straight all the way to the armhole. After you're familiar with the basics, try charting different combinations. Look at sweaters in magazines or stores for possibilities. Almost any sleeve you'll find will be a variation of one of the styles included here.

Sleeves can be knit one at a time or both at the same time on the same needles. If they're knit at the same time and your needles aren't long enough to hold all of the upperarm stitches, you can knit back and forth on a circular needle.

On most sweaters the left and right sleeves and sleeve caps are exactly alike. For a garment where the front and back armholes are not shaped identically, chart each cap edge to match its respective armhole. Remember to work each sleeve cap as a mirror image of the other, or you will have two left sleeves!

Sleeve Ease

We've already discussed ease under "Determining Ease," but let's go over it once more.

One inch of ease is a standard amount to add to your Wrist Measurement so that a sleeve can fit easily over your hand. You can double-check this fit by measuring your hand circumference around the knuckles. If this measurement is greater than the Wrist Measurement plus 1″ ease, then use it, without adding ease, when calculating for the sleeve cuff.

In order to keep the sleeve in proportion to the body of the sweater, add from one-half up to the full amount of the Body Ease (page 37) to your Upperarm Measurement. For instance, if the Body Ease is 2″, between 1″ and 2″ should be added to the Upperarm Measurement, depending on the fullness desired. In general, a greater amount of Sleeve Ease is needed in sweaters for work or sports than in dressier garments. Note that this is a minimum guideline and that your sleeve cap choice (a Gathered or Pleated Cap, for example) may influence the amount of ease you use.

If the sleeve is full and has a tight cuff, blousing can be achieved by adding between 1″ and 3″ to the sleeve length.

Shorter Sleeves

Our sleeve instructions are written for long sleeves, but are easily adaptable for shorter sleeves, with the addition of two new measurements.

1. Measure the circumference of the arm at the point where the sleeve will begin. This measurement plus a minimum of 1″ ease, multiplied by the stitch gauge, will give you the number of stitches to cast on.
2. Measure the distance from the start of the short sleeve to the Measurement String (see "Taking Measurements") for the Sleeve Length Measurement. Increases can be worked along this entire length if the sleeve is full, or can stop 3″ to 4″ below the armhole shaping if the sleeve is narrow.

Use any sleeve cap suited to your yoke. If you're making a very short sleeve but require a lot of fabric for shaping the cap, increase immediately after the ribbing or other border finish to obtain the necessary fullness (see "Lantern Sleeve").

Set-In Sleeve Caps

No part of charting creates greater confusion for the average knitter than Set-In Sleeve Caps. Many knitters regard charting sleeve caps as a hit-or-miss operation; if the finished cap doesn't fit the armhole nicely, ripping out and starting from scratch is taken as a matter of course. Very few of us are big fans of unravelling and re-knitting. There is another way!

We believe that every knitter can knit a front and back yoke, choose a specific sleeve cap style, chart and knit that cap right down to the last stitch—and have it fit the armhole perfectly. It can be done.

The only requirements are a little time and concentration. You will need a general understanding of the Set-In Cap and how it fits into an armhole. If you take the following information bit by bit and digest each section before proceeding to the next, the basics will click into your mind and you will never need to "guesstimate" a Set-In Cap again.

We will begin by dropping the term sleeve from sleeve cap, to avoid confusion when we require specific information about the sleeve itself. From now on we will simply call it the cap.

Which Styles are Set-In Caps? We have made every effort to include guidelines for every basic Set-In Cap style we could find. Some may not be in vogue at the moment, but we really can't understand why. Perhaps they have been forgotten for a while in the dusty archives of old knitting magazines. Still, they're bound to reappear some day.

Our collection includes:

1. Classic Set-In Cap
2. Gathered Cap
3. Pleated Cap
4. Box Cap
5. T-Square Cap
6. Designer's Choice Cap
7. Saddle Shoulder Cap
8. Semi-Raglan Cap

They appear different as a result of their final shaping. Specific shaping details are covered in the guidelines for each style, and don't concern us at this point. First, we will examine their similarities.

THE TYPICAL SET-IN CAP

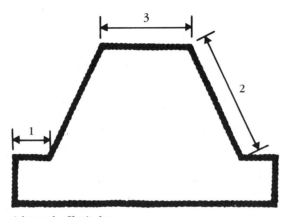

1 bound-off stitches
2 tapered side edges
3 finished width at the top of the cap

HOW A SET-IN CAP FITS INTO AN ARMHOLE

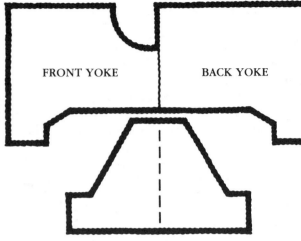

FRONT YOKE   BACK YOKE

The "Typical" Set-In Cap. Let's begin by looking at a "typical" Set-In Cap. Its outer edges have three distinct parts.

1. Bound-off stitches. Every Set-In Cap begins by binding off the same number of stitches per edge as were bound off for the armholes of the yoke sections (CB/Step 8). Our example has five stitches, so we would begin shaping our cap by binding off five stitches at each edge. Likewise, if the Alternate Set-In Armhole shaping is used for a sweater yoke, the first few levels of the cap would be shaped to correspond to it.
2. Tapered side edges. The two tapered (slanted) edges are formed by decreasing a specific number of stitches over the height of the cap. The actual number of stitches per edge depends on the individual cap.

3. Finished width at the top of the cap. The finished width will vary from style to style. We provide guidelines for each style of cap.

How a Set-In Sleeve Fits into an Armhole. A finished cap must fit comfortably within the armhole opening formed by the front and back yokes. Armhole or yoke shapings that might be used include: Set-In Armhole (CB) shaping, Shaped Yoke, Extended Shoulder shaping, and Full-Fashioned Shoulder shaping.

If you divide a typical cap in half lengthwise, one side should fit the back armhole, and the other should fit the front. Neither the cap fabric nor the yoke fabric should need to be pulled or stretched to make the pieces fit when they are joined.

MEASURING THE CURVE OF THE BACK ARMHOLE

MEASURING HALF THE CURVE OF THE CAP (INCLUDING HALF THE STITCHES ON THE NEEDLE)

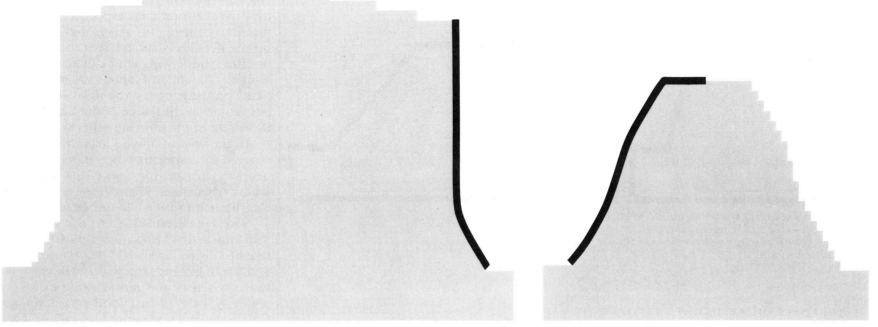

The Curve Measurement. To achieve that perfect fit, we will measure the curve of the back armhole and compare it to half the curve of the cap. Both curves are shown as heavy lines in the illustration.

Use a tape measure to determine the length of the yoke curve along the armhole edge. This measurement is not the same as the Armhole Depth Measurement, which is measured in a straight line. Rather, the Curve Measurement is equivalent to the length of the armhole edge of the yoke.

If the back yoke of your sweater is already complete, measure the armhole curve directly on it, as shown in the illustration. Measure from the marker placed after the last group of bound-off stitches to the beginning of the shoulder shaping. The bound-off stitches at the start of the armhole are not included. Place the tape on edge to measure accurately. If your tape isn't flexible enough, use a piece of string, then measure the length of the string.

If your front and back yokes are not identical, measure both front and back curves, add both together, and divide the result by two for your Curve Measurement.

Now glance at the graph and observe the heavy line along the outside edge of half the cap. If the cap is to fit, then the length of that line on your cap must be equal to, or just barely longer than, the Curve Measurement of your yoke.

Before you proceed, take a minute to *remeasure the stitch and row gauge,* using a portion of the body or yoke as your

WHAT DETERMINES THE HEIGHT OF A CAP?

NARROW SLEEVE   WIDE SLEEVE

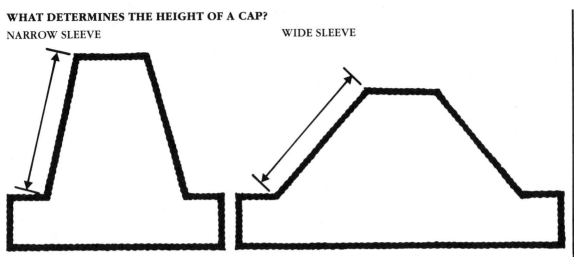

The tapered edges of both caps are identical in length, but the wider sleeve requires more decreases per edge to reach the same finished width at the top.

THE UNFINISHED WIDTH AT THE TOP OF THE CAP

FINISHED WIDTH   UNFINISHED WIDTH

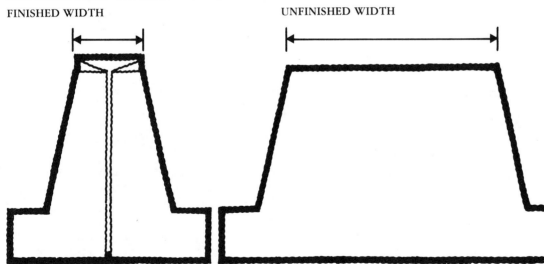

The pleated cap is a good example of the difference between the unfinished and finished width at the top of the cap.

swatch. It is very important that the cap taper be charted from the gauge of the fabric at the time the armhole curve is measured. Sometimes, especially in machine knitting, the fabric that comes off the needles is much larger than it will be after laundering. Your calculations for your cap height and taper should not be based on the gauge of the finished piece, but rather on the gauge of the fabric at this point in the knitting process.

Every Set-In Cap you make will be charted for a specific yoke. It will be necessary to take the Curve Measurement on every garment. We will use a Curve Measurement of 8½″ in our examples.

The Finished Width of the Cap. The Finished Width at the top of an adult Classic Set-In Cap should be between 3″ and 5″. In general, the width will vary with the size of the garment. For example, 3″ to 3½″ is a good measurement for a women's size petite to small, 4″ for a women's medium or a men's small, 4½″ for a women's large or men's medium, and 5″ for a men's large or extra large. We use 3″ in our examples.

Finished Widths for the tops of children's caps vary as follows: infants' (birth to 24 months), 1½″ to 2½″; toddlers' (sizes 2 through 6), 1½″ to 3″; older children's, 2″ to 4″.

What Determines the Height of the Cap? Our illustration shows two caps designed to fit the same yoke, one with a narrow sleeve, the other with a wide sleeve. Both have the same finished width at the top of the cap.

The tapered edges of each cap are identical in length. However, the wider sleeve requires more decreases per edge to reach the same Finished Width at the top. The result is a greater slant and a shorter cap height than on the narrow sleeve.

As you can see, the cap height is determined not only by the Armhole Curve Measurement of the yoke, but by the width of the sleeve at the upperarm as well.

The Unfinished Width at the Top of the Cap. Classic Set-In, Semi-Raglan, and Saddle Shoulder Caps do not require special shaping techniques, so you only will need to know a Finished Width for the top of the cap. On all of the other styles, an Unfinished or Unshaped Width will be needed in addition to the Finished Width.

Let's examine our Set-In Cap more closely. We have a 3″ Finished Width at the top, but perhaps this width is made up of gathers or pleats, or includes darts. Each one of these shaping techniques requires extra fabric at or near the top.

A Pleated Cap is a good example. To pleat a 3″ Finished Width requires three times that width of fabric; or, put another way, it takes 9″ of fabric to make 3″ of pleats. Therefore, in all caps which require additional shaping, we will need to determine an Unfinished Width for the cap top as well as a Finished Width.

The Cap Triangle. To chart the cap, you will need to determine not only the height and the top and bottom dimensions, but also the length of the side slope and the width over which this slope occurs. For this purpose, it helps to think of the cap shape as a central rectangle plus two right-angled triangles on each side. We have diagrammed this in our illustration, labelling the triangle sides as *a, b,* and *c*. When you have determined the length of each side of the triangle, you will be ready to chart your sleeve cap.

Note that for Side *b,* we are working with the Unfinished Width at the top of the cap; for Side *c,* we are working with the Finished Width. In some styles (such as the Classic Set-In Cap used in our example) these measurements are the same. Later in this chapter, we have provided individual guidelines for each style of cap.

When charting, it is important to keep in mind that you will always be working with one-half of the cap width. That is why half measurements are used.

Side *a* is the finished height of the cap. We will show you how to calculate this, using the measurements for sides *b* and *c*.

Side *b* is the width over which the cap will be decreased at each tapered edge. The bound-off stitches at the bottom of the cap are not included in this width.

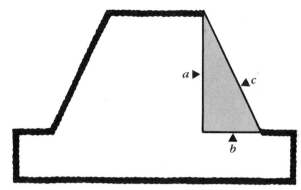

This measurement is figured as follows:

(½ the number of stitches on the needle after the bind-off ÷ stitch gauge) − ½ of the Unfinished Width at the top of the cap = Side *b*
Example: (23 ÷ 5 = 4.6) − 1.5 = 3.1   3.1″

Side *c* is the length of the tapered edge. For it, calculate as follows:

Curve Measurement − ½ of the Finished Width at the top of the cap = Side *c*
Example: 8.5 − 1.5 = 7   7″

With sides *b* and *c* we can determine Side *a,* the cap height. This can be accomplished in either of two ways, the paper-and-ruler method or the math method.

THE PAPER-AND-RULER METHOD

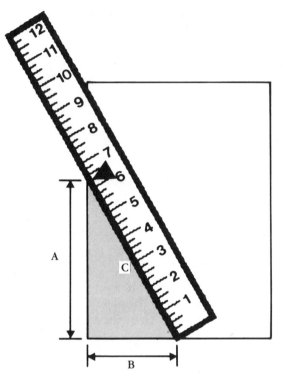

THE PAPER-AND-RULER METHOD

With this simple paper-and-ruler trick, Side *a* can be determined quickly and easily.

At the bottom edge of a sheet of paper, measuring from the corner, mark the width of Side *b*. Place the corner of your ruler at that mark, and pivot the ruler so that you can draw a line the length of Side *c*, connecting the bottom and side edges of the paper and forming a triangle. You then can measure the remaining side of the triangle, giving you the length of Side *a*, the cap height, in inches.

Convert this measurement to rows by multiplying it by the row gauge. If the result is not an even number or contains a fraction, use the next higher even number. It is better to ease in excess fabric from the cap than it is to stretch the yoke during assembly.

THE MATH METHOD

We've labelled our triangle sides *a, b,* and *c* for a very specific reason. Those who studied geometry may recall the formula used for determining the hypotenuse—the diagonal line—of a right triangle: $a^2 + b^2 = c^2$ [that is, $(a \times a) + (b \times b) = c \times c$]. With this formula and the measurements of two sides of a given right triangle, it is possible to figure out the third.

In the present case, we already know the lengths of sides *b* and *c*. To calculate Side *a*, we'll adjust the basic formula to $c^2 - b^2 = a^2$. Then, $a = \sqrt{c^2 - b^2}$ (the square root of c squared minus b squared). If your pocket calculator has a square root symbol, it can do the work for you very easily.

Our guidelines for each cap style go through the math calculations to obtain the length of Side *a*. If you follow step by step, you should have no problem. If you do run into difficulty, you can always use the paper-and-ruler method.

Let's give our formula a tryout.

Math Method

STEP 1
$c^2 = c \times c = ?$
Example: 7 × 7 = 49

49

STEP 2
$b^2 = b \times b = ?$
Example: 3.1 × 3.1 = 9.6

9.6

STEP 3

Step 1 − Step 2 = $c^2 - b^2$ = ?
Example: 49 − 9.6 = 39.4

39.4

STEP 4

The square root of Step 3 = Side *a* = the height of the cap
To determine a square root with a calculator, put the number (here, the number calculated in Step 3) on your screen, then press the square root symbol.
Example: $\sqrt{39.4}$ *= 6.27*

6¼"

STEP 5

Step 4 × row gauge = number of rows for cap
Make this an even number (the next higher one).
Example: 6.27 × 6 = 37.62

38 rows

Tapering the Cap. The cap is tapered by decreasing one stitch on each end of a row a specific number of times. Once you establish the number of rows in the sleeve cap (as above), you can calculate the rate of decrease by means of the Taper Formula.

Although we used a straight-sided, right-angled "cap triangle" as a means to calculate the number of rows in the cap, a "real-life" Set-In Cap should have a domed, bell shape. To get this shape, some portions of the cap edge will be decreased at a faster rate (spreading pairs of single decreases over a smaller number of rows—usually every other row), and some at a slower rate (spreading a given number of decreases over a larger number of rows).

The general rule for distributing decreases over the height of the cap is to work one-half of the "faster" decreases at the start of the taper, then work all of the "slower" decreases, and finish with the remaining "faster" decreases. If the total number of "faster" decreases is odd, work the extra decrease at the start of the taper, as illustrated in Cap *a*.

To soften the change from the decreases to the final bind-off at the top of the cap, one or two two-stitch bind-offs (or double decreases, see "How Tos") can be worked in place of the last one or two single decreases. If this is done, increase the number of "slower" decreases by an equivalent amount, as illustrated in Cap *b*. For instance, if you substitute one pair of double decreases for a pair of single decreases at the top of a cap, then you will also substitute one pair of "slower" decreases for a pair of "faster" decreases at the centers of the side edges. It often helps to calculate and graph the cap using the method in Cap *a,* then make the changes for Cap *b* on the graph.

If you have chosen the Alternate Set-In Armhole shaping for the body of the garment, start your cap with the same number of shaping bind-offs as the armhole. The distribution of the decreases can be done in either of the methods described above. Cap *c,* our example, is done with the method used for Cap *a*.

The tapers described above will give you a nicely shaped Set-In Cap. Two knitters charting from identical numbers could work different tapers, but each finished cap would fit the armhole perfectly.

One more word before we proceed to the actual charting. If you're knitting by hand, measure the cap against the yoke before binding off the final row. If any adjustments need to be made, it's better to find out and make them at this point, rather than when you are assembling the garment.

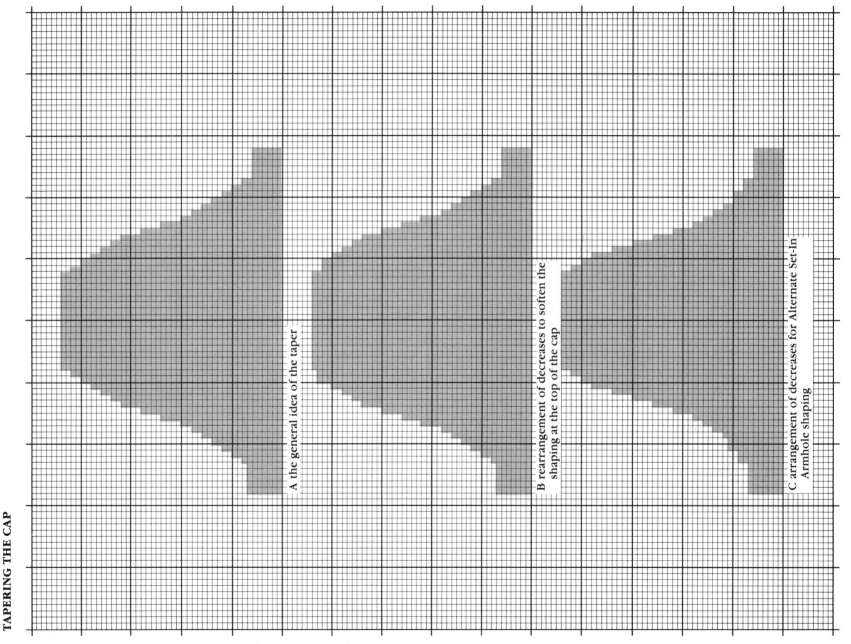

TAPERING THE CAP

A the general idea of the taper

B rearrangement of decreases to soften the shaping at the top of the cap

C arrangement of decreases for Alternate Set-In Armhole shaping

Tapered Sleeve and Classic Set-In Cap, labelled TS

The Tapered Sleeve with Classic Set-In Cap is the most traditional of all sleeve shapes, and is never out of style.

The sleeve can have a hem, border, ribbing, or turned-up cuff. In most cases, the hem, border, or ribbing is worked on needles two or three sizes smaller than those used for the sleeve itself.

When charting the cap, we will refer to the Curve Measurement of the back armhole and to the Cap Triangle. Both are explained above.

A thorough understanding of both Tapered Sleeve and Classic Set-In Cap is important before charting other styles. Like the Classic Body (CB), this combination will be a reference style for other patterns. We will refer to it as "TS" for "Tapered Sleeve."

Note: In the fundamental sections on the Classic Body (page 57) and the Tapered Sleeve, we've put a mark (*) next to the steps which result in actual numbers necessary for knitting.

Tapered Sleeve

*TS/STEP 1

(Wrist Measurement + Ease) × stitch gauge = number of stitches to cast on
- If the knuckle measurement is larger than (Wrist Measurement + Ease), use it instead; add no ease.
  For flat knitting, add two stitches for sleeve seam.
Example: (5.75 + 1 = 6.75) × 5 = 33.75   *34 stitches*

TS/STEP 2

(Upperarm Measurement + Ease) × stitch gauge = number of stitches at top of sleeve section
- If Step 1 is an even number, make Step 2 even. If Step 1 is odd, make Step 2 odd.
  For flat knitting, add two stitches for sleeve seam.
Example: (10.25 + 1 = 11.25) × 5 = 56.25   *56 stitches*

TS/STEP 3

TS/Step 2 – TS/Step 1 = total number of stitches to increase along side edges
Example: 56 – 34 = 22   *22 stitches*

*TS/STEP 4

TS/Step 3 ÷ 2 = number of stitches to increase per side edge
Example: 22 ÷ 2 = 11   *11 stitches*

TS/STEP 5

(Sleeve Length Measurement – 3″ to 4″) – length of ribbing or cuff finish, if applicable = number of inches over which increases will be made
On a narrow or medium-fitting sleeve, the taper should end 3″ to 4″ below the armhole bind-off, in consideration of the thickness of the arm at that point. On very wide sleeves, the taper can continue to the armhole bind-off level. The 1″ difference in Step 5 will give you room to play with your calculations in order to arrive at the smoothest possible taper.
Example: (17.5 – 3 = 14.5) – 3 = 11.5
(17.5 – 4 = 13.5) – 3 = 10.5   *10½″ to 11½″*

TS/STEP 6

TS/Step 5 × row gauge = number of rows over which increases will be made
Make this an even number.
Example: 10.5 × 6 = 63
11.5 × 6 = 69   *64 to 70 rows*

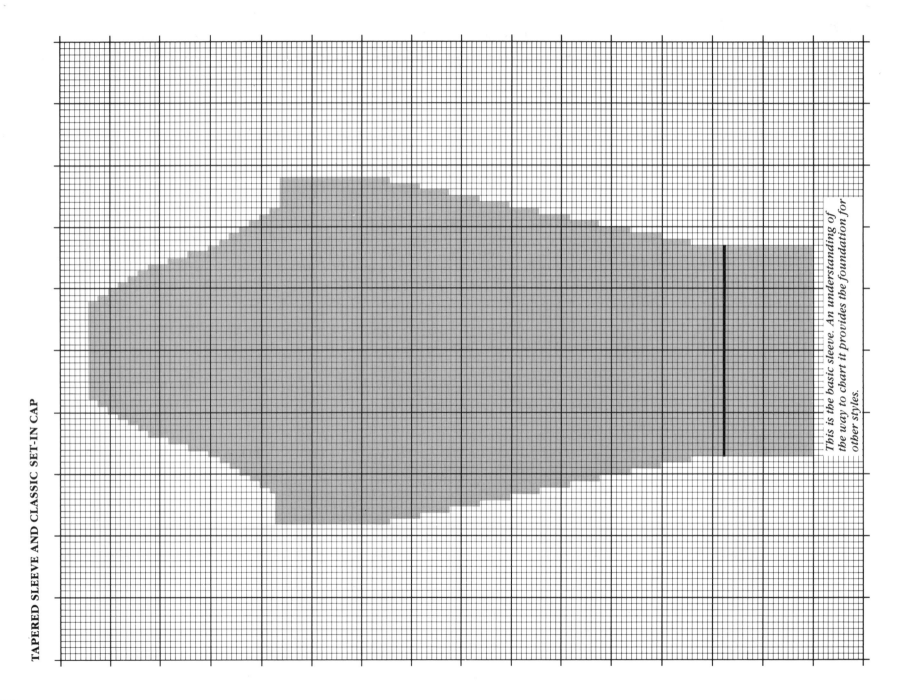

TAPERED SLEEVE AND CLASSIC SET-IN CAP

This is the basic sleeve. An understanding of the way to chart it provides the foundation for other styles.

198

*TS/STEP 7
TS/Step 6 ÷ TS/Step 4 = position of rows on which to work increases
See Taper Formula to figure the distribution of the increases.
In our example, if we increase 1 stitch per edge on every 6th row, we will complete our taper within the 3″ to 4″ below the armhole shaping.
Example: 64 ÷ 11 = 5.8
70 ÷ 11 = 6.3   *Every 6th row*

*TS/STEP 8
After the increases are complete, work even for 3″ to 4″, to the Sleeve Length Measurement.
Example: *17½″*

Classic Set-In Cap

*TS/STEP 9
Bind off the same number of stitches per armhole as for Set-In Armhole shaping (CB/Step 8).
- If you have used the Alternate Set-In Armhole shaping on the yoke, work the start of your cap taper to match.
Example: *5 stitches*

TS/STEP 10
Finished Width at top of cap × stitch gauge = number of stitches at top of cap
- If TS/Step 2 is an even number, make TS/Step 10 even.
- If TS/Step 2 is odd, make TS/Step 10 odd.
Example: 3 × 5 = 15   *16 stitches*

TS/STEP 11
TS/Step 2 – (TS/Step 9 × 2) = number of stitches at start of cap taper
Example: 56 – (5 × 2 = 10) = 46   *46 stitches*

TS/STEP 12
(TS/Step 11 – TS/Step 10) ÷ 2 = number of stitches to decrease per cap edge
Example: (46 – 16 = 30) ÷ 2 = 15   *15 stitches*

TS/STEP 13
a. Curve Measurement of the back armhole – ½ Finished Width at top of cap = Cap Triangle Side *c*
Example: 8.5 – 1.5 = 7   *7″*
b. TS/Step 12 ÷ stitch gauge = Cap Triangle Side *b*
Example: 15 ÷ 5 = 3   *3″*

c. Take square root of: [(TS/Step 13a × TS/Step 13a) − (TS/Step 13b × TS/Step 13b)] = Cap Triangle Side *a*

■ or, if you wish, use the "Paper-and-Ruler Method."

Example: (7 × 7 = 49) − (3 × 3 = 9) = 40
$$\sqrt{40} = 6.32$$

6.32"

d. Side *a* × row gauge = number of rows for cap height
Make this an even number.
Example: 6.32 × 6 = 37.92

38 rows

TS/STEP 14

TS/Step 13d ÷ TS/Step 12 = position of rows on which to work decreases
Make this an even number.
Example: 38 ÷ 15 = 2.5

Every 2nd or 4th row

*TS/STEP 15

a. Use Taper Formula to determine distribution of decreases.
Example: *4 decreases every 4th row, 11 every 2nd row*
b. Group decreases to make bell shape.
Example: *6 every 2nd row, 4 every 4th row, 5 every 2nd row*

*TS/STEP 16

Bind off remaining stitches.

If we translate our Tapered Sleeve and Set-In Sleeve Cap instructions to read like a printed pattern, this is how they would look.

Sleeve: Using smaller needles, cast on 34 stitches (*TS/Step 1*). K1, P1, in ribbing for 3". Change to larger needles and work in pattern stitch, increasing 1 stitch at each end of the needle every 6 rows (*TS/Step 7*) 11 times (*TS/Step 4*). Work even for 3" to 4" until sleeve measures 17½" (Sleeve Length Measurement).

Sleeve Cap: At the beginning of the next 2 rows, bind off 5 stitches (*TS/Step 9*). Decrease 1 stitch at each end of the needle on every other row 6 times; decrease 1 stitch at each end of the needle on every fourth row 4 times; decrease 1 stitch at each end of the needle on every other row 5 times (*TS/Step 15*); and bind off the remaining stitches (*TS/Step 16*).

Lantern Sleeve

A Lantern Sleeve is distinguished by the gathers immediately above a snug-fitting cuff. The cuff treatment can be a ribbing or any type of border stitch.

On a Full Lantern Sleeve, all of the increases are made immediately above the cuff. For less fullness, combine a Lantern Sleeve with a Tapered Sleeve; make half of the increases directly above the cuff, and taper the remainder along the side edges.

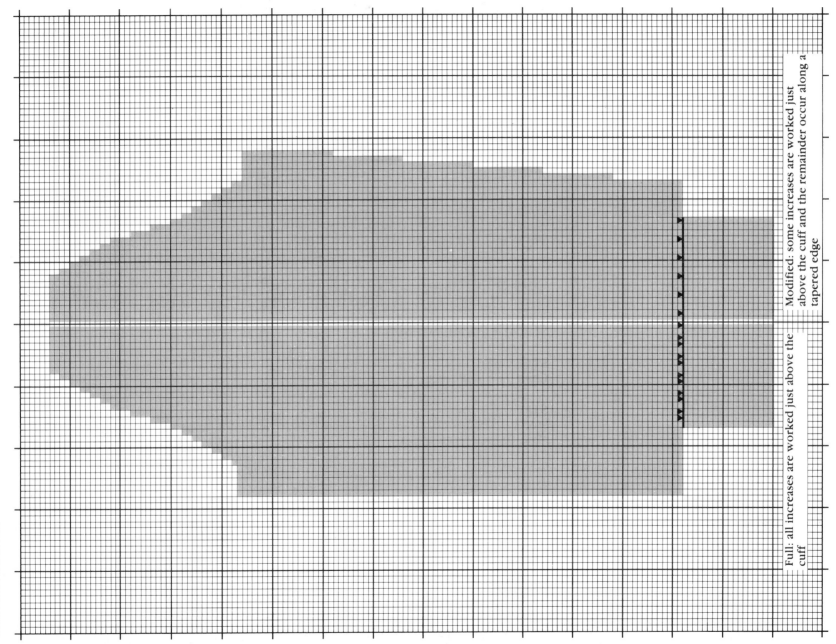

Modified: some increases are worked just above the cuff and the remainder occur along a tapered edge

Full: all increases are worked just above the cuff

Full Lantern Sleeve

STEPS 1-3
Chart Tapered Sleeve through TS/Step 3.

STEP 4
TS/Step 1 ÷ TS/Step 3 = position of stitches in which to work increases
Distribute increases evenly across sleeve width, directly above the cuff (see Gathers Formula).
Example: 34 ÷ 22 = 1.5   *Increase every 1 or 2 stitches*

STEP 5
Work even to the Sleeve Length Measurement.
An extra 1″ to 3″ can be added to the Sleeve Length Measurement, to create a bloused effect.

Modified Lantern Sleeve

STEPS 1-3
Chart Tapered Sleeve through TS/Step 3.

STEP 4
Step 3 ÷ 2 = number of stitches to increase immediately above the cuff
Make this an even number.
Example: 22 ÷ 2 = 11   *12 stitches*

STEP 5
Step 1 ÷ Step 4 = number of stitches between increases directly above the cuff
See Gathers Formula for help in spacing increases.
Example: 34 ÷ 12 = 2.8   *Increase every 2 or 3 stitches*

STEP 6
(TS/Step 3 − Step 4) ÷ 2 = number of stitches to increase at each side edge of sleeve
Example: (22 − 12 = 10) ÷ 2 = 5   *5 stitches*

STEPS 7-10
Work TS/Step 5 through TS/Step 8.
Consider adding extra length for blousing, as in Full Lantern Sleeve, Step 5.

Bishop Sleeve

On a Bishop Sleeve, very full gathers are made immediately above a tight-fitting cuff by increasing in every stitch. The sleeve then tapers inward to the armhole shaping.

The cuff treatment can be ribbing or any type of border stitch, with or without an opening. (For knitted openings, see "Plackets.")

Bishop Sleeve

STEP 1

Cast on TS/Step 1 number of stitches, and knit cuff.

STEP 2

TS/Step 1 × 2 = number of stitches on needle after increases are made

Distribute increases evenly across width of sleeve, directly above cuff (see Gathers Formula).

Example: 34 × 2 = 68   *68 stitches*

STEP 3

(Step 2 − TS/Step 2) ÷ 2 = number of stitches to decrease per side edge

Example: (68 − 56 = 12) ÷ 2 = 6   *6 stitches*

STEP 4

(Sleeve Length Measurement − length of cuff − 1″) × row gauge = number of rows over which decreases will be made

The taper should end about 1″ below the armhole bind-off.

Make this an even number.

■ If you wish, you can add 1″ to 3″ of ease to the sleeve length, for blousing.

Example: (17.5 − 3 − 1 = 13.5) × 6 = 81   *82 rows*

STEP 5

Step 4 ÷ Step 3 = number of rows on which to work decreases. See Taper Formula to determine exact placement of decreases.

Example: 82 ÷ 6 = 13.6   *Every 12th or 14th row*

STEP 6

Work to Sleeve Length Measurement.

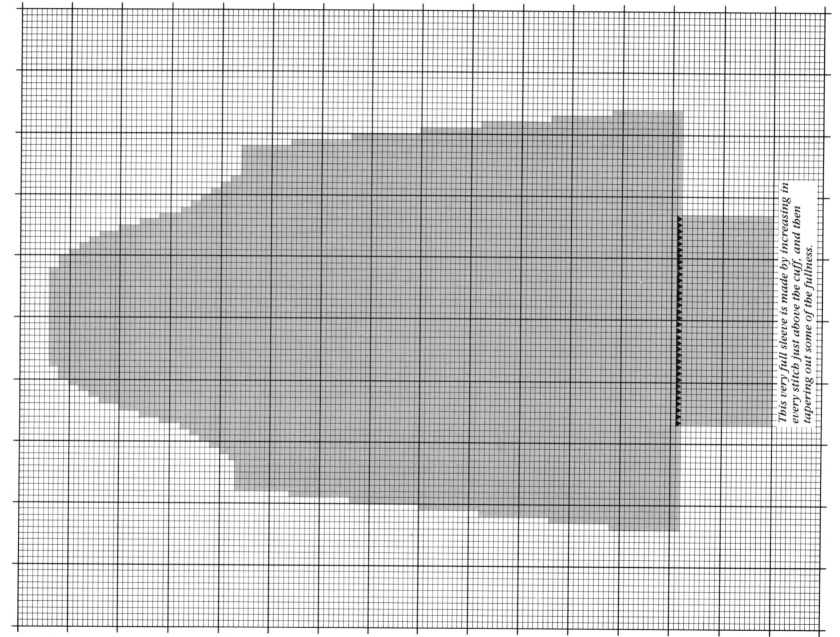

This very full sleeve is made by increasing in every stitch just above the cuff, and then tapering out some of the fullness.

BISHOP SLEEVE

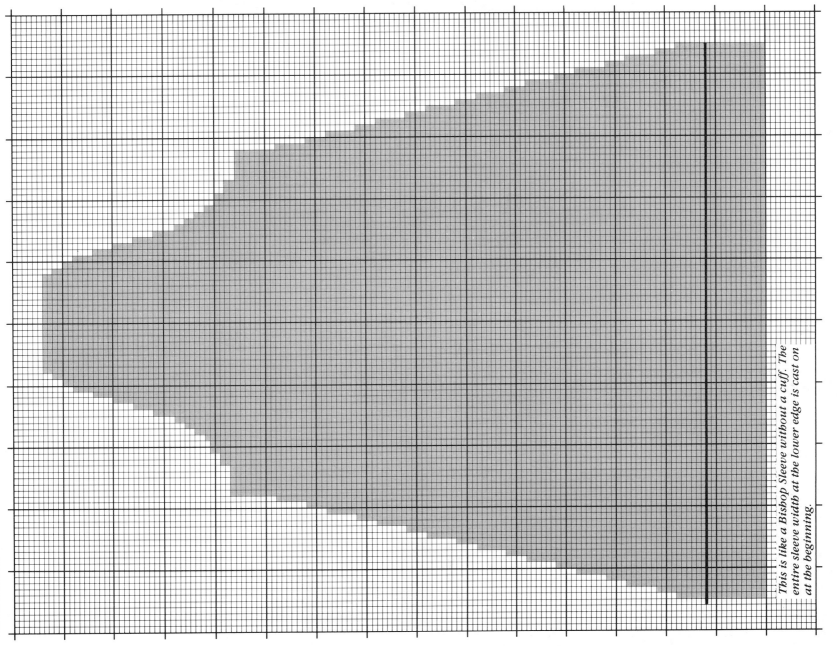

BELL SLEEVE

This is like a Bishop Sleeve without a cuff. The entire sleeve width at the lower edge is cast on at the beginning.

Bell Sleeve

A Bell Sleeve is similar in its tapering to a Bishop Sleeve, but does not have a tight-fitting cuff. The stitch equivalent of the entire sleeve width at the lower edge is cast onto your needle, and the sleeve tapers inward to the armhole shaping.

The cuff treatment can be a hem or border stitch.

The bottom sleeve width is up to you. Our example will be 18″ wide and have a 2″ deep border.

Leg o' Mutton Sleeve

The Leg o' Mutton begins as a close-fitting tapered sleeve, and blouses out at any point of the arm you choose. The entire tapered portion can be worked in ribbing for a tighter fit.

For the Leg o' Mutton Sleeve, you'll need to take two new measurements.

a. Measure from the wrist straight up the arm to where the sleeve fullness will begin.
b. Measure the circumference of the arm where the sleeve fullness will begin.

For our example, Measurement *a* will be 6½″, and Measurement *b* will be 7¾″.

We give directions for knitting both a Full Leg o' Mutton Sleeve and a Modified (less full) version.

Because of its fullness at the upper-arm, the Leg o' Mutton Sleeve should be finished with either a Gathered, Pleated, or Designer's Choice Sleeve Cap.

Bell Sleeve

STEP 1
Width of sleeve at lower edge × stitch gauge = number of stitches to cast on
- If knitting flat, add two stitches for sleeve seam.
Example: 18 × 5 = 90   *90 stitches*

STEP 2
(Upperarm Measurement + Ease) × stitch gauge = number of stitches at top of sleeve
- If Step 1 is an even number, make Step 2 even.
- If Step 1 is odd, make Step 2 odd.
- If knitting flat, add two stitches for sleeve seam.
Example: (10.25 + 1 = 11.25) × 5 = 56.2   *56 stitches*

STEP 3
(Step 1 − Step 2) ÷ 2 = number of stitches to decrease per side edge
Example: (90 − 56 = 34) ÷ 2 = 17   *17 stitches*

STEP 4
(Sleeve Length Measurement − length of cuff if applicable − 1″) × row gauge = number of rows over which decreases will be made
The taper should end about 1″ below the armhole bind-off.
Make this an even number.
Example: (17.5 − 2 − 1 = 14.5) × 6 = 87   *88 rows*

STEP 5
Step 4 ÷ Step 3 = number of rows between increases
See Taper Formula for distribution of increases.
Example: 88 ÷ 17 = 5.1   *Every 4th or 6th row*

STEP 6
Work even to Sleeve Length Measurement.

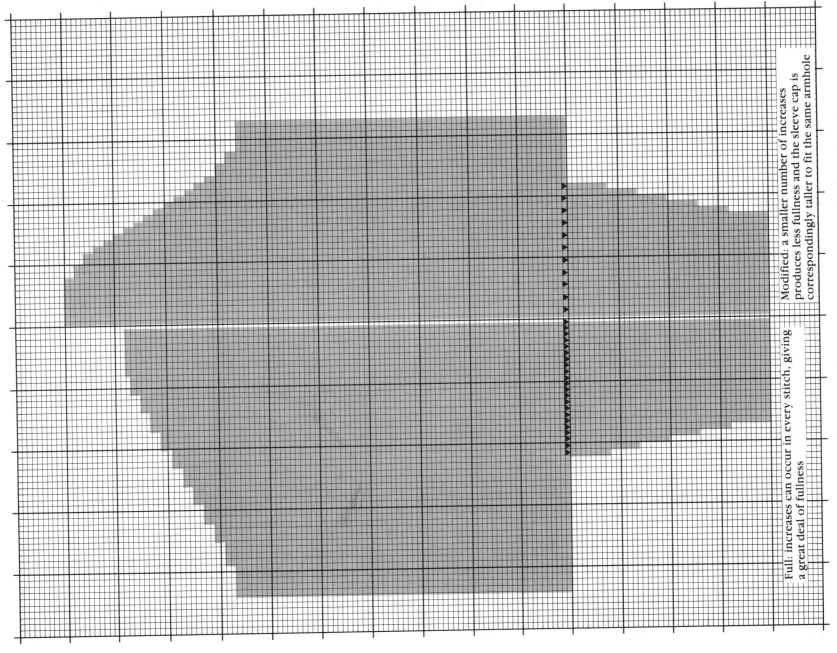

Modified: a smaller number of increases produces less fullness and the sleeve cap is correspondingly taller to fit the same armhole

Full: increases can occur in every stitch, giving a great deal of fullness

VARIATIONS OF THE LEG O' MUTTON SLEEVE

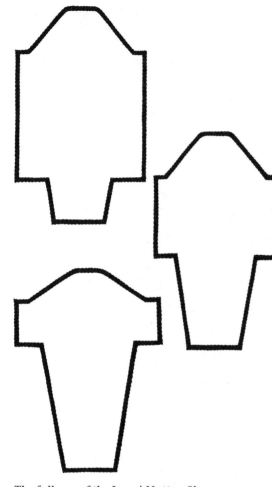

The fullness of the Leg o' Mutton Sleeve can occur at any point on the arm. Because of this sleeve's fullness, it should be finished with a Gathered, Pleated, or Designer's Choice Cap.

Leg o' Mutton Sleeve

STEP 1
TS/Step 1 = number of stitches to cast on
Example: *34 stitches*

STEP 2
(Measurement b + 1″ ease) × stitch gauge = number of stitches where sleeve fullness will begin
- If Step 1 is an even number, make Step 2 even.
- If Step 1 is odd, make Step 2 odd.
- If knitting flat, add two stitches for sleeve seam.

Example: (7.75 + 1 = 8.75) × 5 = 43.75   *44 stitches*

STEP 3
(Step 2 − Step 1) ÷ 2 = number of stitches to increase per side edge
Example: (44 − 34 = 10) ÷ 2 = 5   *5 stitches*

STEP 4
Measurement a × row gauge = number of rows to the start of sleeve fullness
Make this an even number.
Example: 6.5 × 6 = 39   *40 rows*

STEP 5
Step 4 ÷ (Step 3 + 1) = number of rows between increases
See Taper Formula to determine exact sequence.
The sleeve fullness increases will occur on the row where you normally would work your last taper increases. In order to make the correct number of increases within the number of rows in the tapered section on the sleeve, an extra increase (the " + 1") is used in the calculations. *No taper increase is actually worked on this row.*
Example: 40 ÷ (5 + 1 = 6) = 6.7   *Every 6th or 8th row*

STEP 6
a. **Full Leg o' Mutton Sleeve:**
   Make one increase in every stitch.
b. **Modified Leg o' Mutton Sleeve:**
   Make one increase in every other stitch.

STEP 7

Work even to the Sleeve Length Measurement.

- If you wish, 1″ to 3″ of ease can be added to the sleeve length, in the wider sleeve portion, to allow for blousing.

Straight Sleeve

A Straight Sleeve has no taper along the side edges. It is worked even on the cast-on stitches to the beginning of the cap shaping.

The wrist finish can be a border pattern, a rolled cuff, or a hem. This last finish can serve as a casing for elastic, or, if buttonholes are worked into the hem, a drawstring can be inserted to gather the sleeve.

Straight Sleeve

STEP 1

(Upperarm Measurement + Ease) × stitch gauge = number of stitches to cast on

- If working flat, add two stitches for sleeve seam.

Example: (10.25 + 1 = 11.25) × 5 = 56.2   *56 stitches*

STEP 2

Work even on Step 1 number of stitches to the Sleeve Length Measurement.

Funnel Sleeve

Some styles require a large number of stitches at the top of the sleeve, for instance, a Gathered or Pleated Sleeve Cap, or a Basic or Modified T.

However, you may prefer not to have an even taper or a very wide sleeve below the elbow. The solution is a Funnel-Shaped Sleeve. From the wrist to the elbow, this sleeve can be Tapered, Lantern, or Straight. Above the elbow, the shape takes on a broad taper, reminiscent of the top of a funnel.

To chart this sleeve, use the guidelines for a Tapered Sleeve, then gradually increase from the number of stitches on your needle at the elbow to the number of stitches needed at the top of your sleeve. (Use the Taper Formula to work out where the increases should occur.)

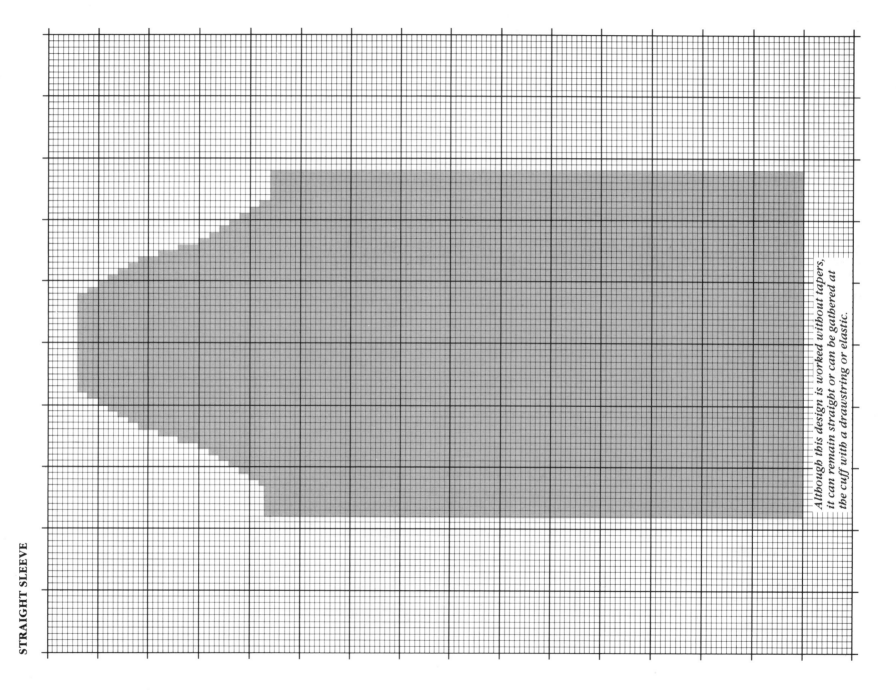

Although this design is worked without tapers, it can remain straight or can be gathered at the cuff with a drawstring or elastic.

STRAIGHT SLEEVE

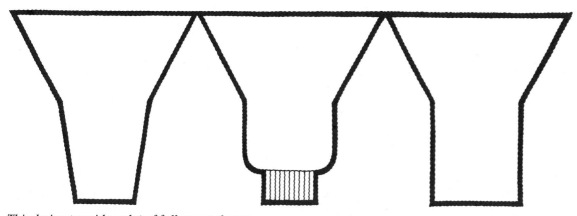

This design provides a lot of fullness at the top of the sleeve. Below the elbow, it can be Tapered, Lantern, or Straight.

Since the sleeve at the upperarm will be wide, the taper can continue to the armhole shaping.

Increases do not have to occur at the edges of the sleeve only. Decorative increases can be planned within the body of the sleeve, either alone or in combination with edge increases.

Gathered Cap

This cap has extra fullness at the top, which is decreased to the Finished Width within the last two rows of knitting.

The Finished Width at the top of an adult Gathered Cap should be between 2″ and 4″, with 1½″ to 3″ for youths, and 1″ to 2″ for children. Remember that you are working with a Finished Width when calculating your cap height.

The Unfinished width at the top of a Gathered Cap is four times the Finished Width. For instance, a gathered Finished Width of 2″ requires an 8″ width of stitches, 3″ requires 12″, and 4″ requires 16″. It is wise to plan the upper width of your sleeve with that in mind. We will use a Finished Width of 2″ in our example.

Because of the rather wide Unfinished Width, many Gathered Caps require no taper along the edges. We do, however, recommend several single decreases per edge on every other row at the top, just before the gathers are worked. This softens the corners, avoiding an abrupt angle where the side edges and gathers meet. As a rule of thumb, we recommend that you decrease the same number of stitches per edge as you decreased for the armhole shaping on your yoke (CB/Step 9).

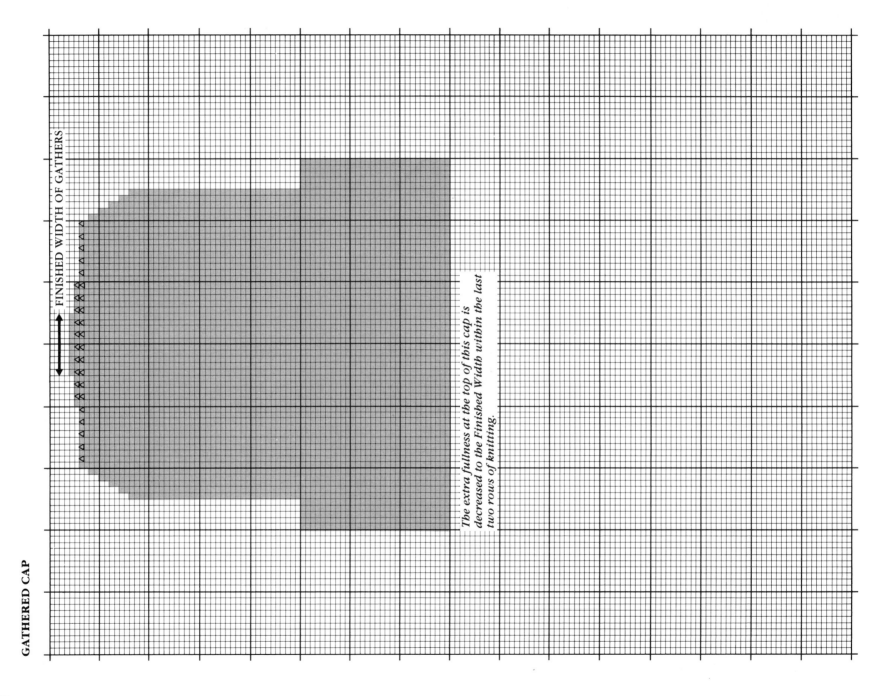

FINISHED WIDTH OF GATHERS

The extra fullness at the top of this cap is decreased to the Finished Width within the last two rows of knitting.

GATHERED CAP

212

Gathered Cap

STEP 1

(Finished Width of gathers × 4 × stitch gauge) + total number of armhole shaping stitches on yoke (CB/Step 6) = minimum number of stitches for top of sleeve

Your sleeve can be wider. Decrease any additional stitches by tapering along the side edges as on any Set-In Cap.

Example: (2 × 4 × 5 = 40) + 20 = 60   *60 stitches*

STEP 2

Bind off the same number of stitches per armhole as for Set-In Armhole shaping (CB/Step 8).

Example: *5 stitches*

STEP 3

Number of stitches at top of sleeve − (Step 2 × 2) = number of stitches at start of cap taper

Example: 60 − (5 × 2 = 10) = 50   *50 stitches*

STEP 4

Finished Width of gathers × 4 × stitch gauge = number of stitches required for gathers

- If Step 3 is an even number, make Step 4 even.
- If Step 3 is odd, make Step 4 odd.

Example: 2 × 4 × 5 = 40   *40 stitches*

STEP 5

(Step 3 − Step 4) ÷ 2 = number of stitches to decrease per side edge

Example: (50 − 40 = 10) ÷ 2 = 5   *5 stitches*

STEP 6

a. Curve Measurement of the back armhole − ¹/₂ Finished Width at top of cap = Cap Triangle Side *c*

Example: 8.5 − 1 = 7.5   *7.5"*

b. Step 5 ÷ stitch gauge = Cap Triangle Side *b*

Example: 5 ÷ 5 = 1   *1"*

c. Take square root of [(Step 6a × Step 6a) − (Step 6b × Step 6b)] = Cap Triangle Side *a*

Example: (7.5 × 7.5 = 56.25) − (1 × 1 = 1) = 55.25
$\sqrt{55.25}$ *= 7.43*   *7.43"*

d. Step 6c × row gauge = number of rows for cap
   Make this an even number.

Example: 7.43 × 6 = 44.58   *46 rows*

STEP 7

Plan the taper (see "Tapering the Cap"), working several of the decreases near the top of the cap to soften the corners.

Plan the decreases to end two rows short of the number of rows in Step 6d. The top two rows of a Gathered Cap are used to work the gathers.

STEP 8

Work 2 together across the next row.
Example: 40 ÷ 2 = 20   *20 stitches*

STEP 9

Repeat Step 8, binding off as you work across.
Example: 20 ÷ 2 = 10   *10 stitches*

EXPANDED CAP SHAPING

How do you put a full cap on a narrow sleeve? When you're familiar with the ideas in this guide, you'll be able to solve your way out of any knitting problem.

Expanded Cap Shaping

We are including this cap shaping as an excellent example of problem solving. It shows how an understanding of charting can lead to a solution for a particular problem.

The problem is how to knit a narrow sleeve with a very full Gathered, Pleated, or Designer's Choice Cap.

The solution is to expand the cap after the initial bind-off by working increases within the fabric. By increasing within the fabric, the side edges are fanned out rather than tapered. (On Gathered and Pleated Caps, we do still recommend edge decreases at the top, as explained in the individual guidelines.)

Charting the cap height is simple. From your Curve Measurement, subtract the Finished Width at the cap top. The result is the cap height.

Pleated Cap

Pleated Caps are similar to Gathered Caps, in that they incorporate extra fullness at the top. They differ in the way they reduce that fullness down to the Finished Width of the cap and also in the amount of fullness: Gathered Caps have greater Unfinished Widths than Pleated Caps.

The Finished Width of pleats at the top of an adult cap should be between 2" and 4", with 1½" to 3" for youth sizes and 1" to 2" for children. Remember that you are working with a Finished Width when calculating your cap height. We will use a Finished Width of 2" in our example.

The Unfinished Width at the top of a Pleated Cap is three times the finished width. In other words, 2" of pleats require a 6" width of knitting, 3" require 9", and 4" require 12". Make sure that your upper sleeve will be wide enough for the pleated width you want.

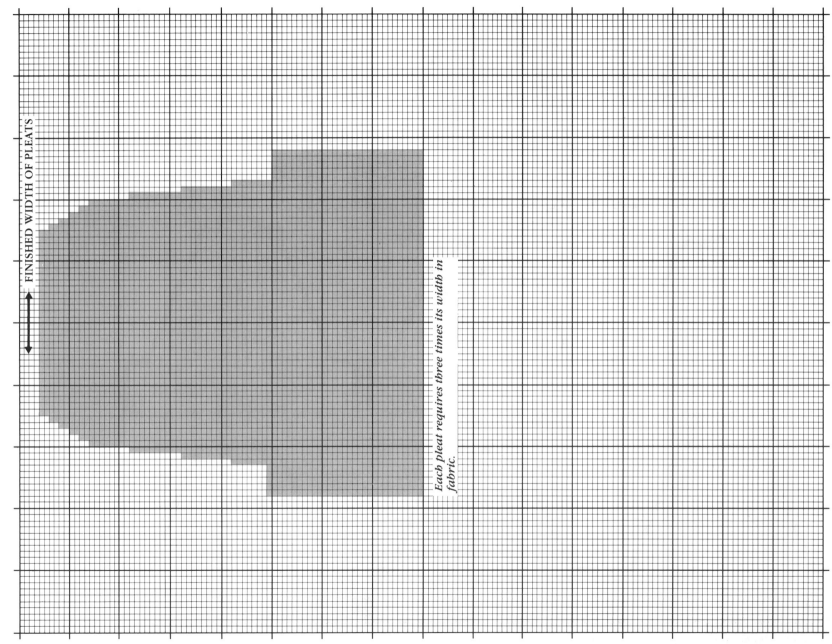

FINISHED WIDTH OF PLEATS

Each pleat requires three times its width in fabric.

PLEATED CAP

VARIATIONS OF THE PLEATED CAP

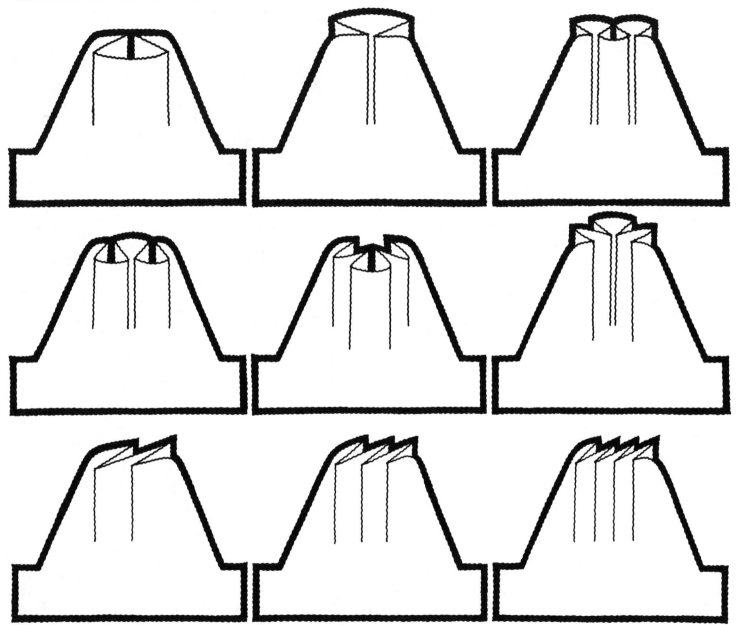

Pleats can be single, double, triple, or more. They can be folded to the inside, the outside, the right or left, or symmetrically from the center.

As with a Gathered Cap, we recommend working several single decreases per edge on every other row at the top, right before the bind-off. This softens the corners, avoiding an abrupt angle where the side edges and pleats meet.

Decrease approximately the same number of stitches per edge as you decreased for the armhole shaping on your yoke (CB/Step 9).

Pleated Cap

STEP 1
(Finished Width of pleats in inches × 3 × stitch gauge) + total number of armhole shaping stitches on yoke (CB/Step 6) = minimum number of stitches for top of sleeve (at beginning of cap)
Your sleeve can be wider. Decrease any additional stitches by tapering along the side edges as on any Set-In Cap.
Example: (2 × 3 × 5 = 30) + 20 = 50   *50 stitches*

STEP 2
Bind off the same number of stitches per armhole as for Set-In Armhole shaping (CB/Step 8).
Example: *5 stitches*

STEP 3
Number of stitches at top of sleeve − (Step 2 × 2) = number of stitches at start of cap taper
Example: 56 − (5 × 2 = 10) = 46   *46 stitches*

STEP 4
Finished Width of pleats in inches × 3 × stitch gauge = number of stitches required for pleats
■ If Step 3 is an even number, make Step 4 even. If Step 3 is odd, make Step 4 odd.
Example: 2 × 3 × 5 = 30   *30 stitches*

STEP 5
(Step 3 − Step 4) ÷ 2 = number of stitches to decrease per side edge
Example: (46 − 30 = 16) ÷ 2 = 8   *8 stitches*

STEP 6
a. Curve Measurement of the back armhole − $\frac{1}{2}$ Finished Width at top of cap = Cap Triangle Side *c*
Example: 8.5 − 1 = 7.5   *7$\frac{1}{2}$"*
b. Step 5 ÷ stitch gauge = Cap Triangle Side *b*
Example: 5 ÷ 5 = 1   *1"*

c. Take square root of [(Step 6a × Step 6a) – (Step 6b × Step 6b)] = Cap Triangle Side *a*
Example: (7.5 × 7.5 = 56.25) – (1 × 1 = 1) = 55.25
$\sqrt{55.25}$ *= 7.43*   *7.43"*
d. Step 6c × row gauge = number of rows for cap.
   Make this an even number.
Example: 7.43 × 6 = 44.58   *46 rows*

STEP 7
Plan the taper (see "Tapering the Cap"), working several of the decreases near the top of the cap to soften the corners.

STEP 8
Bind off remaining stitches. (For a method of binding off and pleating at the same time, see "How Tos".)

STEP 9
Pleat in any manner you wish, from one large pleat to several small ones across the top. Remember, if your pleats face in one direction, each cap must be a mirror image of the other.

VARIATIONS OF THE BOX CAP

CLASSIC BODY
WITH SET-IN
BOX CAP

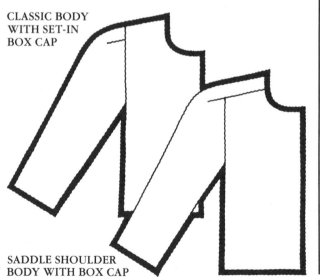

SADDLE SHOULDER
BODY WITH BOX CAP

Box Cap

Just as its name implies, the Box Cap results in a garment with a boxy look, due to the fact that the cap extends straight out past the normal shoulder line.

   This cap is formed by a dart on either side of the bound-off stitches at the top. The Finished Width of these bound-off stitches should be between 1″ and 3″. The amount varies with your choice of yarn: 1″ to 2″ is suitable for fine- to medium-weight yarns, 2″ to 3″ for heavy and bulky-weight yarns. We will use 2″ in our example.

   You will also need to decide on the depth of the darts. We recommend 1″, with 2″ as a maximum if you're aiming for extreme shoulder emphasis. This will be the distance the cap sits away from each shoulder, and shoulder pads usually are required for proper shaping. We will use 1″ in our example.

   The Unfinished Width of a Box Cap is the Finished Width plus the depth of both darts. For example, a cap with a 2″ Finished Width and 1″ darts would have an Unfinished Width of 4″.

   The height of the cap is calculated to the dart shaping, and does not include the extension above the bound-off dart edges. All taper decreases must be made before these bind-offs occur.

   Because this cap extends past the normal shoulder line, the shoulder width can be narrowed by subtracting 1″ to 2″ from the Shoulder Width Measurement. *Use this Adjusted Shoulder Width Measurement when charting the yoke of the garment.*

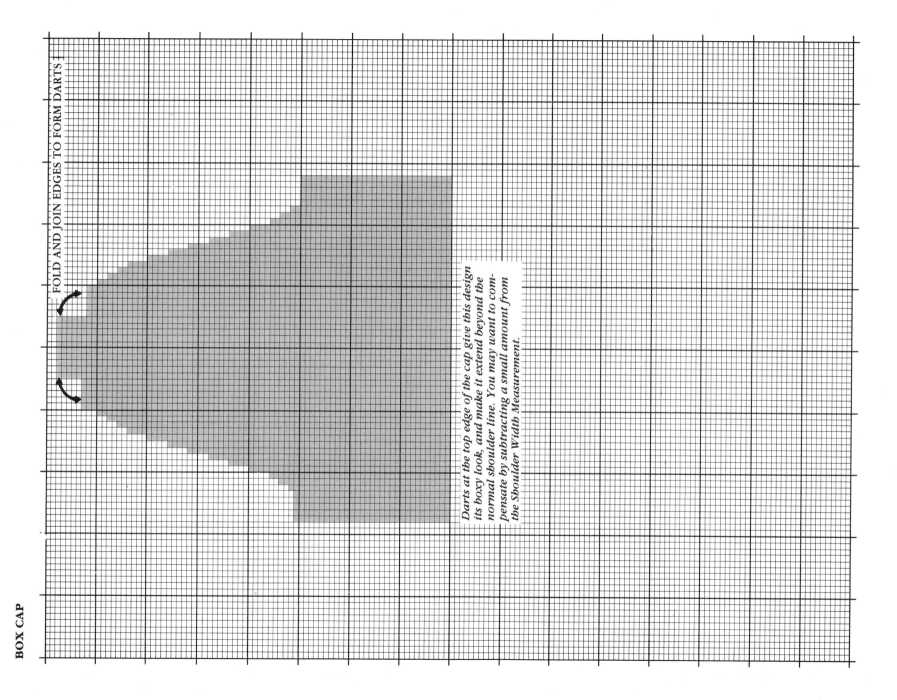

FOLD AND JOIN EDGES TO FORM DARTS

BOX CAP

Darts at the top edge of the cap give this design its boxy look, and make it extend beyond the normal shoulder line. You may want to compensate by subtracting a small amount from the Shoulder Width Measurement.

219

Box Cap

STEP 1

Bind off the same number of stitches per armhole as for Set-In Armhole shaping (CB/Step 8).
Example: *5 stitches*

STEP 2

Number of stitches at top of sleeve (TS/Step 2) − (Step 1 × 2) = number of stitches at start of cap taper
Example: 56 − (5 × 2 = 10) = 46   *46 stitches*

STEP 3

Finished Width of cap in inches + (depth of dart in inches × 2) × stitch gauge = number of stitches at top of cap for box shaping
■ If Step 2 is an even number, make Step 3 even. If Step 2 is odd, make Step 3 odd.
Example: 2 + (1 × 2 = 2) × 5 = 20   *20 stitches*

STEP 4

(Step 2 − Step 3) ÷ 2 = number of stitches to decrease per side edge
Example: (46 − 20 = 26) ÷ 2 = 13   *13 stitches*

STEP 5

a. Curve Measurement of the back armhole − ½ Finished Width at top of cap = Cap Triangle Side *c*
Example: 8.5 − 1 = 7.5   *7½"*
b. Step 4 ÷ stitch gauge = Cap Triangle Side *b*
Example: 13 ÷ 5 = 2.6   *2.6"*
c. Take square root of [(Step 5a × Step 5a) − (Step 5b × Step 5b)] = Cap Triangle Side *a*
Example: (7.5 × 7.5 = 56.25) − (2.6 × 2.6 = 6.76) = 49.49
$\sqrt{49.49} = 7$ *7"*
d. Step 5c × row gauge = number of rows for cap
   Make this an even number.
Example: 7 × 6 = 42   *42 rows*

STEP 6

Plan and work your cap taper. (See "Tapering the Cap.")

STEP 7
Depth of dart in inches × stitch gauge = number of stitches to bind off at the beginning of the next 2 rows
Example: 1 × 5 = 5   *5 stitches*

STEP 8
Work even on remaining stitches to the depth of the darts.
Example: *1″*

STEP 9
Bind off remaining stitches.

STEP 10
Sew edges together to form darts.

T-Square Cap

The top of this cap has two short bound-off sections which fold inward to make an interesting dart, reminiscent of an upside-down T-square. The dart will extend the cap away from the shoulder and probably will require a shoulder pad for proper fit.

The T-Square Cap differs from a "typical" Set-In Cap in a very important way. All of the stitches at the top are utilized for the dart, and none are sewn directly onto the yoke. This means that there is no Finished Width to consider when charting the cap height. The T-Square Cap will be taller than a "typical" Set-In Cap, in fact, almost as tall as the yoke itself.

There is, however, an Unfinished Width to determine for the dart shaping. The Unfinished Width will be *four times the depth of the dart.*

The average dart is about 1″ deep, but can be 1½″ to 2″ on very heavy garments or where extreme shoulder emphasis is desired. We will use 1″ in our example.

Because this cap extends past the normal shoulder line, the shoulder width can be narrowed by subtracting 1″ to 2″ from the Shoulder Width Measurement. *Use this Adjusted Shoulder Width Measurement when charting the yoke of the garment.* This is especially important if the fabric is stiff, since stiffness makes the sleeve quite boxy.

T-SQUARE CAP

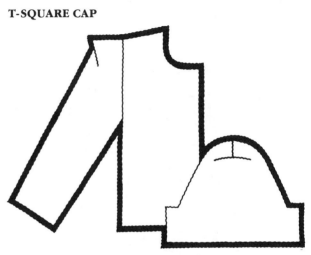

The top seam of the T-Square Cap looks like an extension of the shoulder seam.

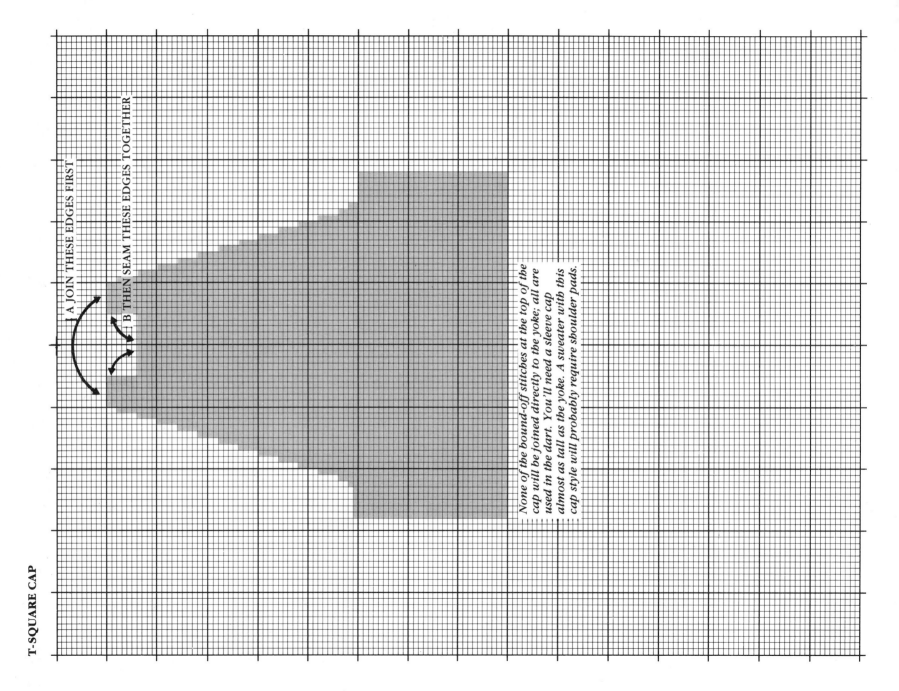

T-SQUARE CAP

A JOIN THESE EDGES FIRST

B THEN SEAM THESE EDGES TOGETHER

None of the bound-off stitches at the top of the cap will be joined directly to the yoke; all are used in the dart. You'll need a sleeve cap almost as tall as the yoke. A sweater with this cap style will probably require shoulder pads.

T-Square Cap

STEP 1
Bind off the same number of stitches per armhole as for Set-In Armhole shaping (CB/Step 8).
Example: *5 stitches*

STEP 2
Number of stitches at top of sleeve (TS/Step 2) − (Step 1 × 2) = number of stitches at start of cap taper
Example: 56 − (5 × 2 = 10) = 46   *46 stitches*

STEP 3
Depth of dart × 4 × stitch gauge = number of stitches at top of cap for dart shaping
■ If Step 2 is an even number, make Step 3 even.
■ If Step 2 is odd, make Step 3 odd.
Example: 1 × 4 × 5 = 20   *20 stitches*

STEP 4
(Step 2 − Step 3) ÷ 2 = number of stitches to decrease per side edge
Example: (46 − 20 = 26) ÷ 2 = 13   *13 stitches*

STEP 5
a. Curve Measurement of the back armhole = Cap Triangle Side *c*
Example: *8½"*
b. Step 4 ÷ stitch gauge = Cap Triangle Side *b*
Example: 13 ÷ 5 = 2.6   *2.6"*
c. Take square root of [(Step 5a × Step 5a) − (Step 5b × Step 5b)] = Cap Triangle Side *a*
Example: (8.5 × 8.5 = 72.25) − (2.6 × 2.6 = 6.76) = 65.49
        $\sqrt{65.49}$ *= 8.09*   *8.1"*
d. Step 5c × row gauge number of rows for cap
   Make this an even number.
Example: 8.1 × 6 = 48.6   *50 rows*

STEP 6
Depth of dart × row gauge = number of rows for dart shaping
Example: 1 × 6 = 6   *6 rows*

STEP 7
Plan and work your cap taper (see "Tapering the Cap") to the number of rows from the top calculated in Step 6. Your edge decreases will not necessarily be complete at this point.

STEP 8

Depth of dart × 2 × stitch gauge = number of stitches to bind off at center
- If you have an odd number of stitches on your needles, bind off an odd number. You must have an equal number of stitches remaining on each side of your needle after the bind-off.

Example: 1 × 2 × 5 = 10   *10 stitches*

STEP 9

1. Join an extra ball of yarn to one side, and work for depth of dart (Step 6). Work even at center edge. Complete decreases on side edges if necessary.
2. Using original yarn, complete second side as a mirror image of the first.

STEP 10

Bind off remaining stitches.

STEP 11

a. Sew bound-off edges of last stitches on needle together, or graft using kitchener stitch (see "How Tos").
b. Sew side edges of last-knit sections to center bound-off stitches.

Designer's Choice Cap

This cap is one of our favorites. It is an extended-shoulder variation of the Set-In Cap. After it is knit, the designer has a choice of various pleating or draping options for its finish. We have given you seven different versions of this cap. Inventive minds may come up with even more possibilities than we show here.

Assembly for all finishes is simple. You may find it a good idea to lightly baste each cap to try out different styles and see which you prefer for the particular garment.

In planning the cap height, there is no Finished Width to consider. All of the bound-off stitches at the top will be used in the shaping, rather than being set into the armhole. The cap will be taller than a typical Set-In Cap; it could even be as tall as the armhole is deep.

You will need to determine an Unfinished Width for the shaping. This Unfinished Width will vary slightly among the different versions. We will use 6″ in our example.

Because these caps extend past the normal shoulder line, the shoulder width can be narrowed by subtracting 1″ to 2″ from the Shoulder Width Measurement. Use this Adjusted Shoulder Width Measurement when charting the yoke of the garment. This is especially important if the fabric is stiff, since that makes the sleeve quite boxy.

Designer's Choice Cap Versions 1, 2, 3, 4, and 7 are suitable for any type of yarn, although the finished shape will be more pronounced with stiffer fabric. Versions 5 and 6 require a soft yarn such as rayon, silk, or alpaca to create a fabric with enough drape for the cap to fall into soft folds.

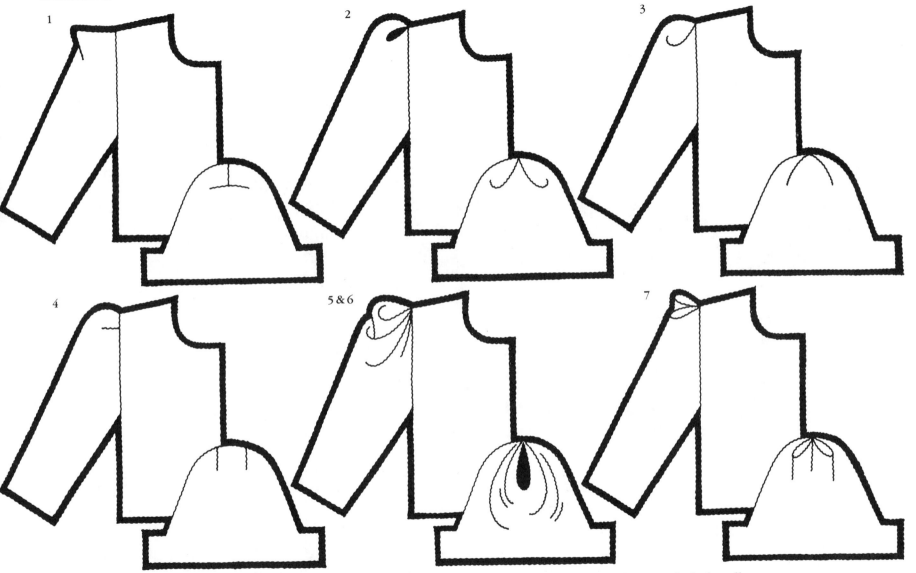

Most of these structures can be used with any type of yarn. Versions 5 and 6 do require a soft yarn that will drape particularly well.

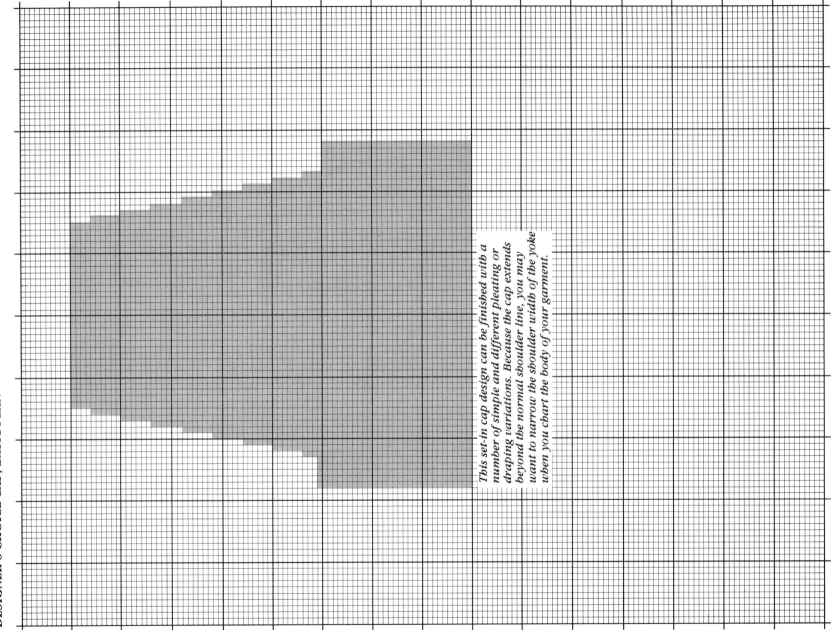

This set-in cap design can be finished with a number of simple and different pleating or draping variations. Because the cap extends beyond the normal shoulder line, you may want to narrow the shoulder width of the yoke when you chart the body of your garment.

Designer's Choice Cap Knitting Guidelines

STEP 1
Bind off the same number of stitches per armhole as for Set-In Armhole shaping (CB/Step 8).
Example: *5 stitches*

STEP 2
Number of stitches at top of sleeve (TS/Step 2) – (Step 1 × 2) = number of stitches at start of cap taper
Example: 56 – (5 × 2 = 10) = 46   *46 stitches*

STEP 3
Unfinished Width at top of cap in inches × stitch gauge = number of stitches to bind off at top of cap
- If Step 2 is an even number, make Step 3 even.
- If Step 2 is odd, make Step 3 odd.

Example: 6 × 5 = 30   *30 stitches*

STEP 4
(Step 2 – Step 3) ÷ 2 = number of stitches to decrease per side edge
Example: (46 – 30 = 16) ÷ 2 = 8   *8 stitches*

STEP 5
a. Curve Measurement of the back armhole = Cap Triangle Side *c*
Example: *8¹/₂"*
b. Step 4 ÷ stitch gauge = Cap Triangle Side *b*
Example: 8 ÷ 5 = 1.6   *1.6"*
c. Take square root of [(Step 5a × Step 5a) – (Step 5b × Step 5b)] = Cap Triangle Side *a*
Example: (8.5 × 8.5 = 72.25) – (1.6 × 1.6 = 2.56) = 69.69
        $\sqrt{69.69}$ = 8.34   *8.34"*
d. Step 5c × row gauge = number of rows for cap
   Make this an even number.
Example: 8.34 × 6 = 50   *50 rows*

STEP 6
Plan and work your cap taper. (See "Tapering the Cap.")

STEP 7
Versions 1, 2, 3, 4, and 5: Bind off remaining stitches.
Versions 6 and 7: Work a horizontal turning row (see "How Tos"), then knit a 1″ hem. Bind off.

STEP 8
Assemble your cap as described above.

Designer's Choice Cap Version 1

In this version, when the cap is set into the armhole the seam which forms the pleat on top appears to be an extension of the shoulder seam. The depth of this extension will be one-fourth of the Unfinished Width. This depth should be between 1″ and 2″, which will result in 4″ to 8″ of stitches to be bound off at the top.

This version is similar in appearance to the T-Square Cap, with the added benefit of "built-in shoulder pads" due to the thickness of the folds. Assembling instructions are as follows.

STEP 1
Fold the cap in half with the right sides together, and sew across the top (a).

STEP 2
Take hold of the point at the folded edge and bring it to the open end of the seam (b). Tack it down at the edge (c).

STEP 3
Turn the cap to the right side.

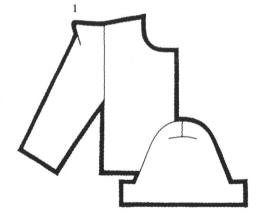

CONSTRUCTION OF THE DESIGNER'S CHOICE CAP VARIATIONS

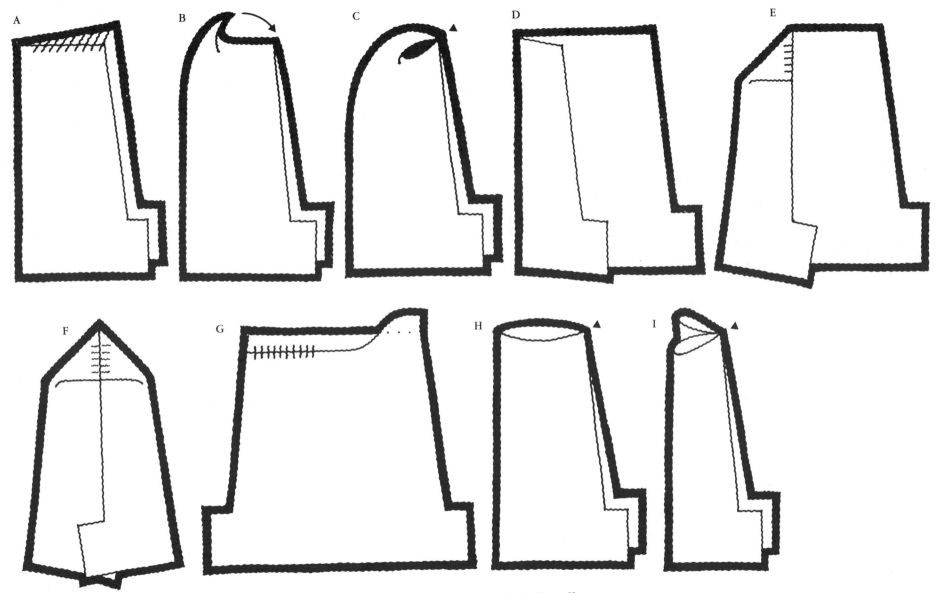

These steps are used in varying sequences, described in the text, to produce the Designer's Choice Cap effects.

Designer's Choice Cap Version 2

In this version, an inverted V is formed at the top of the cap, with the point of the V at the shoulder seam. An opening is formed beneath the V which you can leave open or stitch closed.

This variation requires an Unfinished Width of 4" to "8. Assembling instructions are as follows.

STEP 1
Fold the cap in half (right sides together) and sew across the top (a).

STEP 2
Turn the cap to the right side.

STEP 3
Take hold of the point at the folded edge and bring it to the open end of seam (b). Tack it down at the edge (c).

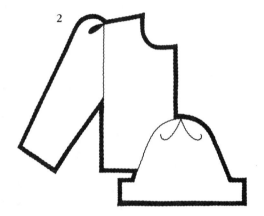

Designer's Choice Cap Version 3

In this version, there are two diagonal pleats which meet at the shoulder seam.

An Unfinished Width of 4" to 6" should be bound off for a sweater, and up to 8" for a jacket or coat. Assembling instructions are as follows.

STEP 1
With right sides together, fold one corner of the cap to the center at the top (d).

STEP 2
Fold the top down (forming a triangle) so that the top edge lines up with the armhole edge. Stitch the open edges together through all three thicknesses (e).

STEP 3
Repeat with other corner (f).

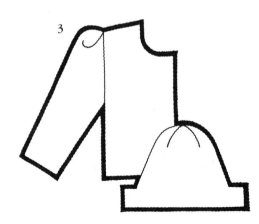

STEP 4
Turn cap to the right side.

Designer's Choice Cap Version 4

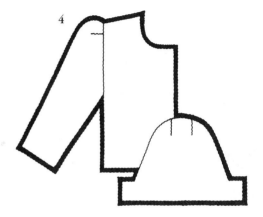

This appears similar to a Box Cap, but, again, the fold of the fabric makes shoulder pads unnecessary for shaping.

An Unfinished Width of approximately 4″ of stitches should be bound off for a lightweight sweater; between 4″ to 6″ for a medium-weight garment, and a maximum of 8″ for a heavy-weight jacket or coat. Assembling instructions are as follows.

STEP 1
With wrong sides together, fold one corner of the cap to the center at the top (d).

STEP 2
Fold the top down (forming a triangle) so that the top edge lines up with the armhole edge. Stitch the open edges together through all three thicknesses (e).

STEP 3
Repeat with the other corner (f).

Designer's Choice Cap Version 5

Cowl folds, draping from the shoulder seam, make this version suitable for dressy sweaters in soft fabrics.

An Unfinished Width of 6″ to 10″ is required. Assembling instructions are as follows.

STEP 1
Fold the cap in half (right sides together) and sew across the top (a).

STEP 2
Turn the cap to the right side. Allow the fabric to drape, tucking the seam to the inside.

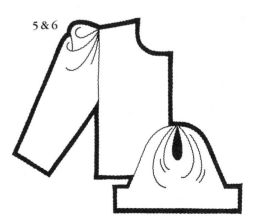

Designer's Choice Cap Version 6

This is an open variation of Version 5. It includes a hem at the top of the cap, to keep the purl side of the fabric from showing through the opening. Assembling instructions are as follows.

STEP 1
Fold the hem at the top of the cap (Designer's Choice Cap Knitting Guidelines, below, Step 7) to the wrong side and tack down (g).

STEP 2
Fold the cap in half (wrong sides together) and stitch the corners together (h). Allow the fabric to drape into folds.

Designer's Choice Cap Version 7

This version has two small open pleats at the top. In stiff fabrics, the pleats will stand up; in soft fabrics, the pleats will drape.

The depth of each pleat is one-fourth of the Unfinished Width (for instance, 1″ deep pleats require a bound-off width of 4″). Like Version 6, this cap includes a 1″ hem at the top. Assembling instructions are as follows.

STEP 1
Fold the hem at the top of the cap (Designer's Choice Cap knitting guidelines, below, Step 7) to the wrong side and tack down (g).

STEP 2
Fold the top edge into two equal-size pleats (wrong sides together), and stitch the corners together (i).

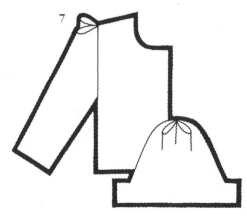

Standard Saddle Shoulder Cap and Band

This sleeve cap is used with the Saddle Shoulder Yoke.

The maximum width of a Standard Saddle Shoulder Band should be 3″ for an adult or 2″ for a child. Wider bands require Modified Saddle Band charting. We will use a 2″ band in our example.

For charting purposes, the width of the band can be considered the Unfinished Width of the cap (but note that in Step 5 this width is not subtracted when determining the length of Cap Triangle Side *c*).

The left and right caps and bands are usually identical. If the optional back neckline shaping (as shown on the graph) is added, the bands should be mirror images. The optional back neckline shaping should be about 1″ deep and one-half the Saddle Band in width.

Standard Saddle Shoulder Cap and Band

STEP 1
Bind off the same number of stitches per armhole as for Set-In Armhole shaping (CB/Step 8).
Example: *5 stitches*

STEP 2
Number of stitches at top of sleeve (CB/Step 2) − (Step 1 × 2) = number of stitches at start of cap taper
Example: 56 − (5 × 2 = 10) = 46   *46 stitches*

STEP 3
Width of Saddle Band in inches × stitch gauge = number of stitches for Saddle Band
■ If Step 2 is an even number, make Step 3 even.
■ If Step 2 is odd, make Step 3 odd.
Add two stitches for seams (not included in calculations).
Example: 2 × 5 = 10   *10 stitches*

STEP 4
(Step 2 − Step 3) ÷ 2 = number of stitches to decrease per side edge
Example: (46 − 10 = 36) ÷ 2 = 18   *18 stitches*

STANDARD SADDLE SHOULDER SWEATER

OPTIONAL BACK NECKLINE SHAPING

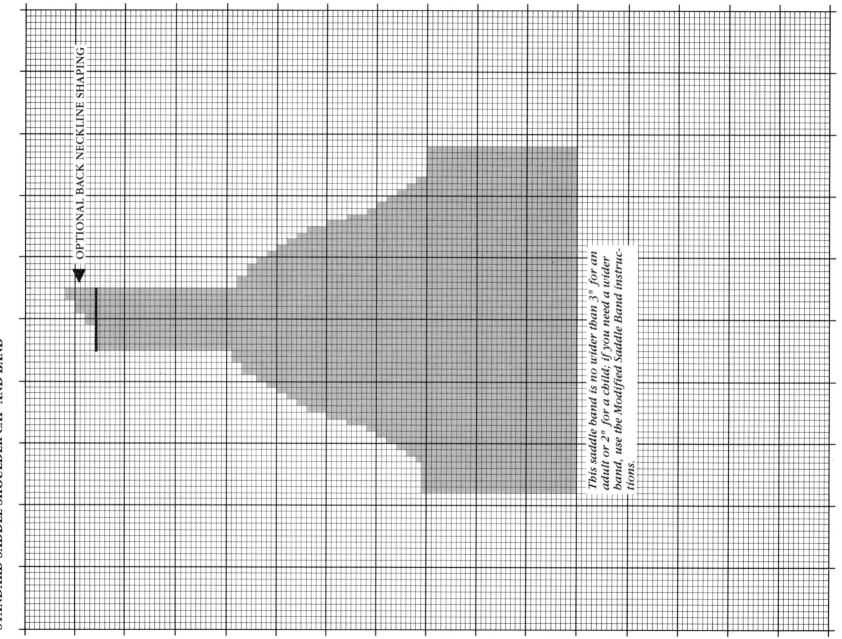

This saddle band is no wider than 3" for an adult or 2" for a child; if you need a wider band, use the Modified Saddle Band instructions.

234

STEP 5

a. Curve Measurement of the back armhole = Cap Triangle Side c

Example: 7½"

b. Step 4 ÷ stitch gauge = Cap Triangle Side b

Example: 18 ÷ 5 = 3.6   3.6"

c. Take square root of [(Step 5a × Step 5a) – (Step 5b × Step 5b)] = Cap Triangle Side a.

Example: (7.5 × 7.5 = 56.25) – (3.6 × 3.6 = 12.96) = 43.29

$\sqrt{43.29}$ *= 6.6*   6.6"

d. Step 5c × row gauge = number of rows for cap

   Make this an even number.

Example: 6.6 × 6 = 39.6   *40 rows*

STEP 6

Plan and work your cap taper (see "Tapering the Cap").

STEP 7

Work even on remaining stitches until the Saddle Band equals the shoulder length of the back yoke, measured along the slant of the shoulder.

STEP 8

Bind off front stitches to the center of the Saddle Band.

STEP 9

Work even on remaining stitches for a depth equal to half the width of the back neckline.

■ If you wish to include optional back neckline shaping (see graph), make it about 1" deep and one-half the Saddle Band in width.

STEP 10

Leave stitches on needle or holder. Knit second Saddle Band as a mirror image of first one, and graft the two bands together (see "How Tos").

Modified Saddle Shoulder Cap and Band

In this style, the Saddle Shoulder Band is broader than for the Standard Saddle Shoulder Cap and Band: wider than 3" for an adult, or wider than 2" for a child. The greater width of this Saddle Band means that it overlaps into the shoulder and neckline areas of the back and front yokes. The shoulder shaping is still worked on the yoke, but the Modified Saddle Band will contain part of the neckline shaping. We recommend that you chart the shaping on graph paper.

A saddle band lowers the back neckline by one-half the band width. For example, a 5" saddle band will lower the back neckline by 2½". This would result in a very deep neck opening if left "as is."

To fill it in, an extension is added to the band. This extension may be worked even or shaped slightly, as shown on our graph.

The front neckline is affected in the same way. To find out the degree to which your Modified Saddle Shoulder Band cuts into the neckline shaping, first chart and graph a Classic Yoke with the neckline of your choice. (We have graphed both a Round Neckline and a Wide V Neckline.) Superimpose your Modified Saddle Shoulder Yoke on your graph. The resulting graph is the pattern for the front yoke of your garment.

If the neckline is incomplete on your Modified Front Yoke, work the unfinished portion into the saddle band, in a taper or slope equivalent to the original shaping. Count the number of shaping stitches and rows needed to finish one neckline edge. For our Round Neckline, the graph shows that the equivalent of 3 stitches and 6 rows must be shaped on the Modified Saddle Band. Adjust the stitches by converting them to the number of rows for that width, and convert the rows into stitches. Chart the front neckline shaping of the saddle band with these new figures.

These modifications mean that you will have right and left saddle bands which will be mirror images. The two bands will meet at the center back and be joined with a seam or grafting (see "How Tos"). Grafting is recommended, as long as it works with your stitch pattern.

We will chart a 5"-wide band in our example. While the band is also the Finished Width of your cap, note that it is not subtracted from the curve measurement when figuring the length of Cap Triangle Side c in Step 5.

Modified Saddle Shoulder Cap and Band

STEP 1
Bind off the same number of stitches per armholes as for Set-In Armhole shaping (CB/Step 8).
Example: *5 stitches*

STEP 2
Number of stitches at top of sleeve (CB/Step 2) − (Step 1 × 2) = number of stitches at start of cap taper
Example: 56 − (5 × 2 = 10) = 46   *46 stitches*

STEP 3
Width of Saddle Band in inches × stitch gauge = number of stitches for Saddle Band
■ If Step 2 is an even number, make Step 3 even.
■ If Step 2 is odd, make Step 3 odd.
Add two stitches for seams (not included in calculations).
Example: 5 × 5 = 25   *26 stitches*

STEP 4
(Step 2 − Step 3) ÷ 2 = number of stitches to decreases per side edge
Example: (46 − 26 = 20) ÷ 2 = 10   *10 stitches*

STEP 5
a. Curve Measurement of the back armhole = Cap Triangle Side c
Example: *6"*
b. Step 4 ÷ stitch gauge = Cap Triangle Side b
Example: 10 ÷ 5 = 2   *2"*

MODIFIED SADDLE SHOULDER SWEATER

MODIFIED SADDLE SHOULDER CAP AND BAND

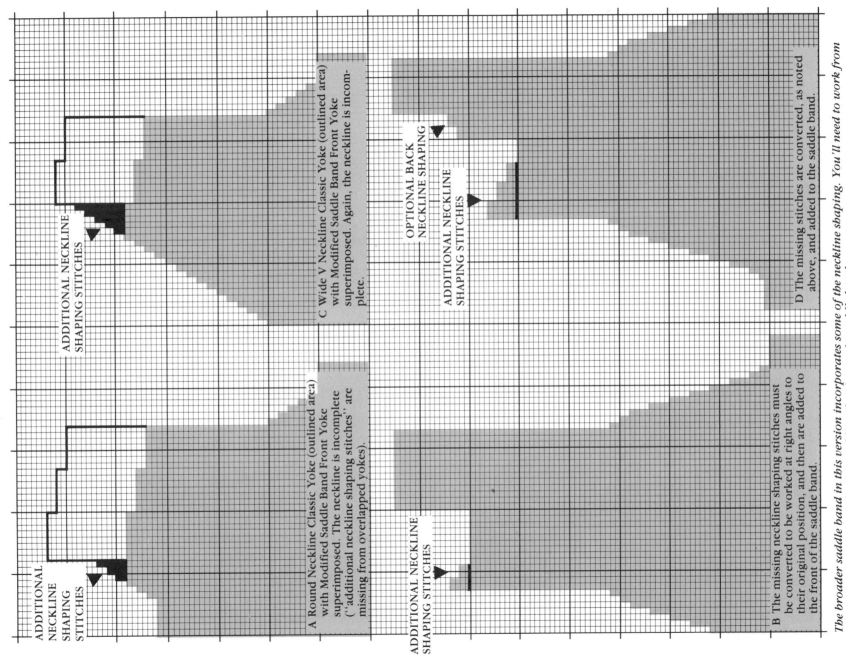

ADDITIONAL NECKLINE SHAPING STITCHES

ADDITIONAL NECKLINE SHAPING STITCHES

C Wide V Neckline Classic Yoke (outlined area) with Modified Saddle Band Front Yoke superimposed. Again, the neckline is incomplete.

OPTIONAL BACK NECKLINE SHAPING

ADDITIONAL NECKLINE SHAPING STITCHES

D The missing stitches are converted, as noted above, and added to the saddle band.

A Round Neckline Classic Yoke (outlined area) with Modified Saddle Band Front Yoke superimposed. The neckline is incomplete ("additional neckline shaping stitches" are missing from overlapped yokes).

ADDITIONAL NECKLINE SHAPING STITCHES

B The missing neckline shaping stitches must be converted to be worked at right angles to their original position, and then are added to the front of the saddle band.

The broader saddle band in this version incorporates some of the neckline shaping. You'll need to work from your yoke chart to transfer this neckline shaping to the saddle band.

237

c. Take square root of [(Step 5a × Step 5a) − (Step 5b × Step 5b)] = Cap Triangle Side *a*
Example: (6 × 6 = 36) − (2 × 2 = 4) = 32
$\sqrt{32} = 5.66$ 5.66"

d. Step 5c × row gauge = number of rows for cap
   Make this an even number.
Example: 5.66 × 6 = 33.96   34 rows

STEP 6
Plan and work your cap taper (see "Tapering the Cap").

STEP 7
Work even on remaining stitches until the saddle band equals the shoulder length of the back yoke, measured along the slant of the shoulder.

STEP 8
- If additional neckline shaping is required, determine the number of stitches and rows to be added on the band. The calculations can be done mathematically, but the actual shaping is easiest to chart on graph paper. Essentially, you will be turning your knitting 90 degrees, converting rows to stitches and stitches to rows so that you can knit your neckline sidewise instead of bottom-to-top.

a. Number of additional shaping stitches per edge (from graph) ÷ stitch gauge = width of un-completed neckline shaping
Example: 3 ÷ 5 = 0.6   0.6"

b. Number of additional shaping rows (from graph) ÷ row gauge = depth of uncompleted neckline shaping
Example: 6 ÷ 6 = 1   1"

c. Step 8b × stitch gauge = new number of stitches
Example: 1 × 5 = 5   5"

d. Step 8a × row gauge = new number of rows
Example: 0.6 × 6 = 3.6   4 rows

STEP 9
Bind off front stitches to the center of the Saddle Band (working neckline shaping, as charted in Step 8, if needed).

STEP 10
Work even on remaining stitches for a depth equal to one-half the width of the back neckline.
- If you wish to include optional back neckline shaping (see graph), make it about 1" deep and one-half the Saddle Band in width.

Remember that your bands must be mirror images!
Leave stitches on needle and graft the two bands together (see "How Tos").

Semi-Raglan Cap

Semi-Raglan Caps are used with Semi-Raglan Yokes. The cap is charted directly from Steps 1 through 4 of the Semi-Raglan Armhole shaping. For the cap, you will bind off the same number of stitches per edge and work the same number of single decreases over the same number of rows as for the yoke. The top of the cap will be sewn to the straight portion of the Semi-Raglan Armhole opening, which is equal in length to the Armhole Depth Measurement, so the width of the cap top must be equal to that measurement as well. The cap is bound off in a straight line, as soon as the decreases are complete.

The yoke and cap decreases will be aligned when the garment is assembled. Consider making maximum design use of this alignment by working the yoke and cap decreases several stitches in from the edge.

The Semi-Raglan Cap is unique, in that its top width determines the width of the sleeve at the upperarm, rather than being determined after the sleeve width is known. The top width is equal to the Armhole Depth Measurement. The lower sleeve width, then, equals the Armhole Depth Measurement plus the armhole shaping stitches.

If you find that the sleeve will be too narrow for comfort, it is possible to add a few extra stitches and taper with double

Semi-Raglan Cap

STEP 1

(Armhole Depth Measurement × stitch gauge) + total number of stitches for armhole shaping (CB/Step 6) = number of stitches at top of sleeve
Example: (8.25 × 5 = 41.25) + 20 = 61.25   *62 stitches*

STEP 2

Bind off the number of stitches in CB/Step 8 at each sleeve edge.
Example: *5 stitches*

STEP 3

Follow Semi-Raglan Armhole Shaping, Steps 3 and 4 (page 82).
Example: Decrease one stitch at each side of the sleeve every 4th or 6th row over 24 rows, for a total of 5 decreases.

STEP 4

After the decreases are complete, bind off remaining stitches straight across.

(or triple) decreases. If the sleeve still will be too narrow, you will need to consider an alternative style of cap.

Standard Raglan Cap

A Standard Raglan Cap—used with a Standard Raglan Yoke—has 1" of stitches remaining at the top which become part of the neckline. These stitches can either be bound off or placed on a stitch holder, depending upon how the stitches at the front and back neckline were handled.

The sleeve cap decreases over the same number of rows as calculated for the Standard Raglan Yoke. Decreases should be worked in the same method as on the yoke, so that they match visually.

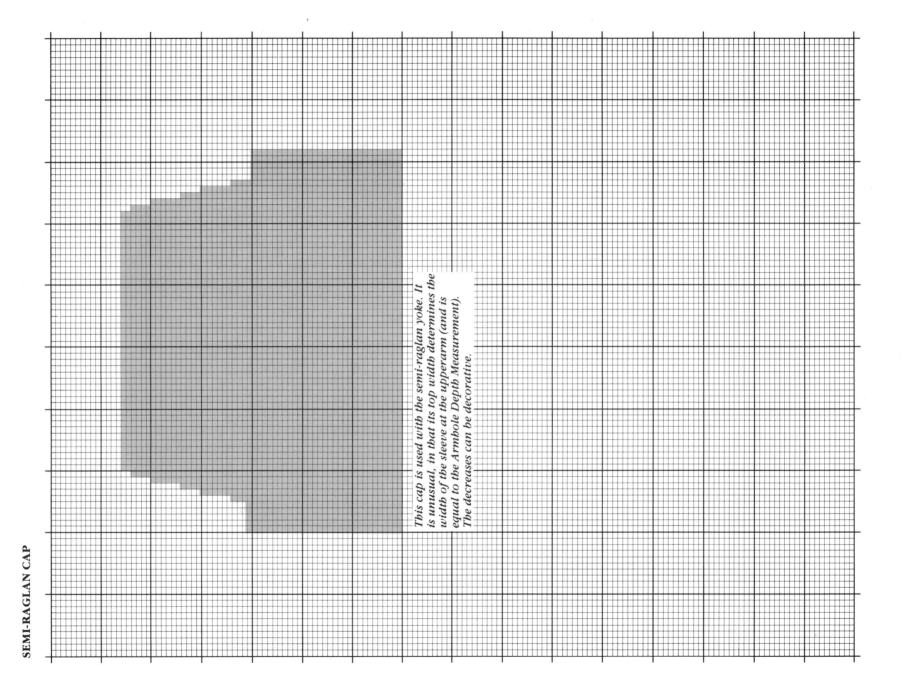

SEMI-RAGLAN CAP

This cap is used with the semi-raglan yoke. It is unusual, in that its top width determines the width of the sleeve at the upperarm (and is equal to the Armhole Depth Measurement). The decreases can be decorative.

240

This cap is used with the standard raglan yoke, and is worked to match that yoke.

Standard Raglan Cap

STEP 1
Bind off the same number of stitches per armhole as for the Set-In Armhole shaping (CB/Step 8).
Example: *5 stitches*

STEP 2
Number of stitches at top of sleeve (TS/Step 2) − (Step 1 × 2) = number of stitches at start of Raglan shaping
Example: 56 − (5 × 2 = 10) = 46 *46 stitches*

STEP 3
Width at top of sleeve cap × stitch gauge = number of stitches remaining at top of sleeve cap
- If Step 2 is an even number, make Step 3 even.
- If Step 2 is odd, make Step 3 odd.

Example: 1 × 5 = 5 *6 stitches*

STEP 4
(Step 2 − Step 3) ÷ 2 = number of Raglan decreases per edge
Example: (46 − 6 = 40) ÷ 2 = 20 *20 stitches*

STEP 5
Decrease over the same number of rows as calculated in Step 7 of the Standard Raglan Yoke.
Example: *52 rows*

STEP 6
Step 5 ÷ Step 4 = number of row on which to work decreases
Make this an even number.
See Taper Formula to work out distribution of decreases.
- If your result is not a round number (and it seldom is), decrease "slower" at the start of the shaping (over the greater number of rows) and "faster" near the neckline (over the lesser number of rows.)
- An exception to this rule can occur if your calculations include two-stitch bind-offs or double decreases (see "How Tos"). If you feel that the bind-offs or double decreases will be visually intrusive if they are made near the neck, work them immediately after the armhole bind-off, where they will be less visible.

Example: 52 ÷ 20 = 2.6 *Every 2nd or 4th row*

STEP 7
Bind off remaining stitches or place them on a stitch holder.

Modified Raglan Cap

The Modified Raglan Cap is used with the Modified Raglan Yoke.

Right and left Modified Raglan Caps are mirror images of each other. The edges of each cap must decrease over the same number of rows as charted for the front and back yokes; that is, one cap edge must correspond to the front yoke and the other edge to the back yoke.

Jot down the number of rows on your front and back Modified Raglan Yokes. Our example (pages 97–98) has 56 rows on the back and 50–51 rows on the front.

Also jot down the number of inches you decided will remain at the top of your sleeve cap (to become part of the neckline). In charting our yoke, we used 3″.

The top of the cap is easiest to shape with the aid of graph paper. Our graph shows a left sleeve cap. The right one will be its mirror image.

We have charted two versions for the shape of the cap top. Modified Raglan Cap Version 1 has a slope occurring only at the back portion of the sleeve cap. Modified Raglan Cap Version 2 has an even slope across the entire cap top. You can use either one. The Stitches at the top can be bound off or worked in short rows and placed on a stitch holder, depending on how you handled the stitches at the back neckline.

Modified Raglan Cap

STEP 1

Bind off the same number of stitches per armhole as for the Set-In Armhole shaping (CB/Step 8).
Example:

5 stitches

STEP 2

Number of stitches at top of sleeve (TS/Step 2) – (Step 1 × 2) = number of stitches at start of Raglan shaping
Example: 56 – (5 × 2 = 10) = 46

46 stitches

STEP 3

Width at top of sleeve cap × stitch gauge = number of stitches remaining at top of sleeve cap
■ If Step 2 is an even number, make Step 3 even. If Step 2 is odd, make Step 3 odd.
Example: 3 × 5 = 15

16 stitches

STEP 4

(Step 2 – Step 3) ÷ 2 = number of Raglan decreases per edge
Example: (46 – 16 = 30) ÷ 2 = 15

15 stitches

STEP 5

Decrease over the same number of rows as calculated in Step 7 of the Modified Raglan Yoke.
Example:

56 rows

STEP 6

(Step 5 – 2) ÷ Step 4 = number of row on which to work decreases
Make this an even number.
See Taper Formula to work out distribution of decreases.

- If your result is not a round number (and it seldom is), decrease "slower" at the start of the shaping (over the greater number of rows) and "faster" near the neckline (over the lesser number of rows).

Example: (56 – 2 = 54) ÷ 15 = 3.6

Every 2nd or 4th row

STEP 7

Chart the sleeve cap on graph paper, decreasing the Step 4 number of stitches per edge over the number of rows on your back yoke (Step 5).

STEP 8

On your graph, mark the row at which the front yoke ends (50–51 rows in our example), then chart the shape of the cap top.

a. **Version 1:** Draw a line straight across half of the cap stitches, from the front to the center of the sleeve cap. Slope the remaining stitches to the top back of the cap (see Slope Formula).

b. **Version 2:** Slope the entire width of stitches from the front to the top back of the cap (see Slope Formula). If your stitches do not divide evenly, decrease over the greater number of stitches first.

The resulting graph drawing is your pattern to follow. Remember to make your second sleeve a mirror image of the first one!

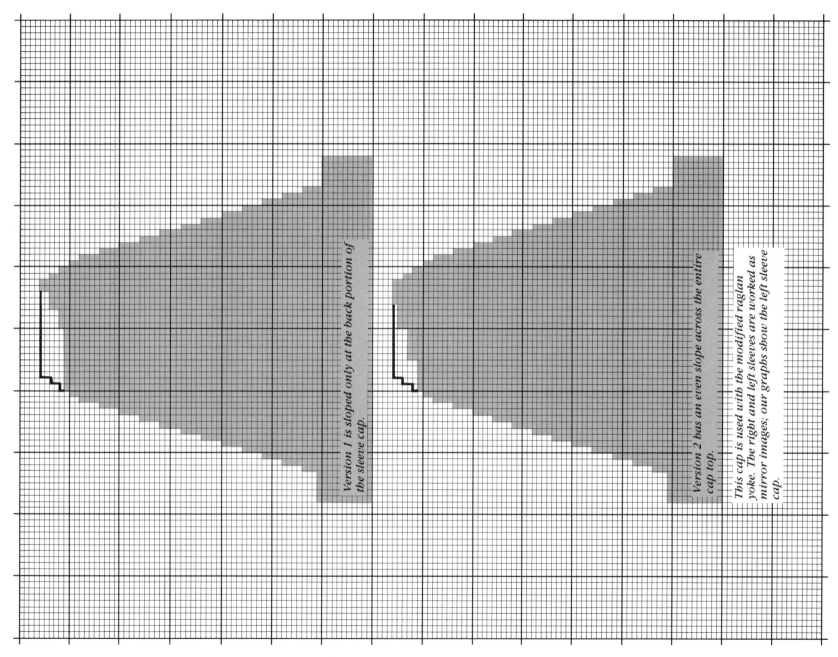

Version 1 is stoped only at the back portion of the sleeve cap.

Version 2 has an even slope across the entire cap top.

This cap is used with the modified raglan yoke. The right and left sleeves are worked as mirror images; our graphs show the left sleeve cap.

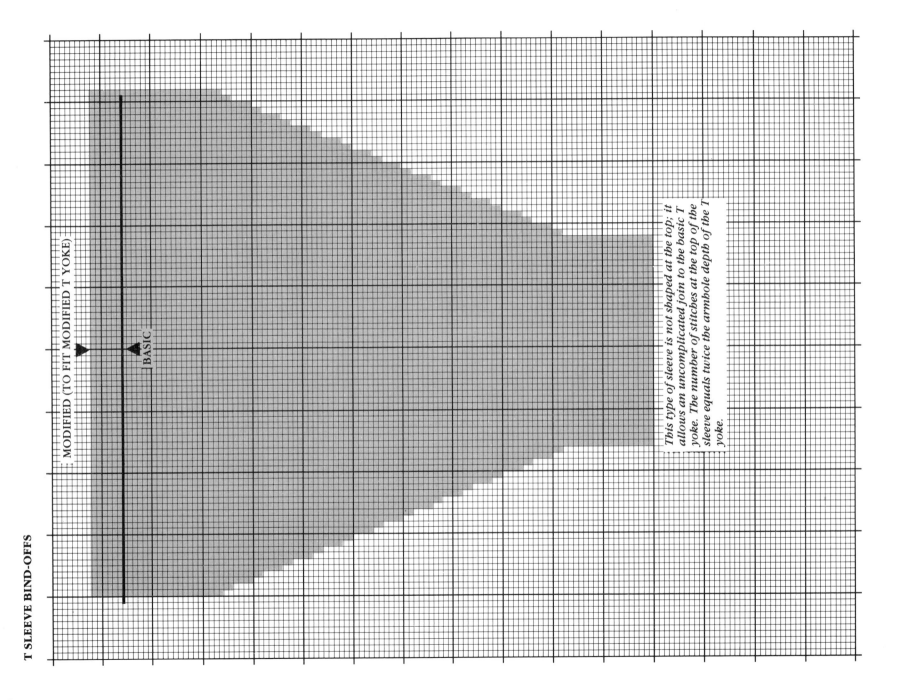

T SLEEVE BIND-OFFS

MODIFIED (TO FIT MODIFIED T YOKE)

BASIC

This type of sleeve is not shaped at the top; it allows an uncomplicated join to the basic T yoke. The number of stitches at the top of the sleeve equals twice the armhole depth of the T yoke.

246

Basic and Modified T Sleeve Bind-Offs

Rather than having a tapered cap, the Basic or Modified T Sleeve is shaped in a straight line across the top; this makes an uncomplicated join to the Basic T Yoke. Although the Straight Sleeve is the shape most commonly used with the T Yoke, other shapes can be used as well.

In this style, the number of stitches at the top of the sleeve is equivalent to twice the Armhole Depth of the T Yoke. On the Basic T Body, measure this distance from the yarn or safety pin marker, or on the Modified T from the armhole bind-off to the shoulder bind-off. Sleeve shapes other than the Straight Sleeve taper from the cuff to this width.

Basic and Modified T Sleeve Bind-Offs

STEP 1
Armhole Depth Measurement × 2 × stitch gauge = number of stitches at upper sleeve
Example: 8.25 × 2 × 5 = 82.5   *82 stitches*
Add 2 seam stitches when working flat.

STEP 2
Chart your choice of sleeve shape, and work to the T Sleeve Length Measurement.
A Straight Sleeve is traditional for a T Sweater, but any sleeve which can taper to the Step 1 number of stitches can be used.
Example: *17³/₄"*

STEP 3
a. **Basic T Sleeve:** Bind off all stitches at the T Sleeve Length measurement.
b. **Modified T Sleeve:** Knit sleeve to the T Sleeve Length Measurement. Then work even for the amount subtracted on the yoke (in our example, this was 1"). Bind off all stitches.

Modified T Sleeve with Gathers or Pleats

Gathers or pleats can be added at the top of a Modified T Sleeve by increasing the number of stitches at the top of the sleeve.

You'll first need to determine the Finished Width of your gathers or pleats. As a general rule, use 2" to 4" for gathers, 1" to 4" for pleats. The finer the yarn, the less the finished width can be. We will use 3" for both examples.

T SLEEVE WITH GATHERS OR PLEATS

GATHERS   PLEATS

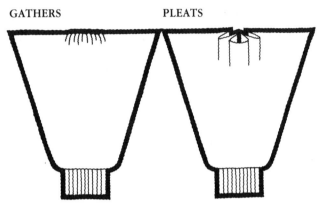

By increasing the number of stitches at the top of a modified T sleeve, you can produce gathers or pleats.

Modified T Sleeve with Gathers or Pleats

STEP 1
(Armhole Depth Measurement × 2) – Finished Width of gathers or pleats = ungathered or unpleated width at top of sleeve
Example: (8.25 × 2 = 16.5) – 3 = 13.5   *13½″*

STEP 2
Step 1 × stitch gauge = number of stitches at top of sleeve (except for pleated or gathered section)
Make this an even number.
Example: 13.5 × 5 = 67.5   *68 stitches*

STEP 3
a. **Gathers:** Finished Width of gathers × stitch gauge × 4 = number of stitches to add for gathers at top of sleeve
Example: 3 × 5 × 4 = 60   *60 stitches*
b. **Pleats:** Finished Width of pleats × stitch gauge × 3 = number of stitches to add for pleats at top of sleeve
Example: 3 × 5 × 3 = 45   *45 stitches*

STEP 4
Step 2 + Step 3 = number of stitches at upper sleeve
Example (Gathered): 68 + 60 = 128   *128 stitches*
Example (Pleated): 68 + 45 = 113   *113 stitches*

STEP 5
When you have increased your sleeve to its full width (Step 4), work across half of the Step 2 number of stitches (34) and attach a marker, work across the Step 3 number of stitches (60 or 45) and attach a marker, and work across the remaining stitches (34) to the end of the row.
a. **Gathers:** For a Gathered Sleeve, place markers on your needle which can be removed on the bind-off row.
b. **Pleats:** For a Pleated Sleeve, attach removable pieces of contrasting yarn to the fabric of your sleeve.
Continue knitting.

STEP 6
a. **Gathers:** Work a Modified T Sleeve to two rows short of its final length. *Row 1:* Work in pattern stitch to marker, work 2 together to next marker, work in pattern stitch to end of row. *Row 2:* Repeat Row 1. *Row 3:* Bind off all stitches.
b. **Pleats:** Work sleeve to the desired Modified T length, and bind off all stitches. Pleat fabric between markers in any manner you wish, to your finished pleated width. Remove markers.

Folded T Sleeve

This fun sleeve is knit as a rectangle, then its shape is formed by folding.

One word of caution: make sure that the body of your garment is long enough to accommodate this sleeve. The body, from the top of the ribbing or border to the shoulder, should be no shorter than the T Sleeve Length Measurement plus half the cuff diameter.

For special emphasis at the seam, knit this sleeve in vertical colored stripes or a horizontal stitch pattern.

Folded T Sleeve

STEP 1

T Sleeve Length Measurement − length of ribbing or cuff finish = width of stitches to cast on
For number of stitches to cast on, multiply by stitch gauge.
Example: 17.75 − 3 = 14.75   *14³/₄″*

STEP 2

Wrist Measurement + Ease + Step 1 = length to knit
■ Use up to twice your Wrist Measurement if you intend to have gathers at the cuff.
Example: 5.75 + 1 + 14.75 = 21.5   *21¹/₂″*

STEP 3

Knit a rectangle, bind off, and fold as follows.
a. From the top, fold down half your Wrist Measurement plus Ease, including half of the fabric allowed for gathers, if any.
b. Fold the bottom portion into a triangle by bringing up one corner. (Fold from one corner for one sleeve, the opposite corner for its mate.) Sew into place.

STEP 4

Pick up the equivalent of your Wrist Measurement plus Ease at the opening, and knit for the length of your cuff.

Cap Sleeves

Cap Sleeves are relatively short, worked along with the yoke of the sweater as an extension to it. Front and back are identical.

In a close-fitting Cap Sleeve, the sweater body is knit up to the normal armhole position (where you would work your armhole bind-off). At that point, an outward slope or taper is worked for about 1″ in depth, to form the sleeve.

Many variations of a cap sleeve are possible. We have graphed several of them. Each graph illustrates one side (front or back) of a sleeve. The dots show

FOLDED T SLEEVE
A FOLD DOWN HALF WRIST MEASUREMENT PLUS EASE

B FOLD BOTTOM PORTION INTO A TRIANGLE BY BRINGING UP ONE CORNER

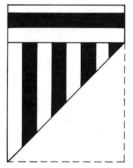

C PICK UP AND ADD CUFF

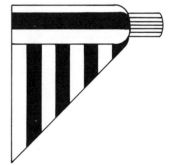

Worked as a rectangle, this sleeve takes its shape from a folding process. The body of your sweater will need to be long enough to accommodate the deep armhole.

CAP SLEEVES

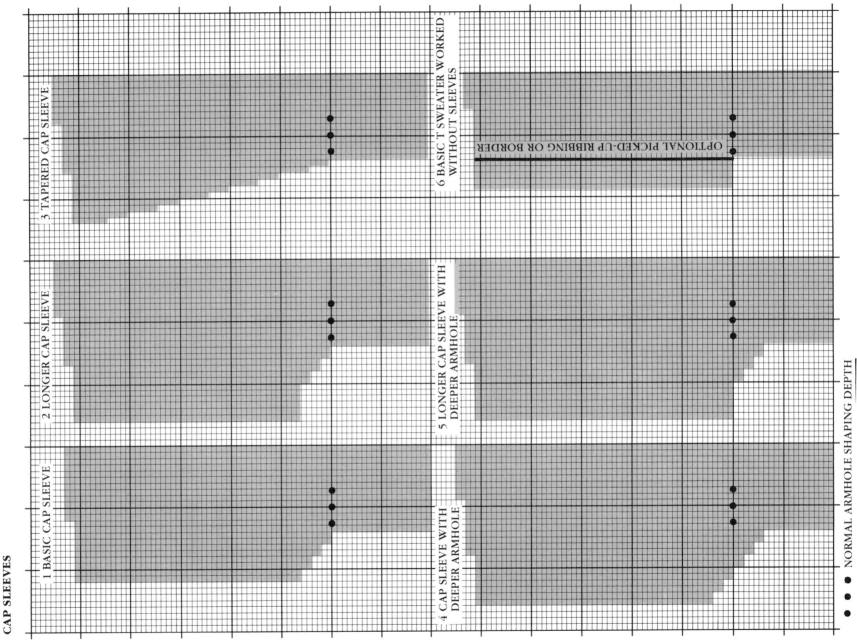

3 TAPERED CAP SLEEVE

2 LONGER CAP SLEEVE

1 BASIC CAP SLEEVE

6 BASIC T SWEATER WORKED WITHOUT SLEEVES

OPTIONAL PICKED-UP RIBBING OR BORDER

5 LONGER CAP SLEEVE WITH DEEPER ARMHOLE

4 CAP SLEEVE WITH DEEPER ARMHOLE

● NORMAL ARMHOLE SHAPING DEPTH

● These sleeves are worked as an extension to the yoke and are relatively short. Many variations are possible, as demonstrated by these possibilities. Each graph shows one side (front or back) of a sleeve. The dots show where the

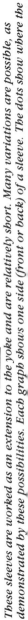

250

the position where the armhole bind-off would have occurred if a cap sleeve had not been added.

For all versions, begin shaping the shoulders when you have reached the top of the Armhole Depth Measurement, but add half again as many shoulder shaping levels for your bind-off. This is calculated as:

(row gauge × 1.5) ÷ 2 = number of shoulder shaping levels.

In our examples, we bind off shoulders and Cap Sleeves in five levels instead of three.

CAP SLEEVE VERSION 1. In this version, two-stitch cast-ons are worked for 1″ in depth, then the sleeves are knit even to the shoulder shaping.

CAP SLEEVE VERSION 2. Likewise, two-stitch cast-ons are worked for 1″ in depth. Then, however, additional stitches are cast onto the needle (between 1″ and 3″ of stitches, depending upon how long you want the sleeves to be), and the sleeves are knit even to the shoulder shaping.

CAP SLEEVE VERSION 3. A taper, beginning at the Armhole Depth Measurement position, is worked along the full depth of the yoke to the shoulder shaping. Decide how wide you want the cap to be (between 1″ and 3″ as a general rule), and determine the rate of increase as you would for any other taper (see Taper Formula).

CAP SLEEVE VERSION 4. The slope is about 2″ deep, with the increases beginning below the normal armhole shaping depth.

CAP SLEEVE VERSION 5. This is similar to Version 2, but has a deeper opening. The slope begins below the Armhole Depth Measurement, and the additional stitches are cast on at the normal armhole shaping depth instead of 1″ higher.

CAP SLEEVE VERSION 6. This is a Basic T sweater worked without sleeves. While not a true Cap Sleeve, it will produce a yoke which extends past the shoulder line. An optional rib or border can be picked up around the armhole if you wish.

ONE- AND TWO-PIECE GARMENTS

One- and Two-Piece Ts and Dolmans, because of their simplicity, offer great freedom to the designer. Because they have few seams and can be worked vertically or horizontally, they can be thought of as blank canvases on which the knitter can paint. Fabric design rather than garment shaping can take center stage.

Once you understand the basic charting of these two styles, you can consider variations on their themes. For instance, Ts and Dolmans do not have to be made in one or two pieces, but can be worked in three, four, or more sections. To cover all the design options is impossible. What can be done is to list their common elements and how they vary.

General Information

Vertical versus Horizontal. We will call a garment being worked from the bottom of a body section to the neckline a "vertical" garment (a). Stitches are cast on at both edges for the sleeves.

A garment being worked from sleeve to sleeve will be referred to as a "horizontal" garment (b). Stitches are cast on at both edges for the body sections.

Stitch Gauge versus Row Gauge. Until now, we have calculated both body and sleeve length using the row gauge. Now one or the other (depending upon whether you are working vertically or horizontally) will be calculated by means of the stitch gauge.

If you are knitting vertically, the sleeve length will be calculated with your stitch gauge (in other words, you'll be casting on a specific number of stitches for the sleeve length).

If you are knitting horizontally, the body length will be calculated with the stitch gauge.

Make sure you use the right gauge for the right calculation!

Charting the Garment. While charting in many cases can be done with numbers alone, graph paper can be an invaluable aid.

Only one-quarter of the sweater needs to be graphed. The remainder of the garment is just a mirror image or shaping in reverse. For instance, if you are knitting vertically and casting on stitches for the sleeves, you'll bind off the sleeve slope in reverse on the opposite edge.

VARIATIONS OF THE DOLMAN SWEATER

One- and two-piece Ts and dolmans are simple to shape and knit. They offer the designer a lot of freedom in fabric design. Once you understand the idea, you can work them in more than one or two pieces if other divisions suit your design.

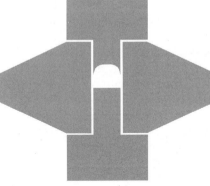

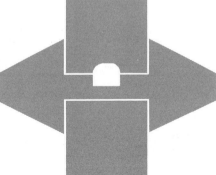

A graphed pattern will help substantially if you have decided to knit your sweater in many sections. Remember to add selvedge stitches wherever there will be seams.

Measuring for Ts and Dolmans. In a number of ways, T and Dolman measurements differ from those for garments with Set-In Sleeves. Important measurements are described below.

1. T/Dolman Body Width. This is charted according to the normal guidelines: bust or chest measurement plus desired ease, divided by two. If only one-quarter of the garment is being charted, divide by four instead of two.

2. T/Dolman Sleeve Length. In "Taking Measurements," we showed you how to take your Neck-to-Wrist Measurement. This measurement is used to establish the Sleeve Length Measurement in Ts and Dolmans. By subtracting the portion of the measurement that is part of the body of the garment, you determine the actual length of the sleeve, taking into account the amount of ease added to the body. Two sweaters with the same total garment width from sleeve edge to sleeve edge (twice the Neck-to-Wrist Measurement) can have different sleeve lengths, for instance, if one of the garments has 4″ of ease in the body while the other has 8″. The T/Dolman Sleeve Length also may need to be adjusted to accommodate the depth of a sleeve finish (such as a cuff) to be worked later.

3. Sleeve Width at the Wrist. This measurement becomes very important when charting a Dolman, since the underarm on this style is obscured by the gusset. The usual ease of 1″ is added to the Wrist Measurement, establishing the minimum width of the sleeve at the wrist. If the sleeve will be finished with a cuff in a border stitch, this minimum can be doubled to establish the maximum width of the sleeve at the wrist. In order to reduce the cuff to the standard of Wrist Measurement plus 1″, a sleeve of greater than minimum width requires decreases just above the cuff when working the finish of the sleeve. On a Basic T, with no sleeve shaping, twice the Raglan Armhole Depth is the maximum width or knitted depth at the wrist.

4. Garment Length to Underarm. The Garment Length to Underarm Measurement is taken according to the guidelines in "Taking Measurements." When a garment is worked horizontally, the garment length becomes the width of the stitches cast on for the body.

5. Armhole Depth. Because a one- or two-piece garment has no shoulder shaping, the Raglan Armhole Depth is used to calculate the depth of the armhole on vertically worked Ts and Dolmans. On horizontal garments it is the basis for calculating the width of the upper sleeve. The Armhole Depth Measurement is used for calculating neckline depths.

6. T/Dolman Total Garment Length. The Total Garment Length—the finished length of the front or back from the bottom edge to the shoulder—is the sum of the Raglan Depth Measurement and the Garment Length to Underarm Measurement.

BASIC DOLMANS

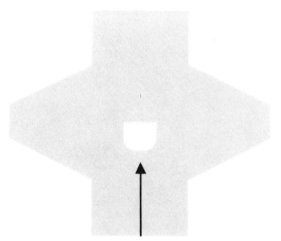

A vertical: begin knitting at bottom of sweater body

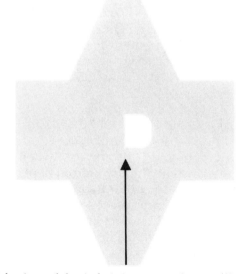

B horizontal: begin knitting at one sleeve cuff

SPECIAL T OR DOLMAN SLEEVE MEASUREMENT

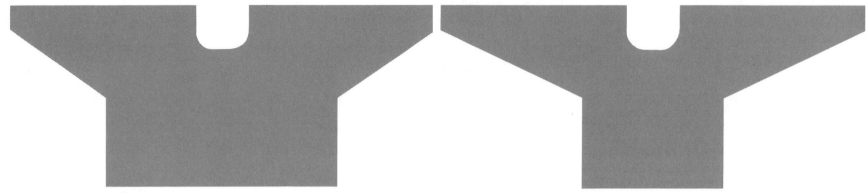

The Neck-to-Wrist is essential to accurate charting of Ts and Dolmans. By using it and our guidelines, you can make garments in these styles with varying amounts of body ease. For example, a garment with a small amount of body ease will have longer sleeves than a garment with more ease. However, the total garment width of both sweaters will be the same.

Finishes. Borders on the sleeves or body of one- or two-piece garments need to be given some thought. The stitch pattern can affect whether the border stitches will be worked as one with the sleeve or body, or will be picked up and worked later.

Ribbing, for example, has a definite vertical line and could not be worked along with a cast-on body or sleeves. In this situation, you will need to shorten the sleeve or body by the knitted depth of the border. On the other hand, seed stitch looks much the same placed vertically or horizontally, and borders in this pattern could be worked along all the edges at the same time as the rest of the garment.

Calculate the number of stitches for picked-up borders using the stitch gauge of the garment. If the piece is very wide, do not leave gaps as you pick up stitches along its edge. Instead, pick up more

stitches than you need, and correct the number of stitches by working evenly spaced decreases in the first row of the border.

If a hem is the finish of your choice, it can be worked vertically, much like a facing, or horizontally, with a purl row forming a turning ridge. For a vertical hem on a sleeve or body which is cast on straight, simply add the number of stitches for the width of the hem, plus an extra stitch for the vertical turning ridge. On a sleeve or body which slopes, figure the slope formula using the number of stitches for the sleeve or body length only, then add the stitches of the hem and the turning ridge stitch to the last group of cast-on stitches.

Necklines. Any neckline shaping can be used for Ts and Dolmans, including cardigan openings. However, do pay attention to neckline placement for these garments.

No new information needs to be digested for neckline shaping. Everything already has been covered under ''Necklines.'' But remember that, just as with other styles, a typical neckline is shaped on the front of the garment, and little or no shaping occurs on the back. Every so often, we come across a knitter who has placed the neck shaping right in the center of a one-piece sweater rather than within the front half. Please, don't let that happen to you!

If you begin knitting with the back, bind off for the back neckline when you have reached the Total Garment Length. Add the depth of the shoulder slope (the Raglan Depth Measurement minus the Armhole Depth Measurement) to the standard neckline depth guidelines when charting the front neckline. You will be working the neckline shaping from the top down; decreases will become increases and stitches bound off will change to stitches cast on.

If you are knitting the sweater from sleeve to sleeve, the neckline will be located on the front half of your work (left or right side, from the knitter's point of view). You will be starting at an edge of the neckline and working it sideways. Shaping that, when worked vertically, is calculated as a taper, changes to a slope when worked horizontally. Let the number of rows and stitches be your guide—tapers have more rows than stitches, and slopes have an equal number or more stitches than rows. Remember to add the depth of the shoulder shaping (Raglan Depth Measurement minus Armhole Depth Measurement) to the neckline depth when charting the neckline.

Gussets are triangular pieces of fabric added at the underarm for ease of movement. They also add growing room to children's sweaters. On Ts, they are optional. However, on Dolmans gussets are an integral part of the design of the sleeve.

Knitting Needles. If you are knitting a one- or two-piece garment, you will be working with a large number of stitches when you have the sleeves and body on the needle. To hold them all comfortably, work the garment, in rows, on a long circular needle.

T-Shapes

One- and Two-Piece Ts. The simplest style to chart is a Classic Body with Straight Sleeves—a very basic T. Front and back can be worked together as one piece, horizontally or vertically. The sleeve width at the upperarm is based on the Raglan Depth Measurement, since there is no shoulder shaping on a one-piece garment. When this style is worked horizontally, the sleeve is charted by the Basic T guidelines (page 247), substituting the Raglan Depth Measurement for the Armhole Depth Measurement in the calculations for the width of the sleeve at the top.

Simple gussets can be added to any T-shaped garment. For a gusset, increase or cast on one stitch on every other row, starting 2" to 4" below the armhole. Remember to account for the gusset stitches when figuring the number of stitches to cast on for the sleeves (or the body, if you are working horizontally).

A tapered sleeve on a vertical one- or two-piece sweater is shaped with a slope rather than a taper, since the number of stitches added for the sleeve length will be greater than the number of rows over which to add the stitches. If you are working vertically, the front and back can be worked separately and then sewn together along the center of the sleeves and across the shoulders. This seam can become a decorative element if closed with an embroidery stitch or crochet.

Vertically Knit Ts

These are worked from bottom back, across the sleeves, to bottom front.

STEP 1
Work the garment to the armholes.

STEP 2
Chart the sleeves.
a. **Straight Sleeves.** Neck-to-Wrist Measurement × stitch gauge − (number of stitches on needle ÷ 2) = number of stitches to cast on per sleeve
Cast on this number of stitches at the beginning of the next two rows.
Remember to adjust the sleeve length by the depth of the finish and the gusset stitches, if any.

b. **Tapered Sleeves.** Cast on the same total number of stitches as for the Straight Sleeve, but not all at once. Use the Slope Formula to determine how to distribute the increases, with the following numbers of stitches and rows.
i. [Neck-to-Wrist Measurement – ½ the Body Width – 3″ to 4″ (optional for an untapered upperarm) length of wrist finish] × stitch gauge = number of stitches in the slope of the sleeve.
ii. [Raglan Depth Measurement – (½ Wrist Measurement + 1″ ease)] × row gauge = number of rows in the slope of the sleeve

STEP 3
Complete the knitting.
a. **Two-Piece Garment.** Work to the Raglan Depth Measurement (top of the shoulders), and bind off straight. Join the front to the back across the sleeves and shoulders.
b. **One-Piece Garment.** Work the sweater back to the Raglan Depth Measurement, bind off as needed for the neckline, and continue on the front of the garment, working the neckline and all other shapings in reverse.

Horizontally Knit Ts

These are worked from wrist to wrist.

STEP 1
Chart and work any sleeve style, using your T/Dolman Sleeve Length Measurement (Neck-to-Wrist Measurement – ½ Body Width Measurement) for figuring the length of the sleeve.

STEP 2
Garment Length to Armhole × stitch gauge = number of stitches for each side of the body
Cast on this number of stitches at the beginning of the next two rows.
Adjust the garment length by the depth of the bottom border and the gusset, if needed.

STEP 3
Work the body of the garment, including the neckline shaping, to a knitted depth equal to the T/Dolman Body Width Measurement.

STEP 4
Bind off the Step 2 number of stitches at the beginning of the next two rows.

STEP 5
Continue on the second sleeve, working the shaping in reverse.

Dolmans

The T is an angular, boxy garment. The Dolman, on the other hand, is a style with softer lines, and curves. All Dolman versions include a gusset which extends the armhole depth, creating a smoothly curved line between body and sleeve. The full styling of the Dolman can hide a myriad of figure flaws, but comfort of fit is its main attraction.

There are many variations on the Dolman, along with the multiple ways to chart them. First, let's go over some of the considerations common to all of these variations.

General Considerations. The Dolman Armhole Depth is the sum of the Raglan Armhole Depth and the depth of the gusset. The easiest way to figure the start of the underarm shaping that gives this style its name is to subtract at least 2″ (the minimum depth of a Dolman gusset) from the Garment Length to Underarm Measurement. This establishes the length to knit before starting the sleeve.

As mentioned in "Measuring for Ts and Dolmans," the *Sleeve Width (or Depth) at Wrist* becomes an important measurement in the charting of the Dolman Sleeve. Once the depth of the armhole is established, the shaping itself is charted along the outer edge of the sleeve, to the wrist. The knitted depth of the sleeve at the wrist is used in figuring the depth of the shaping at the underarm on Vertical Dolmans. On Horizontal Dolmans, the width of the sleeve at the wrist is used in figuring the number of stitches to increase or decrease when shaping the sleeves.

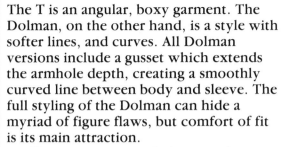
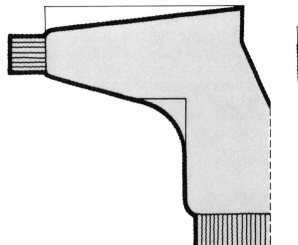

VERSION 1 is a vertical two-piece dolman; this sketch shows it with an optional shoulder slope.

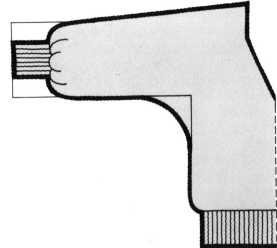

VERSION 3 is a vertical two-piece dolman with a gathered cuff, instead of the sloped underarm.

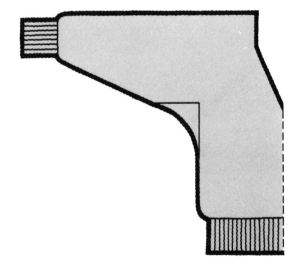

VERSION 2 is a vertical one-piece dolman.

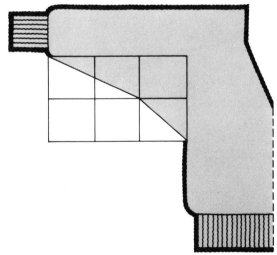

VERSION 4 incorporates a nicely shaped sleeve which can be developed through a simple formula. It can be worked vertically or horizontally.

Shoulder shaping as we know it does not occur on Dolmans. If the entire garment is worked in one piece, it will be charted with a straight line along the top from the neckline to the wrist. If the front and back are worked separately, a slope can be worked along that length, if you wish. While exceptions do exist, we recommend that the slope be only 2″ to 3″ deep so the arms can be raised without undue pull on the garment.

Charting the Dolman. Dolman Sleeves begin a minimum of 2″ below the normal armhole position, with a gusset of that depth. The gusset creates a smooth curved line between the body and the sleeve.

If you like, you can chart your gusset on graph paper. But, for those knitters who prefer an easier method, we have designed a Curve Guide that will work for most Dolmans, regardless of stitch or row gauge (see "How Tos"). Read the chart to see how many stitches to add or subtract per edge, and at what rate to do this. The Curve Guide is designed to work for both Vertical and Horizontal Dolmans.

On some Dolman styles the gussets are charted separately. For such styles, first chart the underarm as a T, then adjust for the gusset stitches and rows when determining the number of stitches to cast on for the sleeve or body length. Other variations include gusset shaping within the actual charting of the sleeves.

Below, we give two charting examples: a Vertical Two-Piece Dolman (with or without a shoulder slope), and a Vertical One-Piece Dolman. These are Dolman Version 1 and Dolman Version 2, respectively. After that, we describe construction of six more versions, including Horizontal Dolmans.

Dolman Version 1: Vertical Two-Piece Dolman

STEP 1
Work the sweater body and gussets (see Curve Guide in "How Tos") to the start of the sleeves.

STEP 2
Raglan Armhole Depth – ½ Sleeve Width at Wrist – 2″ to 3″ for shoulder slope (optional) = depth of sleeve underarm slope
Example: 9.25 – 3.5 – 2 = 3.75   3¾″

STEP 3
Step 2 × row gauge = number of rows for sleeve underarm slope
Round down to the next lower even number (rounding down keeps the sleeve a bit wider, instead of narrowing it).
Example: 3.75 × 6 = 22.5   *22 rows*

STEP 4
Neck-to-Wrist Measurement – ½ sweater T/Dolman Body Width = Dolman Sleeve Length
Example: 26.5 – (17.5 ÷ 2) = 17.75   17¾″

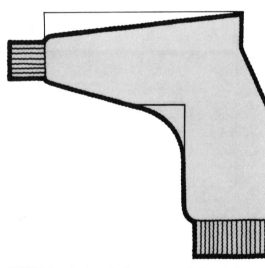

VERSION 1 is a vertical two-piece dolman; this sketch shows it with an optional shoulder slope.

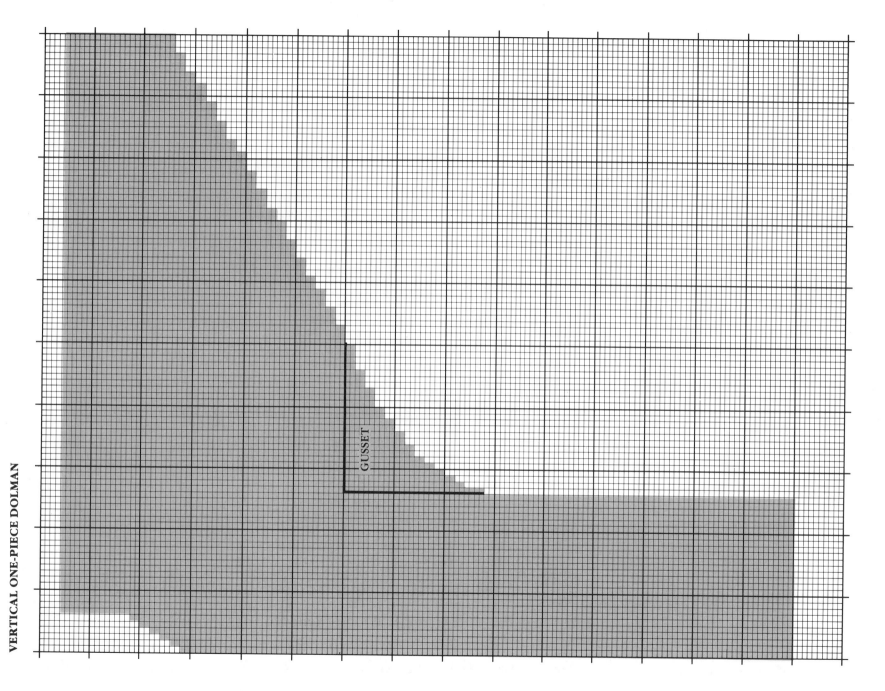

VERTICAL ONE-PIECE DOLMAN

GUSSET

STEP 5

Dolman Sleeve Length − cuff finish length = adjusted sleeve length
Example: 17.75 − 3 = 14.75

14³/₄"

STEP 6

(Step 5 × stitch gauge) − gusset stitches = number of stitches across underarm slope
Example: (14.75 × 5 = 73.75) − 24 = 49.75

50 stitches

STEP 7

Step 6 ÷ (Step 3 ÷ 2) = number of stitches to cast on per sleeve edge on every other row
See Slope Formula to determine exact distribution.
■ If your armhole is very deep, you may be tapering stitches instead of sloping them. In this case, use the Taper Formula to calculate the spacing of the increases.
Example: 50 ÷ (22 ÷ 2 = 11) = 4.5

4 or 6 stitches

STEP 8

Work even for one-half the Sleeve Width at Wrist.

STEP 9

Depth of shoulder slope × row gauge = number of rows of shoulder slope
Use the same shoulder slope depth as chosen in Step 2.
■ If you wish to omit the shoulder slope, see Vertical One-Piece Dolman, Step 9.
Example: 2 × 6 = 12

12 rows

STEP 10

Number of stitches on the needle from the sleeve edge to the neckline ÷ (Step 9 ÷ 2) = number of stitches to bind off at each sleeve edge on every other row
Use Slope Formula to determine exact distribution of decreases.
Example: 94 ÷ (12 ÷ 2 = 6) = 15.6

15 or 16 stitches

STEP 11

Work a front to match the back but *include the front neckline*, assemble the garment at the two seams, pick up and work the neck finish, pick up and work the sleeve finish, and close the underarm seams.

Dolman Version 2: Vertical One-Piece Dolman

STEP 1

Work the sweater body and gussets (see Curve Guide in "How Tos") to the start of the sleeves.

STEP 2

Raglan Armhole Depth – ¹/₂ Sleeve Width at Wrist = depth of underarm slope
Example: 9.25 – 3.5 = 5.75   *5³/₄"*

STEP 3

Step 2 × row gauge = number of rows for sleeve underarm slope
Round down to the next lower even number.
Example: 5.75 × 6 = 34.5   *34 rows*

STEP 4

Neck-to-Wrist Measurement – ¹/₂ T/Dolman Body Width = Dolman Sleeve Length
Example: 26.5 – (17.5 ÷ 2) = 17.75   *17³/₄"*

STEP 5

Dolman Sleeve Length – cuff finish length = adjusted sleeve length
Example: 17.75 – 3 = 14.75   *14³/₄"*

STEP 6

(Step 5 × stitch gauge) – gusset stitches = number of stitches across underarm slope
Example: (14.75 × 5 = 73.75) – 24 = 49.75   *50 stitches*

STEP 7

Step 6 ÷ (Step 3 ÷ 2) = number of stitches to cast on per sleeve edge on every other row
See Slope Formula to determine exact distribution.
- If your armhole is very deep, you may be tapering stitches instead of sloping them. In this case, use the Taper Formula to calculate the spacing of the increases.

Example: 50 ÷ (34 ÷ 2 = 17) = 2.9   *2 or 3 stitches*

STEP 8

Work even for one-half the Sleeve Width at Wrist.

STEP 9

a. **One-Piece Dolman:** Continue working even for the full width of the sleeve at the cuff edge. Then begin your sleeve shaping in reverse (binding off at the same rate as you cast on). Shape the gussets in reverse to match the gussets on the opposite side, and complete the body. Assemble the garment at the underarms and, if necessary, pick up and work the neck finish and the sleeve finish.

b. **Two-Piece Dolman without Shoulder Slope:** Work as for Vertical One-Piece Dolman through Step 8. Bind off. Work front to match the back, remembering to add the front neckline. Assemble the garment at the top, pick up and work the neck finish, pick up and work the sleeve finish, and close the underarm seams.

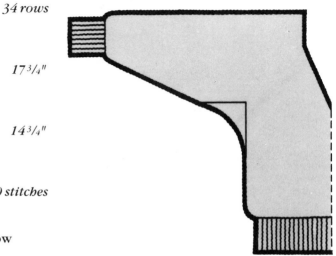

VERSION 2 is a vertical one-piece dolman.

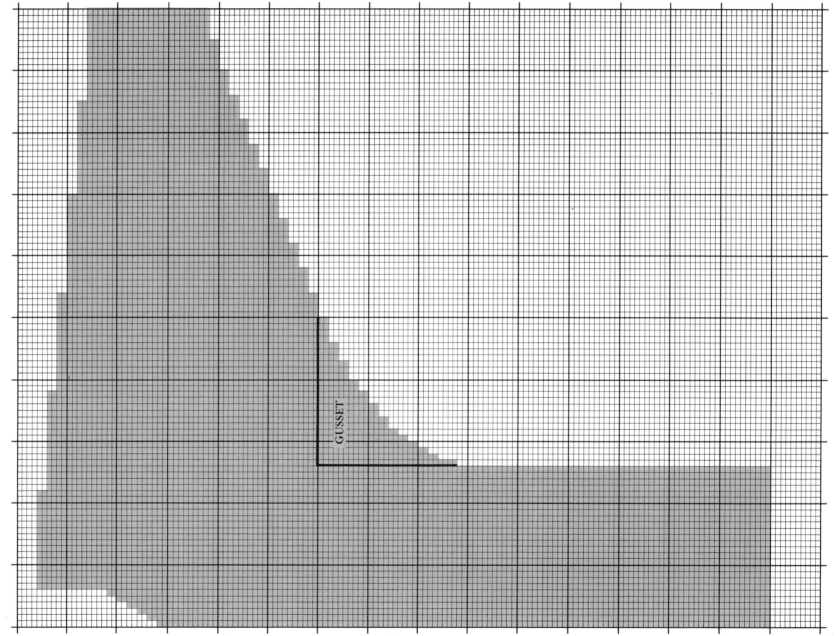

GUSSET

Dolman Version 3

This Vertical Two-Piece Dolman has a gathered cuff rather than a sloped underarm.

STEP 1
Work the body and gusset to the desired garment length.

STEP 2
Cast on the T/Dolman Sleeve Length number of stitches at the beginning of the next two rows (there is no slope or taper under the arm).

STEP 3
Knit the number of rows equivalent to one-half of the Sleeve Width at Wrist.

STEP 4
Raglan Depth Measurement – $1/2$ Sleeve Width at Wrist = depth of shoulder slope
Work an even slope from the wrist to the neckline, using this depth (see Slope Formula).

STEP 5
For cuff finish, sew front and back together along shoulder slope, pick up stitches along the sleeve edge, then decrease evenly to cuff width (Wrist Measurement + Ease) and knit the cuff.

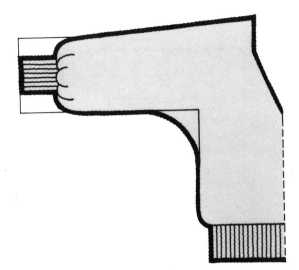

VERSION 3 is a vertical two-piece dolman with a gathered cuff, instead of the sloped underarm.

Dolman Version 4

This version uses a simple formula which produces a nicely shaped sleeve. First establish where on the side seam the sleeve will start. This can be anywhere from 2″ below the normal armhole, down as far as to the waist. The curve of the Dolman is charted from this point to the start of the sleeve depth at the wrist. Separately charted gussets are not needed.

Vertically Knit
STEP 1
(Total Garment Length – garment length to start of sleeve – $1/2$ Sleeve depth at Wrist) × row gauge = number of rows for sleeve shaping

STEP 2
(Neck-to-Wrist Measurement – ¹/₂ T/Dolman Body Width – length of sleeve finish) × stitch gauge = number of stitches for sleeve length

STEP 3
Taper one-third of the Step 2 stitches over one-half of the Step 1 rows, at the part of the sleeve closest to the body. (See Taper Formula for procedure.)

STEP 4
Taper (or slope) the remaining two-thirds of the stitches over the remaining one-half of the rows (extending the sleeve out to the wrist).

STEP 5
Finish knitting top of sleeves and body.

Horizontally Knit
STEP 1
Work the sleeve finish, then any needed increases, to the final Sleeve Width at Wrist.

STEP 2
(Neck-to-Wrist Measurement – ¹/₂ T/Dolman Body Width – length of sleeve finish) × row gauge = number of rows for sleeve length

STEP 3
(Total Garment Length – garment length to start of sleeve – ¹/₂ Sleeve Width at Wrist) × stitch gauge = number of stitches for sleeve shaping (on each side of the sleeve)

STEP 4
Taper one-half of the Step 3 stitches (at both sides of the sleeve) over two-thirds of the Step 2 rows. (See Taper Formula for procedure.)

STEP 5
Taper (or slope) the remaining one-half of the stitches over the remaining one-third of the rows, completing the entire sleeve length.

STEP 6
Knit the sweater body, then the second sleeve as a mirror image of first (in other words, knit in reverse).

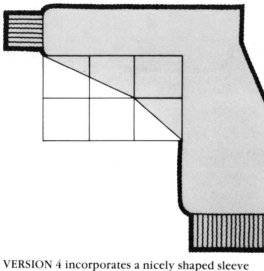

VERSION 4 incorporates a nicely shaped sleeve which can be developed through a simple formula. It can be worked vertically or horizontally.

DOLMANS

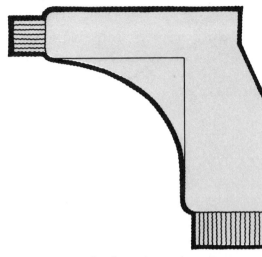

VERSION 5 is a freeform shape, charted on knitting graph paper.

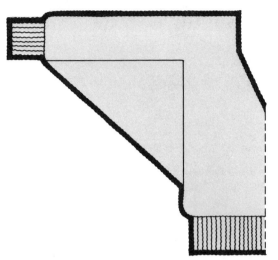

VERSION 7 is similar to Version 6, with a deeper taper.

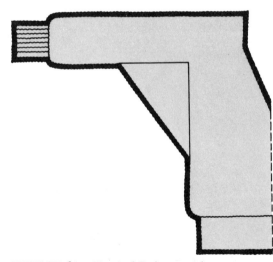

VERSION 6 is a Vertical Dolman with an angular shape.

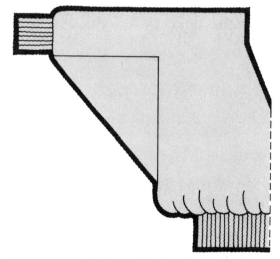

VERSION 8 is similar to Version 6, with extra ease in the body of the sweater.

Dolman Version 5

A "freeform" Dolman can be charted on knitting graph paper, perhaps with the aid of French curves, dishes, or other curved edges.

STEP 1
Lightly graph a Basic T garment shape to scale, marking the Armhole Depth and one-half of the Sleeve Width at Wrist.

STEP 2
Draw a pleasing curve between those marks.

STEP 3
Following the curve as closely as possible, mark off the stitches to be shaped. Remember that it's easier to work the shaping on every even-numbered row.

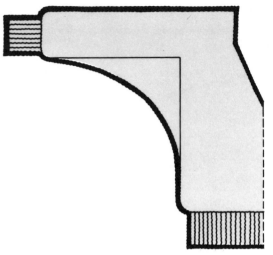

VERSION 5 is a freeform shape, charted on knitting graph paper.

Dolman Version 6

This vertically knit style is more angular than previous versions. The taper of the underarm can begin as low as the waist.

STEP 1
Establish where on the side seam the sleeve shaping will begin, and the depth of the taper.

STEP 2
Taper one-half of the Sleeve Length stitches (excluding the cuff) over the depth of Step 1, then cast on the remaining stitches of the sleeve all at one time.

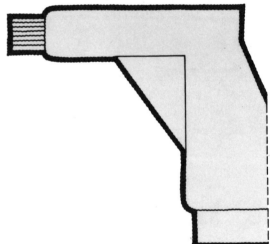

VERSION 6 is a Vertical Dolman with an angular shape.

Dolman Version 7

This is similar to Version 6, but with a deeper taper; it is charted from the waist to the wrist. Add 1″ to 3″ to the garment length for ease when raising the arms.

Dolman Version 8

This is another variation of Versions 6 and 7. Its shaping includes extra ease for a Blouson Body.

STEP 1
Work a border, then increase for a Blouson Body.

STEP 2
Work even on the body for a depth of approximately 2″.

STEP 3
Taper the sleeves to the wrist.

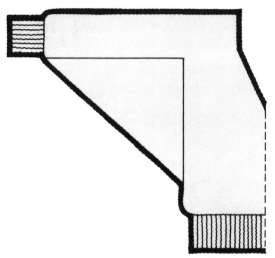

VERSION 7 is similar to Version 6, with a deeper taper.

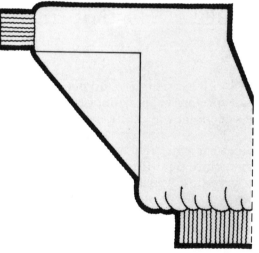

VERSION 8 is similar to Version 6, with extra ease in the body of the sweater.

Finishing Details

NECKLINE FINISHES

Both garment use and personal preference play important roles in the selection of necklines and their finishes. How will the garment be worn? Outerwear sweaters, jackets, and coats may require tight-fitting collars designed for warmth; for instance, turtlenecks, shawl collars, or hoods. A vest or sweater meant to be layered over a special shirt or blouse might need only a simple band. A dressy sweater may utilize a plain crochet or piped edge if jewelry will be worn, or fancy ruffles or a soft cowl collar if the sweater alone will frame the wearer's face.

Yarn thickness and fiber must also be considered when selecting a neckline finish. Some yarns have body, while others provide softness and drape. Most finishes can be made with a wide variety of yarns.

Of course, one of the delights of designing your own garment is selecting the most comfortable and flattering neckline style. Because there are so many possibilities, an attractive variation can always be found for each sweater.

Be sure to select your neckline finish before charting the front and back necklines, since the finish often defines the width and depth of the neckline shaping.

General Information

Picking Up the Neck Finish. While most collars and bands can be worked separately, then sewn onto the neckline, we recommend picking up rather than sewing whenever possible, to reduce the extra work of seams.

In most cases, stitches are picked up with the right side of the garment facing the knitter. The ridge that results is then on the wrong side of the fabric, and is hidden by most finishes. A few collars, however, fold to the outside right at the neck edge. For such a finish, you must decide on which side of the garment the ridge will be least visible.

On circular knit finishes, begin picking up stitches at either shoulder seam unless specifically instructed to begin at another point on the neckline. On open finishes, begin picking up stitches at the opening.

Pick up one stitch for each bound-off stitch (or use all stitches on a holder), and three stitches for every four rows. Or, better yet, mark each inch of your neckline circumference and pick up the equivalent of your stockinette stitch gauge in each inch (see "How Tos"). When two edges are equal in length, be sure to pick up the same number of stitches along each of them.

Seam Stitches. If the collar, or a portion of the collar, requires assembly with a seam, remember to include seam stitches along the edges to be joined. If you do not, stitches from the collar and neckline will be "lost" when the pieces are joined. This is especially problematical on V and Square Necklines with sewn collars and bands. Round Necklines and picked-up finishes on any type of neckline do not require seam stitches.

Machine knitters, in particular, may need to work the entire collar separately and assemble it with seams. Consider which portions of the finish will be visible when the garment is worn, and make sure the seams are on the inside. A flat-knit Turtleneck or Cowl, for example, should have its lower half sewn on the inside and its upper half sewn on the outside to ensure that all seams will be hidden when the collar folds.

Band and Collar Depths. The terms width (a horizontal measurement) and depth (a vertical measurement) often are used interchangeably when describing collars and bands (a 4"-wide collar, or a 4"-deep collar). For the sake of consistency, we will use the term depth in all cases when referring to collars or neckline bands. If a mental picture helps, imagine the band or collar across the back neck-

line where the depth is measured vertically.

Finished band and collar depths can vary significantly: from a single row of slip stitch or crochet, to a 1" band, to a 4–6" collar, to a 10" or deeper cowl. Where possible, we have given standard measurements. These are averages, which may be adjusted to suit individual preferences. Make children's neck finishes one-half to three-quarters of the depth of adults'.

Many finishes are the same depth around the entire neckline circumference. However, they generally fit highest at the back since the front neckline is usually lowered by shaping.

Other finishes, such as some styles of collars, may taper from narrowest at the center front to deepest across the back. Tapering usually is planned to be completed 1–4" below the shoulder, along the edges of the front neckline. (These several inches allow room for adjustments when charting taper rates.) The back of the collar is worked even.

Tapered collars can be knit either horizontally or vertically. On *horizontally worked collars,* stitches are picked up around the neckline circumference. The collar depth is determined by the number of rows knit. Tapering is accomplished by working short rows (see "How Tos"). On *vertically knit collars,* stitches are picked up at the center front. The width of the stitches on the needle equals the depth of the collar; the number of rows is equivalent to the neckline circumference. Tapering for this type of collar is achieved by increasing and decreasing the number of stitches. The collar is sewn to the neckline after completion.

OVERLAPPED FINISHES

MAN'S COLLAR   WOMAN'S COLLAR

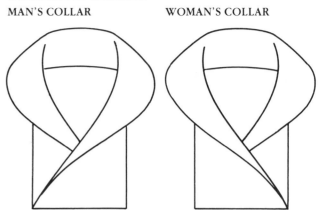

When charting a collar or band, consider whether it will be a single thickness, or whether it will be folded to the inside or outside. Folded collars, of course, will be charted and worked to twice the finished depth.

Overlapped Finishes. Bands, collars, and plackets that overlap at the front bring up the question of which direction to cross the fabric. We opt for tradition. When worn, the left side should overlap the right on a man's collar, and for a woman's collar, the right should overlap the left. Remember when you are assembling the sweater that you are facing the garment, and the "right" and "left" sides are reversed.

If the collar overlaps at the side edge or shoulder, the rules are not as hard-and-fast. Base your decision on what works or looks best. In many cases the overlap is stitched down after the collar is complete, so you can try out both ways.

Knitting Needles. Many neckline finishes can be worked in the round. This eliminates a seam, and makes the working of some finishes—V Necklines, for example—much simpler. Certain finishes can only be worked in rows. This is true on cardigans and for picked-up overlapped bands.

The circumference or width of the neckline will influence the type of knitting needle to use. On High Round Necklines, where the circumference is small, double-pointed needles work best. A circular needle is an excellent choice for most other necklines, since its flexibility allows it to follow the curve of the neck shaping. Since stretching the neckline is something to be avoided, choose the circular knitting needle length closest to the circumference of your neckline. Use a 16″ needle for most bands and collars, a 24″ needle for deep or wide necklines, and a 29″ or longer needle if your finish includes the front bands of a cardigan. Straight needles can be used for knitting overlapped band or shawl collars made separately and sewn to the neckline.

Unless specifically mentioned, neck finishes are worked on your border (smaller) size needle.

Stitch Patterns. The standard stitch patterns for borders—ribbing, seed stitch, or garter stitch—are the most commonly used patterns for neck finishes. The alternation of knit and purl stitches makes these patterns stable and noncurling. Being reversible, they are well suited for collars that fold and show both sides of the fabric.

Stockinette stitch, even with its tendency to roll, should not be ignored. This stitch pattern can be used effectively either by controlling the roll with a hem or a facing, or by taking advantage of the curl and using it for a rolled collar or piping.

Always look for other possibilities—crocheted edgings, brioche patterns, cables, or lace patterns—when they seem applicable. Hems and facings are effective ways to stabilize stitch patterns other than the traditional ones. Be sure that the total number of stitches on your needle matches the requirements of your pattern repeat. A finish worked in the round must contain full repeats. A 1/1 ribbing requires an even number of stitches, and a 2/2 rib must have a multiple of four.

Circularly knit V bands must be planned differently. The stitch pattern must be centered on the back neckline. A 1/1 rib needs an odd number of stitches across the back neck edge to ensure that the two center stitches at the point of the V (one stitch from each side) will both be the same—knits or purls. A 2/2 ribbing needs an even number of stitches across the back neck edge, and the two stitches at center back—and subsequently at center front—must both be the same—knits or purls.

Split (open) collars are planned in the same manner as the circularly knit Vs. By centering the stitch pattern at the back, the edge stitch on each side of the collar will be the same. Think your pattern through, and add or subtract stitches accordingly.

Always work the bind-off of a patterned area in the pattern stitch.

Crochet Finish. The simplest finish for any neckline is to work a row of single crochet, reverse single crochet, or slip stitch around the entire circumference. A decorative crocheted edging can be an effective finish for a sweater knit in a lace pattern.

Round Necklines

Narrow Bands. The traditional finish for a Round Neckline is a 1″ band worked in the round (Crewneck). The depth of the band may be subtracted from each shoulder and added to the neckline width to make the finish lie more smoothly on the shoulders and not ride so high on the neck. Bands of this kind can be worked in any yarn.

The basic procedure is to pick up stitches around the neckline, work the finish in the round to the desired depth, and bind off in pattern.

For a softer edge, double the depth of the band, fold it to the inside, and stitch in place with herringbone stitch (see "How-Tos"). Another method is to fold it to the outside and stitch it in place with backstitch (see "How Tos"). If you wish, use a contrasting color for the backstitching to make it a decorative element. You may or may not wish to place a turning ridge (see "How Tos") at the fold.

Deep Round Necklines can be finished with any of the types of bands mentioned above, but the finish is often narrower, to accent the dressier look of this neckline. The depth of the finish ordinarily is subtracted from the shoulders. This widens the neckline slightly and gives it better

SOME FINISHES FOR ROUND NECKLINES

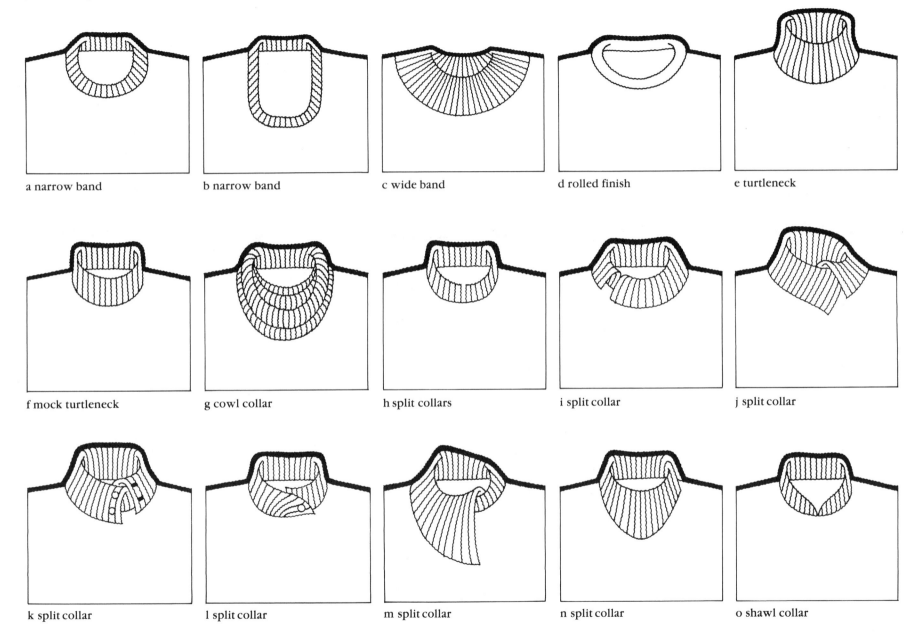

a narrow band

b narrow band

c wide band

d rolled finish

e turtleneck

f mock turtleneck

g cowl collar

h split collars

i split collar

j split collar

k split collar

l split collar

m split collar

n split collar

o shawl collar

SOME FINISHES FOR ROUND NECKLINES (cont.)

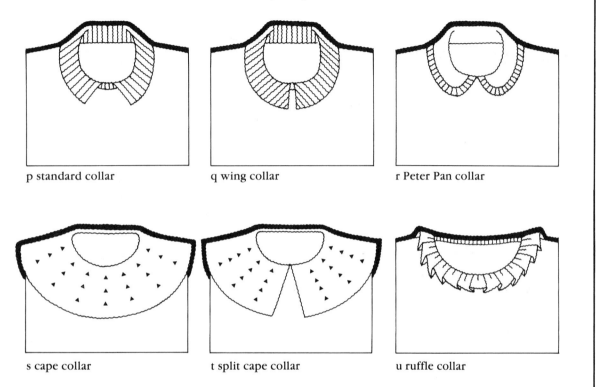

p standard collar

q wing collar

r Peter Pan collar

s cape collar

t split cape collar

u ruffle collar

proportion. If the band is as much as 1″ wide, decreases may need to be worked on the bind-off row at the tightest parts of the curve to prevent gapping. If you are decreasing in ribbing, be sure that the knit stitch ends up on top. (At the neckline's right edge, work to a knit stitch, SSK or SKPO. At the left edge, work to a purl stitch and K2 together. See "How Tos.")

Wide Bands. Wide Bands of 2–5″ depth are worked in the round on deep, wide necklines. Chart your neckline as you would for a Crewneck, then subtract the band depth from the front, shoulders, and back.

Take a Neckline Circumference Measurement around your neck at the point of the wearer's body where the finish will end. The band must be decreased to this measurement.

Decreasing can be worked in two ways, by decreasing stitches or by decreasing needle sizes. Choose the one that works best for your stitch pattern. Both methods are suitable for any yarn and any border stitch.

Decreasing Stitches

STEP 1
Pick up stitches around the neckline and count the stitches on the needle.

STEP 2
Neckline Circumference Measurement × stitch gauge = number of stitches at bind-off row

STEP 3
Step 1 – Step 2 = number of stitches to decrease

STEP 4
Band depth × row gauge = number of rows for band

STEP 5
Step 3 ÷ Step 4 = number of stitches to decrease per row
Determine the rate of decreasing which works best for your pattern stitch. You can decrease as calculated in Step 5 on every row, or decrease twice that number of stitches on every other row, or four times the number every fourth row, etc.
- If you are knitting a ribbing, one way to hide your decreases is to work additional purl stitches between the knit stitches, then decrease the purls while keeping the knit stitches intact.

STEP 6
Bind off, or continue working even for a Turtleneck, a Split Collar, or a Standard Collar.

Decreasing Needle Size

STEP 1
On border size needles, pick up stitches around the neckline and count the stitches on the needle.

STEP 2
Step 1 ÷ Neckline Circumference Measurement = stitch gauge on bind-off row

STEP 3
Work test swatches on smaller needles until you find the size that gives you the Step 2 gauge.

STEP 4
Work even to the desired collar depth, decreasing the needles by one size at regularly spaced intervals to the size established in Step 3.

STEP 5
Bind off, or continue working even for a Turtleneck, Split Collar, or Standard Collar.

NARROW BAND

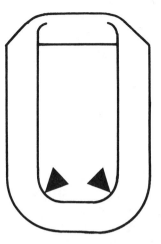

A deep round neckline with a band less than 1" wide does not require extra attention. But a wider band may call for decreases on the bind-off row, at the locations marked, to prevent gapping.

Rolled Finishes. The tendency of stockinette stitch to curl forms the basis for Rolled Collars, Purl Welt Edging, and Piping. The latter two finishes are relatively narrow, while the Rolled Collar is somewhat wider.

Piping and Rolled Collars are worked on needles of the same size as used for the sweater body. Purl Welt Edgings are worked on needles one size smaller than the body needles.

PIPING. With the wrong side facing you, pick up stitches around the entire neckline. Turn the work. Working on the right side of the garment and in the round, knit four rounds, then bind off. Let the piping roll to the right side of the garment (covering the unfinished edge), then stitch it down.

PURL WELT EDGING. With the right side facing you, pick up stitches around the neckline. Working in the round, purl between four and six rounds, then bind off.

ROLLED COLLAR. With the right side facing you, pick up stitches around the neckline. Working in the round, knit to the desired depth (approximately 3″ to 4″ minimum), then bind off loosely.

The Purl Welt Edging and the Rolled Collar do not need to be stitched down. They simply roll and are finished. The Rolled Collar can be whip stitched (see "How Tos") with a yarn of a contrasting color or texture, if you wish. If stitched down, this collar can be stuffed to make a thicker roll.

Turtleneck. This tightly fitting, high collar is a popular finish for a High Round Neckline. However, if it is to be used as the basis for a Turtleneck, the High Round Neckline shape needs to be widened by 1″ to 2″ to enable the collar to fit over the head.

TRADITIONAL TURTLENECK. Pick up stitches around the neckline, work in the round for 4″ to 6″ (or the desired depth), then bind off loosely in pattern.

MOCK TURTLENECK. Pick up stitches around the neckline, work in the round for 1″ to 1½″, then bind off. If you want a firmer collar, work for 2″ to 3″ before binding off, then fold the collar to the inside and stitch it down.

The **Cowl Collar** is a deep, folded-over finish, looser-fitting than a Turtleneck. It is suitable for any Round Neckline, from a High Round Neckline to a Deep Wide one. This is a finish that is best worked in the round, since that eliminates any seams which could show when the collar is rolled.

There are various factors that affect the final form of a Cowl Collar. The first has been mentioned: the shape of the neckline. The second and third factors are the depth of the collar and its circumference at the outer edge. As well, the thickness and fiber composition of the fabric will affect the collar shape.

Influenced by these various elements, a Cowl can take many forms. When knit in a heavy yarn, a Cowl can be a wide, low, standing collar. Or it can be a deep, soft collar knit of a fine, draping yarn.

Variation of different elements—weight and hand of the yarn, shape of the neckline, and depth and circumference of the collar itself—will give you many possible looks.

On wide, deep necklines, pick up the stitches for the collar, work even to the desired depth, and bind off. Increasing the collar's outer circumference is optional.

If this finish is worked on a High Round Neckline, the neckline will need to be widened by 1″ to 2″ to enable it to fit over the head with ease. In this case, increasing the circumference of the outer edge of the collar is necessary for proper drape. This can be accomplished in one of three ways.

GRADUAL FLARING. Increase the needle size by one size every 1″ to 1½″. Bind off when you reach the desired depth.

SUDDEN FLARING. Work even on the picked-up stitches for approximately ¾″ to 1″. Change needle size drastically (3–4 sizes larger).

or

Increase 2″ to 4″ of stitches, evenly spaced, in the next row.

or

Change to a pattern stitch that knits to a looser gauge without needing a change in needle size (for example, brioche ribs or lace).

TAPERED INCREASES. Determine the finished depth of the Cowl and the circumference you wish to have at the top:

(Final circumference × stitch gauge) – number of stitches picked up at neckline = number of stitches to increase

Place a marker at the center back, and increase two stitches per round, one on each side of the marker, evenly spaced over the depth of the finish. Bind off.

Your method of increasing a Cowl can be influenced by your choice of pattern stitch. Any reversible border stitch is appropriate. Pick up the collar on your border size needles and increase in a way that maintains the integrity of the pattern.

Cowls also can be worked as a continuation of the stitch pattern of the sweater body. For example, you might knit both body and collar in stockinette stitch or in lace. In this case, work the entire collar on the body size needles, and select an increase method that does not require a change in needle size.

There are additional things to consider if your collar is worked in the same stitch as the rest of the garment. When a Cowl is folded, the wrong side of the fabric shows. To avoid this and at the same time prevent the fabric from curling, you can knit to twice the collar depth, fold the collar to the inside, and stitch it in place.

If a Cowl Collar is made deep enough, it can become a Hood. Measure for it as follows. With the head bent forward, measure from the back neckline, over the head, to the forehead. This is the minimum depth of the collar.

If worked separately in the round, a Cowl can be a removable collar for sweaters with simpler finishes, such as Crewnecks or Boatnecks. Drape a string around your neck to determine the desired circumference of the cowl. If

COWL COLLARS

GRADUAL FLARING

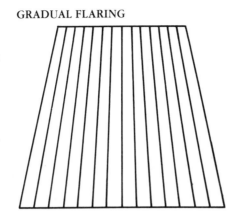

SUDDEN FLARING

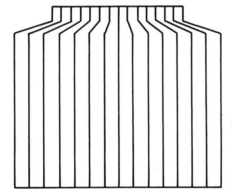

TAPERED FLARING

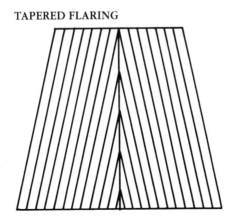

HOODED COWL COLLAR

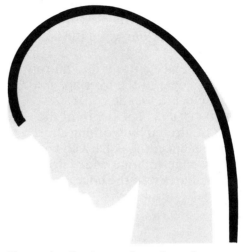

If a cowl collar is very deep, it can become a hood. To determine the minimum depth of the collar, measure from the back neckline, over the head, to the forehead.

your pattern stitch curls, work a border of 1/2″ to 3/4″ in a non-curling stitch at both edges. Another method to prevent the Cowl from curling is to sew the cast-on and bound-off edges together to form a tube.

Split Collars. Splitting a Turtleneck, Mock Turtleneck, or Cowl Collar creates a new set of neckline design possibilities.

To start, determine where on the neckline you want the opening—at the center front, off-center on an edge, or at a shoulder. Begin picking up stitches at that point, and work the collar in rows on a circular needle or double-pointed needles.

Some design variations include the following.

OVERLAPPED EDGES. Cast on 1″ or more of stitches at the beginning and/or end of the picked-up row. Sew the overlap to the neckline when the collar is complete.

BUTTONS. Place buttons and button-holes on the edges of the overlap, as a decorative closure for the collar.

SHAPED COLLAR. The depth of the collar can be altered by working short rows. For instance, the collar can have one narrow edge and one wide edge, or it can go from narrow at the edges to wide in the center, or it can slope in the opposite direction.

SEPARATELY KNIT COLLAR. A separate collar can be worked either horizontally or vertically. Placement of the opening can then be decided after the collar is complete. The short edges of the rectangle will equal the collar depth; the long edges will equal the neckline circumference plus any overlap. Join it to the neckline with a seam.

A **Shawl Collar** is highest at the back, decreasing to zero at the center front. It can be charted for any Medium or High Round Neckline. The finished depth at the back should be from 1″ to 2″. This Round Neckline finish may be knit in any weight of yarn and in any border stitch. If the collar is doubled, it is possible to use stockinette stitch.

There are two versions of the Shawl Collar for a Round Neckline. The first is worked directly on the sweater by picking up stitches around the neckline edge. The collar is knit using the short row technique (see "How Tos"). The second version is a separately knit collar which is shaped by casting on.

Picked-Up Shawl Collar

STEP 1
Mark the center front (F) and center back (B) of the neckline. Mark points at the right (R) and left (L), halfway between F and B. These divide the neckline into four equal sections.

STEP 2
Beginning at L, pick up stitches around the entire neckline.

STEP 3
Count the total number of stitches between R and L, across the front of your neckline. There should be an equal number of stitches between R–F and F–L.

STEP 4
Finished collar depth × row gauge = number of rows for collar shaping

STEP 5
Step 3 ÷ Step 4 = number of additional stitches to work per row for collar shaping

STEP 6
Work the first row across the back neckline, from R to L. *Turn the work. Knit across the previously worked stitches, remove the marker, work Step 5 number of stitches, and replace the marker at this point.* Repeat between asterisks (*) until all of the neckline stitches have been worked. You will be at F.

SPLIT COLLARS

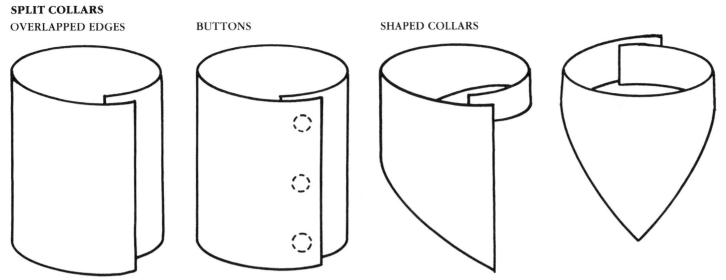

OVERLAPPED EDGES BUTTONS SHAPED COLLARS

A turtleneck, mock turtleneck, or cowl collar can be split, producing a new set of design possibilities. The split can occur at the front, off-center, at the shoulder, or at the back. The collar can be closed, shaped, or otherwise modified.

STEP 7

a. **Single Thickness Collar:** Bind off in the next row.

b. **Double Thickness Collar:** Continue knitting to produce a mirror image of the collar, working the short rows in reverse over the Step 4 number of rows. Bind off.

or

Work the additional rows, but bind off the Step 5 number of stitches each row using the bias bind-off method (see "How Tos").

Fold the fabric to the inside and stitch in place, or let the collar roll to the outside.

Separate Shawl Collar

STEP 1

Neckline circumference in inches × stitch gauge = number of stitches for the width of the collar

STEP 2
Step 1 ÷ 2 = total number of shaping stitches
Make this an even number.

STEP 3
Finished collar depth × row gauge = number of rows for the collar

STEP 4
Step 2 ÷ Step 3 = number of shaping stitches per row

STEP 5
Step 1 − Step 2 = number of stitches to cast on

STEP 6
Cast on the Step 5 number of stitches, work 1 row, and turn the work.

STEP 7
Cast on the Step 4 number of stitches at the beginning of the next row, and work to the end of the row. Repeat between asterisks (*) until the Step 1 number of stitches is on your needle.

STEP 8
a. **Single Thickness Collar:** Bind off all stitches. Sew the collar to the neckline along the tapered edge.
b. **Double Thickness Collar:** Work an additional Step 3 number of rows, binding off Step 5 number of stitches each row, using the bias bind-off method (see "How Tos").

The **Standard Collar** is a fold-over collar with a split front.

Pick up stitches around the neckline, beginning at the center front, and work in the round for $1/4''$ to $3/4''$ in ribbing or garter stitch. Divide the work at the center front and work in rows in any reversible border stitch for $2''$ to $4''$, or to the desired depth. Bind off.

If the stitch pattern needs to be balanced at the collar edges, one or two stitches can be bound off at the center front on the dividing row.

The **Wing Collar** has a smaller front opening than the Standard Collar.

Knit this collar like the Standard Collar, but work a single increase, at least one stitch in from the edge, on each edge every other row.

SHAWL COLLAR FOR A ROUND NECKLINE

A Basic shape

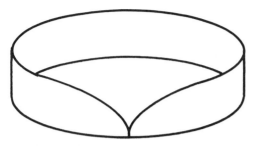

The shawl collar for a round neckline is highest at the back, and decreases to zero at the center front. It can be worked with short rows on picked-up stitches, or can be knit separately and sewn into place.

B Before picking up stitches, mark collar in four equal sections.
R (right) B (back) F (front) L (left)

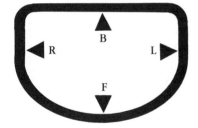

C Begin at R and work first row across the back neckline to L. Work back and forth (as described in Step 6) until all neckline stitches have been worked and you are at F.

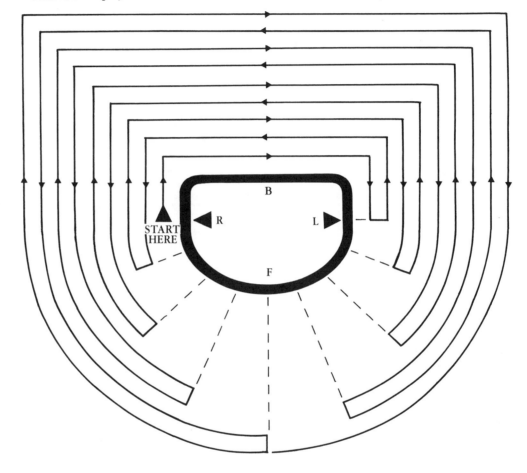

D To knit a double-thickness collar, continue knitting to produce a mirror image, working the short rows in reverse.

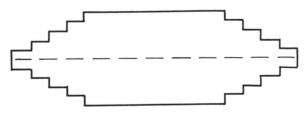

PETER PAN COLLAR

A Begin 1/4" to 1/2" left of center front and pick up stitches, ending the same distance right of center front. The distance left without stitches will determine the depth of the patterned border.

B Work even for 1/4" to 1/2" less than desired collar depth.

C Change to smaller needles; cast on, at each edge, the number of stitches equal to the depth of the collar you have worked. Work border pattern and bind off.

D Sew cast-on edges of border to front edges of collar.

E You can make rounder front corners by shaping the front edges with decreases between b and c as shown above.

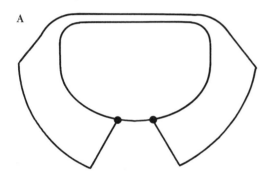

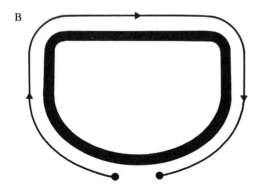

The Peter Pan collar is like a standard collar with rounded front corners, and includes a narrow patterned border around its edges.

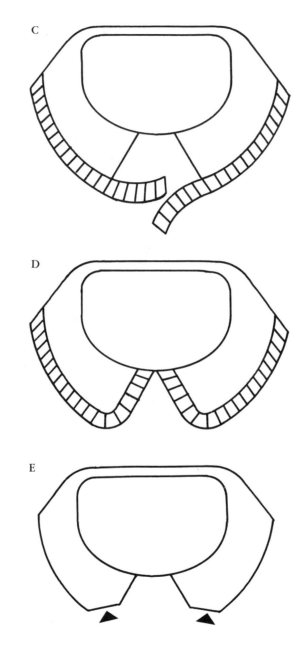

A **Peter Pan Collar** resembles a Standard Collar with rounded front corners, and includes a narrow patterned border around all edges. It is worked on a bound-off High Round Neckline, and can be knit in any weight of yarn.

Turn the sweater inside out. Using the same size needles as for the sweater body, start 1/4" to 1/2" left of center front and pick up stitches around the neckline to the same distance right of center front. Start the pattern with a wrong-side row, and work in any stitch pattern for 1" to 2", or to 1/4" to 1/2" less than the desired collar depth.

Change to smaller needles and cast on, at both edges, the equivalent of your collar depth in stitches (1–2" × stitch gauge). Change to a border pattern and work it for a depth equal to half the width of the space at the center front (1/4"–1/2"). Bind off in pattern.

Sew the cast-on edge of the border pattern section to the side edges of the collar, then sew its ends to the center front, filling the space.

If you wish, you can round the corners of the collar even more by decreasing or binding off at the collar's front edges. Start the shaping a few rows before casting on and knitting the border.

A **Cape Collar** is deep, often extending to the shoulder line. It can be worked in the round, or split at the center front or back and worked in rows.

Any yarn is appropriate, as are most stitch patterns, including stockinette, lace, and designs using the various color techniques. If you wish, the edges can be stabilized by a narrow border.

CAPE COLLAR

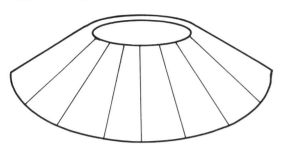

This is a deep collar, worked in the round or split at center front or back and worked in rows.

Determine the collar depth and take a circumference measurement around your body at that point, equivalent to the edge circumference of the collar. The collar width will be increased from the neckline circumference to the edge circumference measurement.

This collar also can be knit in reverse—from the wide edge to the neckline, working decreases instead of increases—then sewn onto the neckline.

Ruffled Collar. This is a collar with extra width, so that it does not lie flat. It can be any depth, and can be continuous or split.

Working in the round, pick up and work a minimum of two rows of ribbing or garter stitch to stabilize the neckline. *On the next row, double the number of stitches on your needle by increasing in every stitch or between every two stitches.* Work one row even, then repeat between asterisks (*) once more. Work even for 1″ or to the desired depth of the ruffle.

Border patterns, stockinette, and laces are good stitch choices for ruffles. An easy way to stabilize the edge is to bind off in knit on the wrong side of the ruffle. Consider the yarn, and work a test swatch to see how a ruffle in this size and fiber reacts. Fine, soft, draping yarns are best; heavier weights of yarn or yarns with more body are not always suitable.

Note that ruffles can be worked at the wrist, as well as at the neckline.

V Neckline Finishes

There are two versions of the V Neckline, the Traditional V and the Blunt V. The Traditional V Neckline begins with a point. When the sweater front has an odd number of stitches, a single stitch is bound off or placed on a holder at the center front. On a Blunt V Neckline, from 1″ of stitches up to one-third of the neckline stitches are bound off or placed on a holder at center front.

Don't wait until you have finished knitting your sweater to decide on the finish for your V Neckline. The finish you select can determine which neckline version you should use, as well as whether you bind off the neckline stitches or leave them open on a holder.

In a **Self-Finished V Neckline**, the border finish is worked at the same time as you knit the front and shape the neckline. Choose a suitable stitch pattern for the finish, and work the decreases of the neckline to the inside of the border stitches. The front neckline must be charted to include the border. Chart the neckline narrower and shallower than you would if a border were to be added

SELF-FINISHED V NECKLINES

A   B

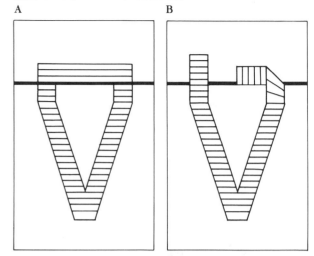

There are two ways to work the back neckline finish, either as a separate back finish worked along with the body (a), or as an extension of the front border (b).

later. The back neckline can be finished in one of two ways.

SEPARATE BACK FINISH. Work a border along the back neckline in the same stitch and to the same depth as the front neckline. To complete the garment, sew the front and back together at the shoulders, lining up the border stitches.

EXTENSION OF FRONT BORDER. Bind off only the stitches of the body in the shoulder shaping, and continue even on the stitches of the borders for a length equal to one-half the width of the back neckline. Sew or graft the ends together, and sew the band to the back neckline. When charting the back neckline of this version, subtract the width of the border from each shoulder; your shoulder shaping should have the same number of stitches on the back and the front.

SOME FINISHES FOR V NECKLINES

A self finish
B-C decreased bands
D-E decreased bands with standard
    collar and turtleneck
F foldover collar
G cowl collar
H rolled finish
I band with collar
J band with wing collar

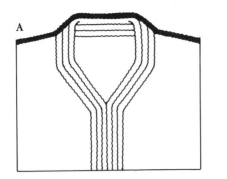

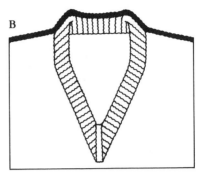

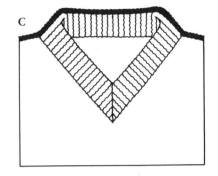

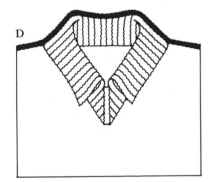

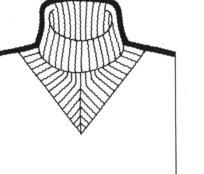

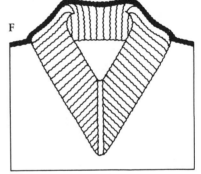

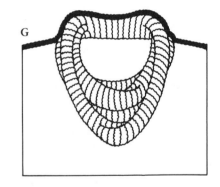

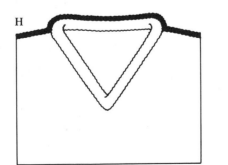

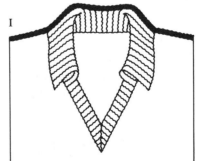

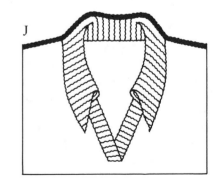

(More V-Neckline finishes on page 290)

Decreased Band. Perhaps the most popular V finish is a ribbed band with decreases at the center front.

On Traditional V Neck sweaters, neckline shaping begins at a level near the armhole bind-off, and the added band is about 1″ deep. Don't be shy about making changes. A V can be a wider and shallower neckline, and the band can be narrower or deeper than 1″. This finish is suitable for any yarn.

Below, we give you four slightly different versions of the V Neckline Decreased Band. All of them start the same way: Beginning at the right shoulder and working in the round, pick up stitches around the entire neckline. Be sure to pick up equal numbers along both front edges. Remember to center the stitch pattern at the back neckline. For a 1/1 rib, pick up an odd number of stitches; for a 2/2 rib, pick up an even number of stitches.

Decreased Band Versions 1 and 2

These variations require a *center stitch*. A center stitch is one remaining on a holder at the front center. If your sweater was knit with an odd number of stitches, you automatically have a center stitch. If not, you can create one with a lifted increase or a picked-up stitch.

Decreased Band Version 1 incorporates a raised double decrease at the center of the neckline.

In Decreased Band Version 2, the center stitch is less prominent, and you may find it appropriate for dressier sweaters. A variation especially suited for a 2/2 rib is to leave two center stitches on a holder as you shape the neckline. Both center stitches, then, are knit as you work the finish.

STEP 1
Place a yarn marker around the center stitch(es).

STEP 2
Pick up stitches around the neckline, knitting the center stitch when you come to it.

STEP 3
Begin working a 1/1 or 2/2 rib.

STEP 4
Work the decreases.
a. **Version 1:**
    Stop one stitch before the center stitch.
    Slip two stitches together knitwise, K1, and pass the two slipped stitches over (together or one at a time).

b. **Version 2:**
Stop two stitches before the center stitch(es).

- If the first stitch on your left needle is a knit stitch, work as follows: SSK or SKPO (see "How Tos"), knit center stitch(es), K2 tog.
- If the first stitch on your left needle is a purl stitch, work as follows: P2 tog, knit center stitch(es), P2 tog.

STEP 5
Continue with the rib.

STEP 6
Repeat Step 4 every round (or every other round on wider neckline), including the bind-off row.

Decreased Band Versions 3 and 4

These variations are worked on V Necklines without a center stitch.
　　Decreased Band Version 3 is similar to Version 2.
　　Decreased Band Version 4 creates a band of two stitches at the center front of the finish. This makes an effective finishing detail for a 2/2 rib.

STEP 1
Pick up stitches around the entire neckline, placing a marker on the needle at the center front point.

STEP 2
Work in ribbing to two stitches before the marker.

STEP 3
Work the decreases.

a. **Version 3:**

- If the first stitch on the left needle is a knit stitch, work as follows: SSK or SKPO (see "How Tos"), slip the marker, K2 tog.
- If the first stitch on the left needle is a purl stitch, work as follows: P2 tog, slip the marker, P2 tog.
　　Work the second decrease very tightly, so that a gap does not form between the decreases. If necessary, tighten by pulling on the yarn after the decrease is made.

b. **Version 4:**
K2 tog, slip the marker, SSK or SKPO (see "How Tos").
Here, too, work the second decrease tightly to avoid a gap.

STEP 4

Continue with the rib.

STEP 5

Repeat Step 3 on every round (every other round on wider necklines), including the bind-off row.

Decreased Band with Standard Collar or Turtleneck. These Decreased Band combination collars are close-fitting finishes that can be worked in any yarn.

Both variations require a wide, shallow neckline. Begin your V Neckline decreases after the armhole shaping is complete, and widen the neckline by approximately 4″ (2″ per shoulder). In addition, shape the back neckline by at least 1″.

To start either of these styles, work any version of a decreased band to a 2″ depth. You may need to work the decreases on every other row.

STANDARD COLLAR. Bind off the center stitch, if necessary to match your pattern. Continuing in a rib pattern, work in rows for the desired collar depth. Bind off.

TURTLENECK. Continue working even in the round for the desired depth of your Turtleneck. Make sure that the Turtleneck begins with an appropriate pattern repeat. For example, if you have been working a 1/1 rib with a center stitch, make sure that you have alternating knit and purl stitches there. If you have no center stitch, you may need to make one.

The **Foldover Collar** begins with a Decreased Band. When that is complete, the finish continues into a mirror-image Increased Band. The increased portion of the band will fold to the outside. If your neckline is wide and you are planning a deep decreased portion for this finish, consider shaping the back neckline to the depth of the Decreased Band.

Using a 1/1 or a 2/2 rib, work a Decreased Band with a center stitch for a depth of one to several inches, filling in as much of the neck opening as you wish.

At this point, begin the increased portion. Change the center stitch to a purl, since you are working on the wrong side of the fabric for this portion of the collar. When the collar is folded, the center purl will show as a knit.

Continuing in your rib pattern, increase one stitch on each side of the center purl. Work the increases at the same rate as you worked the decreases. When your pattern requires a knit stitch, work an M1 Knit Increase. When a purl stitch is required, work an M1 Purl Increase. (For M1 Increases, see "How Tos.")

Knit until the increased portion is at least 1/2″ deeper than the decreased portion, and bind off. This finish can be worked in any yarn.

A **Cowl Collar** can be worked on any V Neckline by picking up stitches and working in the round for the desired collar depth. For details, see "Round Neckline Finishes."

DEEP V BAND WITH COLLAR

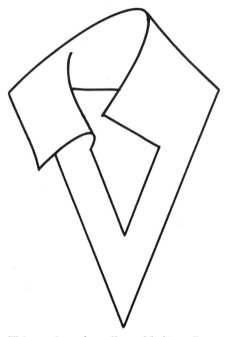

This version of a collar added to a Decreased Band works best with a narrow, deep traditional V neckline.

THE PAPER TRICK FOR OVERLAPPED BANDS

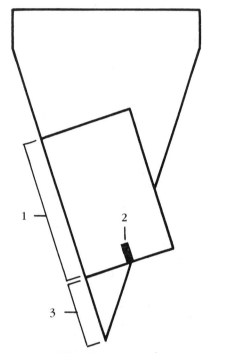

A tapered finish at the end of an overlapped band allows the finish to fit perfectly into the angle of the V. You can figure the amount to taper with a simple paper trick.

1 Mark desired depth of band on a rectangular piece of paper.
2 Place bottom of paper flat along one edge of neckline taper, so mark touches opposite edge of neckline taper.
3 Measure fabric between point of V and edge of neckline taper to determine the number of stitches to taper at the V.

Rolled Finishes are worked the same as for a Round Neckline. If the finish will be more than a few rows deep, consider working a decrease at the point of the V on every other row, so that the finish will lie flat. For detailed information on Rolled Finishes, see "Round Neckline Finishes."

Deep V Band with Collar. This finish superimposes a collar on the top of a Decreased Band. Unlike the Decreased Band with Collar discussed above, in this variation the collar does not extend all the way down to the point of the V.

This style works best with a narrow, deep Traditional V Neckline. The edges of the collar should start 3″ to 4″ below the shoulder. Any yarn can be used.

Pick up and work a Decreased Band to a 1″ depth. (An Overlapped Band, as described below, also can be used.) Bind off all the stitches at the front that are not required for the collar. Remaining on your needle will be 3″ to 4″ of stitches below each shoulder, plus all of the stitches across the back. Continuing in the pattern of the band, work even, in rows, for 2″ to 4″ or to the desired collar depth. Bind off in pattern.

For a Wing Collar variation, work single increases at least one stitch in from the edge, at each edge, on every other row.

Overlapped Band. In this finish, the two sides of the border band are overlapped at the center front, rather than being worked continuously.

This is an easy, yet very versatile, finish for a V Neckline. It is worked in rows, in any yarn, with a wide range of stitch possibilities for the fabric. The finished band can be any depth you want—from less than 1″ up to several inches. Wide Bands can be folded to become a Shawl Collar.

As to the direction of the overlap, we will stay with a left overlap (as worn) on a man's garment, and a right overlap on a woman's garment. Be sure to cast on an additional seam stitch on the appropriate side if the band is to be sewn to the neckline.

Either a Vertical Band (worked in the same direction as the stitches of the sweater body) or a Horizontal Band (worked on picked-up stitches, at an angle to the stitches of the sweater body) can be used for this finish. There are slight differences to consider in planning it for a Traditional V or a Blunt V Neckline.

TRADITIONAL V NECKLINE. If your neckline has an odd number of stitches, bind off or decrease the center stitch.

For deeper bands, we recommend tapering the ends of the finish, except when the neckline itself is so wide that it forms a right angle at the point of the V. This taper will allow the finish to fit perfectly into the angle of the V.

Determine the amount to taper by means of a simple paper trick. On a sheet of paper, measure up from the right-hand corner and mark your desired band depth on the edge (1). Lay the sweater flat and place the bottom of the paper (2) along the left edge of the neckline so that the mark touches the opposite edge. The width of fabric between the edge of the paper and the point of the V (3) equals the width of stitches to taper.

Traditional V Neckline

Vertical Band
STEP 1
Starting at the point, pick up on the right edge (for a woman) or on the left edge (for a man), a number of stitches equal to the width of the band. Cast on a seam stitch at the seam edge of the band.

STEP 2
Knit a length approximately 1″ shorter than the neckline circumference. If needed, slope the ends with short rows. Bind off.

STEP 3
Sew the band in place, stretching it to fit and tucking the bound-off end to the inside.

Horizontal Band
STEP 1
Cast on one stitch for a seam stitch. With the seam stitch on the needle and starting at the point on the left edge of the neckline, pick up stitches around the entire neckline. Cast on another seam stitch.

STEP 2
Work the band to the desired depth, tapering it at the ends if needed.

STEP 3
Bind off, then overlap and sew the ends at the center front.

OVERLAPPED BANDS

TRADITIONAL V   BLUNT V

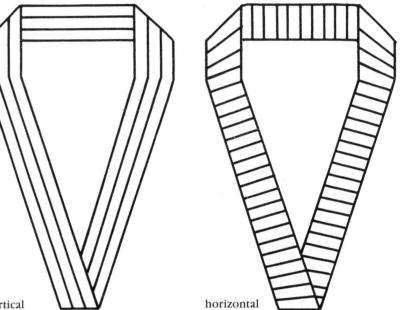

vertical   horizontal   vertical   horizontal

*The two sides of the border band can be
overlapped at the center front, on either a
traditional or a blunt V neckline. The border
band can be worked either vertically (along
with the sweater body) or horizontally (from
picked-up stitches).*

BLUNT V NECKLINE. Measure the width of the stitches bound off or left on a holder at the center front of the V Neckline. Horizontal Bands can vary in depth from one-half this width to the entire width. Vertical Bands will have the same number of stitches as the blunt edge.

Blunt V Neckline

Vertical Band
STEP 1
The center neckline stitches should have been left on a holder. Place them on the needle and add a seam stitch on the appropriate side of the needle (at your right, as you face the sweater, for a man; at your left for a woman).

STEP 2
Knit the band to a length equal to the neckline circumference minus $1/2''$ to $1''$, and bind off.

STEP 3
Sew the band to the neckline edge, stretching it to fit and tucking the bound-off end to the inside.

Horizontal Band
STEP 1
Pick up in the same way as for the Traditional V Neckline.

STEP 2
Work to the desired depth, bind off, and stitch the ends in place in front.

A little imagination opens up a whole realm of possible variations for the Overlapped Band. Let's look at several ideas.

The **Gathered Overlapped Band** includes extra width, which is gathered together at the point of the V so that the fabric of the band lies in folds around the neckline circumference. Best worked in fine to medium yarns with a fair amount of drape, this version of the Overlapped Band results in a soft finish suitable for dressier sweaters. The entire collar can be worked in stockinette stitch. The outer edge will roll to the inside, but that is fine.

On a Blunt V Neckline, knit the stitches from the holder. On a Traditional V Neckline, pick up $2''$ to $4''$ of stitches along the left edge. Increase in every stitch on the next two rows. There will be four times the original number of stitches on the needle. Work even until the collar length equals the circumference of the neckline. Knit two stitches together across the next two rows, and bind off. Stitch the collar into place around the neckline.

MORE FINISHES FOR V NECKLINES

K-O overlapped bands
P gathered overlapped band
Q pleated overlapped band
R-S shawl collars
T-V reverse taper collars
W ruffle collar
X band with insert

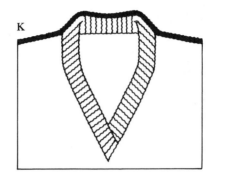

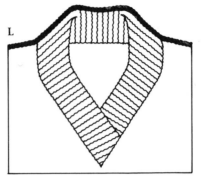

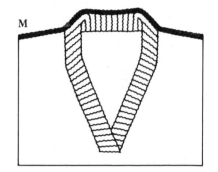

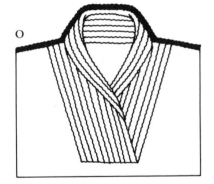

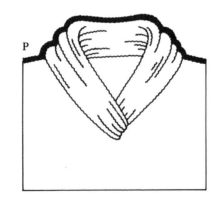

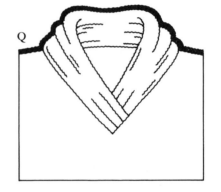

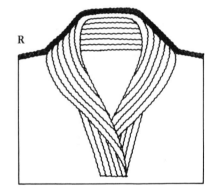

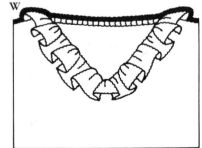

(More V-Neckline finishes on page 282)

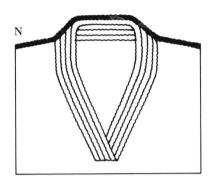

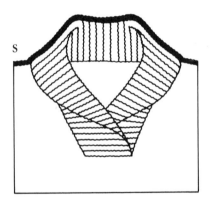

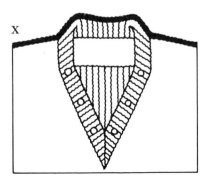

The **Pleated Overlapped Band** is similar in concept to the gathered band, but is worked separately.

If the band is knit in stockinette, work the last few stitches on the outer edge in a border stitch to stabilize the edge. Another option is to work a vertical turning ridge (see "How Tos") ½" in from the edge, for a hem.

Cast on three times the finished band width, work even until the band length equals the neckline circumference, and bind off. Pleat both ends and stitch the collar to the neckline.

Shawl Collar. A tapered Overlapped Band provides still more possibilities for new neckline designs. The Shawl Collar— higher at the back, lower at the front—is a variation familiar to most knitters. Work this finish in any noncurling, reversible pattern stitch. All weights and types of yarn are appropriate for this collar.

Careful thought should be given to the planning of the neckline. A Shawl Collar is quite full, and if the neckline is too narrow or shallow the addition of the collar may make its fit uncomfortably snug. The depth of a V Neckline of standard width (one-third the Shoulder Width) should at least equal the Raglan Depth Measurement. Wider necklines can begin higher.

If you use a Traditional V Neckline shape, you may want to taper the corners of the ends of the collar, as described above for a plain Overlapped Band.

Decide on the unfolded depth of the collar at the back of the neck—4" to 6" is average. From that measurement, subtract the width or depth of the band at the front. The difference between these two measurements equals the width of the taper on a Vertical Shawl Collar or the depth of the slope on a Horizontal Shawl Collar. The shaping on the front can end at the shoulder seam, 4" below it, or anywhere in between. Generally, the collar depth is even across the back.

Note that Shawl Collars for cardigans are discussed separately, in connection with cardigan front finishes. For additional information on Shawl Collar shaping, look through that section, as well as the section on Shawl Collars for Round Necklines.

VERTICAL SHAWL COLLAR. On a vertically knit collar (stitches knit in the same direction as those of the sweater body), the taper is created by working single increases along one front portion and mirrored decreases along the other. The increases and decreases can be worked at the inside edge of the collar (the part that will be sewn to the neckline), at the outside edge, or at both edges. Work the shaping at least one stitch in from the edge.

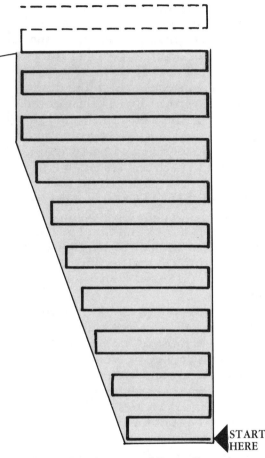

VERTICAL SHAWL COLLAR FOR A V NECKLINE

START HERE

This shawl collar for a V-neckline pullover is worked along with the sweater body.

Vertical Shawl Collar

STEP 1
Pick up stitches at the point or blunt part of the V as you would for an Overlapped Band.

STEP 2
(Finished collar depth at the back × stitch gauge) − Step 1 number of stitches = number of increases or decreases

STEP 3
Length of tapered portion of band × row gauge = number of rows over which to work increases or decreases

STEP 4
Step 3 ÷ Step 2 = position of row on which to work increase or decrease
Make this an even number, so that increases or decreases always are worked on the same side of the fabric.
■ If you decide to increase (and decrease) at both edges of your collar, multiply this number by 2. (Since you will be increasing two stitches instead of one on a given row, you will work the increases half as many times, and twice as far apart.)

STEP 5
Working the collar in rows, increase one stitch (or two stitches) at the rate determined in Step 4. After the increases are complete, work even until the collar reaches across the back neckline to the start of the reverse taper. Decrease at the same rate as you increased, until you have the original number of stitches on your needle. Bind off and sew collar into place.

TWO-PIECE VERTICAL SHAWL COLLAR. If you wish, you can knit this collar in two pieces. Follow the instructions through the first sentence of Step 5. After completing the increases, work even until this portion reaches to the middle of the back neckline. Bind off or place the stitches on a holder. Work the second half of the collar as a mirror image of the first. Sew or graft (see "How Tos") the two pieces at the top, and sew the collar to the neckline.

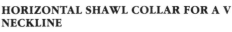

Horizontal Shawl Collar

STEP 1

Using a circular needle and starting on the left edge of the V, pick up stitches around the neckline as you would for a Horizontal Overlapped Band. As you pick up the stitches on the left edge, place a marker on your needle where you wish to complete your collar depth increase (anywhere from 4″ below the shoulder seam to the shoulder seam itself), and another marker at the same place on the right side. These mark the start of the short row shaping. Break off the yarn at the end of the picked-up row.

STEP 2

Count the total number of stitches below the markers along both front edges. The number of stitches on each side of the front should be equal.

STEP 3

(Finished collar depth at the back − finished depth at the front) × row gauge = number of rows over which to work the shaping

STEP 4

Step 2 − Step 3 = number of additional stitches per shaping row

STEP 5

With the right side of the sweater facing you, slip the stitches of the left neckline edge onto the right-hand needle to the first marker. Join the yarn and work the stitches across the back neckline to the second marker. *Turn the work. Knit across the previous row to the marker, work the Step 4 number of stitches, and place the marker at this point.* Repeat between the asterisks (*) until all of the neckline stitches have been worked.

STEP 6

Continue working even on all of the stitches of the collar for the depth of the band at the front. Bind off and sew the ends to the front.

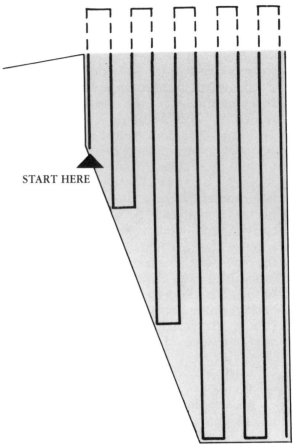

START HERE

This Shawl Collar for a V-Neckline Pullover is worked from picked-up stitches and shaped with short rows.

HORIZONTAL SHAWL COLLAR. On a horizontally knit Shawl Collar, the taper changes to a slope, and is shaped by short rows.

Reverse Taper Variations. If you taper an Overlapped Band opposite to the way a Shawl Collar is shaped—deeper at the front and shallower at the back—you have opened the door to another group of design possibilities. In finishes T and U, the taper ends at the shoulder. The deeper portion of the front can be buttoned or stitched to the opposite edge, or folded over into a collar.

Reverse Tapered Bands can be worked vertically, with edges shaped by increasing and decreasing, or horizontally, with the shaping worked in short rows. If the latter method is your choice, each front portion initially will be worked separately, then joined by working across the stitches of one front side, the stitches of the back neckline, and the stitches of the other front side. Continue on all stitches to the desired depth of the band at the back neckline. Bind off and finish as you choose. For design variation V, shape only one side and work the other edge to the same depth as the back.

Ruffled Collar. This is analogous to the Round Neckline Ruffled Collar.

Plan the depth and width of the neckline for this collar as you would like it to be when worn. The depth of the finish is minimal, and it does not fill in the neckline opening to any significant degree.

The ruffle can be worked in the round and increased at the point of the V, or it can be split at the center front and worked in rows, in the manner of an overlapped band. See the Ruffled Collar directions in "Round Neckline Finishes" for the method of working the increases.

INSERTS

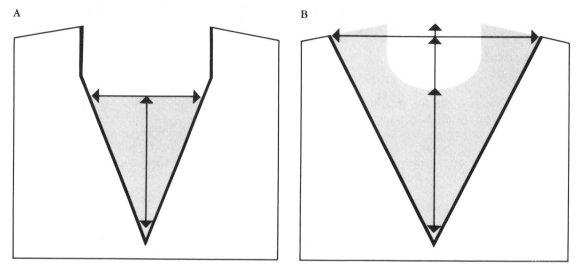

A

B

A mock insert can be worked at the same time as the front. For a separate insert, work the front and block it. Then measure for the height and width of the insert (a and b). On a wide neckline, you may need to chart neckline and shoulder shaping as part of the insert (b).

Inserts. An Insert can be planned as an addition to a V neckline, either as a design element or as a filling for a deep opening. It can be worked in the same yarn as the body, perhaps in a contrasting color or stitch pattern, or it can be worked in a totally different yarn.

MOCK INSERT. This can be knit at the same time as the front, as long as the stitch and row gauges remain constant. Its shape is defined simply by changing the pattern stitch along a diagonal line. Chart the front with the actual neckline of your choice, then chart an additional V Neckline on the front to determine the rate at which to change the pattern stitches to create the illusion of an insert.

SEPARATE INSERT. If the gauge for the insert is different from that of the sweater body, due to a change in stitch pattern or yarn thickness, the insert will have to be knit separately. The insert can be bound off straight at the desired depth, or a shaped neckline can be charted on the insert if it fills the V entirely. For necklines that are quite wide, neckline and shoulder shaping are charted as part of the insert.

Knit and block the front of the sweater, lay it flat, and measure for the height and width of the insert. The height is measured from the central point of the V to the highest point on the insert. The width is measured across the widest portion of the insert. If the insert does not completely fill the neckline opening, these measurements will be less than the height and width of the actual neckline.

REMOVABLE INSERTS. This addition can increase a sweater's versatility. For instance, a sweater with a deep V Neckline and a Narrow Band finish can be worn with a blouse or shirt, or the same sweater can be worn alone if an insert is added to fill the opening.

Chart and knit the insert, guided by the dimensions of the neckline shaping. Pick up and knit the finish of the neckline, working buttonholes in the band, then sew buttons on the insert. If buttonholes are not desired on the band, work them on the insert and place the buttons on the inside of the band. Several inserts in varying colors, stitch patterns, or yarns can be made for the same sweater.

The neckline finish on a Removable Insert is worked at the top edge of the insert, before it is added to the sweater. On sweaters with a Mock Insert, the neckline finish is worked along the actual neckline shaping. Separate Inserts can be self-finished or finished with a narrow edging or border before being sewn in place, or the garment can be completely assembled and a finish worked around the final neckline shape. This means that the final shape could be a Round, Square, or Boat Neckline, or even another V.

Square Neckline Finishes

Self-Finishes. The simplest Square Neckline finish is the Self-Finish, knitted at the same time as the body of the garment.

Start by charting the neckline to its finished width and depth, keeping in mind that the finish will not affect the

SOME FINISHES FOR SQUARE NECKLINES

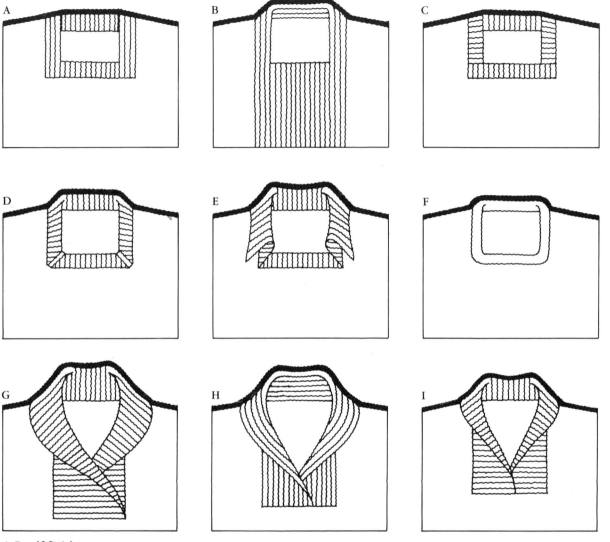

A-B self finishes
C butted band
D decreased band
E decreased band with collar
F rolled finish
G-I shawl collars

SELF-FINISHED SQUARE NECKLINE

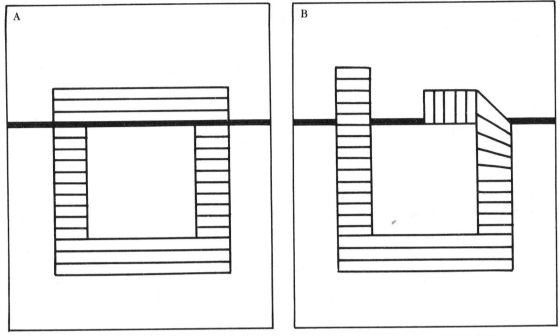

There are two ways to work the back neckline finish, either as a separate back finish worked along with the body (a), or as an extension of the front border (b).

size of the opening. Choose the width and depth of the Self-Finish border. Compute the number of stitches in the width of the border by multiplying the neckline width plus twice the border width by the stitch gauge. To determine where on the yoke to start working these border stitches, subtract the neckline depth and the depth of the finish from the Armhole Depth. When the finish is completed, bind off the neckline stitches at the center front,

and continue working the remaining border stitches on the sides of the neckline through the shoulder shaping. If your Square Neckline is tapered, work the decreases on the body of the sweater, at the inside of the border stitches. Work the back neckline to match, following guidelines given for the Self-Finished V Neckline.

This finish does not need to be worked just around the neckline. Try knitting the entire yoke of the sweater in ribbing, seed stitch, or garter stitch. Another option is to chart a Square Neckline for your sweater, then chart a Mock Insert to be worked in a stitch pattern that will serve as a self-finish.

In the **Butted Band** finish, all border bands are rectangular in shape.

First choose the knitted depth of the bands. Shape the back neckline to a depth at least equal to the depth of the finish.

The front and back edges of the neckline can be worked in one of two ways. In the first, the neckline stitches are bound off or left on a holder, and the border is worked or picked up as part of the finishing. In the second method, the front and back borders are worked along with the body of the garment, and bound off. The latter method eliminates the need for seams at the sides of the border, but limits you to stitches that can be worked on the same needles as the body of the sweater.

After the finish is worked on the front and back edges, stitches are picked up along the two side edges and knit in the border stitch to a depth equal to the front and back bands. The side bands will be sewn to the front and back, so remember to add a seam stitch at the beginning and end of the picked-up row. If you wish, the side bands can overlap the top and bottom bands, or vice versa.

Decreased Band. This neckline finish has mitered corners, which can be worked in any of the four ways described in the Decreased Band finishes of the V Neckline. The difference here is that the decreases are worked on every other round instead of every round.

Knit front and back body sections, and join them at the shoulder. Starting at the center back, pick up stitches around the neckline, making sure that opposite sections have equal numbers of stitches, and that the number of stitches allows for the centering of the border pattern in each section. If your choice of decrease method requires a center stitch, pick up one in each corner.

If the softer edge of a Doubled Band is desired, work a Decreased Band to the desired depth, work one row even, then work increases at the corners on every other round until the depth of the band is doubled. Bind off, fold the band to the inside, and stitch it in place.

Any weight or type of yarn is appropriate for this finish. The neckline has better proportions if the depth of the band is subtracted from each shoulder and added to the neckline width.

Rolled Finishes. Piping and Purl Welting have a softening effect on the Square Neckline. They are of such minimal depth that often there is no shaping needed at the corners, except possibly on the bind-off row. This serves to round out the corners.

Work these finishes according to the guidelines under "Round Neckline Finishes."

Shawl Collars. Several variations of the Shawl Collar can be worked on a Square Neckline. This is a favorite finish for children's, especially toddlers', outerwear pullovers. The wide neckline needed for children of this age is filled in nicely by the collar, making it snug and warm, yet it is easy to get off and on.

The fullest version of this collar overlaps across the entire center front of the neckline, and tapering usually is not required for its shaping. The neckline should be deep, with shaping starting at the level of the armhole bind-off or slightly higher. If a shallower neckline depth is desired, the neckline will need to be wider than the standard of one-third of the Shoulder Width. The fullness of this finish fills in the neckline opening substantially, and can make its fit uncomfortably tight if the opening is not big enough.

One way to correct, or avoid, too snug a fit is to have only a partial overlap, across two-thirds to three-quarters of the front neckline. This way the neckline does not need to be as deep, and tapering along the collar edges can be included if more fullness is desired for the folded portion of the collar.

It also is possible to work the collar with a minimal overlap, or none at all. This often is the choice for a toddler's pullover, due to the shallow depth of the neckline on so small a garment. For such a variation, work the collar to one-half the front neckline width plus an optional $1/2''$. Tapering remains an option if greater fullness is desired around the neck.

Like other Shawl Collars, this finish can be worked in any yarn in a reversible border pattern. Work it vertically or horizontally, depending on the directional appearance desired for the stitch of the collar. Both versions of the Square Neckline Shawl Collar are worked in rows.

SHAWL COLLARS FOR A SQUARE NECKLINE

HORIZONTAL

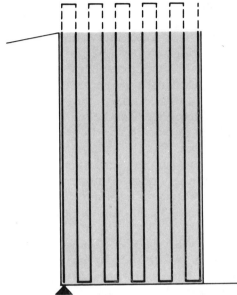

START HERE

VERTICAL

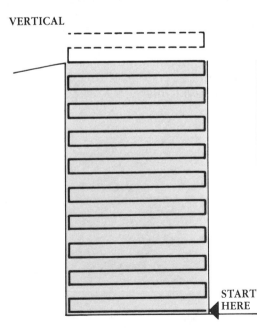

START HERE

Horizontal Shawl Collar

STEP 1
Pick up the stitches for the collar as follows. Cast on one stitch for a seam stitch. With the seam stitch on the needle, pick up stitches along the left neckline edge, across the back, and along the right neckline edge, then cast on another seam stitch.

STEP 2
Work to the desired depth of the collar and bind off. This can vary from one-half the width of the front to the whole width, depending on the general design of the garment.
- If a taper is planned, work it according to the V Neckline Horizontal Shawl Collar guidelines.

STEP 3
Stitch the edges into place across the front, overlapping as planned.

Vertical Shawl Collar

STEP 1
Pick up stitches across the front neckline edge, according to the degree of overlap planned.
- If the overlap includes the full width of stitches at the front, these stitches could be left on a holder to be knit directly. Otherwise, the stitches on the front should be bound off and stitches picked up across the partial width. Cast on a seam stitch at the appropriate edge for a male or female overlap.

STEP 2
Work the collar for a length equal to the sum of the lengths of the two sides plus the width of the back neckline. Bind off.

STEP 3
Stitch the collar to the neckline, overlapping at center front as planned.

A successful sweater begins with the design process. We knit sample patterns and measured our gauge. We took body measurements. Then we worked out body shape, neckline, collar, and sleeve possibilities, keeping in mind the total look we wanted. Knitters' graph paper, measuring tools, and a calculator helped us to translate the ideas into stitches and rows.

It's easy to shape edges and place pattern motifs when you use the Taper Formula and plot your results on graph paper. In our diagram, the Xs along the edges of alternate rows mark the right-side rows. Along the edges, we worked a seam stitch by always knitting the first and last stitches in each row. This technique produces a series of bumps at the edge of the fabric which correspond to the Xs on the graph.

At this point, we made more samples to find a companion pattern to use on the yoke—an afterthought, to make the sweater more interesting. We started our long swatch with a lattice worked around the cobnut stitch. Then we changed the lattice to twisted stitches, to clarify the design, and experimented with variations of the interlacement. However, we abandoned this pattern because its gauge did not match that of our original stitch and we wanted to keep the number of stitches consistent. The twisted-stitch lattice by itself was compatible in both gauge and appearance, so we made more samples to explore some of its variations.

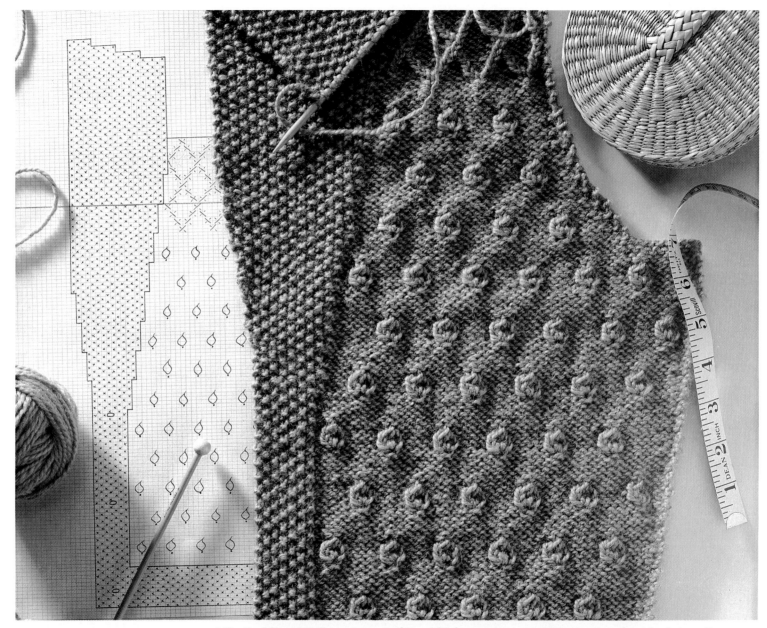

A Vertical Shawl Collar gets most of its width by moving one stitch at a time from body to collar; we added a little extra width by making increases along the outer edge. Note that we graphed only half of the front; all shaping on the other side is a mirror image, with buttonholes added.

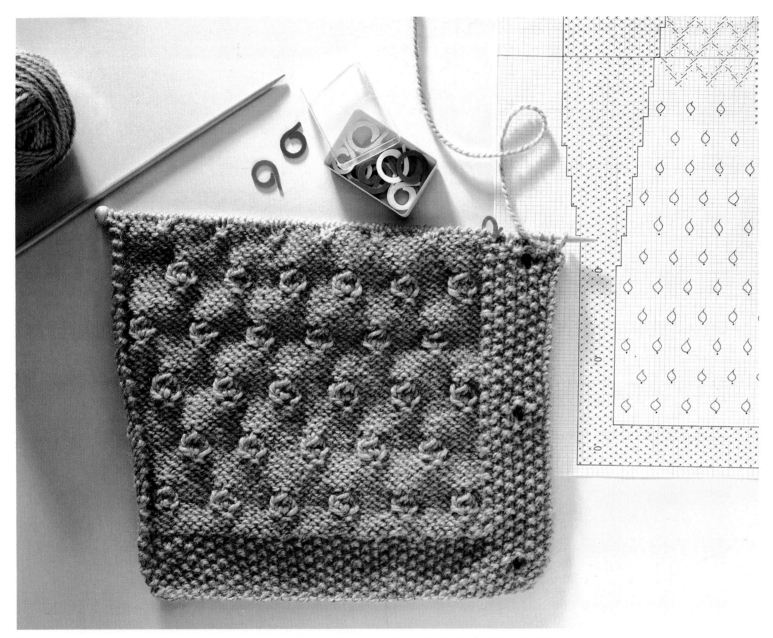

Markers are handy for keeping track of changes in stitch patterns, like this one at the front band. When the collar shaping begins, the marker becomes essential for coordinating the stitch changes. Note that the shaping on this front section has been reversed from the graph, and the buttonholes have been worked.

Yarn markers make it easier to measure the yoke length. Knit a 6" piece of contrasting yarn into the last bound-off stitch for the first marker. Place another marker toward the center of the yoke on the bind-off row. Use this one as a reference point when measuring the depth of the yoke.

Measuring the curve of the back armhole from the end of the bound-off stitches to the shoulder provides the number which you use in the formula for shaping the sleeve cap. It is Cap Triangle Side c (the hypotenuse of the right triangle) in the calculations.

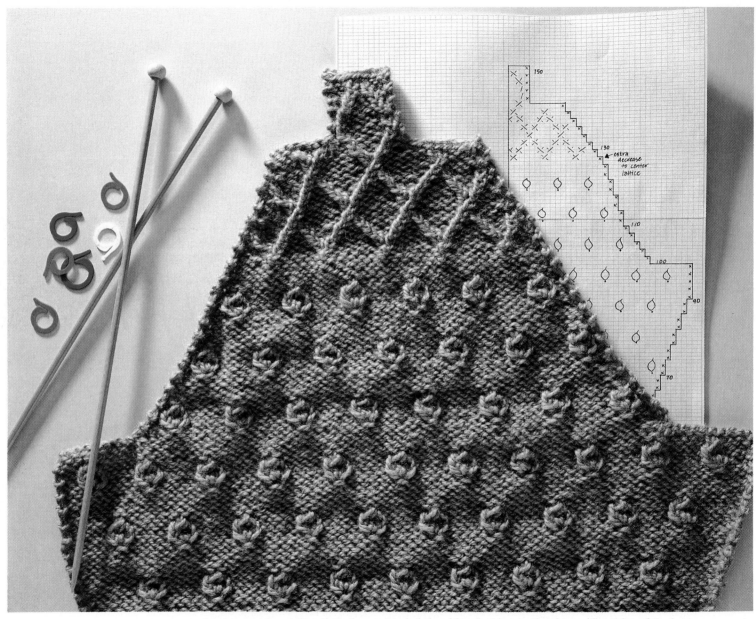

In our sweater, a Box Cap gives extended shoulder shaping to the sleeve. The sides of the box are sewn to the bound-off sections just below. We shaped the sleeve cap according to the sleeve cap formula, and it fits the armhole perfectly.

CHARTING THE SAMPLE SWEATER

Stitch and Symbol Glossary

...: repeat sequence between these marks

RS: right side

WS: wrong side

right cross: Slip next stitch to cable needle and hold to back, K1 through back loop, K1 through back loop from cable needle.

right purl cross: Slip next stitch to cable needle and hold to back, K1 through back loop, P1 from cable needle.

left purl cross: Slip next stitch to cable needle and hold to front, P1, K1 through back loop from cable needle.

K: knit

P: purl

st: stitch

inc: increase

beg: beginning

yo: yarn over

tog: together

Classic Body

CB/STEP 1

Chest Measurement + Ease = total circumference of garment body

35 + 5 = 40   40″

CB/STEP 2

Step 1 ÷ 2 = width of garment back or front

40 ÷ 2 = 20   20″

CB/STEP 3

Step 2 × stitch gauge = number of stitches to cast on

Add 2 stitches for seams, plus 1 stitch to center pattern.

20 × 4.5 = 90 + 2 + 1   93 sts

CB/STEP 4

Work even on (number in step 3) stitches for desired Garment Length to Armhole shaping   12½"
or
Garment Length to Armhole × row gauge = number of rows to armhole shaping
12.5 × 6 = 75   76 rows

CB/STEP 5

Shoulder Width Measurement × stitch gauge = number of stitches for yoke
If Step 3 is an odd number, make Step 5 odd.
Add 2 stitches for seams.
13.5 x 4.5 = 60.75; 61 + 2 = 63   63 sts

CB/STEP 6

Step 3 − Step 5 = total number of stitches for armhole shaping
93 − 63 = 30   30 sts

CB/STEP 7

Step 6 ÷ 2 = total number of shaping stitches per armhole
30 ÷ 2 = 15   15 sts

CB/STEP 8

Step 7 ÷ 2 = number of stitches to bind off at each armhole edge
If the result includes a fraction, round off to the next higher number. Knit in a 6" piece of
contrasting yarn along with the last bound-off stitch, to use as a marker. Place another yarn
marker toward the center of the yoke in the bind-off row. Use this as a reference point when
measuring the depth of the yoke (Step 10) or the start of the front neckline shaping.   8 sts

CB/STEP 9

Step 7 − Step 8 = number of stitches to single-decrease per armhole edge
Decrease 1 st at each armhole edge on every other row, on the right side of the fabric only.
15 − 8 = 7   7 sts

CB/STEP 10

Work even on remaining (number in Step 5) stitches until Depth of Armhole is reached   8"
or
Armhole Depth Measurement × row gauge = number of rows in yoke
8 × 6 = 48   48 rows

CB/STEP 11

Step 5 ÷ 3 = number of stitches per shoulder
If the result includes a fraction, use the whole number only. Do not increase to the next higher
number. Use any extra stitch(es) within the neckline.
Note: The yoke was decreased to 62 stitches in order to center the lattice pattern, and the
neckline was widened 1'' for the shawl collar.
62 ÷ 3 = 20.6   18 sts

CB/STEP 12

Step 5 - (Step 11 × 2) = number of stitches for neckline

62 – (18 × 2 = 36) = 26   26 sts

CB/STEP 13

Raglan Depth Measurement – Armhole Depth Measurement = height of shoulder slope in inches

8.5 – 8 = .5 $1/2''$

CB/STEP 14

Step 13 × row gauge = total number of rows for shoulder shaping

.5 × 6 = 3   3 rows

CB/STEP 15

Step 14 ÷ 2 = number of bind-off levels per shoulder
A bind-off level consists of 2 rows.

3 ÷ 2 = 1.5   2 levels

CB/STEP 16

Step 11 ÷ Step 15 = number of stitches per level to bind off on each shoulder
These stitches are bound off on every other row, or left on a stitch holder to be grafted or knit to its opposite shoulder.

18 ÷ 2 = 9   9 sts

CB/STEP 17

Back neckline: bind off remaining (number in Step 12) stitches, or place them on a stitch holder.

Tapered Body

STEP 1

($1/2$ Waist Measurement + $1/2$ optional Ease) x stitch gauge = number of stitches to cast on
Add 2 stitches for seams. We need an odd number for our pattern stitch.

(13 + 4 = 17) × 4.5 = 76.5 + 2 = 78.5   79 sts

STEP 2

($1/2$ Chest Measurement + $1/2$ Ease) × stitch gauge = number of stitches at upper body
Add 2 stitches for seams. Because Step 1 is odd, Step 2 will be odd.

17.5 + 2.5 = 20 × 4.5 = 90 + 2 = 92   93 sts

STEP 3
(Step 2 − Step 1) ÷ 2 = number of stitches to increase at each side edge for taper
93 − 79 = 14 ÷ 2 = 7   7 sts

STEP 4
Garment Length to Armhole Measurement − 3–4″ = number of inches over which increases
will be made
12 − 3 = 9 or 12 − 4 = 8   8–9″

STEP 5
Step 4 × row gauge = number of rows over which increases will be made
Make these even numbers.
8 × 6 = 48 or 9 × 6 = 54   48 to 54 rows

STEP 6
Step 5 ÷ Step 3 = rows on which to work increases
See Taper Formula.
48 ÷ 7 = 6.86 or 54 ÷ 7 = 7.71   Every 7th or 8th row

STEP 7
After the taper is complete, work even for the remaining 3–4″ to armhole shaping

---

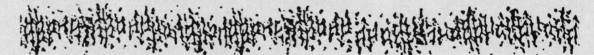

Cardigan, Preliminary Calculations

STEP 1
Body stitches for Tapered Body (Step 1) ÷ 2 = Starting Number of body stitches for cardigan
front
79 ÷ 2 = 39.5   39 sts

STEP 2
Front Overlap Width in inches × stitch gauge = number of Front Overlap Width stitches
1.5 × 4.5 = 6.75   7 sts

Cardigan Version 1 (with Vertical Band)

STEP 1

Starting Number of body stitches + $\frac{1}{2}$ the number of Front Overlap stitches = number of stitches to cast on

We need an odd number for our pattern.

39 + 3.5 = 42.5   **43 sts**

STEP 2

Work the bottom border to the desired depth.

$1.75'' \times 6$ rows = 10.5   **11 rows**

STEP 3

Work the band pattern stitch (seed stitch) at the center front edge over the total number of Front Overlap Width stitches (7). Work the remaining stitches in the body pattern stitch.

Standard Vertical Shawl Collar

Our directions are for a Standard Shawl Collar for a cardigan. In it, the stitches of the neckline shaping are not decreased but are simply moved to the front band, by changing the pattern stitch from that of the body to that of the band. The widened front band becomes the shawl collar.

Standard Vertical Shawl Collar

STEP 1

Work Steps 1 through 3 of Cardigan Version 1 (noted above).

STEP 2

Adjust the front neckline stitches as follows. Because we are working with one section of the cardigan front, we use one-half of the stitches in CB/Step 12.

$\frac{1}{2}$ starting number of stitches in the neckline (CB/Step 12) − $\frac{1}{2}$ the number of Front Overlap Width stitches = adjusted number of neckline stitches for calculating the V Neckline taper

13 − 4 = 9   **9 sts**

Recalculate the neckline taper with the adjusted number of neckline stitches.

72 rows ÷ 9 = 8   **Every 8th row**

Wide Vertical Shawl Collar

If you wish, you may increase the standard width of a shawl collar 1″ or more by working evenly spaced increases on the collar at the same time that you widen the collar area by changing the stitch pattern, as described above.

For a 1″ increase in width for this sweater, 4 stitches will be increased at the front edge.

For a wider roll to the collar, work a slope with short rows from the back neck edge of the collar to the outer edge.

STEP 3
Place a marker between the stitches of the body and the stitches of the band.

STEP 4
Following the graph of the neckline taper, move the marker one stitch toward the shoulder every time the taper indicates a decrease. As you knit, the number of stitches on your needles will remain the same, but the band will widen to become the Shawl Collar and the number of body stitches will decrease to the number of stitches for the back shoulder shaping.

STEP 5
Work through the shoulder shaping.

STEP 6
Continue knitting the stitches of the collar for one-half the width of the back neckline. Place the stitches on a holder or bind them off.

STEP 7
Work the other front in the same manner, reversing the shapings.

STEP 8
Join the fronts and the back at the shoulders.

STEP 9
Graft or sew the two sides of the collar together, and sew the collar to the back neckline.

Tapered Sleeve

TS/STEP 1
(Wrist Measurement + Ease) × stitch gauge = number of stitches to cast on
(When knitting, add 2 stitches for sleeve seam. For calculations, use unadjusted number.)
(5.5 + 1) = 6.5 × 4.5 = 29.25   29 sts

TS/STEP 2
(Upperarm Measurement + Ease) × stitch gauge = number of stitches at top of sleeve section
(When knitting, add 2 stitches for sleeve seam.) Because Step 1 is odd, Step 2 will be odd.
(10.5 + 4.5) = 15 × 4.5 = 67.5   69 sts

TS/STEP 3
TS/Step 2 − TS/Step 1 = total number of stitches to increase along side edges
69 − 29 = 40   40 sts

TS/STEP 4
TS/Step 3 ÷ 2 = number of stitches to increase per side edge
40 ÷ 2 = 20   20 sts

TS/STEP 5
(Sleeve Length Measurement – 3–4″) – length of ribbing or cuff finish, if applicable =
number of inches over which increases will be made
On a narrow or medium-fitting sleeve, the taper should end 3–4″ below the armhole bind-off,
in consideration of the thickness of the arm at that point. On very wide sleeves, the taper can
continue to the armhole bind-off level.
16.75 – 3 = 13.75 or 16.75 – 4 = 12.75   13–14″

TS/STEP 6
TS/Step 5 × row gauge = number of rows over which increases will be made
Make these even numbers.
13 × 6 = 78 or 14 × 6 = 84   78–84 rows

TS/STEP 7
TS/Step 6 ÷ TS/Step 4 = position of rows on which to work increases
See Taper Formula.
78 ÷ 20 = 3.9 or 84 ÷ 20 = 4.2   Every 4th row

TS/STEP 8
After the increases are complete, work even to the Sleeve Length Measurement (see graph).

Box Cap

Refer to section on Box Cap for comments on shaping.

STEP 1
Bind off the same number of stitches per armhole as for Set-In Armhole shaping (CB/Step 8).   8 sts

STEP 2
Number of stitches at top of sleeve (TS/Step 2) – (Step 1 × 2) = number of stitches at start of
cap taper
69 – (8 × 2 = 16) = 53   53 sts

STEP 3
Finished Width of cap in inches + (depth of dart in inches × 2) × stitch gauge = number of stitches at top of cap for box shaping
Because Step 2 is odd, Step 3 will be odd.
2 + (1¹/₂ × 2 = 3) × 4.5 = 23

23 sts

STEP 4
(Step 2 − Step 3) ÷ 2 = number of stitches to decrease per side edge
(53 − 23 = 30) ÷ 2 = 15

15 sts

STEP 5
Determine the number of rows for the cap as follows:
a. Determine Triangle Side *c* in inches: Curve Measurement of the back armhole − ¹/₂ Finished Width at top of cap = Cap Triangle Side *c*
   8.5 − 1 = 7.5

7.5″

b. Determine Triangle Side *b* in inches: Step 4 ÷ stitch gauge = Triangle Side *b*
   Triangle Side *b*
   15 ÷ 5 = 3

3″

c. Take square root of [(Step 5a × Step 5a) − (Step 5b × Step 5b)] = Cap Triangle Side *a*
   (7.5 × 7.5 = 56.25) − (3 × 3 = 9) = 45.25
   √45.25 = 6.73

6.75″

d. Step 5c × row gauge = number of rows for cap
   Make this an even number
   6.75 × 6 = 40.5

40 rows

STEP 6
Plan and work your cap taper.
Determining the Rate of a Taper:
a. The total number of rows over which decreases will be made is found in Step 5d; the number of stitches to decrease per edge is found in Step 4.
b. Step 5d ÷ Step 4 = unadjusted rate of decrease
   If this result contains a fraction, write down the next lower even number and the next higher even number. These will be the rows on which to work the decreases.
   40 ÷ 15 = 2.67

Every 2nd or 4th row

c. [(Step 4 × higher even number) − Step 5d] ÷ 2 = number of decreases to be worked on lower-even-numbered rows
   [(15 × 4 = 20) ÷ 2] = 10

10 decreases every 2nd row

d. Step 4 − Step 6c = number of decreases to be worked on higher-even-numbered rows
   15 − 10 = 5

5 decreases every 4th row

STEP 7
Depth of dart in inches × stitch gauge = number of stitches to bind off at the beginning of the next 2 rows
1.5 × 4.5 = 6.75

7 sts

STEP 8
Work even on remaining stitches to the depth of the darts.

1¹/₂″ or 9 rows

STEP 9
Bind off remaining stitches.

STEP 10
Sew edges together to form darts.

Stitch Patterns

Seed Stitch: Multiple of 2 sts, 2 rows. For an odd number of stitches, all rows: *K1, P1,* K1.

Cobnut Pattern: Multiple of 6 sts, 16 rows.
Note: this pattern centers on an odd number of stitches.
Row 1 (RS): P5, (K1, yarn over to make one, K1) in the next stitch.
Row 2: P3, K5.
Row 3: P5, K3.
Row 4: P3 tog, K5.
Rows 5 & 7: P.
Rows 6 & 8: K.
Row 9: P2, (K1, yarn over to make one, K1) in the next stitch, P3.
Row 10: K3, P3, K2.
Row 11: P2, K3, P3.
Row 12: K3, P3 tog, K2.
Row 13 & 15: P.
Rows 14 & 16: K.

Lattice Pattern: Multiple of 6 sts, 12 rows.
Note: this pattern centers on an even number of stitches.
Row 1 (RS): P2, right cross, P2.
Row 2: K2, P2 through the back loops, K2.
Row 3: P1, right purl cross, left purl cross, P1.
Row 4: K1, P1 through the back loop, K2, P1 through the back loop, K1.
Row 5: Right purl cross, P2, left purl cross.
Row 6: P1 through the back loop, K4, P1 through the back loop.
Row 7: K1 through the back loop, *P4, right cross,* P4, K1 through the back loop.
Row 8: P1 through the back loop, K4, P1 through the back loop.
Row 9: Left purl cross, P2, right purl cross.
Row 10: K1, P1 through the back loop, K2, P1 through the back loop, K1.
Row 11: P1, left purl cross, right purl cross, P1.
Row 12: K2, P2 through the back loops, K2.

Cobnut and Lattice Sweater

Size: Misses' 12. Finished bust measurement at underarm 40″, length 21″, sleeve width at upperarm 15″.

Materials: Approximately 24 ounces 100% wool, 2-ply New Zealandspun from Ironstone Warehouse, at approximately 760 yards/pound, in color B (light gray). One pair size 7 needles, or size to obtain gauge. Three ⅝″ buttons.

Gauge: 4½ stitches and 6 rows per inch on size 7 needles.

Seam stitch: On all edges except the front edge, knit the first stitch of every row, to produce a seam stitch. This stitch makes a bump every second row, which aids counting. The K stitches on the RS are marked with Xs on the graph.

Back: Cast on 79 sts. Work seed st for 11 rows, ending on a RS row. K 1 row, P 1 row, K 1 row. Start cobnut pattern, increasing 1 st at each edge on each occurrence of pattern rows 1 and 9 (93 sts). Work even, ending on WS row 76. *Armhole shaping:* Bind off 8 sts at the beginning of the next two rows. Continue in pattern; decrease 1 st each edge 7 times. Work even on 63 sts, ending on WS row 102. Start lattice pattern, decreasing 1 st to make an even number of sts. Work even on 62 sts, ending on WS row 126. *Shoulder shaping:* Bind off 9 sts at beginning of next 4 rows. Bind off remaining 26 sts for neck.

Left front: Cast on 43 sts. Work seed st for 11 rows, ending on a RS row. Next row: Work 7 sts in seed st for front band, place a marker on the needle, K to end of row. Continuing front band in seed st, P 1 row, K 1 row. Start cobnut pattern, increasing 1 st at side edge on rows 1 and 9 to match the back. AT THE SAME TIME: Start shawl collar shaping on row 55 by moving the front band marker over 1 st. Continue to move the marker over 1 st at a time every 8 rows 8 more times. On the 2nd through 5th marker moves, inc 1 st at the front edge to give the collar more width. *Armhole shaping:* On RS row 77, bind off 8 sts. Continue in pattern and decrease 1 st on the armhole edge 7 times. On RS row 103, start lattice pattern. *Shoulder shaping:* Keeping in pattern, begin shoulder shaping on RS row 127. Bind off 9 sts on the first level and 10 sts on the second level. Continue seed st on 20 sts to WS row 150. Slope back of collar by working 4 levels of 5 sts each, leaving all sts on the needle for grafting.

Right front: Knit as for left side, reversing all shaping. Start buttonholes on rows 5, 29, and 53. To work buttonhole rows: K1, P1, K1, yarn over twice, K2 tog, P1, K1, finish row in pattern. Second row: Work row to seed st band, K1, P1, K1, P1, and let the second yo drop off needle, K1, P1, K1. Third row: K1, P1, K1, P1 through the hole below the stitch, drop next stitch, K1, P1, K1. At end of collar, omit 4-level slope unless you want the collar to lie flatter. Leave sts on needle for grafting.

Sleeves: Cast on 29 sts. Work seed st for 11 rows, ending on a RS row. K 1 row, P 1 row, K 1 row. Start lattice pattern, increasing 1 st each edge every 4 rows until there are 69 sts and 98 rows. *Underarm shaping:* Bind off 8 sts at the beginning of the next 2 rows. Continue in pattern; decrease 1 st each edge every other row 5 times, every 4th row 5 times. AT THE SAME TIME: Start lattice pattern on RS row 127, decreasing 1 st to make an even number of sts. Continue decreasing 1 st at each edge every other row 5 times (22 sts). *Box sleeve shaping:* Bind off 7 sts at beginning of next 2 rows. Work final lattice on remaining 8 sts. On row 151, bind off remaining sts.

Finishing: Block pieces. Sew shoulder seams. Graft sts at back of collar and sew back neck seam. Sew side seams and sleeve seams. On sleeve cap, bring side edges of the box to the bound-off sts and stitch together. Set in sleeves. Sew on buttons.

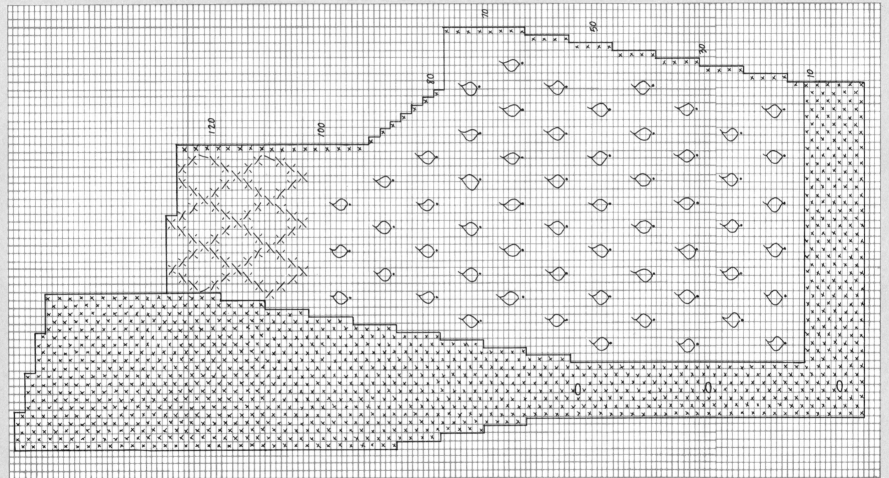

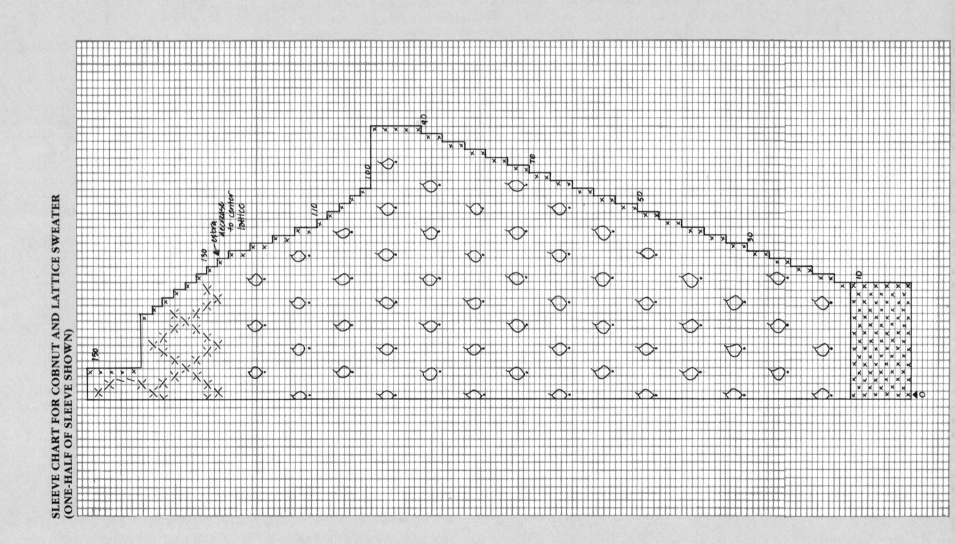

SOME FINISHES FOR BOATNECKS

SELF FINISH

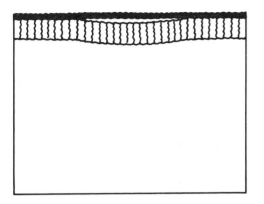

ROLLED FINISH

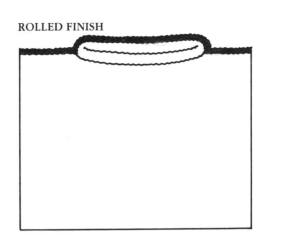

DECREASED BAND

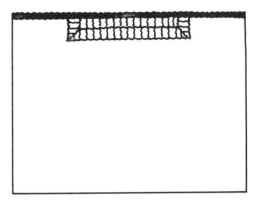

FOLDOVER COLLAR

STAND-UP COLLAR

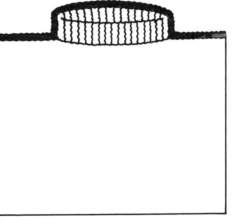

COWL COLLAR

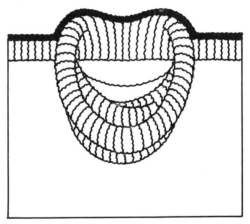

Boat Neckline Finishes

Self-Finishes. The most common finish for a Boat Neckline is the Self-Finish. This is easily worked along with the front and back. Specifics are covered in the charting guidelines for Boat Neckline shaping.

Crocheted Edgings. If the fabric stitch of the sweater is continued through the shoulder and neckline shaping, a row of slip stitch, single crochet, or reverse single crochet can be worked around the neckline edge to stabilize it. Knitted lace patterns can be finished with a narrow crocheted lace edging, if the Shaped Boat Neckline style is chosen.

Rolled Finishes. Any of the rolled finishes discussed for the Round Neckline can be used for a Boat Neckline. They even can be combined with a Self-Finished edge as a decorative element. Try working a Purl Welt Edging before assembling the front and back, so that the welt crosses the entire shoulder width. Or work Piping in a Square or Shaped Boat Neckline as the sole finish to the neckline edge. The Rolled Collar can be worked on the Shaped or Butted versions of the Boatneck. These finishes can be knit in any yarn.

The **Decreased Band** finish can be used for a Shaped or Square Boatneck. Starting at the center back, pick up stitches around the entire neckline. On the Shaped Boat Neckline, decreases are worked every round at each shoulder seam, in any of the four ways explained for V Neckline Finishes. If a Doubled Band finish is your choice, work the band to the desired depth, then work one round even and start working increases every round to double the depth. Bind off, and stitch down on the inside.

The Square Boat Neckline's finish is decreased every other round and, just like the Shaped Boatneck, can be doubled by working an increased portion to fold to the inside.

Foldover Collar. Taking the idea of the Shaped Boat Neckline with a Doubled Band a step further, the band can be folded to the outside to create the Foldover Collar. Follow the guidelines given for the Foldover V Collar. Work the decreased inner portion of the band for several rows,

just enough to stabilize the neckline, then switch to the increased band. Since this collar spreads across the shoulder area, consider increasing the needle size every inch or so if you are working the collar to a depth of more than 1".

Stand-Up Collar. This finish works well for the Butted and Shaped Boatnecks. On the Butted Neckline, the finish can be worked at the same time as the garment pieces by simply continuing on the neckline stitches for 2" to 3" after binding off for the shoulders. Fold the collar in half to the inside, and stitch in place. Stand-Up Collars for Shaped Boatnecks are worked in short rows and can have the finish knit directly on the open stitches. If the neckline shaping is bound off, stitches can be picked up. In yarns with body, the collar will stand up. If softer yarns are used, the collar will drape slightly.

Cowl Collar. The ever-popular Cowl fits well into Butted or Shaped Boat Necklines. With a Boatneck, it is very easy to work the collar separately and extend your use of the garment by wearing it with or without the collar. Buttons can be sewn to the inside of the neckline at the seams, and buttonholes or button loops can be a part of the Cowl to help hold it in place. Follow the directions given for Cowl Collars in the Round Neckline Finishes section.

Combinations of Neckline Finishes

Earlier, we discussed ways of changing neckline shapes by means of inserts; we have also mentioned neckline finishes, such as the V Neckline Decreased Band with Collar or Turtleneck, which combine two different neckline shapes. Just a step beyond this is the trick of combining two neckline finishes on the same garment. For instance, you can work a Standard Collar inside a Crewneck . . . a Narrow Band or Piping along with a Ruffle or Cape Collar . . . a Turtleneck within a separate V Neckline Decreased Band . . . only your imagination is the limit.

To combine neck finishes, complete one finish, then pick up stitches along the outside of the neckline and work the other. Alternatively, work one of the finishes separately and stitch it into place.

Some styles lend themselves to being worked separately and used as optional add-on collars. Making a separate collar can double the use of a sweater. Separate Cowls can be worn over Boatnecks and Crewnecks. Peter Pan, Standard, and Cape Collars can be worn over High Round Neckline finishes, such as crocheted edgings or even Turtlenecks. Inserts can be knit for V Necklines and fastened with hidden snaps or buttons. These individual collars can be worked in different collars or yarns from the sweater body. Anything you can envision, you can design and knit!

SEPARATE COLLARS AND INSERTS

SEPARATE COWL

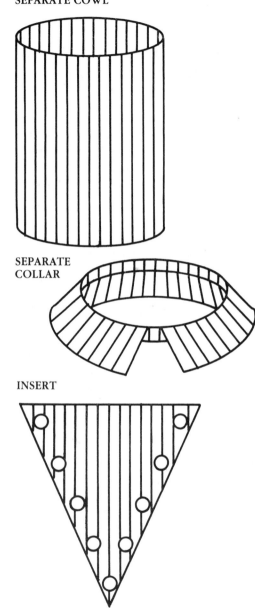

SEPARATE COLLAR

INSERT

Some styles can be worked separately and used as optional accessories.

HOODS

Hoods are practical additions to children's jackets and coats, but also should be considered for men's and women's outerwear garments such as sweatshirt-style pullovers and jackets, and women's coats.

Hoods can be added to cardigans or to pullovers with or without front openings. The neckline shaping can be a High to Medium Round neckline or a shallow Traditional or Blunt V. A hood also can be worked in a manner similar to the Vertical Shawl Collar; here, the front neckline stitches are not shaped, but worked even through the shoulder shaping, with the band widening gradually to include the neckline stitches.

You can knit the hood separately and sew it to the neckline edge, or you can pick up stitches and work the hood attached to the neckline. You also have the option of placing the neckline stitches on holders, then working the hood after the sweater is assembled.

The last alternative is the preferred method when working a hood on an unshaped (straight) neckline. Always bear in mind the neckline's need for stability when deciding whether to bind off or leave stitches open. It is possible to leave the neckline stitches open on the front but to bind off on the back. This will eliminate a picked-up ridge on the front where it could show, but will still stabilize the back neckline.

Integrate the hood into the design of the sweater. Carry fabric elements such as cables, stripes, or color designs onto the hood. Several of the styles lend themselves to different ways of accomplishing this.

TAKING MEASUREMENTS FOR HOODS

1 HEAD HEIGHT AT THE BACK
2 HEAD HEIGHT AT THE FRONT
3 HEAD DEPTH

Before charting can begin, three **Hood Measurements** will need to be taken. Ease will be added to these measurements. Remember that all ease allowances are the minimum required. We will label the measurements 1, 2, and 3, and refer to them as such in the guidelines for the hoods.

For best results, first knit, block, and assemble the body of the sweater, then take these measurements while wearing the sweater body.

1. Head Height at the Back. Placing a ruler or a book on top of the head so that it is horizontal, measure straight up from the level of the back neckline to the ruler or book. Add a minimum of 1½″ ease.

2. Head Height at the Front. Measure from the top of the head at the center front, along the side of the head at the temple, to the center front of the neckline shaping. Add a minimum of 1½″ of ease.

3. Head Depth. Standing with the head against a wall and using a ruler, measure from the front hairline straight back to the wall. Add a minimum of 1″ of ease.

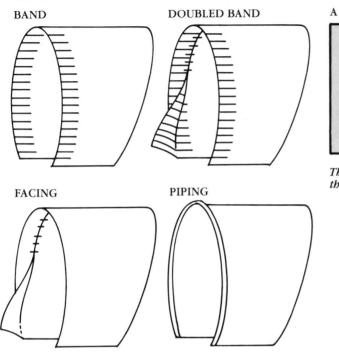

HOOD FINISHES

BAND

DOUBLED BAND

FACING

PIPING

BASIC HOODS

A

There are two basic shapes for the hood: the Rectangle (a) and the T-Shape (b).

B

Finishes. The face edge of the hood needs a finish. This can be a simple Band in the border stitch of the garment, or a Doubled Band if a softer edge is desired. A Doubled Band can also serve as a casing for a drawstring if you work a buttonhole at each end of the band, either on the outside or inside. Hems and Facings are other ways to stabilize and finish the face edge and can also serve as casings with the addition of buttonholes. Piping and Purl Welt Edging are other finishes which can be used.

The method that you select for working the hood will determine the amount of planning needed in the charting of the hood. Separately knit hoods are the simplest ones to chart. You cast on at the face edge and work your chosen finish directly on the hood, adjusting the depth of the hood when the finish is a Hem or Doubled Band.

Attached hoods require more planning. A Self-Finish or Facing could be worked along with the hood. Other finishes need to be sewn on or picked up and worked after the hood is assembled. If the sweater is a cardigan or a pullover with an opening, the finish of the front opening and the hood may be worked as

one. If the garment does not have an opening, you must leave space to either side of center front equal to the depth of the finish, as you would for a Peter Pan Collar. Another option for a self-finished hood is to work the finish in the manner of an Overlapped Split Collar: start picking up stitches slightly off-center, pick up around the neckline edge, and cast on stitches for the underlap.

Basic Hoods. There are two basic shapes for a hood, the Rectangle and the T-Shape. The guidelines for working the two basic hoods, and variations of each, are divided into hoods worked separately and sewn on, and hoods worked from picked-up or open stitches.

Since it is easier to visualize a hood worked separately, we give the guidelines for this type first. Once you have a clear idea of the variations possible for the basic hoods, applying that knowledge to attached hoods will be easier.

Separate Rectangular Hoods

The simplest hood is a rectangle. Its long edge is folded and sewn together at the back of the head, and the short edges are sewn to the neckline. If the neckline edge of the hood is longer than the neckline itself, you can gather the hood to the neckline's length or use pleats to make it fit.

In all of these variations, the hood width is the longer dimension of the rectangle. (This is because of the direction in which the hood is knit, from one long edge to the other.)

Hood Version 1

This is the simplest rectangular hood, knit with four perpendicular sides. Slightly different instructions are given for hoods intended to be attached to unshaped (straight) or shaped necklines.

For an Unshaped Neckline

STEP 1
(Hood Measurement 1 + Ease) × 2 = hood width

STEP 2
Hood width × stitch gauge = number of stitches to cast on

STEP 3
Measure the neckline circumference of the sweater and divide it by 2. Compare this length to (Hood Measurement 3 + Ease), and work the hood to the longer of the two. Bind off.
■ If working a hem or a Doubled Band, remember to add the extra depth here.

STEP 4
Fold the hood in half and close the seam at the back. Sew the hood to the neckline, easing any excess to the neckline's length (see "Easing a Seam").

For a Shaped Neckline

STEP 1
(Hood Measurement 2 + Ease) × 2 = hood width

STEP 2
Follow the guidelines for the unshaped neckline hood, above, Steps 2 through 4.

HOOD VERSION 1

FOR UNSHAPED NECKLINE

FOR SHAPED NECKLINE

A separately worked rectangular hood with four perpendicular sides. For use with an unshaped neckline, the hood width is determined by the head height at the back. For use with a shaped neckline, the width is determined by the head height at the front.

HOOD VERSION 2

A separately worked rectangular hood with tapered neckline edges, which fit better on a shaped neckline.

Hood Version 2

In this version of the rectangular hood, the neckline edges are tapered. This produces a better fit for a shaped neckline.

STEP 1
(Hood Measurement 2 + Ease) × 2 = starting width of the hood

STEP 2
(Hood Measurement 1 + Ease) × 2 = finished width of the hood

STEP 3
Step 1 × stitch gauge = number of stitches to cast on

STEP 4
Step 2 × stitch gauge = final number of stitches

STEP 5
(Step 3 – Step 4) ÷ 2 = number of stitches to taper at each edge of the hood

STEP 6
(Hood Measurement 3 + Ease) – depth of the finish = depth of the taper

STEP 7
Step 6 × row gauge = number of rows over which to taper

STEP 8
Taper the Step 5 number of stitches over the Step 7 number of rows.
See Taper Formula for procedure.
Cast on Step 3 number of stitches, work the face edge finish, continue knitting over the Step 7 number of rows while decreasing at each edge as determined in Step 8, and bind off.

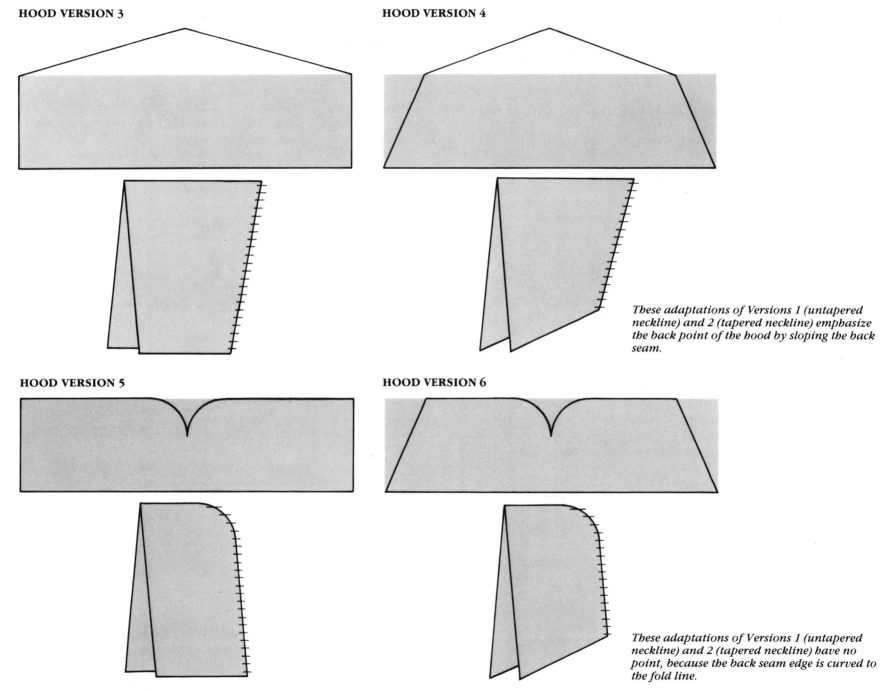

HOOD VERSION 3

HOOD VERSION 4

These adaptations of Versions 1 (untapered neckline) and 2 (tapered neckline) emphasize the back point of the hood by sloping the back seam.

HOOD VERSION 5

HOOD VERSION 6

These adaptations of Versions 1 (untapered neckline) and 2 (tapered neckline) have no point, because the back seam edge is curved to the fold line.

Hood Version 5

STEP 1
Chart as in Version 1, Steps 1 and 2.

STEP 2
Using the Curve Guide (see "How Tos"), chart two mirror-image curves, 2" to 4" deep, at the foldline of the hood.

STEP 3
Compare (Hood Measurement 3 + Ease) with one-half the neckline circumference of the sweater. Choose the larger measurement.

STEP 4
Work to the Step 3 measurement minus the depth of the curve.

STEP 5
Working each side separately, shape the center curves.

STEP 6
Bind off.

Hood Version 6

STEP 1
Chart as in Version 2, Steps 1 through 8.

STEP 2
Using the Curve Guide (see "How Tos"), chart two mirror-image curves, 2" to 4" deep, at the foldline of the hood.

STEP 3
Work to (Hood Measurement 3 + Ease) minus the depth of the curve.

HOOD VERSIONS 3 AND 4. If you wish to emphasize the point of the hood at the back, you can slope the back seam of the hood to a point at the center fold line.

To knit these shapes, work either Version 1 or Version 2, but instead of binding off straight, work a slope from each neckline edge to the center, adding the extra depth desired for the point.

HOOD VERSIONS 5 AND 6. These hoods are very similar to Versions 1 and 2, but the back seam edge is curved to the fold line, eliminating the point.

HOOD VERSIONS 7 AND 8. These are two variations of a fully shaped hood for a sweater where the measurement of the neckline circumference is less than (Hood Measurement 3 + Ease) × 2. The back seam edge is sloped in to the neckline, and a curve shapes the hood to the head. Version 7 is for unshaped necklines, Version 8 for shaped necklines.

Charting this hood on graph paper makes it easier to work.

STEP 4
Work each side separately, shaping the center curves.

STEP 5
Bind off.

Hood Version 7

STEP 1
(Hood Measurement 1 + Ease) × 2 = hood width

STEP 2
Using the Curve Guide (see "How Tos"), chart two mirror-image curves, 2″ to 4″ deep, at the foldline of the hood.

STEP 3
(Sweater neckline circumference ÷ 2) – depth of hood finish = knitted depth to the start of the slope

STEP 4
(Hood Measurement 3 + Ease) – Step 3 = depth of the slope of the back seam

STEP 5
Step 4 × row gauge = number of rows of slope

STEP 6
(Step 1 × stitch gauge) ÷ 6 = number of stitches of the slope

STEP 7
Starting at each side edge of the hood, slope the Step 6 number of stitches over the Step 5 number of rows (see Slope Formula). This results in an outward slope at the bottom of the back seam line.

STEP 8
When knitting, work the two sides of the hood separately after you reach (Hood Measurement 3 + ease) minus the depth of the curve.

Hood Version 8

STEP 1
(Hood Measurement 2 + Ease) × 2 = starting width of the hood

STEP 2
(Hood Measurement 1 + Ease) × 2 = finished width of the hood

STEP 3
Step 1 × stitch gauge = number of stitches to cast on

STEP 4
Step 2 × stitch gauge = number of stitches in finished hood width

STEP 5
(Step 3 − Step 4) ÷ 2 = number of stitches to taper at each neckline edge of the hood

STEP 6
(Sweater neckline circumference ÷ 2) − depth of hood finish = depth of the taper of the neckline edge

STEP 7
Step 6 × row gauge = number of rows over which to taper

STEP 8
Chart the taper at the sides (neckline edges) of the hood, using the Step 5 number of stitches over the Step 7 number of rows (see Taper Formula).

STEP 9
Using the Curve Guide (see "How Tos"), chart two mirror-image curves, 2″ to 4″ deep, at the foldline of the hood.

STEP 10
(Hood Measurement 3 + Ease) − (sweater neckline circumference ÷ 2) = depth of the slope of the back seam

STEP 11
Step 4 ÷ 6 = number of stitches in the back seam shaping

STEP 12

Step 10 × row gauge = rows over which to slope back seam

STEP 13

At each edge of the hood, slope the stitches of Step 11 over the rows of Step 12 (see Slope Formula). This results in an outward slope at the bottom of the back seam line.

STEP 14

When knitting, work the two sides of the hood separately after you reach (Hood Measurement 3 + Ease) minus the depth of the curve.

Separate T-Shaped Hoods

T-Shaped Hoods are more appropriate for adults' garments than the basic rectangle. The T-shape forms darts at the back of the head, making the hood more rounded and eliminating the point. A very effective way to integrate a design element of the garment with a hood of this style is to continue a design from the back up the center of the hood.

HOOD VERSION 9. This version of the T-Shaped Hood works for garments in which the neckline circumference measurement is equal to or less than (Hood Measurement 3 + Ease) × 2. If the neckline circumference is less than the hood measurement, the extra fabric of the hood can be eased or pleated when it is sewn to the neckline edge.

Slightly different instructions are given for hoods intended to be attached to unshaped (straight) or shaped necklines.

Hood Version 9

For an Unshaped Neckline

STEP 1

(Hood Measurement 1 + Ease) × 2 = front hood width

STEP 2

Determine the width of the back portion. 2″ is the minimum width for a child, and 3″ is the minimum width for an adult. Maximum width is the width of the back neckline of the garment.

STEP 3

(Hood Measurement 3 + Ease) − (Step 2 ÷ 2) = depth of the front portion of the hood

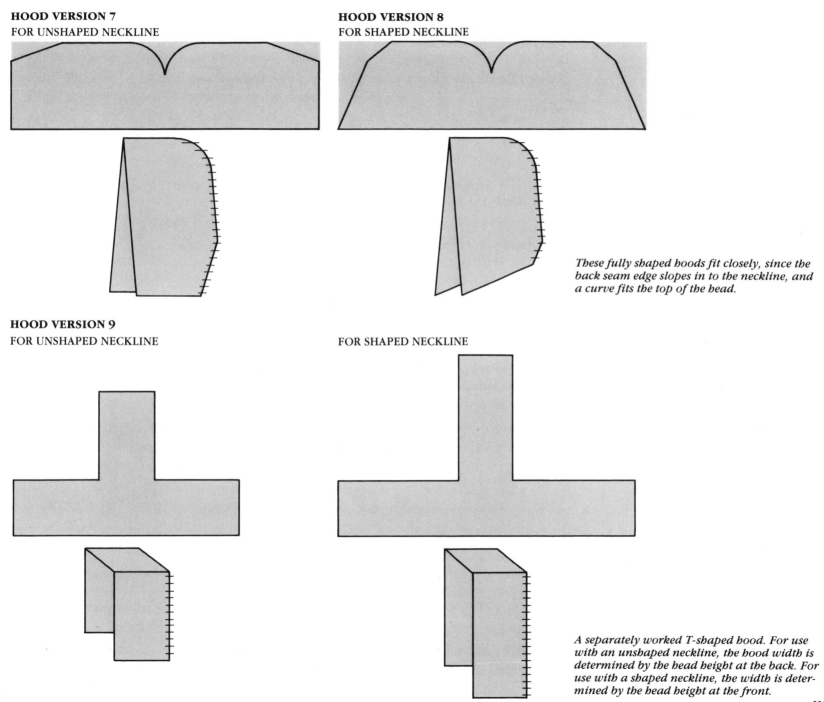

HOOD VERSION 7
FOR UNSHAPED NECKLINE

HOOD VERSION 8
FOR SHAPED NECKLINE

These fully shaped hoods fit closely, since the back seam edge slopes in to the neckline, and a curve fits the top of the head.

HOOD VERSION 9
FOR UNSHAPED NECKLINE

FOR SHAPED NECKLINE

A separately worked T-shaped hood. For use with an unshaped neckline, the hood width is determined by the head height at the back. For use with a shaped neckline, the width is determined by the head height at the front.

STEP 4

Step 1 × stitch gauge = number of stitches to cast on

STEP 5

Cast on Step 4 number of stitches, and work to the depth of Step 3.

STEP 6

[(Step 1 − Step 2) ÷ 2] × stitch gauge = number of stitches to bind off at the beginning of the next 2 rows

STEP 7

Work even on the remaining stitches until the back portion is equal in length to the width of the stitches in Step 6. Bind off.

STEP 8

Sew the equal-length edges of the back portion and the front portion together at each side of the hood. Sew hood to neckline along bottom edge.

For a Shaped Neckline

STEP 1

(Hood Measurement 2 + Ease) × 2 = front hood width

STEP 2

Work following the guidelines for the unshaped neckline hood, above, Steps 2 through 8.

Hood Version 10

Similar to Version 2, Version 10 works for shaped neckline only.

STEP 1

(Hood Measurement 2 + Ease) × 2 = starting width of the hood

STEP 2

(Hood Measurement 1 + Ease) × 2 = finished width of the hood

STEP 3

Determine the width of the back portion. 2″ is the minimum width for a child, and 3″ is the minimum width for an adult. Maximum width is the width of the back neckline of the garment.

STEP 4

(Step 1 − Step 2) × stitch gauge ÷ 2 = number of stitches to taper at each side edge of the hood

STEP 5

(Hood Measurement 3 + Ease) − (Step 3 ÷ 2) − depth of hood finish = depth of the taper

STEP 6

Step 5 × row gauge = number of rows of the taper

STEP 7

Taper the Step 4 number of stitches over the Step 6 number of rows (see Taper Formula), to form a slope along the front neckline edge.

STEP 8

[(Step 2 − Step 3) ÷ 2] × stitch gauge = number of stitches to bind off at the beginning of the next two rows

STEP 9

Work even on the remaining stitches until the back portion is equal in length to the width of the stitches in Step 8. Bind off.

STEP 10

Assemble hood as in Version 9, Step 8.

HOOD VERSION 10

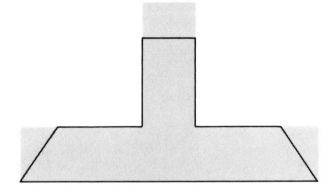

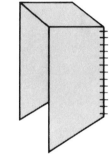

A separately worked T-shaped hood with tapered neckline edges, which fit better on a shaped neckline (a T-shaped Version 2).

HOOD VERSIONS 11 AND 12. When the sweater neckline circumference is less than (Hood Measurement 3 + Ease) × 2, or if you want more fullness in the hood, work these versions of the T-Shaped hood.

On both versions, the back of the hood slants outward from the neckline. Version 12 has a sloping side front edge, to better fit a shaped neckline.

Hood Version 11

STEP 1

a. **For an Unshaped Neckline**
   (Hood Measurement 1 + Ease) × 2 = starting width of the hood

b. **For a Shaped Neckline**
   (Hood Measurement 2 + Ease) × 2 = starting width of the hood

STEP 2

Determine the width of the back portion. 2″ is the minimum width for a child, and 3″ is the minimum width for an adult. Maximum width is the width of the back neckline of the garment.

STEP 3

(Sweater neckline circumference ÷ 2) − (Step 2 ÷ 2) = depth of the front portion of the hood to the beginning of the outward slope

STEP 4

Calculate and cast on stitches for the width of the hood (Step 1a *or* Step 1b × stitch gauge). Work to the depth of Step 3.

STEP 5

[(Step 1a *or* Step 1b − Step 2)] ÷ 2 × stitch gauge = number of stitches to slope on each side of the back portion

STEP 6

(Hood Measurement 3 + Ease) − (sweater neckline circumference ÷ 2) = depth of the slope of the back (seam) edges of the front portion of the hood

STEP 7

Step 6 × row gauge = number of rows for slope

STEP 8

Chart the slope of the seam edges of the front portion, using the Step 5 number of stitches and the Step 7 number of rows (see Slope Formula).

STEP 9

Work the slope on both sides of the hood until you reach a number of stitches equal to (Step 2 × stitch gauge).

STEP 10

Work even on the remaining stitches until the back portion is equal in length to the measurement of the sloped edges of the front portion. Bind off.

Hood Version 12

Taper the neckline edges as in Version 10, and slope the seam edge of the front portion as in Version 11, using the Step 1b measurement.

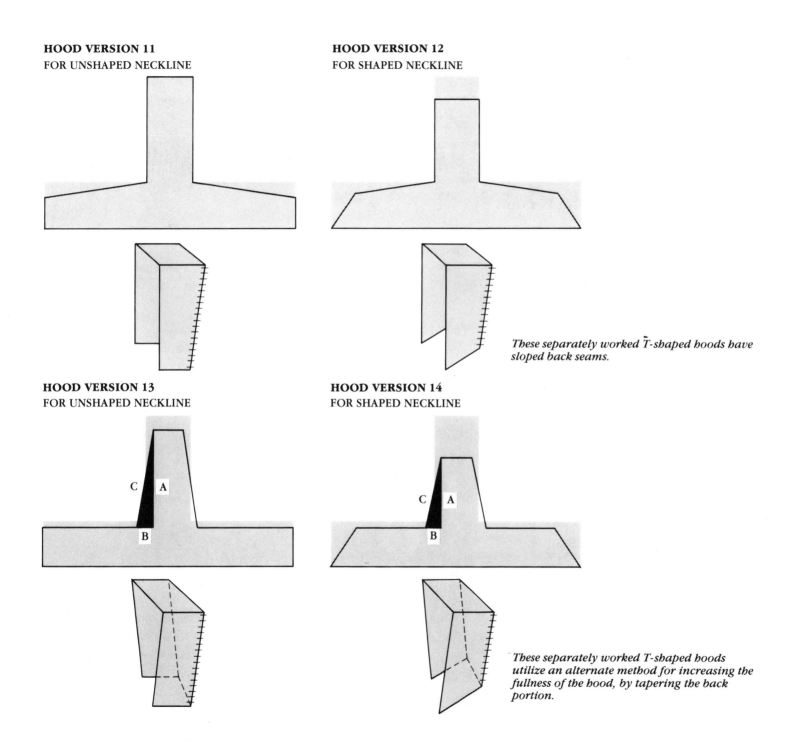

HOOD VERSION 11
FOR UNSHAPED NECKLINE

HOOD VERSION 12
FOR SHAPED NECKLINE

These separately worked T-shaped hoods have sloped back seams.

HOOD VERSION 13
FOR UNSHAPED NECKLINE

C   A
B

HOOD VERSION 14
FOR SHAPED NECKLINE

C   A
B

These separately worked T-shaped hoods utilize an alternate method for increasing the fullness of the hood, by tapering the back portion.

HOOD VERSIONS 13 AND 14. These versions utilize an alternate method for increasing the fullness of the hood. In it, the back portion of the hood tapers from an Unfinished Width—after the binding off of the front portion—to a smaller Finished Width at the back neckline edge. Version 14 has a sloping side front edge, to better fit a shaped neckline.

Hood Version 13

STEP 1
Determine the Finished Width of the back portion of the hood. 2″ is the minimum width for a child, and 3″ is the minimum width for an adult. Maximum width is the width of the back neckline of the garment.

STEP 2
Calculate the number of stitches to cast on, using Version 9, Steps 1 and 4.

STEP 3
([(Hood Measurement 3 + Ease) × 2] – sweater neckline circumference) + Step 1 = Unfinished Width of the back portion of the hood.

STEP 4
(Sweater neckline circumference ÷ 2) – (Step 1 ÷ 2) = depth of the front portion of the hood

STEP 5
Step 3 – (Step 2 × stitch gauge) = number of stitches to bind off at the beginning of the next two rows

STEP 6
Use Sleeve Cap Formula (or paper-and-ruler method) to determine the length of the back portion of the hood.
a. Side *c*: Step 5 ÷ stitch gauge = the width of the stitches bound off in Step 5
b. Side *b*: (Step 2 – Step 1) ÷ 2 = the width of stitches to taper
c. Side *a*: Square root of [(Side *c* × Side *c*) – (Side *b* × Side *b*)] = the depth of the back portion of the hood

STEP 7
Step 6b × stitch gauge = number of stitches to decrease at each side of the back portion of the hood

STEP 8
Step 6c × row gauge = number of rows over which to work decreases

STEP 9
Taper the back portion using the numbers calculated in Steps 7 and 8 (see Taper Formula).

STEP 10
Bind off.

Hood Version 14

Taper the side edges of the front portion as in Version 10, Steps 1 through 7, and the back portion as in Version 13, Steps 5 through 10.

Attached Hoods

The major difference between Attached and Separate Hoods is that the seam(s) of the Attached Hood will be at the top of the head, instead of at the back. The direction of the knitting allows you to continue design elements from the body or from the sleeves of Raglans and Saddle Shoulders onto the hood without a break in the fabric.

The Attached Hood variations described below are based on those versions (1, 3, 5, 7, 9, 11, 13) of the Separate Hood which do not taper at the neckline edge.

Choose with the Shaped or Unshaped variation of a given hood version, depending on the neckline shaping you have chosen for your sweater.

The instructions for the Attached Hoods are somewhat abbreviated; if necessary, refer to the corresponding version of the Separate Hood for more detail.

If it is difficult to pick up the number of stitches needed for the width of the hood, then instead pick up the number of stitches in your stockinette stitch gauge over every inch around the neckline edge. After that, work evenly spaced increases (see Gathers Formula) to reach the required number of stitches.

ATTACHED HOOD VERSION 1

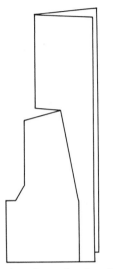

A rectangular hood.

ATTACHED HOOD VERSION 3

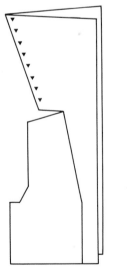

The point is emphasized by sloping the back seam.

Hood Version 1, Attached

STEP 1

(Hood Measurement 3 + Ease) × 2 × stitch gauge = number of stitches to pick up around the neckline for the hood

Adjust Hood Measurement 3 by the depth of the finish if necessary, and allow space on the neckline edge for the finish if needed.

STEP 2

a. **For an Unshaped Neckline**
   Work to (Hood Measurement 1 + Ease), and bind off.

b. **For a Shaped Neckline**
   Work to (Hood Measurement 2 + Ease), and bind off.

STEP 3

Fold hood at center back, and sew top edges together.

Hood Version 3, Attached

STEP 1

(Hood Measurement 3 + Ease) × 2 × stitch gauge = number of stitches to pick up around the neckline for the hood

Adjust Hood Measurement 3 by the depth of the finish if necessary, and allow space on the neckline edge for the finish if needed.

Place a marker at center back.

STEP 2

a. **For an Unshaped Neckline**
   Determine the extra length desired for the point. Increase the number of stitches equal to that length on both sides of the marker over the depth of (Hood Measurement 1 + Ease). Bind off.

b. **For a Shaped Neckline**
   Determine the extra length desired for the point. Increase the number of stitches equal to that length on both sides of the marker over the depth of (Hood Measurement 2 + Ease). Bind off.

STEP 3
Fold hood at center back, and sew top edges together.

Hood Version 5, Attached

STEP 1
(Hood Measurement 3 + Ease) × 2 × stitch gauge = number of stitches to pick up around the neckline for the hood
Make this an even number.
- If necessary, adjust Hood Measurement 3 by the depth of the finish, and if needed allow space on the neckline edge for the finish.

STEP 2
Choose the depth of the curve at the back (2″ to 4″).

STEP 3
Using the Curve Guide (see ''How Tos''), chart two mirror-image curves at the foldline of the hood, to the chosen depth.

STEP 4
a. **For an Unshaped Neckline**
   Work to (Hood Measurement 1 + Ease) − Step 2.
b. **For a Shaped Neckline**
   Work to (Hood Measurement 2 + Ease) − Step 2.

STEP 5
Work the shaping of the curve on either side of center back, and bind off the remaining stitches.

STEP 6
Fold hood at center back, and sew top edges together.

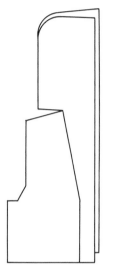

There is no point, because the back seam edge is curved to the fold line.

Hood Version 7, Attached

STEP 1

Sweater neckline circumference × stitch gauge = number of stitches to pick up for the hood
Make this an even number. Place a marker at center back.

■ If necessary, adjust Hood Measurement 3 by the depth of the finish, and if needed allow space on the neckline edge for the finish.

STEP 2

(Hood Measurement 3 + Ease) × 2 − Step 1 = number of stitches to increase at center back
Make this an even number.

STEP 3

a. **For an Unshaped Neckline**
   [(Hood Measurement 1 + Ease) ÷ 3] × row gauge = number of rows for the taper
b. **For a Shaped Neckline**
   [(Hood Measurement 2 + Ease) ÷ 3] × row gauge = number of rows for the taper
Make this an even number.

STEP 4

Calculate the taper at the center back, using the Step 3 number of rows and one-half of the Step 2 number of stitches. Work the increases for the taper on both sides of the marker (one-half of the Step 2 stitches on each side of the marker), over the number of rows calculated in Step 3.

STEP 5

Choose the depth of the curve (2″ to 4″) at the top back corner of the hood.

STEP 6

a. **For an Unshaped Neckline**
   Work even on the increased width to (Hood Measurement 1 + Ease) − Step 6.
b. **For a Shaped Neckline**
   Work even on the increased width to (Hood Measurement 2 + Ease) − Step 6.

STEP 7

Work the shaping of the curve (determined from the Curve Guide, as for Version 7, Step 2) on either side of the center back, and bind off the remaining stitches.

STEP 8

Fold hood at center back, and sew top edges together.

ATTACHED HOOD VERSION 7

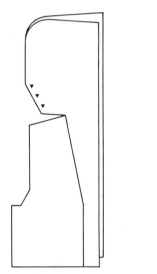

This fits closely, since the back seam edge slopes in to the neckline, and a curve fits the top of the head.

Hood Version 9, Attached

STEP 1

(Hood Measurement 3 + Ease) × 2 × stitch gauge = number of stitches to pick up around the neckline for the hood

- If necessary, adjust Hood Measurement 3 by the depth of the finish, and if needed allow space on the neckline edge for the finish.

STEP 2

Determine the width of the back portion. 2″ is the minimum width for a child, and 3″ is the minimum width for an adult. Maximum width is the width of the back neckline of the garment.

STEP 3

a. **For an Unshaped Neckline**

Work the hood to (Hood Measurement 1 + Ease) – (Step 2 ÷ 2).

b. **For a Shaped Neckline**

Work the hood to (Hood Measurement 2 + Ease) – (Step 2 ÷ 2).

STEP 4

[Step 1 – (Step 2 × stitch gauge)] ÷ 2 = number of stitches to bind off at the beginning of the next 2 rows

STEP 5

Work even on the remaining stitches until the back (top) portion is equal in length to the width of the stitches of Step 4. Bind off.

STEP 6

Sew side edges of top portion to top edges of side portions.

ATTACHED HOOD VERSION 9

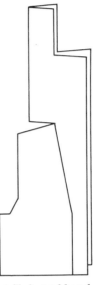

A T-shaped hood.

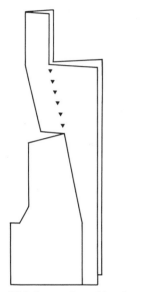

ATTACHED HOOD VERSION 11

This has a sloped back seam.

Hood Version 11, Attached

For this version, markers are placed on the needle to indicate the stitches of the back portion. The increases of the hood are worked at the outside of these markers, on the front portion of the hood.

STEP 1
Sweater neckline circumference × stitch gauge = number of stitches to pick up around the neckline for the hood

STEP 2
Determine the width of the back portion. 2″ is the minimum width for a child, and 3″ is the minimum width for an adult. Maximum width is the width of the back neckline of the garment.

STEP 3
Step 2 × stitch gauge = number of stitches in back portion
Place markers on the needle, equidistant from the center back, to indicate the stitches of the back portion.

STEP 4
(Hood Measurement 3 + Ease) × stitch gauge = number of stitches equivalent to the finished depth of the hood

STEP 5
Step 4 − (Step 1 ÷ 2) = number of stitches to increase on the outside of each marker

STEP 6
a. **For an Unshaped Neckline**
   (Hood Measurement 1 + Ease) − (Step 2 ÷ 2) = depth of the shaping of the hood × row gauge = number of rows for shaping
b. **For a Shaped Neckline**
   (Hood Measurement 2 + Ease) − (Step 2 ÷ 2) = depth of the shaping of the hood × row gauge = number of rows for shaping

STEP 7
Use Steps 5 and 6 to calculate the taper of the hood (see Taper Formula).

STEP 8
Step 4 − (Step 3 ÷ 2) = number of stitches to bind off at the beginning of the next 2 rows

STEP 9

Work even on the remaining stitches until the back (top) portion is equal in length to the width of the stitches of Step 8. Bind off.

Hood Version 13, Attached

Chart hood and place markers on the needle as for Hood Version 11, Attached, but work the increases to the inside of the markers, on the back portion of the hood.

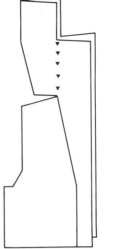

This incorporates an alternate method for increasing the fullness of the hood, by tapering the back portion.

PLACKETS

When a neckline has an opening, whether for reasons of fit or to enhance the design, the opening has to be finished. The finish might be a row of slip stitch or single crochet or a piped edging, but when it is wide enough to overlap it is called a placket. A placket can be worked in any of the noncurling border stitch patterns, or it can be hemmed or faced to stabilize its edge. If the opening is to be fastened with buttons, the underlap of the placket will hold the buttons and the overlap will have buttonholes.

Plackets have much in common with the finishes of cardigan fronts. Read through the information on necklines and finishes in the Cardigans section for guidelines on determining the maximum and minimum amount of overlap for a placket. As for length, the neckline placket can start anywhere above the bottom border and run the length of the body to the neckline, or it can be as short as 1″ if it is purely decorative.

Remember that men's and women's garments traditionally overlap in opposite directions: right side over left side (from the wearer's point of view) for women, and left over right for men. We have given separate instructions for each style.

Neckline openings can be sorted into two types. The first is actually a slot in the fabric. This often is called a Keyhole Opening since, when paired with the neckline opening, that is what it resembles. A Keyhole slot can be worked at the front or back neckline, at the top of Raglan sleeves and Saddle Bands, or on the shoulders of One-Piece Dolmans and Ts.

The second type of opening is a Seam Opening. Any seam that ends at the neckline edge can be finished with a placket, then closed with buttons or other fasteners. Possible locations include shoulder seams, Saddle Band seams, and Raglan seams.

Although our discussion here centers on neckline plackets, these openings also can be added to sleeve or body openings.

PLACKET VARIATIONS

BOATNECK WITH BUTTONS ON BACK

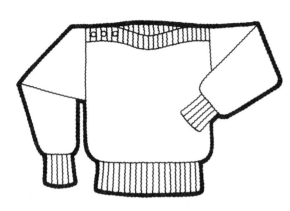

SADDLE BAND SEAM PLACKET, WITH OVERLAP ON FRONT SHOULDER

FACED FINISH WITH BUTTONHOLES

ROUND NECKLINE WITH SELF-FINISHED KEYHOLE PLACKET

SQUARE NECKLINE WITH SELF-FINISHING BAND AND KEYHOLE PLACKET

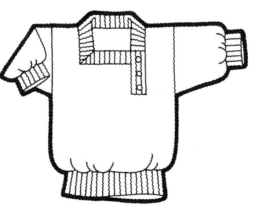

V NECKLINE WITH SHAWL AND SELF-FINISHED KEYHOLE PLACKET

BLUNT V NECKLINE WITH OVERLAPPING INSERT

ROUND NECKLINE WITH FACED PLACKET AND PIPING FINISH

RAGLAN WITH PLACKET IN SEAM

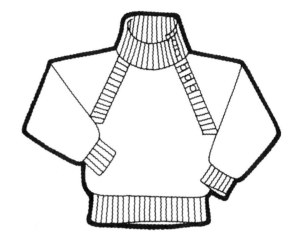

ROUND NECKLINE WITH PLACKET FROM SHOULDER

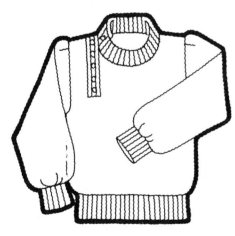

ROUND NECKLINE WITH PLACKET ON SHOULDER

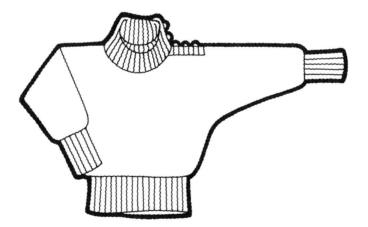

Like neckline plackets, sleeve plackets can be of any length, from 1″ to the full length of the sleeve.

Keyhole Openings

The dimensions of the slot are based on the depth of the opening and the width of the placket. Preliminary procedures for plackets are as follows.

1. Chart and graph the graph piece, and determine the placement of the Keyhole Opening on the graph.

2. Cast on and work the garment piece to the base of the opening.
3. Bind off or place on a stitch holder the number of stitches equal to the width of the placket.
4. Finish garment piece, working each side separately on either side of the slot.

Horizontal Placket. This placket is worked sideways. For it, a number of stitches equivalent to the width of the placket needs to be bound off on the sweater body. After the body has been completed, stitches are picked up to work the placket.

Horizontal Placket

STEP 1
Pick up stitches along one (vertical) side of the opening.

STEP 2
Knit to a depth equal to the width of the opening, and bind off.

STEP 3
On the opposite side of the opening, pick up and knit overlap in the same way, working buttonholes at regular intervals if desired.

STEP 4
Sew the overlap to the bound-off edge of the garment piece, and stitch the underlap to the same edge on the inside of the garment.

KEYHOLE OPENINGS

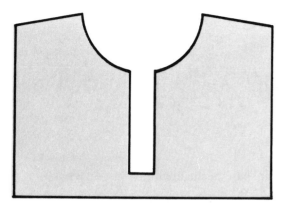

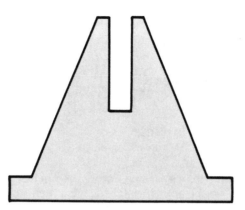

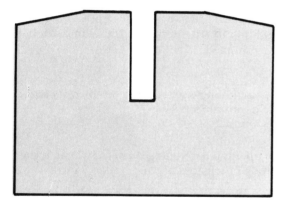

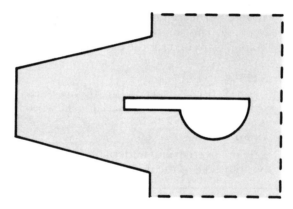

These plackets can ease the opening of a sweater, making it easier to get off and on, or can be simply decorative.

HORIZONTAL PLACKET

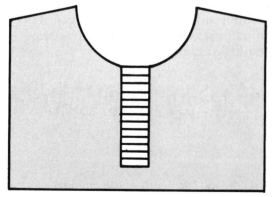

VERTICAL PLACKET

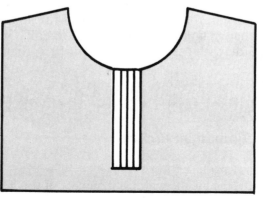

SELF-FINISHED PLACKET

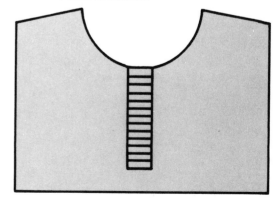

Vertical Placket. Like the Horizontal Placket, the Vertical Placket is picked up and worked after the sweater body has been completed (with an opening left for the placket). For this version, the stitches for the width of the placket can be bound off or placed on a holder.

Vertical Placket

STEP 1
Pick up stitches, or knit across the open stitches, at the base of the opening. Cast on a seam stitch on the appropriate side for a men's or women's overlap.

STEP 2
Work a vertical finish, with buttonholes if desired, to a length just short of the depth of the opening. This can be up to 1″ less on a deep opening. Bind off stitches or put these on a stitch holder as needed for the neckline finish.

STEP 3
Cast on stitches equal to the stitches worked in Step 1 (including a seam stitch on the *opposite* side to Step 1) for the underlap, and work to the same depth as Step 2.

STEP 4
Sew the overlap and underlap to the side edges of the opening, stretching them to fit. Stitch the bottom edge of the underlap in place on the wrong side of the garment.

Self-Finished Placket. If seed stitch, garter stitch, or another noncurling stitch is used, the placket can be self-finished, that is, knit along with the garment. The side with the underlap is knit first, then the overlap is picked up at the base of the placket and worked together with the remaining side of the garment piece. This eliminates stitching the underlap to the base of the placket.

Woman's Placket

STEP 1
Determine the width and number of stitches of the placket, and the depth of the opening.

STEP 2
Chart and graph the garment piece and determine the placement of the placket on the graph.

STEP 3
Work just short of the base of the opening, and place markers on the needle to indicate the stitches included in the placket.

STEP 4
Work to the base of the opening, ending with a wrong-side row.

STEP 5
Knit to the first marker. Work the pattern of the placket to the second marker and place the remaining stitches of the piece on a holder.

STEP 6
Complete this side of the piece (the left side as worn), knitting the placket pattern stitch along the right edge (as worn).

STEP 7
Inserting the right needle into the placket stitches at the base of the underlap, pick up the stitches for the overlap, then place a marker. With the same yarn, work the stitches from the holder.

STEP 8
Continue to knit, working the placket pattern stitch between the marker and the left edge of the piece (as worn). Work buttonholes on the placket as desired.

Man's Placket

STEP 1
Work Steps 1 through 4 of the Woman's Self-Finished Placket.

STEP 2
Work to the first marker and place the stitches just worked on a holder. Break off the yarn, leaving a 12″ to 15″ tail.

STEP 3
Join the yarn, work the pattern of the placket to the second marker, resume the pattern of the garment, and finish the row.

STEP 4

Complete this side of the piece. This is the underlap side.

STEP 5

Place the stitches from the holder on the needle and, inserting the right needle into the placket stitches at the base of the underlap, pick up the stitches of the overlap using the 12″ to 15″ of yarn still attached.

STEP 6

Join the yarn and complete this side of the piece, working buttonholes in the placket if desired.

Faced Placket. When you need an opening, but you want a design element— a stripe, for example—to cross the fabric unbroken, then a Faced Placket is your best option. The fabric of the facing can be worked in the stitch pattern of the piece, or in stockinette stitch if the gauges are compatible.

Consider the thickness of the fabric. If the fabric is heavy, you may choose to work a Self-Finished Underlap and a Faced Overlap. This would give you only three layers of fabric in the placket instead of four. Work the pattern of the self-finish on one to three stitches less than the stitches for the width of the placket, so that it will be hidden by the overlap.

Our instructions are for facings on both underlap and overlap.

Woman's Placket

STEP 1

Work Steps 1 through 4 of the Woman's Self-Finished Placket.

STEP 2

Work to the second marker, and place the remaining stitches on a holder.

STEP 3

Cast on one stitch for a vertical turning ridge (see "How Tos"), and an additional number of stitches equal to the width of the placket. This is the underlap side.

FACED PLACKET

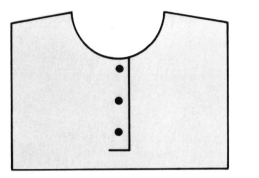 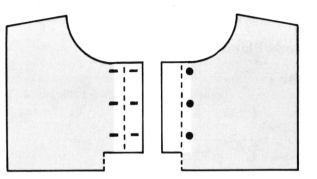

If you need an opening but want a design element to cross the fabric without interruption, use a Faced Placket.

STEP 4
Complete this side of the piece.

STEP 5
For the overlap side, insert the needle into the placket stitches at the base of the underlap, pick up the stitches for the overlap, then work the stitches from the holder.

STEP 6
At the end of the next row, cast on additional stitches equal to the width of the facing plus one stitch for the vertical turning ridge.

STEP 7
Complete this side of the piece, working buttonholes on both placket and facing if required for your garment.

STEP 8
Fold facings of both overlap and underlap to the reverse side of the fabric, and sew down along bottom and side edges. Join buttonholes around edges, as well.

Man's Placket

STEP 1
Work Steps 1 through 4 of Woman's Self-Finished Placket.

STEP 2
Knit to the first marker, and place the stitches just worked on a holder. Break off the yarn, leaving a 12″ to 15″ tail.

STEP 3
Cast on a number of stitches equal to the width of the placket, plus a vertical turning ridge stitch (see "How Tos"), and continue knitting across the row.

STEP 4
Complete this side of the piece.

STEP 5
Place the stitches from the holder on the needle. Insert the needle into the placket stitches at the base of the underlap, and pick up the stitches of the overlap using the 12″ to 15″ of yarn still attached. Turn the work.

STEP 6
On the right needle, cast on the stitches for the facing and the vertical turning ridge, and, with the same yarn, finish the row.

STEP 7
Complete this side of the piece, working buttonholes on both the placket and the facing, if desired.

STEP 8
Fold facings of both overlap and underlap to the reverse side of the fabric, and sew down along bottom and side edges. Join buttonholes around edges, as well.

Seam Openings

Shoulder Seam Openings. The major decision to make when charting a placket in a shoulder seam is where to place the buttons. They can be on the front shoulder, forward of the seamline, or they can be on the seamline itself, at the top of the shoulder. Button placement determines how much to adjust the armhole depth of

PLACKETS AT THE SHOULDER LINE

BUTTONS ON THE FRONT

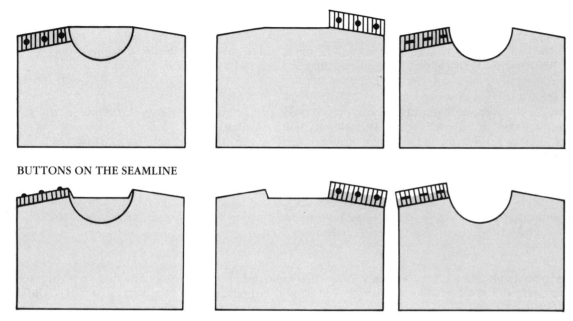

BUTTONS ON THE SEAMLINE

the open shoulder. It also determines whether both the front and back yokes are adjusted, or if changes are needed only on the front.

Which of the shoulders carries the opening is up to you. Once the choice is made, plan the adjustments for that shoulder on the front, and remember that the adjustments on the back yoke will occur on the opposite shoulder (from the knitter's point of view). In order words, if the front's right shoulder carries the overlap of the opening, the back's left shoulder will carry the underlap.

Buttons on the Front

In this version, when the placket is closed the buttons are on the front of the sweater. The underlap (which extends under the sweater front) is worked as part of the back shoulder, and the front shoulder carries the overlap and the buttonholes. The placket depth needs to be at least the width of the buttons. The placket width is equal to the shoulder width. If the fabric is not too thick, the finish can be faced or be worked as a Doubled Band.

STEP 1

Work the back with no adjustments. Bind off the shoulder slope as usual to stabilize the shoulder.

STEP 2

On the front, choose which shoulder will be open and determine its adjusted armhole depth:
Armhole Depth Measurement – depth of the placket = adjusted armhole depth

STEP 3

Knit the front above the armhole bind-offs to the depth determined in Step 2, then work the shoulder slope for the side where the opening will be located.
The shoulder slope can be shaped by binding off or by working short rows (see "How Tos").
Work the other side to the normal armhole depth before shaping its shoulder.

STEP 4

The placket overlap on the front shoulder can be picked up and worked attached, worked separately and sewn on, or, if the slope was shaped by short rows, worked from open stitches.
Chart and work buttonholes on the overlap as desired.

STEP 5

The placket underlap on the back shoulder can be picked up and worked attached, or worked separately and sewn on. Work it straight out from the shoulder, to a depth equal to that of the placket overlap.
■ If the overlap is doubled, consider working only a single thickness on the underlap to eliminate bulk.

STEP 6

When finishing the sweater, join the front and back by overlapping and stitching the armhole edges of the placket together, then set in the sleeve.

Buttons on the Seamline

In this version, buttons are sewn to the underlap at what would have been the seamline. Because of this, both the front and the back sections need to be adjusted to allow for the fabric of the placket.

STEP 1

Determine the adjusted armhole depth for the front and back placket shoulders:
Armhole Depth Measurement – $\frac{1}{2}$ the depth of the placket = adjusted armhole depth

STEP 2

Knit the back above the armhole bind-offs to the depth determined in Step 1, then work the shoulder shaping for the side where the opening will be located.
The shoulder slope can be shaped by binding off or by working short rows (see "How Tos").

STEP 3

Bind off the stitches for the back neckline at the end of the shaping of the placket shoulder. Continue on the remaining shoulder stitches until the full armhole is reached. Work the shoulder shaping.

STEP 4

Work the front, adjusting the placket shoulder in the same manner as the back.

STEP 5

The placket pieces on both front and back can be picked up and worked attached, worked separately and sewn on, or, if the slope was shaped by short rows, worked from open stitches. Chart and work the buttonholes on the overlap so that they lie along the original seam line.

STEP 6

When finishing the sweater, join the front and back by overlapping and stitching the armhole edges of the placket together, then set in the sleeve.

Saddle Band Seam Openings. A sweater with Saddle Shoulder styling can have an opening on the front or back edge of the saddle band. Here, as in the plackets of shoulder seams, the placement of the buttons determines how to work the placket. If the buttons are on the saddle band when the opening is fastened, the saddle band carries the placket overlap and the shoulder carries the underlap. If the buttons are on the shoulder, the placement of the underlap and the overlap is reversed.

Overlap on Saddle Band

For this version, the front and back are charted and worked without adjustment. The placket shoulder can be shaped by short rows (see "How Tos") if you want to work the underlap on open stitches. All of the finishing options for plackets described in the guidelines for plackets along shoulder seams are applicable here as well.

STEP 1

Chart the sleeve through the sleeve cap and saddle band shaping.

PLACKETS ON THE SADDLE-SHOULDER SEAM (WITH OVERLAP ON THE SADDLE BAND)

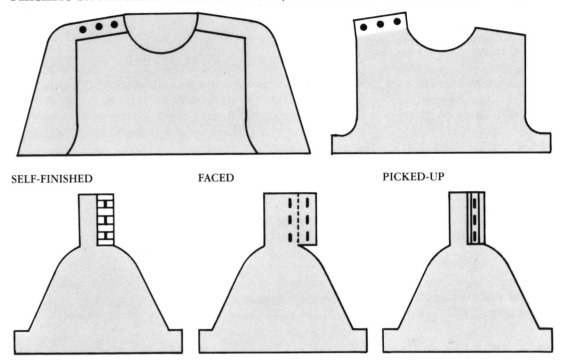

SELF-FINISHED   FACED   PICKED-UP

STEP 2
Determine the width of the placket and adjust the saddle band, starting at the shoulder edge.
a. **Self-finished edge:** Work the stitches for the width of the placket in a stable stitch pattern. Chart and work the buttonholes.
b. **Faced edge:** Cast on stitches equal to the width of the placket for a facing, and work a vertical turning ridge (see "How Tos") on the original edge stitch. Work buttonholes on both the facing and the saddle band.
c. **Picked-up or sewn-in placket:** Bind off stitches equal to the width of the placket and work the saddle band on the remaining stitches. Either pick up and work the placket, or work it separately and sew it on.

STEP 3
On the back or front shoulder section where the underlap will be located, pick up stitches across the width of the shoulder. Work to placket depth, then bind off.

PLACKETS ON THE SADDLE-SHOULDER SEAM (WITH BUTTONS ON THE SADDLE BAND)

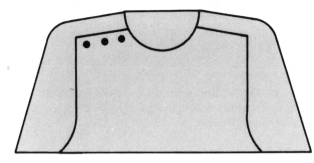 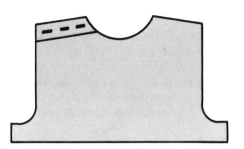

PICKED-UP   CAST ON

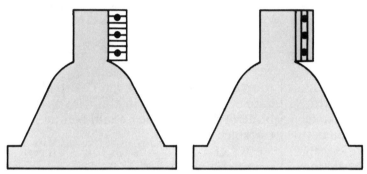

Overlap on Front Shoulder

In this version, extra fabric is added to the saddle band for the underlap.

STEP 1
Chart the front. Choose which shoulder will be open, and determine its adjusted armhole depth:
Armhole Depth Measurement of Saddle Shoulder Yoke − depth of the placket = adjusted armhole depth

STEP 2

Knit the front above the armhole bind-offs to the depth determined in Step 1, then work the slope of the placket shoulder.

The shoulder slope can be shaped by binding off or by working short rows (see "How Tos"). Work the other side to the normal armhole depth before shaping its shoulder.

STEP 3

The placket overlap on the front shoulder can be picked up and worked attached, worked separately and sewn on, or, if the slope was shaped by short rows, worked from the open stitches. Chart and work buttonholes on the overlap, as desired.

STEP 4

Chart and work the sleeves normally to the saddle band. The underlap can be worked in one of two ways. You can either finish the saddle band as charted and work the underlap by picking up stitches, or cast on stitches at the shoulder edge equal to the width of the placket and complete the saddle band with this larger number of stitches.

Raglan Seam Openings. Our guidelines are written with the overlap of the placket worked as part of the front yoke. Because the Raglan Cap and the Raglan Yoke are so similar, these guidelines can easily be adapted to place the overlap on a sleeve, if you wish.

The depth of the opening can vary from 1" (for a purely decorative opening) to two-thirds of the Raglan Depth Measurement. Avoid placing buttons at the underarm, where they could be uncomfortable.

We give directions for four different variations of plackets in Raglan Seam Openings, each of which is initiated in the same way.

Raglan Seam Openings

STEP 1

Width of the button × stitch gauge = number of stitches for the width of the placket

STEP 2

Chart the raglan seam, planning the placement of the decreases at a distance from each edge equal to the number of stitches calculated in Step 1 plus one stitch. Place a marker at each side of the first row of the yoke at (Step 1 + 1) stitches in from the edge, and work the decreases to the inside of the markers.

STEP 3

Work the front to the Raglan Depth Measurement – the depth of the placket opening. At this depth, work the shaping for your chosen style of placket.

Picked-Up Horizontal Placket
STEP 4

Bind off the Step 1 number of stitches at the opening edge. Complete the front.

STEP 5

Chart and work the sleeves.

STEP 6

On the front yoke, pick up stitches for the overlap of the placket along the edge of the opening.

STEP 7

Cast on a seam stitch at the appropriate edge where you cast off previously, and knit the overlap, working the buttonholes. Sew unattached edge in place.

STEP 8

Starting at this depth on the sleeve, pick up the same number of stitches as in Step 6 and work the underlap as a horizontal band.

STEP 9

Sew the sleeve and the front together, up to the base of the opening. Stitch the bottom edge of the underlap to the inside of the overlap.
A Picked-up Vertical Placket can be worked similarly.

Self-Finished Placket
STEP 4

Work the stitches on the outside of the markers in a border stitch for the entire Raglan Depth, along all the raglan shaping (both sides of the yoke), or start the border stitch at the placket depth (Step 3) on only the placket edge. Work buttonholes (as desired) along the open edge of the front, within the border stitch area.

STEP 5

Work the placket sleeve to the depth determined in Step 3. Cast on the number of stitches calculated in Step 1. Complete the sleeve on the adjusted number of stitches, working the added stitches in the chosen border stitch.

STEP 6

Sew the sleeve and the front together, up to the base of the opening. Stitch the bottom edge of the underlap to the inside of the overlap.

PLACKETS ON THE RAGLAN SEAM

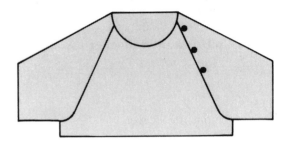

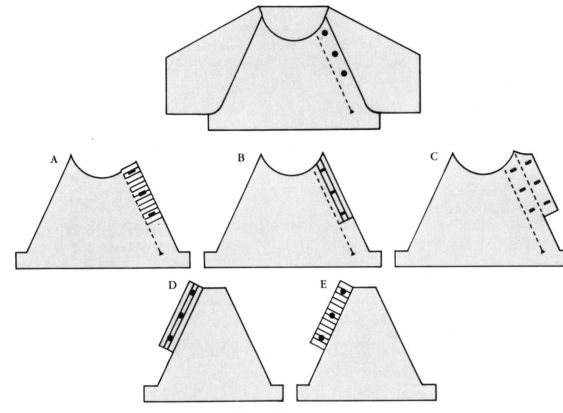

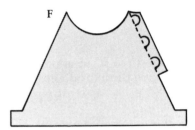

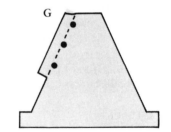

A BODY: placket picked up and knitted
   horizontally
B BODY: placket self-finished
C BODY: placket finished with facing which
   contains buttonholes
D SLEEVE: button underlap worked vertically
E SLEEVE: button underlap picked up and
   worked horizontally

F BODY: faced finished with loop closures
G SLEEVE: buttons along seam line

Plackets on a raglan seam can incorporate buttonholes or loops.

Faced Finish with Buttonholes

STEP 4

To work a faced overlap on the front yoke, cast on the number of stitches determined in Step 1. Work a vertical turning ridge (see "How Tos") on the original edge stitch, and complete the front on the adjusted number of stitches. Remember to work buttonholes on both the placket and the facing.

STEP 5

Work the placket sleeve to the Step 3 depth. Cast on the number of stitches calculated in Step 1. Complete the sleeve on the adjusted number of stitches, working the underlap section in a non-curling border stitch. If you want to have a faced underlap, the width should be twice the number of Step 1 stitches.

STEP 6

Sew the sleeve and the front together, up to the base of the opening. Fold the facing to the inside of the overlap and stitch in place. Stitch the underlap to the inside of the overlap.

Faced Finish with Loop Closures

STEP 4

Cast on ½" to 1" of stitches for the facing. Work a vertical turning ridge (see "How Tos") on the original edge stitch, and complete the front on the adjusted number of stitches.

STEP 5

If the facing extends into the neckline shaping, it will need to be shaped accordingly (see Cardigan Versions 13 and 14).

STEP 6

Sew the sleeve and the front together, up to the base of the opening. Fold the facing to the inside of the overlap and stitch in place. Stitch the underlap to the inside of the overlap.

STEP 7

Work buttonhole loops along the open edge of the overlap. Place the buttons right along the raglan edge line.

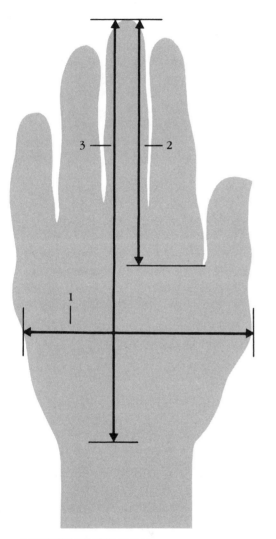

1 WIDTH OF THE HAND
2 LENGTH OF FINGERS AND THUMB
3 LENGTH OF THE HAND

POCKETS

A pocket is a container in a garment that enables you to carry all your treasures close at hand. Ask any child . . . or adult. A coat or jacket must have at least one pocket if it is to be a truly useful garment.

To be practical, the pocket needs to be the right size. Base the size of the pocket on the hand that will use it. The appropriate depth and width will be determined from pocket measurements taken from the hand.

The easiest way to measure the hand is to lay it on a piece of paper palm down, thumb and fingers together, and to trace around it, clearly showing the wrist and the joint at the base of the thumb.

The following three basic measurements for pockets will be referred to by number in the instructions for various pocket styles.

1. Width of the Hand
   Measure across the hand at the thumb joint.
2. Length of Fingers and Thumb
   Draw a line across the hand at the thumb joint and measure from that line to the tip of the middle finger.
3. Length of the Hand
   Measure from the wrist to the tip of the middle finger.

Another useful measurement to have is the *length of the arm and hand* from the shoulder to the middle fingertip. Use this measurement when deciding a pocket's placement. Measured from the start of the shoulder shaping on the front, this length indicates the lowest placement for the bottom edge of a pocket.

Patch Pockets

Patch Pockets are the easiest type to knit. On children's sweaters, they can be used as decorations if they are knit in different colors and/or shapes.

On adults' sweaters, the primary concern is to design the Patch Pocket so that it does not look like an afterthought. This can be a challenge. Placement should be well planned, and sewing should be done with meticulous care. Mark the stitches and rows of the pocket's width and length on the garment's fabric with a basting stitch in a contrasting color, and invisibly whip stitch (see "How Tos") the pocket to the fabric, to coincide row-for-row with the background. If the pocket is knit in stockinette stitch, duplicate stitch (which traces exactly the same path as the knit stitches) can be used to attach it.

Finishing the sewn edges with a small border or hems is another way to improve the appearance of a Patch Pocket. The bottom seam can be eliminated entirely by picking up the stitches of the pocket directly from the fabric. A flap, buttoned or plain, can be added by picking up stitches at least 1/4" above the top of the pocket, then working the flap upside down. Sweatshirt-style Pouch Pockets, sometimes called kangaroo pockets, can be picked up and knit along with the front section, then joined to the background fabric by knitting together (see "How Tos").

Use Pocket Measurements 1 and 2 for charting a Patch Pocket.

Simple Patch Pocket. This is the basic Patch Pocket. Instructions given are for the minimum size. If you want, you can make it bigger.

PATCH POCKETS

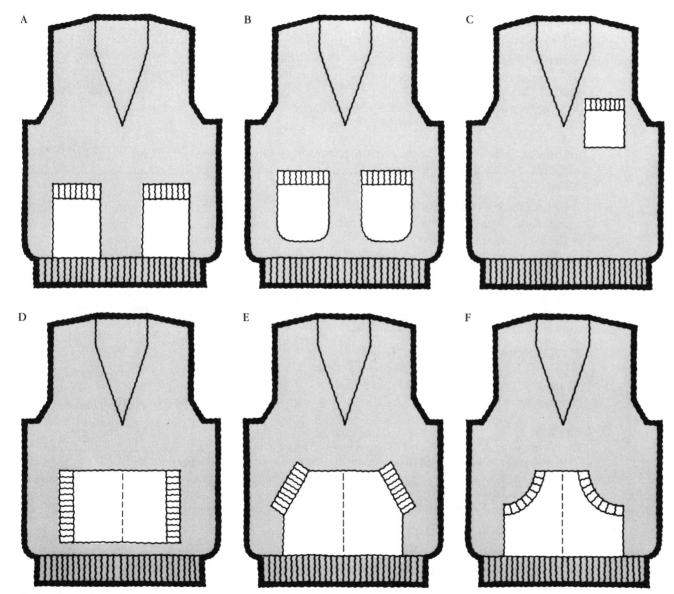

A simple patch pockets
B patch pockets with shaped lower edges
C patch pocket with side hems
D pouch pocket
E pouch pocket with sloped edges
F pouch pocket with curved edges

SIMPLE PATCH POCKET

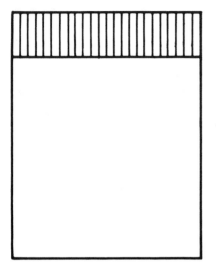

PATCH POCKET WITH SIDE HEMS

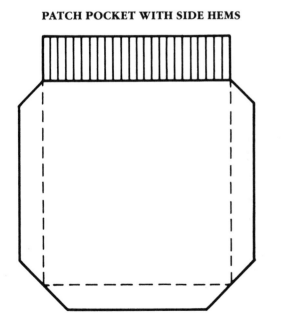

Simple Patch Pocket

STEP 1
(Pocket Measurement 1 + 1″ Ease) × stitch gauge = number of stitches to cast on

STEP 2
Knit the pocket to Pocket Measurement 2, working a border at least ³/₄″ deep at the top.

Patch Pocket with Side Hems.
These directions allow for a two-row hem at the bottom and two extra stitches at each edge for the side hems. The side hems do not extend into the top edge border. At the bottom corners, they are shaped for a mitered fit when folded under.

Patch Pocket with Side Hems

STEP 1
(Pocket Measurement 1 + 1″ Ease) × stitch gauge − 4 stitches = number of stitches to cast on

STEP 2
Increase one stitch at each end of the row every row four times. A vertical turning ridge (see "How Tos") can be worked on the third stitch in from each side edge.

STEP 3
Work to Pocket Measurement 2, plus two rows for the hem, minus the depth of the top edge finish.

STEP 4
Bind off two stitches at each edge, work the top finish on the remaining stitches, and bind off.

STEP 5
Fold the hems to the wrong side, baste them in place, and block the pocket. Stitch along the folded edges when sewing the pocket to the garment.

Pouch Pocket. This is a single, central pocket in the front of a sweater, with openings on both sides. If you wish, the open edges of the pocket can be sloped or curved (see Slanted and Curved Inset Pockets, below).

Pouch Pocket

STEP 1
Decide on the width and depth of the pocket.
a. **Width:** This pocket can extend across the entire front of the sweater if you wish. One simple method of determining width is twice the length of the hand (Pocket Measurement 3 × 2).
b. **Depth:** The top of the pocket should be no higher than 3″ to 4″ below the armhole shaping for an adult, or 1″ to 2″ for a child.

STEP 2
Work the sweater front to the top edge position of the pocket. Place the front stitches on a holder.

STEP 3
Pick up the stitches for the pocket on the front at the bottom edge position of the pocket, and work to the pocket depth.

STEP 4
Return the front stitches to the needle, placing markers on the needle to indicate the placement of the stitches of the pocket.

STEP 5
Holding the pocket stitches in front of the body stitches, work across the row, knitting together the pocket stitches and the corresponding front stitches between the markers (see "How Tos"). Complete the front.

STEP 6
Pick up and work a finish on each side edge of the pocket.

STEP 7
Sew the edges of the finish to the front, and close the bottom 3″ to 5″ of the pocket by sewing the edge of the finish to the background fabric. If you wish, stitch down the center of the pocket with a backstitch seam (see "How Tos").

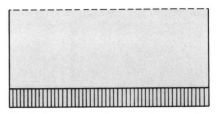

Work the sweater front to the top edge position of the pocket.

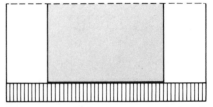

Pick up the stitches for the pocket at the bottom edge position, and work pocket.

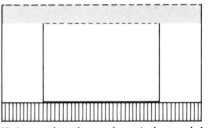

Knit together the pocket stitches and the corresponding front stitches.

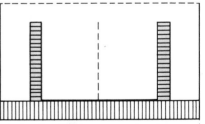

Work edge finishes on pocket; sew seam down center of pocket if you choose.

This single, central pocket has openings on both sides. The open edges can be sloped or curved.

INSET POCKETS

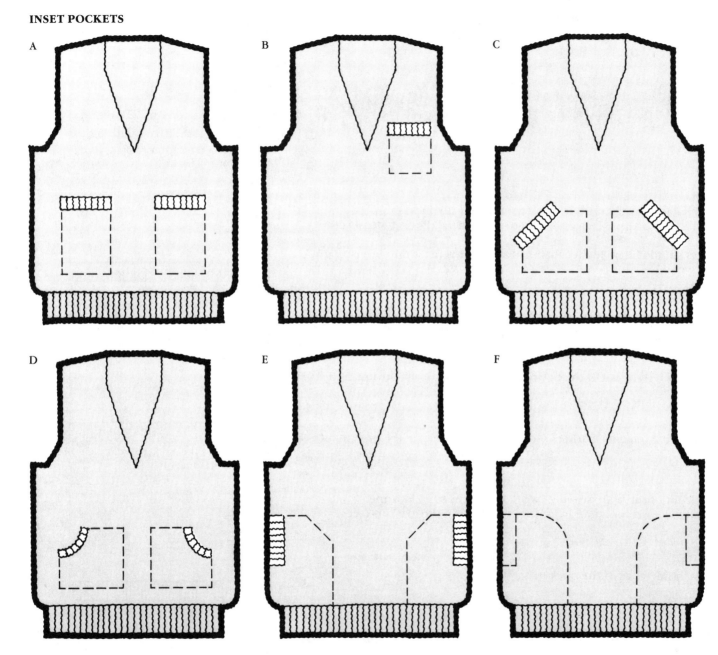

A horizontal openings
B horizontal openings
C slanted opening
D curved opening
E seam opening and self finish
F seam opening and faced finish

Inset Pockets

The Inset Pocket is the style we most often choose. This is because it blends better into the overall design of the sweater than does the Patch Pocket. Inset Pockets can be made obvious and used as a design element in the garment, but they can also be set invisibly into a side seam, serving their function without detracting from the sweater's design.

The pocket opening can be horizontal, vertical, slanted, or curved. Except for the Seam Opening Inset pocket, the liner is knit first and placed on a holder until needed. If the fabric of the garment is textured, either by the stitch pattern or the yarn, knit the liner in stockinette stitch, using a smooth yarn in a matching color. If there is a difference in gauge between the liner and the garment, it may be necessary to adjust the number of stitches by increasing or decreasing when you join the pocket to the fabric of the sweater.

The edge of the opening needs a finish to both strengthen and visually complete the opening. Many of the finishes described for necklines also are appropriate for pocket edges. When the gauge of the finish and the garment are the same, the finish can be worked along with the garment. If the gauges are different, the finish will need to be worked on open or picked-up stitches, or knit separately and sewn on.

Horizontal Inset Pockets require Pocket Measurements 1 and 2. The remaining Inset Pockets need all three pocket measurements.

Inset Pocket with Horizontal Opening. This can be thought of as a hidden Patch Pocket. The opening is slightly smaller than the width of the lining. A finishing border is added to the top edge of the opening after the entire sweater front has been completed.

Inset Pocket

STEP 1
(Pocket Measurement 1 + 1″ ease) × stitch gauge = number of stitches for the pocket opening

STEP 2
Step 1 + 4 = number of stitches for the liner

STEP 3
Cast on and work the liner to a depth equal to (Pocket Measurement 2 − the depth of the finish).

STEP 4
Work the front section of the garment to the row where the pocket opening will be located. Mark the position of the opening with a marker to either side of the Step 1 number of stitches.

STEP 5
Knit to 2 stitches before the marker, place the liner on a needle, and hold it to the wrong side of the work.

INSET POCKET WITH HORIZONTAL OPENING

A Work pocket liners and work front garment section to row where pocket opening will be located.

B On joining row, secure pocket liners and reserve pocket-opening stitches of front to be finished later.

C Pick up reserved stitches of front and work finish.

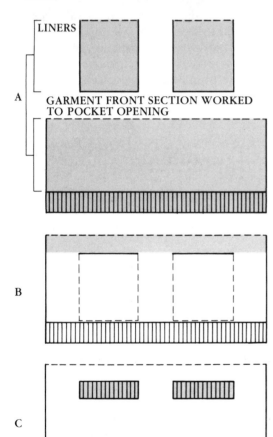

LINERS

A GARMENT FRONT SECTION WORKED TO POCKET OPENING

B

C

This is like a hidden patch pocket, but interrupts the garment's design less than a patch pocket.

STEP 6
Work together the next 2 stitches of the front section with the first 2 stitches of the liner (see "How Tos"), remove the marker, and, after placing the stitches of the pocket opening on a holder, remove the second marker.

STEP 7
Work across the stitches of the liner, knitting together the last 2 stitches of the liner and the next 2 stitches of the front. Complete the front section of the garment.

STEP 8
Place the stitches of the opening on the border size needles and work the finish. Bind off.

STEP 9
Stitch the sides of the finish to the front, and carefully sew the sides and bottom of the liner to the wrong side of the fabric.

Loose Inset Pocket with Horizontal Opening. This version has a free-swinging, bag-like liner rather than a liner consisting of a single layer of fabric.

Loose Inset Pocket with Horizontal Opening

STEP 1
(Pocket Measurement 1 + 1″ ease) × stitch gauge = number of stitches of pocket opening

STEP 2
Work the front section of the garment to just short of the pocket opening position. Place markers on the needle in the next row to indicate the placement of the stitches for the pocket opening.

STEP 3
Work the front to the pocket opening row, ending with a wrong-side row.

STEP 4

Knit across the front section to the second marker, working a horizontal turning ridge (see "How Tos") on the stitches of the opening, if desired. Place the remaining stitches of the front section on a holder, and turn the work.

STEP 5

Work to the first marker, place the remaining stitches of the front on a holder, and turn the work.

STEP 6

(Pocket Measurement 2 – depth of the finish) × 2 = length of the liner

STEP 7

Increase 1 stitch at each end of the next row, then work even for the length determined in Step 6. End with a right-side row, stopping 1 stitch short of the end of the row.

STEP 8

With the right side of the work facing you, place the stitches to the left of the pocket opening on a needle. Fold the liner to the back, and work the last stitch of the liner together with the next stitch of the front section. Finish the row.

STEP 9

Work back across the row (on the wrong side) to the last stitch. Place the remaining stitches of the front on a needle, and work the last stitch of the liner together with the next stitch of the front. Complete the front section.

STEP 10

Pick up and work a border across the fold at the opening.

■ If you worked a turning ridge, pick up below the ridge so that it does not show.

STEP 11

Stitch the side edges of the finish to the front, and close the side seams of the liner. Secure the bottom of the liner to the front with tacking stitches at each corner.

If the garment is knit in a highly textured yarn or stitch pattern, work 1″ of the liner, then change to a smooth yarn or to stockinette stitch, adjusting the number of stitches if necessary to maintain the correct width. Work even for (Step 6 – 2) inches beyond the change. Return to the yarn or stitch pattern of the body, again adjusting the stitches if needed, and work the last 1″ of the liner.

LOOSE INSET POCKET WITH HORIZONTAL OPENING

A Work the front to the pocket opening, then work the pocket liner.
B Fold the pocket to the inside and continue work as described.

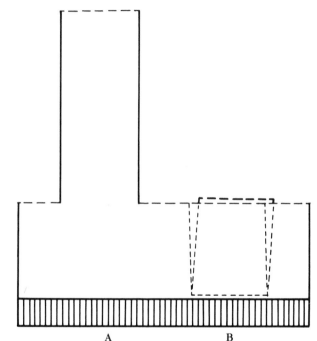

A   B

This pocket consists of a two-layer liner which is not seamed to the sweater along its sides and bottom.

Inset Pocket with Slanted Opening. These directions are written for a right-hand pocket (opening slanting up from wearer's right to wearer's left). To work a left-hand pocket, follow these directions, but end Steps 3, 5, and 7 with right-side rows.

Inset Pocket with Slanted Opening

STEP 1
Determine the dimensions of the pocket:
a. Width = Pocket Measurement 1 + (1″ to 2″ ease)
b. Minimum depth = Pocket Measurement 3

STEP 2
Determine the dimensions of the opening:
a. Width of opening = Pocket Measurement 1. This is the horizontal distance which the pocket will slant across.
b. Depth of opening = Pocket Measurement 1 + 1″. This is the vertical distance which the pocket will slant across.

STEP 3
Work the bottom section of the pocket liner. Cast on a number of stitches equal to (Step 1a × stitch gauge), and work for (Step 1b − Step 2b) inches. End with a wrong-side row. Place the liner stitches on a holder.

STEP 4
Work the front section of the garment to just short of the pocket opening level. Place markers on the needle in the next row to indicate the placement of the stitches of the opening.
The number of stitches will be equal to (Step 2a × stitch gauge).

STEP 5
Work the front to the level where the pocket opening will begin, ending with a wrong-side row.

STEP 6
Work the next row to the second marker (M2). Place the remaining stitches on a holder.

STEP 7
Taper the stitches of the width of the opening over the rows of the depth of the opening (see Taper Formula), binding off at the edge or working short rows (see "How Tos"). Slant the opening up from the M2 position, decreasing as planned until you reach the first marker (M1), ending on a wrong-side row. Place the remaining stitches of the front on a holder.

INSET POCKETS WITH SLANTED OPENINGS

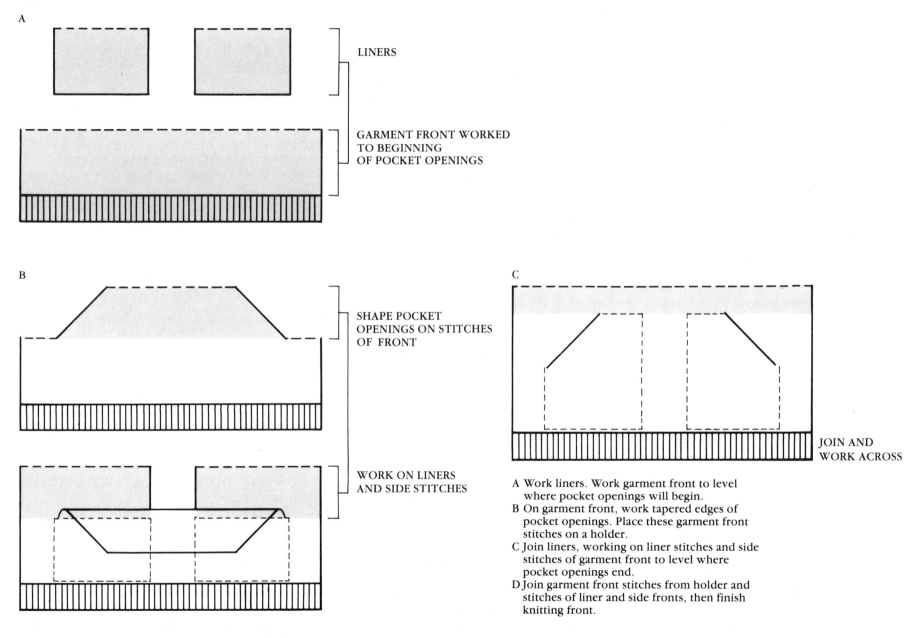

A

LINERS

GARMENT FRONT WORKED
TO BEGINNING
OF POCKET OPENINGS

B

SHAPE POCKET
OPENINGS ON STITCHES
OF FRONT

WORK ON LINERS
AND SIDE STITCHES

C

JOIN AND
WORK ACROSS

A Work liners. Work garment front to level
where pocket openings will begin.
B On garment front, work tapered edges of
pocket openings. Place these garment front
stitches on a holder.
C Join liners, working on liner stitches and side
stitches of garment front to level where
pocket openings end.
D Join garment front stitches from holder and
stitches of liner and side fronts, then finish
knitting front.

STEP 8

(Step 1a × stitch gauge) − (Step 2a × stitch gauge) = number of stitches to be joined to the sweater front, at the sides of the pocket

STEP 9

Place the stitches of the liner on a needle, work across (Step 8 − 2) stitches, place a marker (M3) on the needle, and work to the last 2 stitches.

STEP 10

Transfer the group of front section stitches adjacent to M2 onto a knitting needle. Holding the liner stitches to the back of the slanted section, with the right sides of the fabric facing you, knit together (see "How Tos") the last 2 stitches of the liner and the first 2 stitches of the side front section. Continue knitting across side front section to edge.

STEP 11

Work even across side front section and liner for the depth of the opening, ending on a wrong-side row.

STEP 12

Join the liner and the front center section as follows.
a. Place the remaining front stitches on a needle, and work to the last (Step 8 − 2) stitches.
b. Knit together the remaining stitches of the front and the liner stitches to the M3 marker.

STEP 13

Finish knitting the front.

STEP 14

Pick up and work a finish along the pocket opening. Sew the edges of the finish to the front, and stitch the liner to the wrong side of the fabric.

Inset Pocket with Curved Opening. This is a variation of the Slanted Opening Inset Pocket. The stitches of the width of the pocket opening can be curved over the depth of the opening by any of the following methods.

SET-IN ARMHOLE SHAPING METHOD. Bind off half of the stitches of the opening straight across, then decrease the remaining stitches on every other row. Work even for the remaining depth of the opening.

ALTERNATE SET-IN ARMHOLE SHAPING METHOD. Bind off one-third of the stitches of the opening straight across. Bind off one-third of the stitches in groups of 2–3 stitches every other row. Finally, decrease the remaining stitches at a rate of 1 stitch every other row. Work even for the remaining depth of the opening.

CURVE GUIDE METHOD. Use Curve Guide (see "How Tos") to chart the curve.

Inset Pocket on Seam Opening. This is an extremely versatile pocket that can be planned and worked at the same time as the garment, or picked up and worked on the garment's side edge before assembling. It can even be added to a finished sweater by opening the side seam and picking up and working the lining on the back and a facing on the front.

The top of the opening at the seam line should be placed no lower than 2″ below the waistline. The depth of the pocket should be at least equal to Pocket Measurement 3.

These directions are for pockets at both side seams of a medium-length sweater. Four different sweater front versions are given: Self-Finished, Picked-Up Finish, Faced Edge, and Loose Inset. All of them are used in combination with a single version of the back.

Back with Attached Pocket Liners

STEP 1
Determine the dimensions of the pockets:
a. Width = Pocket Measurement 1 + (1″ to 2″ ease)
b. Minimum depth = Pocket Measurement 3

STEP 2
Cast on and work the back section of the sweater through the border.

STEP 3
Cast on stitches equal to the width of the pocket at the beginning of the next two rows.

STEP 4
Work even for the depth of the pocket (or, if you wish, the pocket liners can be tapered or curved).

STEP 5
Bind off the stitches of the pocket at the beginning of the next two rows.

STEP 6
Complete the back.
■ If the yarn or the stitch pattern is highly textured and you wish to work the liner in a smooth yarn, cast on only 2″ in Step 3 (working in the yarn and/or pattern of the sweater body). Work the pocket liners separately in a smoother yarn and/or pattern, making them 2″ narrower than the width determined in Step 1a, and sew them to the edges of the back pocket headings. Alternatively, pick up stitches along the side of the pocket heading and work the liners horizontally.

INSET POCKET WITH SEAM OPENINGS

The pocket liner is formed as an extension of the back; the edges of the liner can be tapered or curved.

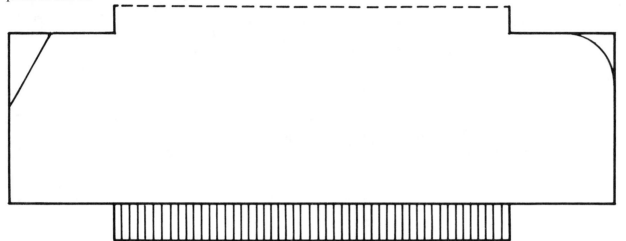

Several front finishes are possible.

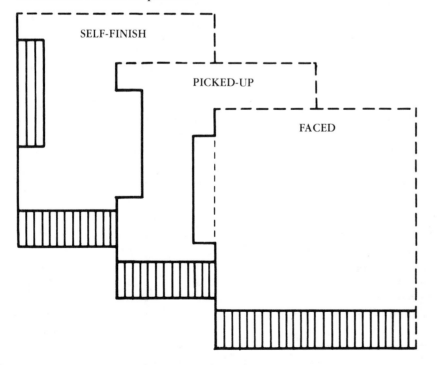

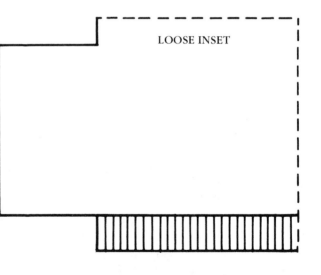

This pocket can be worked along with the garment, or picked up and added just before assembly. It can even be used on a finished sweater.

Self-Finished Front

STEP 1
Pocket Measurement 1 + (1″ to 2″ ease) = depth of pocket opening

STEP 2
Cast on and work the front to (Back/Step 1b − Step 1) inches above the bottom border.

STEP 3
Work a self-finishing pattern stitch on approximately 1″ of stitches at each edge of the front section for the depth of the opening.

STEP 4
Resume working the pattern of the body on all the stitches, and complete the front.

STEP 5
Assemble the sweater. Close the side seams at the bottom border and above the pocket liner and the self-finish. Sew the pocket liner to the inside of the front. Sew the portion of the front selvedge below the opening to the back.

Front with Picked-Up Finish

STEP 1
Pocket Measurement 1 + (1″ to 2″ ease) = depth of pocket opening

STEP 2
Cast on and work the front to (Back/Step 1b − Step 1) inches above the bottom border.

STEP 3
At the beginning of the next two rows, bind off stitches equal to the knitted width of the finish, and work even on the remaining stitches for the depth of the opening.

STEP 4
At the beginning of the next two rows, cast on the same number of stitches as were bound off in Step 2. Complete the front.

STEP 5
Pick up and work the finish, either vertically or horizontally. Remember to add a seam stitch at the appropriate edge. Sew the edges of the finish to the bound-off stitches of the front.

STEP 6
Assemble as in Self-Finished Front, Step 5.

Front with Faced Edge

STEP 1
Pocket Measurement 1 + (1″ to 2″ ease) = depth of pocket opening

STEP 2
Cast on and work the front to (Back/Step 1b − Step 1) inches above the bottom border.

STEP 3
Cast on ³⁄₄″ to 1″ of stitches at the beginning of the next two rows for the pocket facings.

STEP 4
Working vertical turning ridges (see "How Tos") on the original first and last edge stitches of the front, continue even for the depth of the opening.

STEP 5
At the beginning of the next two rows, bind off the stitches cast on in Step 3. Complete the front.

STEP 6
Fold the facings to the inside of the front, and stitch in place.

STEP 7
Assemble as in Self-Finished Front, Step 5.

Front with Loose Inset Pocket

STEP 1

Follow the instructions for Back with Attached Pocket Liners, Steps 1 through 6. Include a vertical turning ridge (see "How Tos") on the original first and last (edge) stitches of the front, at the inside of the stitches cast on for the pockets.

STEP 2

Sew the front and back side seams together along the entire edge, around the outside pocket edges. Push the pockets to the inside and sew the pocket opening edges (at the side seams) together at the bottom, for a depth above the bottom border equal to (Back/Step 1b − Pocket Measurement 1 + 1–2″ ease). The pockets can be tacked to the inside front, to help support weight. Crocheted chains can support the pocket tops.

Favorite How-Tos

Knitting has developed over many centuries and in many countries. Because of this, a wealth of different techniques have been developed, so that often there are several different methods available to accomplish a given task. Every knitter has a favorite method of holding needles and yarn, working increases and decreases, casting on or binding off, learned from teachers and fellow knitters, books and magazines, or trial and error. If your methods work well for you, by all means continue to use them.

In this section, we would like to share some techniques and formulas which we find work well for us. While knitting itself may be a solo endeavor, knitters as a group are delightfully willing to share. A favorite method of today may change by tomorrow, because we may learn a better or easier way.

Keeping an open mind and willingness to learn (and share) makes knitting more relaxing and enjoyable as time goes on. Remember, in knitting there are no "only" ways; there are only the ways which work best for you.

BLOCKING

Blocking of knitwear is sometimes assumed to mean the same thing as pressing. Blocking is *not* pressing! It is most clearly defined as the process of wetting a fabric, then shaping it to size, and allowing it to dry to its new form.

Wetting accomplishes three things:

1. It *smooths and flattens* the fabric. The water softens the yarn, allowing it to conform to the looped shaped of the stitches. When this occurs, the fabric stops twisting and curling.
2. It *sets the hand* of the fabric. As the yarn assumes its new shape, the true texture and drape of the fabric (its "hand") is established. For this reason, even fabrics with dimensional patterns such as cables, bobbles, and popcorns should be blocked.
3. It *shapes* the fabric to size. When damp, the fabric becomes more malleable, and, if needed, the garment pieces can be shaped to their correct dimensions.

There are three methods for wetting the knit fabric: steaming with an iron, wet wrapping, or immersion. We discuss them below, in the order in which we most commonly use them.

If the garment pieces do not conform to their correct measurements by wetting alone, pinning to size may be necessary.

Place the damp pieces on a flat, padded surface, pin them into shape, and allow them to air dry. Be sure to use rustproof pins, placing them close together to get smooth edges. Angle the pins toward the fabric for better holding. If you wish, you can place identically shaped pieces on top of each other and pin them together to dry.

We prefer to block the garment pieces before assembling the garment, because it is much easier to sew the pieces together when they are flat and smooth. Note that any test swatches should be blocked before charting begins, in order to establish the gauge of the fabric in its final form.

Steam-Iron Method

The most important thing to remember here is that the steam is the blocking agent. The iron only produces and disperses the steam. The weight of the iron should never be placed on the fabric. Let the steam do the work!

A Teflon® protector placed on the plate of the iron will allow you to block almost any fiber, even most synthetics (except glitter yarns containing Mylar®). The protector permits the use of the higher setting necessary for heavy steam, without scorching or overheating the fiber. If you don't have a protector, use a clean cotton cloth over the fabric instead.

Even with the protector, the iron should be kept a minimum of $\frac{1}{2}''$ above the fabric, and even higher with synthetics. Take the time to allow the steam to penetrate. With synthetics this time is quite short. Be aware that woolen fabric will not feel particularly wet due to this fiber's capacity to absorb water.

Lay the pieces flat to dry. The drying time is so short that by starting with the front and back of the garment and laying out each piece as you finish steaming it, you will be able to start assembling the sweater after blocking the last piece.

Wet-Wrap Method

Soak a bath towel, squeeze it out lightly and lay it flat. Place the garment pieces on the towel, flattening them out as much as possible. Roll the towel up like a jelly-roll, and let the bundle sit for one to two hours. Unwrap and lay the pieces flat to dry. Pin to shape if necessary, using aluminum or stainless steel pins.

Use this method for heat-sensitive yarns, for garments knit with beads and sequins, and if you have reservations about using the steam method on synthetics such as acrylic, nylon, or polyester.

Immersion Method

Place the sweater pieces in a water-filled tub, soak twenty minutes, and either spin dry in your washing machine or roll in towels and press to dry. Lay the pieces out flat to complete the drying, pinning to size if needed, using rustproof pins.

Use this method on heavily ribbed or cabled fabrics and fabrics that are distorted in shape due either to the stitch pattern or to the twist of the yarn. Handspun yarns or tightly spun singles worked in stockinette stitch may cause "biasing"; that is, distortion to a diagonal rather than rectangular shape. *If you are blocking a biased swatch and the bias cannot be corrected by thorough wetting combined with pinning to shape, switch to another stitch pattern or change yarns.*

ASSEMBLING INSTRUCTIONS

The assembling and finishing phase of designing a sweater is an exciting time. It is here that a concept—your sweater design—achieves reality. You may have made changes to the original design along the way, but, at last, you will be able to see, hold, and wear a sweater which is yours in every sense of the word.

For us, as for many knitters, the ability to enjoy this part of designing sweaters increased as we gained greater skill and confidence in our techniques. Through trial and error, and sometimes pure necessity, we have developed several methods that speed up this process and make it easier. Read them through and try them. We hope that our tips will be ones that add to your knitting enjoyment.

Before beginning to assemble the sweater, block the pieces separately. It is easier to neatly sew and finish a sweater if the fabric is smooth and even. Blocking also insures that edges intended to fit together, such as front and back side seams of the sweater body, are equal in length. After assembly is complete, the seams and finishes can be blocked by a light steaming.

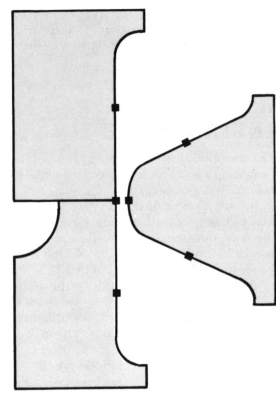

STEP 1 Sew shoulders and finish neckline.
STEP 2 Set in sleeves by marking quarter-points on both sleeve caps and arm-holes.
STEP 3 Close remaining seams.

Tools that you should have on hand are a *tapestry needle* (preferably a metal one), a *measuring tape,* a ball of *yarn in a contrasting color* for marking, and the correct *knitting needles* for working any picked-up finishes.

There are three distinct styles of sweater that need their own assembly instructions, at least to start: the Set-in Sleeve, the Basic T, and the Raglan. Once the sleeves have been joined to the body pieces, the remaining seams are the same for all styles.

Assembling a Sweater with Set-In Sleeves

STEP 1
Sew both shoulders closed, and work the neckline finish. The front finishes on a cardigan can be worked at this time.

STEP 2
Set in the sleeves.
a. Find and mark the halfway point on the curve of the cap. Fold the sleeve cap in half, and place a long yarn marker at the fold on the top of the cap.
b. Find and mark the quarter-points on the curve of the cap. These are found by placing the start of the cap shaping at the halfway marker and bringing the cap's edges together until the fold is reached. Place a marker at the fold for the quarter-point.
c. Quarter and mark the curve of the armhole in the same way.
d. Using the long yarn markers, tie the quarter-points of the cap and armhole together.
e. Sew the cap to the armhole. Work the seam from a side edge to the shoulder seam. Turn the garment around, and again work from a side edge to the shoulder seam.

STEP 3
Close all remaining seams and weave in the ends.

Assembling a Sweater with Basic T Sleeves

STEP 1
Sew both shoulders closed, and work the neckline finish. The front finishes on a cardigan can be worked at this time.

STEP 2

Sew the sleeves to the body.
a. Fold the sleeve in half and mark the halfway point at the top of the sleeve.
b. Find and mark the quarter-points by folding the edge of the sleeve to the halfway marker.
c. Find and mark the halfway point and quarter-points on the armhole edge of the body.
d. Sew the sleeve to the body from the shoulder seam to the underarm. Turn the garment around, and work from the shoulder seam to the underarm to complete the seam.

STEP 3

Close all remaining seams and weave in the ends.

Assembling a Sweater with Raglan Sleeves

STEP 1

Sew the sleeves to the front and back. Raglan Sleeves do not need to be marked since there are the same number of rows in the shaping of the sleeve cap as in the shaping of the yoke.

STEP 2

Work all neckline and cardigan finishes.

STEP 3

Close all remaining seams and weave in the ends.

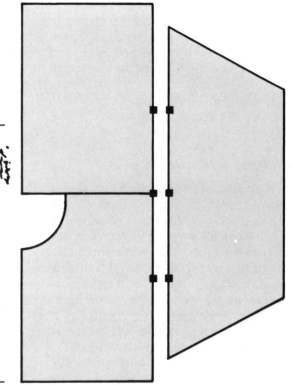

ASSEMBLING A GARMENT WITH BASIC T SLEEVES

STEP 1 Sew shoulders and finish neckline. Finish fronts of cardigan.
STEP 2 Fold and mark half- and quarter-points of sleeves and of armhole edges above markers; attach sleeve to body.
STEP 3 Close remaining seams.

SEAMS AND JOINS

The methods described here include tips for picking up stitches, for marking and positioning edges prior to picking up stitches or joining, for grafting, and for sewing or knitting seams together.

Marking Edges for Picking Up Stitches

The easiest method we've found for marking an edge in preparation for picking up stitches is to use a large-scale whip stitch (see "How Tos") along the edge. This speeds up the finishing process significantly. Lay a measuring tape along the edge being marked, and, using contrasting yarn, stitch back-to-front into the very edge of the fabric at every inch. Be sure to split the yarn of the fabric when you stitch in order to hold the stitch at an exact location. What you are doing is a giant whip stitch in which each stitch measures 1″.

When there are two identical edges to be marked, such as the right and left sides of a V Neckline or the armholes of a vest, mark only one side using the measuring tape. Then fold or place the marked edge on the equivalent unmarked edge, and use the marked edge to show where to stitch. This ensures that both edges are marked identically and will contain the same number of picked-up stitches.

Picking Up Stitches

Pick up stitches by knitting into the fabric below a bind-off ridge, or between the first and second stitches on a selvedge edge. Work all shaping at least one stitch in from the edge. This gives you a clean line to follow when picking up or sewing a seam.

The number of stitches to pick up in each inch ordinarily will be equal to the stockinette gauge of the yarn or the stitch gauge of the border stitch. When the stitch gauge contains a half-stitch, alternate between the whole number of the gauge and the next whole number. For example, with a gauge of 4.5 stitches per inch, pick up 4 stitches in the first inch and 5 in the next, then repeat this pattern to the end. If the gauge contains a quarter-stitch (for instance, 5.25), then three out of four inches will contain the whole number of the gauge (5) and the fourth inch will need the next higher number (6).

When all the stitches are picked up and the finish is completed, pull out the marking yarn.

Easing a Seam

There are times in finishing knitting when the two edges to be sewn together are unequal in length. The most common places that this occurs are in setting in a sleeve, and when joining a separate band to a cardigan. Quartering the two edges and pinning or tying the quarter-points together are the first steps in easing the longer piece to the length of the shorter.

The easing is done by using a technique probably familiar to those of you who have sewn with knit fabric on a sewing machine. Easing is achieved by pinning the ends or the quarter-points of the two pieces together and stretching the pieces until the shorter one is the length of the longer. The fabrics are then sewn together while they are being stretched, with the result that the extra length of the longer piece is evenly distributed along the length of the shorter.

The trick to applying this method to hand knitting is to wear a knee pad (available from sporting goods and hardware stores), and to pin the two pieces being joined to the pad at the top of the seam (or at a quarter-point on sectioned seams). With one hand pulling the two pieces to equal lengths, the other hand is available for working the seam. Rather than using a knee pad, you could pin the work to your jeans or to the arm of a chair, or you could enlist a friend to hold one end of the work while you pull and sew!

Knitted Seams

A knitted seam is a way of *both joining and binding off* two pieces of knitting having equal numbers of open stitches. It is particularly useful for shoulders, because it eliminates bulk while still preventing stretching.

To work a knitted seam, place the stitches of the two pieces on separate double-pointed needles. Hold the two needles parallel to each other with the right sides of the fabric together. Holding the two needles in the left hand, knit together the first stitch on each of the needles. Repeat this with the second stitch on each left-hand needle, then bind off one stitch from the right-hand needle. Continue to knit together the next stitch on each needle on the left, and to bind off a stitch on the right, until all the stitches are joined and bound off. Cut the yarn and fasten off by pulling it through the loop of the last knit stitch.

Pleats can be joined and bound off in this way. Place the stitches of the pleat on three double-pointed needles, fold the fabric between needles, and knit all three layers together. Again, this is an effective way to minimize bulk at a seam.

If you eliminate the bind-off step, you can use this method to join pockets and pocket liners to the fabric of the sweater body (for instance, see the Pouch Pocket illustrated on page 347).

Grafting

Grafting (also called kitchener stitch) is a way to join two pieces without using a seam. The yarn woven through the stitches creates a new row with the appearance of knitting, which "grafts" the two pieces together. This method of joining knitted pieces can be used for the back seam of Vertical Shawl Collars, the seams of hoods, and to connect underarm stitches for sweaters worked in the round. The two pieces should have equal numbers of open stitches.

Place the open stitches of each section on a needle and hold the needles parallel with the wrong sides of the fabrics together. Thread a tapestry needle with the yarn used for the knitted fabric. This yarn should be at least three times as long as the width of each piece being joined.

Starting with the front needles, insert the tapestry needle into the first stitch as if to purl, draw the yarn through, then repeat this on the back needle. *Returning to the front needle, insert the tapestry needle into the first stitch on the needle as if to knit, and slip the stitch onto the tapestry needle. Insert the tapestry needle into the next stitch as if to purl, and leave the stitch on the knitting needle. Draw the yarn through both stitches. Going to the back knitting needle, insert the tapestry needle into the first stitch as if to purl, and slip the stitch onto the tapestry needle. Insert the tapestry needle into the next stitch as if to knit, and leave the stitch on the knitting needle. Draw the yarn through both stitches.* Repeat between the asterisks (*) to the end of the needles, tightening up the yarn as necessary. Fasten off.

This method will produce a row of stockinette stitch. If garter stitch is desired, work the instructions for the front needle on both front and back needles.

Woven Seams

This is our favorite method for sewing seams. Often called mattress stitch, this seam is strong, easy to work, and always looks good. Because it is worked on the right side of the fabric, matching rows and pattern stitches is simple. This is the method we use for almost every seam we work, with a few exceptions, primarily hems and the seams used in securing pocket linings.

There are three versions of the woven seam, covering all the needs of a knitter: for the vertical seams of side selvedges, for the horizontal seams of bound-off stitches, such as shoulder seams, and for seams joining two different types of edges, such as the bound-off stitches of a sleeve and the selvedge edge of an armhole.

Vertical Woven Seam. Place the two pieces to be joined side by side, right side up. Insert the tapestry needle under the horizontal strand between two stitches, from bottom to top. Alternate stitches from side to side, first on one piece, then on the other. On fabrics with few stitches per inch, go under one strand at a time. On fabrics with a gauge of 5 stitches or more per inch, it is possible to go under two strands at a time.

Loosely stitch the pieces together for approximately 2", then close the seam by pulling on the sewing yarn to draw the two pieces of fabric together. Each time you close a section of the seam, tug on both ends of the stitched area to stretch the seam yarn. This will eliminate any gathering and prevent the seam from puckering.

On side edges, work the seam up from the garment border to the underarm. This will place any necessary easing at the underarm, where it is less visible.

Horizontal Woven Seam. This seam is used to join two bound-off edges, and is worked across the tops of the bound-off stitches. Work it at the inside of the ridge formed by binding off, inserting the needle under an entire stitch (under two yarns) regardless of the gauge. Work this seam in the same manner as the vertical seam, alternating the needle between the two pieces being joined.

Combination Seam. On horizontal seams such as shoulder seams, the ratio of front stitches to back stitches is one to one. If you consistently sew under one stitch on each edge, the seam will end evenly. On sleeve and body seams the numbers of rows are not identical, but are only off by one. (This extra row is caused by the fact that binding off can only occur at the beginnings of rows.) Here again, if you stitch under a consistent number of strands (one or two) on each edge, you will finish even at the end of the seam.

In contrast, combination seams are worked to join pieces that don't have this one-to-one ratio of stitches; for instance, where a side edge is joined to an end edge. In this case, since row gauge and stitch gauge are not equal, you will need to stitch under either one or two strands on the vertical edge (regardless of the gauge), while consistently stitching under one stitch on the horizontal edge. Generally a pattern develops on the vertical edge, in which you stitch under one strand twice and two strands once. Once you recognize such a pattern, continue it to the end of the seam.

Particularly along curved and/or eased seams, such as around the top edge of a sleeve, keep your eye on the angle of the seam stitches. If the seam stitch slants up to one side or the other, you are stitching under too many strands per stitch on that side. Take out a few stitches and go under one strand a couple of times until the seam stitches become level. It is less confusing if you keep the bound-off edge consistent and vary the selvedge edge.

Other Useful Stitches

Whip Stitch. This simple stitch is reserved for marking edges in preparation for picking up stitches and for attaching the sides of pocket linings to the inside of the garment. Be sure to stitch sideways through the yarn, splitting it, when sewing a pocket lining to the fabric of the body. This keeps the stitching from showing on the right side of the work.

Back Stitch. This is an excellent seam stitch for knitting, since it is a looped stitch and stretches with the fabric. Its biggest drawback is that it must be worked with the right sides of the fabric held together, making matching of stripes and patterns difficult. In addition, because the seam is not as tight as the woven seam, it is more visible.

In spite of these drawbacks, back stitch is very useful for places where its ability to give and stretch can be put to good use. We use it for stitching down Doubled Bands and Piping at the neckline edge. Another good place to use back stitch is across the bottoms of pockets, where strength and flexibility are needed.

Just as with the whip stitch, split the yarn when stitching through the fabric of the sweater body, to keep the stitches from showing on the right side of the work.

Herringbone Stitch. This is another looped stitch which is useful for attaching hems and Doubled Bands. It stretches with the fabric and keeps a hem from being too binding. This attribute is especially important for necklines.

INCREASING, DECREASING, BEGINNING, AND ENDING

Increases

M1 INCREASE. One of the main reasons the M1 increase has become our preferred increase is that planning its placement is so simple. If you work an increase for the right edge two stitches in from the beginning of the row, you then stop two stitches from the end of the row to work the increase for the left edge.

The M1 increase is worked into the horizontal strand that runs between two stitches. The increase is kept invisible by twisting this strand so that the loop is closed at the bottom. The direction of the twist determines whether the increase has a right or left slant and makes it possible to "pair," or mirror-image, your increases.

If the stitch increased is a purl on the right side of the fabric, use the Purl Right Slant version for all increases. In this case, the direction of the twist does not show, and this version is easier to work than the Purl Left Slant version.

When increasing several stitches evenly spaced on the same row, for example directly above the bottom border on a Blouson body, work the increases in whatever stitch is correct for the stitch pattern of the body. Using the Gathers Formula, plan the spacing of the increases and place markers on the left needle at the calculated locations for increases. Work the next row in the pattern stitch of the body, increasing in knit or purl as needed for the pattern whenever you reach a marker. Remove the markers as you go.

Knit Left Slant Increase

STEP 1
Place the horizontal strand on the left needle by inserting the left needle *front to back* under the strand.

STEP 2
Knit into the back of the resulting loop.

Knit Right Slant Increase

STEP 1
Place the horizontal strand on the left needle by inserting the left needle *back to front* under the strand.

STEP 2
Knit into the front of the resulting loop.

Purl Left Slant Increase

STEP 1
Place the horizontal strand on the left needle by inserting the left needle *front to back* under the strand.

STEP 2
Purl into the back of the resulting loop.

Purl Right Slant Increase

STEP 1
Place the horizontal strand on the left needle by inserting the left needle *back to front* under the strand.

STEP 2
Purl into the front of the resulting loop.

Decreases

Just as increases need to be "paired," so do decreases. There are two basic ways of decreasing, one in which the decreased stitches slant to the right and one in which the decreased stitches slant to the left. The two decreases should be thought of, and worked, as a pair; if one is worked at the beginning of a row, the other is worked at the end of the row. Unless your fabric is knit in a very textured yarn, in which the stitches are not distinguishable, never work the same decrease at both ends of a row.

Decreases can be used as a decorative device by enhancing their visibility and emphasizing the direction of their slant. If the eliminated stitch is stretched by the process of decreasing, its visibility is heightened. On the other hand, if stretching of the decreased stitch is kept to a minimum, then the decrease is less obvious.

The position of a decrease can also serve to emphasize the direction of the slant and the visibility of the decrease. When a Left Slant Decrease is worked at the beginning of a row, and a Right Slant Decrease is worked at the end, the line created by the decrease becomes quite visible. The farther in from the edge the decrease is worked, the more visible it becomes.

The least visible way to combine decreases is to work the Right Slant Decrease, one stitch in from the edge, at the beginning of a row and the Left Slant Decrease, the same distance in, at the end of the row. If the decreases are enhanced by stretching the eliminated stitch, they will be more visible. Working enhanced decreases two or more stitches in from the edge will emphasize them even more.

By working swatches using the different decreases, paired and unpaired, you will be able to see the different effects that decrease placement can have and understand better how to use decreases decoratively.

Our decrease guidelines are written with the decreases located the minimum number of stitches in from the edge of the work. To work the decreases farther in from the ends of the row (for example, two stitches farther in), add the extra stitches in this manner:

K1 (+ 2), dec, work to the last 3 (+ 2) stitches, dec, K1 (+ 2), which works out to: K3, dec, work to the last 5 stitches, dec, K3.

Minimized Single Decreases decrease one stitch at a time with a less visible result than the "enhanced" method.

Minimized Single Decreases

Right Slant Decrease ("K2 tog")
STEP 1
Knit two stitches together.

Left Slant Decrease ("SSK")
STEP 1
Slip 1 stitch knitwise twice.

STEP 2
Insert the left needle into the fronts of the two slipped stitches on the right needle.

STEP 3
From this position, knit the two stitches together.

DECREASES

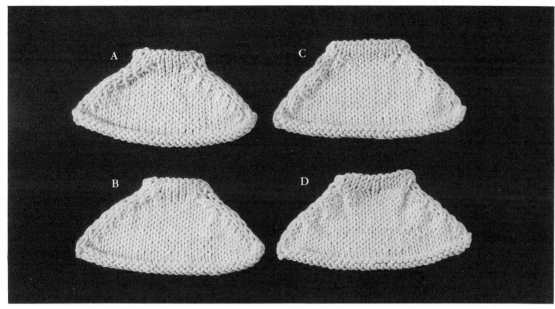

A enhanced decreases: single in lower half of
  swatch, double in upper half
B minimized decreases: single in lower half of
  swatch, double in upper half
C full-fashioned decreases: from bottom—one,
  two, three, and four stitches per edge
D cabled decreases: from bottom—single,
  double, triple, and quadruple

Enhanced Single Decreases

Right Slant Decrease ("K1, pass back, pass 1 over, slip back")
STEP 1
Knit 1 stitch.

STEP 2
Insert the left needle into the front of the resulting stitch on the right needle and pass the stitch
back to the left needle.

STEP 3
With the right needle, reach across the replaced stitch on the left needle and pass the next
stitch over it.

STEP 4
Slip the replaced stitch, purlwise, back to the right needle.

Enhanced Single Decrease
decreases one stitch at a time, with a
highly visible result.

Left Slant Decrease ("Sl1, K1, psso" or "SKPO")

STEP 1
Slip one stitch onto the right needle as if to knit.

STEP 2
Knit the next stitch.

STEP 3
With the left needle, reach across the knit stitch on the right needle and pass the slipped stitch over the knit one.

Minimized Double Decreases

Right Slant Decrease ("K3 tog")
STEP 1
Knit three stitches together.

Left Slant Decrease ("SSSK")
STEP 1
Slip one stitch knitwise three times.

STEP 2
Insert the left needle into the fronts of the three slipped stitches.

STEP 3
From this position, knit the stitches together.

Minimized Double Decreases decrease two stitches at a time, with a less visible result than the "enhanced" method.

Enhanced Double Decreases

Right Slant Decrease ("SSK, pass back, pass 1 over, slip back")

STEP 1
Work the SSK decrease.

STEP 2
Insert the left needle into the front of the resulting stitch on the right needle and pass it back to the left needle.

STEP 3
With the right needle, reach across the replaced stitch on the left needle and pass the next stitch over it.

STEP 4
Slip the replaced stitch, purlwise, back to the right needle.

Left Slant Decrease ("Sl1, K2 tog, psso")

STEP 1
Slip one stitch knitwise.

STEP 2
Knit two stitches together.

STEP 3
With the left needle, reach across the resulting stitch on the right needle and pass the slipped stitch over it.

Enhanced Double Decreases decrease two stitches at a time, with a highly visible result.

Cabled Decreases are decorative decreases especially applicable to the Full-Fashioned Shoulder shaping, since decreasing more than two stitches at a time is easily accomplished by this method.

The decrease is worked using a cable needle. The stitches being decreased are slipped onto the cable needle, and are then placed in front or in back of an equivalent number of stitches on the left needle. They are then decreased by working together the stitches from the cable needle with the stitches on the regular needle, one pair at a time. The slant of the decrease is determined by whether the stitches are placed to the front or to the back of the work. Since full-fashioned decreases generally slant toward the shaped edge, the directions here are written to achieve that effect.

SINGLE DECREASE. When decreasing only one stitch at each edge, use the Enhanced Right Slant Decrease at the beginning of the row and the Enhanced Left Slant Decrease at the end.

DOUBLE DECREASE. K1, slip the next 2 stitches onto a cable needle and put them to the back of the work, work together the next 2 stitches on the regular needle with the 2 stitches on the cable needle, work to the last 5 stitches, slip the next 2 stitches onto a cable needle and put them to the front of the work, work together the next 2 stitches on the regular needle with the 2 stitches on the cable needle, K1.

TRIPLE DECREASE. K1, slip the next 3 stitches onto a cable needle and put them to the back of the work, work together the next 3 stitches on the regular needle with the 3 stitches on the cable needle, work to the last 7 stitches, slip the next 3 stitches onto a cable needle and put them to the front of the work, work together the next 3 stitches on the regular needle with the 3 stitches on the cable needle, K1.

QUADRUPLE DECREASE. K1, slip the next 4 stitches onto a cable needle and put them to the back of the work, work together the next 4 stitches on the regular needle with the 4 stitches on the cable needle, work to the last 9 stitches, slip the next 4 stitches onto a cable needle and put them to the front of the work, work together the next 4 stitches on the regular needle with the 4 stitches on the cable needle, K1.

Decrease Placement for Full-Fashioned Shoulder Shaping. The decreasing of the back shoulders on a sweater with Full-Fashioned shaping often requires working a combination of single and double decreases. The placement of the decreases is important in creating a smooth line despite the different combinations needed to eliminate the correct number of stitches at each edge of the work.

DECREASING ONE STITCH AT EACH EDGE. K2, work Enhanced Right Slant single decrease, work to the last 4 stitches, work Enhanced Left Slant single decrease, K2.

DECREASING TWO STITCHES AT EACH EDGE. K2, work Enhanced Right Slant double decrease, work to the last 5 stitches, work Enhanced Left Slant double decrease, K2.

DECREASING THREE STITCHES AT EACH EDGE. K1, work Enhanced Left Slant single decrease, work Enhanced Right Slant double decrease, work to the last 6 stitches, work Enhanced Left Slant double decrease, work Enhanced Right Slant single decrease, K1.

DECREASING FOUR STITCHES AT EACH EDGE. K1, work Enhanced Left Slant double decrease, work Enhanced Right Slant double decrease, work to the last 7 stitches, work Enhanced Left Slant double decrease, work Enhanced Right Slant double decrease, K1.

Short Row Shaping

Short rows have been mentioned often in the charting guidelines as a means of shaping the work, not only at an edge, but also within the fabric of the sweater. This method of shaping is used for working darts, shaping shoulders that will be closed with a knitted seam, and working picked-up Shawl collars.

Chart the short row shaping using the Slope Formula. The number of stitches that would normally be bound off at the beginnings of the rows will now be left unworked at the ends of the rows. Since the stitches are not eliminated, the number of stitches left unworked will grow until the shaping is complete. At this point, knit two finishing rows in which all the stitches are worked across the entire row.

The problem to avoid in working short rows is having a hole at the point in the row where the piece is turned. This hole can be minimized by slipping, rather than knitting, the first stitch after a turn, but this still leaves a loose stitch in the fabric, which creates a visible hole. The method that best eliminates any sign of the turn is the Wrapped Short Row. Proceed as follows.

Wrapped Short Row

STEP 1
Knit to the stitches being left unworked at the end of the row.

STEP 2
- If the last stitch worked is a knit stitch: bring the yarn to the front, slip a stitch purlwise, put the yarn to the back, and return the slipped stitch to the left needle. Turn the piece.
- If the last stitch worked is a purl stitch: put the yarn to the back, slip a stitch purlwise, bring the yarn to the front, and return the slipped stitch to the left needle. Turn the piece.

STEP 3
Continue to do this on every short row before turning the piece.

STEP 4
Knit two final rows, including all stitches to the end of the row. Every time you come to a wrapped stitch, work the wrap and the stitch together in this manner:
a. **On the Right Side of the Work:**
   - If the wrapped stitch is a *knit,* insert the right needle under the wrap on the front of the work and into the stitch on the needle, then knit the wrap and the stitch together.
   - If the wrapped stitch is a *purl,* slip the stitch, lift the wrap from the front of the work and place it on the left needle, pass the slipped stitch back to the left needle, then purl the stitch and the wrap together.
b. **On the Wrong Side of the Work:**
   There is no difference if the wrapped stitch is a purl or a knit. Lift the wrap on the back of the work and place it on the left needle, then purl or knit the wrap and the stitch together.

Cable Cast-On

This is our preferred method for casting on stitches at the beginning of a row. The Cable Cast-On is used in one- and two-piece garments when adding stitches for the sleeves or body, and when shaping the neckline.

It is possible to eliminate the stair-step effect that occurs when stitches are cast on at an edge on every other row. When casting on the last added stitch, stop after Step 2. With the last cast-on stitch still on the right needle, start working the row. Because the first stitch of the row is not worked, the stair-step effect is eased and a smooth edge is achieved.

Working a Bias Bind-Off

Binding off in a slope often creates a stepped edge. The bias Bind-Off eliminates "steps" and creates a smooth edge. Use this method at all times when working slopes.

Cable Cast-On

STEP 1
Insert the right needle between the first and second stitches on the left needle.

STEP 2
Wrap the yarn as if to knit, and pull the yarn through to the front between the stitches.

STEP 3
Twist the new stitch as you place it on the left needle in this manner: bring the left needle to the front of the new stitch and insert the left needle right to left through the stitch.

STEP 4
Insert the right needle between the new stitch and the previous stitch.
Repeat Steps 2 through 4 until all the stitches are cast on.

Bias Bind-Off

STEP 1
Work the first bind-off of any edge in the usual manner.

STEP 2
On the return row, in preparation for the second bind-off, stop one stitch short of the end of the row, and turn the work.

STEP 3
The unworked stitch is on the right needle. Slip a stitch from the left needle to the right, and pass the unworked stitch over the slipped stitch. This is the first bind-off of this row. Continue to knit and bind off the remaining number of stitches for the row.

STEP 4
Repeat Steps 2 and 3 at the beginning of all the remaining bind-off groups in the slope.

BUTTONHOLES

Horizontal Buttonhole

This single-row buttonhole is firm and strong. A major advantage it has over other horizontal buttonholes is that it re- quires no finishing work. It looks best if worked on the wrong side of the fabric. Plan the buttonhole to begin at least three stitches in from an edge. All the slip stitches are slipped purlwise.

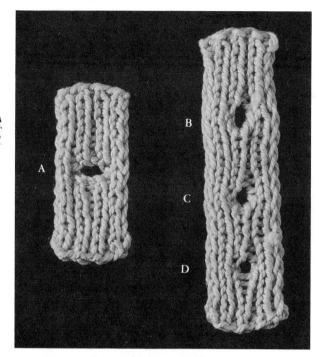

A horizontal (single-row) buttonhole
B eyelet buttonhole
C vertical eyelet buttonhole
D elongated vertical buttonhole

Horizontal Buttonhole

STEP 1

Knit to the stitches for the buttonhole. Bring the yarn to the front and slip a stitch. Put the yarn to the back and slip a second stitch. Drop the yarn, which will not be used again until Step 4.

STEP 2

Pass the first slipped stitch over the second slipped stitch to bind off the first stitch of the but- tonhole. Continue to slip a stitch and pass the previous slipped stitch over it until all of the buttonhole stitches are bound off.

STEP 3

Pass the last slipped stitch back to the left needle. Turn the work.

STEP 4

Pick up the yarn and put it to the back of the work. Working the Cable Cast-On, cast on the number of stitches bound off.

STEP 5

Cast on one extra stitch, but bring the yarn to the front between this extra stitch and the last buttonhole stitch before placing the extra stitch on the left needle. This extra stitch does not need to be twisted when it is placed on the left needle. Turn the work.

STEP 6

Slip a stitch from the left needle, pass the extra stitch over the slipped stitch and tighten the extra stitch firmly. Finish the row.

Vertical Buttonhole

The search for the perfect Vertical Buttonhole has been a lengthy one for us. This version appears to meet the requirements for any buttonhole. It is strong, looks good, and is easy to work. It is based on the Eyelet Buttonhole, and looks best in a 1/1 rib with the hole centered on a purl ridge. On a Vertical Band, the number of stitches in the band must be odd and the center stitch must be a purl. This buttonhole needs to be started on the right side of the work.

The **Eyelet Buttonhole** is simply a hole in the fabric.

The **Vertical Eyelet Buttonhole** is a longer and firmer buttonhole than the Eyelet.

The **Elongated Vertical Buttonhole** is still longer than the Vertical Eyelet buttonhole.

Eyelet Buttonhole

STEP 1
Knit to the center purl, YO, K2 tog, and finish the row.

STEP 2
Work the next row in pattern, knitting into the YO.

STEP 3
Continue the work.

Vertical Eyelet Buttonhole

STEP 1
Knit to the center purl, YO, K2 tog, and finish the row.

STEP 2
Work the next row in pattern, knitting into the YO.

STEP 3
Work the next row in pattern to the buttonhole. Purl into the buttonhole, drop the purl stitch, and finish the row.

STEP 4
Continue the work.

Elongated Vertical Buttonhole

STEP 1
Work to the center purl, YO twice, K2 tog, and finish the row.

STEP 2

Knit the next row in pattern. Knit the first YO and drop the second.

STEP 3

Work the next row in pattern to the buttonhole. Purl into the buttonhole, drop the purl stitch, and finish the row.

STEP 4

Knit the next row in pattern to the buttonhole. Knit into the buttonhole, drop the knit stitch, and finish the row.

STEP 5

Continue the work.

TURNING RIDGES

Vertical Turning Ridge

This turning ridge is based on the fact that the knitted fabric will fold easily at a slip stitch ridge. By slipping a stitch on the right-side rows of the fabric and purling it on the wrong-side rows, you create a smooth foldline at that stitch.

Horizontal Turning Ridge

A **Purl Row on the Right Side of the Fabric** is the most common horizontal turning ridge.

An **Eyelet Row** is a more decorative way of forming a horizontal foldline in a knitted fabric. This finish is known by a variety of names, such as *cat's paw hem, picot edging,* or *sawtooth edge,* all of which are descriptive of its scalloped edge. It is a very effective border for lace garments, but should not be limited to use with openwork patterns.

Eyelet Row

STEP 1

K1, *YO, K2 tog*, repeat between the asterisks (*). If there is an even number of stitches, end with a K1.

STEP 2

K1, purl to the last stitch, K1.

CURVE GUIDE

This is a guide for producing rounded curves on Dolmans, Hoods, Pockets, jacket front edges, or anywhere you can imagine them. It is based on the stitch-to-row ratio for stockinette stitch.

Curve Guide

STEP 1
Determine approximately how deep you want your gusset to be.
Example: 5"

STEP 2
Step 1 × row gauge = number of rows for the desired gusset depth
Example: 5 × 6 = 30 30 rows

STEP 3
Locate the closest number of rows on the gusset guide to the number in Step 2. You may have to make the gusset a little deeper or shallower.
Example: 28 rows

STEP 4
Step 3 ÷ row gauge = actual depth of your gusset
Example: 28 ÷ 6 = 4.6 4.6"

STEP 5
Follow the column of the chart (in our example a white column) around for the number of stitches in your gusset.
Example: 24 stitches

STEP 6
Follow the graphed shape of the curve when working your garment. For instance, in our example, proceed as follows: *Increase/decrease 1 stitch every 4 rows 1 time, and every 2 rows 5 times; then, on every row, increase/decrease 2 stitches 4 times, 3 stitches 2 times, and 4 stitches 1 time.*

CURVE GUIDE

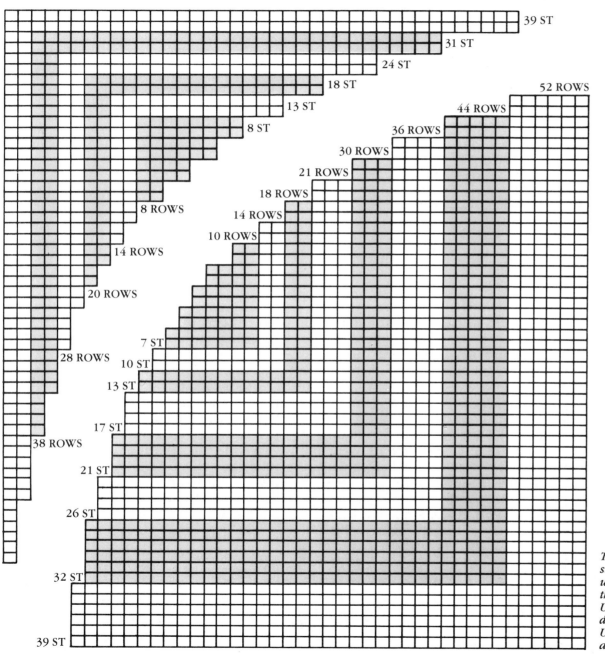

39 ST

31 ST

24 ST

18 ST

13 ST

8 ST

52 ROWS

44 ROWS

36 ROWS

30 ROWS

21 ROWS

18 ROWS

14 ROWS

10 ROWS

8 ROWS

14 ROWS

20 ROWS

7 ST

10 ST

28 ROWS

13 ST

17 ST

38 ROWS

21 ST

26 ST

32 ST

39 ST

This guide is based on the ratio for stockinette stitch, and may need to be adjusted if you are using a pattern stitch which produces a ratio that differs noticeably.
Use guide at top left for curves (gussets) on dolmans.
Use guide at bottom right for curved hoods and pockets.

Appendix

KNITTING ETHNIC

Traditional knitting designs can be a source of inspiration, whether you follow the traditional format as closely as possible or use it as a jumping-off point for your own elaboration. Although knitting traditions have crossed cultural barriers through many generations of colonization, migration, and trade, we still associate certain garment styles with specific ethnic areas. If you're at all familiar with traditional knitting, the names *Jersey* and *Guernsey, Aran* and *Shetland, Scandinavian* and *Icelandic* will bring unique usages of pattern and color to mind.

The traditions with which we are most familiar come from the colder countries of the northern hemisphere. Most of the sweaters from these areas, however different in design, were made for a practical purpose: to keep the wearers warm and dry. Multicolor stranded work, which adds an extra layer to the fabric, adds considerably to a sweater's warmth. Tightly knit stitch patterns also keep the wind out, and cables add bulk and insulating space. Wool was the fiber used traditionally in these northern areas since it was readily available and known for its insulating qualities. It was used either in natural colors or natural-dyed. The wool was sometimes oiled for additional protection against the elements. The shapes of these sweaters were simple and often worked in the round. They fall into two categories, which we call the T-Shape and the Round Yoke.

In order to spark your imagination, we will take a quick look at a few of these knitting traditions. If you are interested in pursuing one of them in depth, there are specialized books which examine their histories and techniques. These fascinating studies will give even greater meaning to your knitting efforts. If you want to recreate a traditional sweater as accurately as possible, you can duplicate the yarns fairly closely at a local shop or through mail order, and you'll find that in some instances authentic skeins are being imported.

Fishermen's Guernseys

Several knitting traditions have developed in the British Isles. Fishermen's "ganseys" derive their name from the Isle of Guernsey. They are knit in a durable five-ply

worsted wool, called "seaman's iron." The most popular color is navy blue.

Stitch patterns include knit/purl combinations, worked in vertical or horizontal panels, or in a combination of these orientations. Simple twisted cables also appear. The decorative stitches are sometimes used only on the yoke and sleeves, with a plain knit body.

The body is T-Shaped, worked in the round with the addition of gussets at the underarm. After the gussets are worked, the front and back yokes are worked back-and-forth. Sleeves are picked up from the finished body and knit down, from shoulders to cuffs.

Fair Isle

Fair Islanders knit a variation of the gansey shape without the gussets, but their designs are produced through color knitting. The patterns are geometric. The yarn is a soft two-ply of about sport weight, worked tightly on small needles to produce a fabric that withstands the elements.

Originally a wide range of natural hues was used, with the addition of reds, blues, and yellows, dyed with local plants and lichens, as accent colors. The invention of synthetic dyes expanded the range of colors, although recently the subtler hues have been rediscovered. Sometimes the background color is composed of several closely related shades, worked in stripes; the patterning itself can also be worked this way.

Yet with all this color complexity, the knitting is kept simple. The sweaters are worked in the round and only two colors are used on each round.

Aran

Unlike the Guernseys and Fair Isles, which are worked in the round with picked-up sleeves, Aran sweaters are made in pieces and then assembled. The traditional style is the Basic T-Shape with sleeves that taper toward the wrist, and the sweaters often feature Saddle Bands across the shoulders. Present fashions feature Set-In and Raglan Yokes as well. The yarn is a thick, hard-wearing, cream colored, three- or four-ply wool.

The patterns incorporate cables, bobbles, and other heavily textured combinations in vertical panels. They produce dense fabrics, extremely well suited to a cold, wet environment.

SCANDINAVIAN

COWICHAN

ICELANDIC

SOUTH AMERICAN

Scandinavian

Scandinavian sweaters are known for their elaborate color designs, featured primarily on the yoke and upper arm sections, with color seeding (repetitive flecks of small patterns) on the body and lower sleeves. A sportweight four- or five-ply wool is worked tightly, to protect the wearer from the cold.

As many as three or sometimes four colors can be used in each pattern row. Designs from Norway are largely geometric, including stylized snowflakes and flowers. Swedish patterns often depict people, animals, leaves, and flowers.

Sweaters are either T-Shaped or based on the Round Yoke style, but all work is done in the round. Necklines, armholes, and front openings are cut into the completed fabric. While the fishermen's garments of Aran, Guernsey, and Fair Isle fit snugly, these garments, designed for skiing, are looser to permit free movement in the snow.

Icelandic

The island nation of Iceland shares in the Nordic tradition of color knitting. Sweaters from Iceland are knit in the round, with Round Yokes.

Natural wool colors are traditional, but dyed yarns have been introduced recently. The intricate color work occurs mainly on the yoke, with smaller repeats above the border ribbings of sleeves and body. The remainder of the garment is worked in a single-color stockinette.

Native Icelandic sheep provide a unique type of wool; the fleece contains both a long, lustrous element and soft, downy undercoat. This spins nicely into a low-twist, bulky singles, called *lopi,* which knits into a shaggy fabric that sheds snow or misty rain.

Cowichan

The Cowichans, a Native American people from the Pacific Northwest, have adapted their traditional designs for use in knitted jackets and pullovers. Cowichan sweaters represent a more recently established knitting style, in keeping with the history of distinctive types of garments.

The people of the geographic area in which Cowichan sweaters developed depend on outdoor activities, and these garments meet the associated requirements for promoting dryness and warmth. The fishing, boating, and mountaineering populations of the region have readily adopted these practical garments.

The Cowichan people spin their own super-bulky, low-twist singles, and make Raglan and Basic T-Shape sweaters. They decorate them with wide bands of color patterning, separated by bands of single-color stockinette.

South American

The Andean countries of South America still abound with the heritage of the Incas, and with their wealth of textile history. Hats, sweaters, shawls, and ponchos are knit from either wool or alpaca.

Garments and articles knit from wool are often brilliantly colored, while alpaca is used in its natural shades. The color knitting features human figures, local animals, and geometric borders.

HATS

Yarn left over from sweaters can be used to make matching hats, scarves, or mittens. Here are two sets of guidelines for popular styles: a Watch Cap and a Tam o' Shanter. For either style, a 100-gram (3.5 ounce) skein of worsted weight yarn usually is sufficient.

Hats are best knit on 16″ circular needles, changing to double-pointed needles as decreasing progresses. If they are worked on straight needles, a seam will be required.

For a totally coordinated outfit, utilize both the same yarn and the same pattern stitch as you did in your sweater.

Two measurements are needed for hats. Those below are standard measurements to use in case actual measurements are unavailable.

1. Head Circumference
   Measure around the head at the level of the forehead (20″ to 21″ for a woman, up to 24″ for a man).
2. Ear-to-Ear Measurement
   Measure from the bottom of one ear, across the top of the head, to the bottom of the other ear (16″ for a woman, 16″ to 18″ for a man).

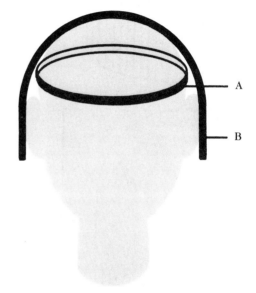

A circumference of head
B ear-to-ear

CONSTRUCTION OF A WATCH CAP

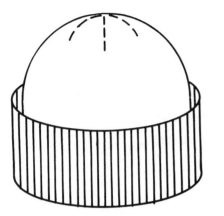

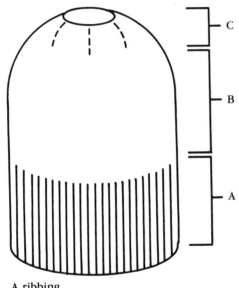

C

B

A

A ribbing
B pattern area
C decrease area

Watch Cap

These guidelines are for a cap which fits over the ears and has a 3″ fold-up brim. If you like, the cap or brim can be shorter. If the yarn is fine, the brim can be knit longer, making a double or triple fold-over. The brim can also be eliminated: work in rib for only 1″ and proceed as explained below.

Our example is worked as follows:

a. Ribbing for 4″,
b. A several-inch depth in pattern stitch,
c. Decreases worked over a 2″ depth.

Use the same size needles as you used for the body of your sweater.

Watch Cap

STEP 1
Head Circumference Measurement × stitch gauge = number of stitches to cast on

STEP 2
Work in ribbing for 4″.

STEP 3
½ Ear-to-Ear Measurement − 3″ = number of inches to work even in pattern stitch

STEP 4
Work evenly spaced decreases on every other row over the next 2″. You can decrease to 6, 8, 10, or 20 stitches—the amount is optional—producing a shaped top to the cap. Or you can work the last 2″ even and have gathers at the top.

STEP 5
Run the end of the yarn through the remaining stitches, tighten, and tie off. Finish with a pompom or tassel if you choose.

Tam o' Shanter

A Tam (beret) is simple to knit, but takes a bit of play with numbers to chart. It is worked in the round on 16″ circular and/or double-pointed needles. Charting is based on a circle.

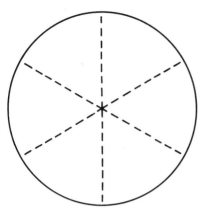

Top of tam

TAM

STEP 1
Begin by determining the following Tam measurements in inches.
a. Diameter: Most tams are 10″ to 12″ in diameter
b. Diameter ÷ 2 = radius
c. Diameter × 3.14 = circumference

STEP 2
Next determine the following stitches and rows:
a. (Head Circumference Measurement − 1″) × stitch gauge = number of stitches for ribbing
b. Step 1c × stitch gauge = number of stitches at widest part
c. (2″ to 2½″) × row gauge = number of rows for increases
d. Step 1b × row gauge = number of rows for decreases

STEP 3
Cast on Step 2a number of stitches. On smaller needles, work in ribbing for approximately 1″.

STEP 4
Divide the stitches into 6, 7, 8, or 9 equal sections. Place markers between the sections to facilitate counting.

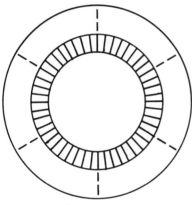

Underside of tam

STEP 5
In pattern stitch, on larger needles, work evenly spaced increases (see discussion below), over a depth of 2″ to 2½″, to reach the Step 2b number of stitches.

STEP 6
Work evenly spaced decreases (see discussion below), down to one stitch per section, over a depth equal to the tam's radius. Switch to double-pointed needles when the stitches become too few for a 16″ circular needle.

STEP 7
Run the end of the yarn through the remaining (6, 7, 8, or 9) stitches, tighten, and tie off.

STEP 8
Block with steam on a dinner size plate.

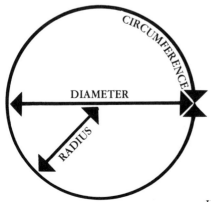

CONSTRUCTION OF A TAM

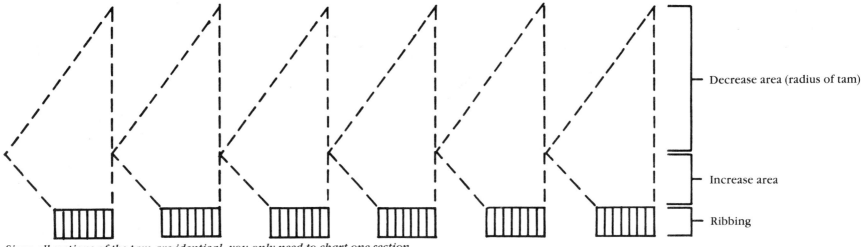

Decrease area (radius of tam)

Increase area

Ribbing

Since all sections of the tam are identical, you only need to chart one section.

It is easiest to chart just one section for the tam to indicate increases and decreases, since all sections will be identical. Divide both rib and circumference stitches by 6, 7, 8, or 9. (Try them all and see which works best for your row count.) You will probably find it necessary to add or subtract a few stitches on both rib and circumference to make the numbers work. Increases and decreases can be worked in different ways to form different patterns. If you're not sure where to begin, try the following.

INCREASES. In each section work to one stitch before the marker, make an M1 increase, knit the final stitch in that section, repeat across round.

DECREASES. In each section, work to last 2 stitches before the marker, knit 2 together, then repeat across round. This creates a graceful curved star on the top of the Tam.

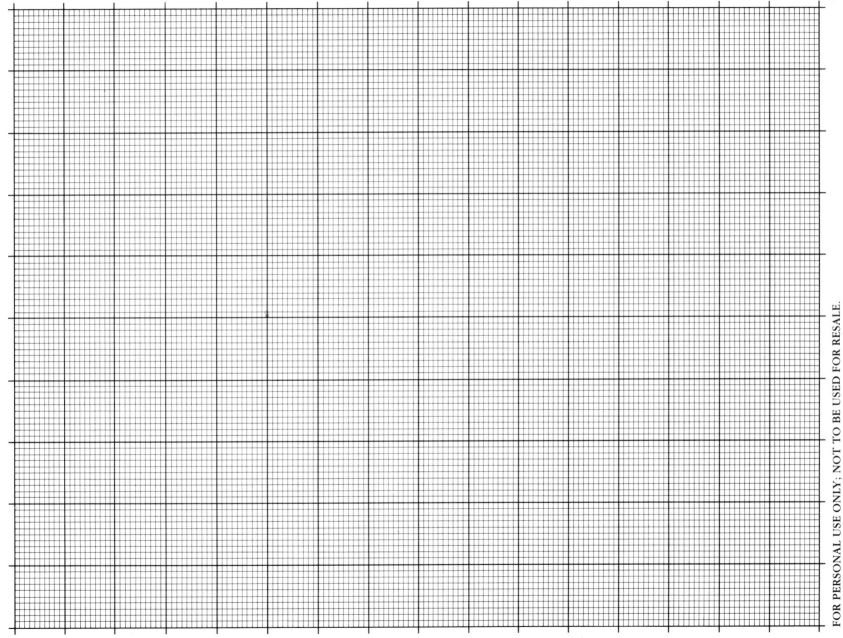

YOUR PERSONAL MEASUREMENT CHART

Review the complete guidelines for the style of garment you are planning to chart (*including body shaping, yoke, neckline, sleeve, sleeve cap and neck finish*) to see if any other measurements are required.

Measurements for _____

1. Chest/Bust   _____
2. Shoulder Width   _____
3. Front Yoke Width   _____
4. Back Yoke Width   _____
5. Armhole Depth   _____
6. Raglan Depth   _____
7. Armhole to Waist   _____
8. Waist Circumference   _____
9. Hip Circumference   _____
10. Upperarm Circumference   _____
11. Wrist Circumference   _____
12. Sleeve Length   _____
13. Special T/Dolman   _____
14. Garment Length to Armhole   _____
15. _____   _____
16. _____   _____
17. _____   _____
18. _____   _____
19. _____   _____
20. _____   _____

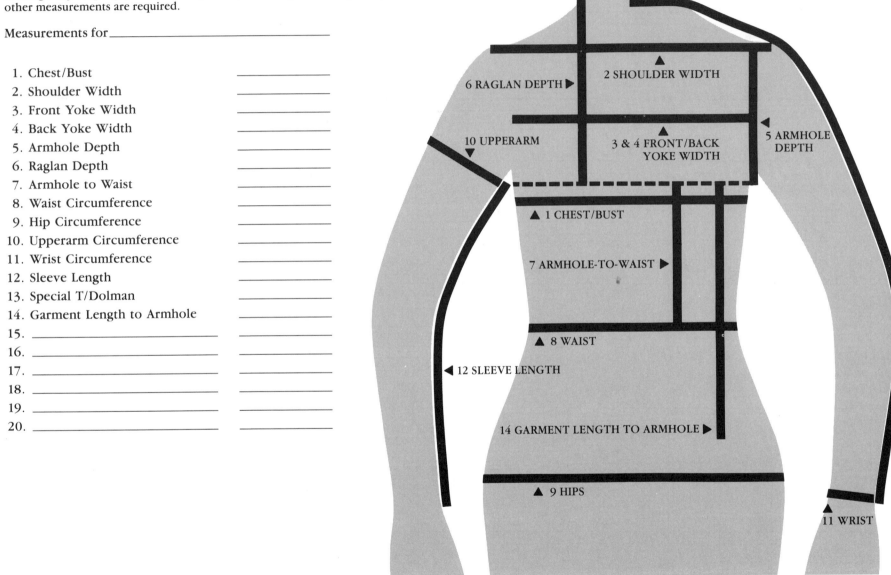

13 NECK-TO-WRIST

6 RAGLAN DEPTH ▶

2 SHOULDER WIDTH ▲

10 UPPERARM ▼

3 & 4 FRONT/BACK YOKE WIDTH ▲

5 ARMHOLE DEPTH ◀

▲ 1 CHEST/BUST

7 ARMHOLE-TO-WAIST ▶

▲ 8 WAIST

◀ 12 SLEEVE LENGTH

14 GARMENT LENGTH TO ARMHOLE ▶

▲ 9 HIPS

11 WRIST ▲

▬ ▬ ▬ ▬ ▬ MEASUREMENT STRING

YARDAGE CHART

Yarn Type	Sport				Worsted				Bulky			
Needle Size	5–6				8–9				10–13			
Stitch Gauge	5½–6				4½–5				3–4			
Garment Size	S	M	L	XL	S	M	L	XL	S	M	L	XL
WOMEN												
Pullover, long sleeves	1200	1400	1600	1800	1000	1200	1400	1600	800	900	1000	1100
Pullover, short sleeves	1000	1200	1400	1600	800	950	1100	1250				
Cardigan	1300	1500	1700	1900	1075	1275	1475	1675	825	925	1025	1125
Vest	800	900	1000	1100	600	700	800	900	400	500	600	700
MEN												
Pullover	1400	1600	1800	2000	1325	1500	1675	1850	900	1000	1100	1200
Cardigan	1575	1750	1925	2100	1400	1575	1750	1925	950	1050	1150	1250
Vest	875	1050	1225	1400	800	950	1100	1250	700	800	900	1000

This chart is a compilation of average amounts of yarn needed to knit simply styled garments. These are approximations only and are intended merely as a guide.

Courtesy of Vernice Brown.

STANDARD MEASUREMENTS

INFANTS	Size		
	Newborn	6 Months	12 Months
Approximate height	22"–25"	26"–30"	31"
Approximate weight (lbs.)	5–10	11–18	19–24
Chest	17"–18"	19"–20"	21"–22"
Shoulder width	7½"	7¾"	8¼"
Armhole depth	3¼"	3½"	3¾"
Raglan depth	3¾"	4"	4¼"
Armhole to waist	3"	3½"	3¾"
Waist	18"	19"	20"
Hips (includes diapers)	19"	20"	21"
Upperarm	4½"	5"	5½"
Wrist	3½"	4"	4½"
Sleeve length	6"	6½"	7"
Head circumference	15"	16"	17"

CHILDREN'S SIZES

					Size				
	2	3	4	6	8	10	12	14	16
Approximate height	2' 10"	3' 1"	3' 4"	3' 10"	4' 3"	4' 5"	4' 9"	5'	5' 2"
Approximate weight (lbs.)					60	66	84	96	110
Chest	21"	22"	23"	24"	26"	28"	30"	32"	34"
Shoulder width	9¼"	9½"	9¾"	10¼"	10¾"	11¼"	12"	12¼"	13"
Armhole depth	4¼"	4½"	4¾"	5"	5½"	6"	6½"	7"	7½"
Raglan depth	4¾"	5"	5¼"	5¾"	6¼"	6¾"	7¼"	8"	8½"
Armhole to waist	4¼"	4½"	4¾"	5"	5½"	6"	6½"	7"	7½"
Waist	20"	20½"	21"	22"	23"	24"	25½"	26½"	28½"
Hips	22"	23"	24"	26"	28"	30"	32"	34"	36"
Upperarm	6"	6¼"	6½"	7"	7½"	8"	8½"	9"	9½"
Wrist	4½"	4½"	4½"	5"	5"	5½"	5½"	6"	6"
Sleeve length	7½"	8½"	9½"	10½"	12"	13½"	15"	16"	16½"
Head circumference	19½"	20"	20½"	20¾"	21"	21¼"	21½"	21¾"	22"

TEEN SIZES

			Size					
	Girls				Boys			
	7/8	9/10	11/12	13/14	14	16	18	20
Approximate height	4' 8"	4' 10½"	5' 1"	5' 4"	5' 2"	5' 4"	5' 6"	5' 8"
Approximate weight (lbs.)	78	89	100	115	105	115	126	138
Bust/chest	29"	30½"	32"	33½"	31½"	33"	34½"	36"
Shoulder width	11½"	12½"	13"	13½"	13"	13½"	14"	14½"
Armhole depth	6"	6¼"	6½"	6¾"	6¾"	7"	7¼"	7¾"
Raglan depth	6¾"	7"	7¼"	7½"	7¾"	7"	8¼"	8¾"
Armhole to waist	6½"	6¾"	7"	7¼"	6¾"	7"	7¼"	7½"
Waist	23"	24"	25"	26"	26½"	27½"	28½"	29"
Hips	32"	33½"	35"	36½"	32"	34"	35½"	37"
Upperarm	8¼"	8¾"	9¼"	9½"	9¼"	9½"	9¾"	10"
Wrist	5¼"	5½"	5½"	5½"	6½"	6¾"	7"	7¼"
Sleeve length	14"	14½"	15"	15½"	16"	16½"	17"	17½"
Head circumference	21"	21½"	22"	22"	22"	22½"	23"	23"

JUNIOR SIZES
5' 2" to 5' 6". Smaller waist. Higher bust. Shorter from shoulder to waist.

	Size							
	3	5	7	9	11	13	15	17
Approximate height	5' 1½"	5' 2"	5' 2½"	5' 3"	5' 3½"	5' 4"	5' 4½"	5' 5"
Approximate weight (lbs.)	85	93	101	108	119	130	142	153
Bust	30"	31"	32"	33"	34½"	36"	37½"	39"
Shoulder width	11¼"	12"	12¼"	12½"	13"	13¼"	13½"	13¾"
Armhole depth	6¾"	6¾"	7"	7"	7¼"	7¼"	7½"	7½"
Raglan depth	7¾"	7¾"	8"	8"	8¼"	8¼"	8½"	8½"
Armhole to waist	7½"	7¾"	7¾"	8"	8¼"	8¼"	8¼"	8½"
Waist	20½"	21½"	22½"	23½"	25"	26½"	28"	29½"
Hips	32"	33"	34"	35"	36½"	38"	39½"	41"
Upperarm	9¼"	9¼"	9½"	10"	10¼"	10½"	11"	11¼"
Wrist	5¼"	5¼"	5¼"	5½"	5½"	5¾"	6"	6"
Sleeve length	16¼"	16¼"	16½"	16½"	16½"	16¾"	16¾"	16¾"
Head circumference	21"	21"	22"	22"	22"	22"	22"	22"

MISSES' SIZES
5' 3" to 5' 7". Average proportions.

	Size								
	6	8	10	12	14	16	18	20	22
Approximate height	5' 2½"	5' 3"	5' 3½"	5' 4"	5' 4½"	5' 5"	5' 5½"	5' 6"	5' 6½"
Approximate weight (lbs.)	98	106	113	125	136	147	161	176	190
Bust	31½"	32½"	33½"	35"	36½"	38"	40"	42"	44"
Shoulder width	12"	12¼"	12½"	13"	13¼"	13½"	13¾"	14¼"	15"
Armhole depth	7"	7¼"	7¼"	7½"	7½"	7½"	7¾"	8"	8"
Raglan depth	8"	8¼"	8¼"	8½"	8½"	8¾"	9"	9¼"	9¼"
Armhole to waist	7¾"	7¾"	8"	8"	8¼"	8½"	8½"	8½"	8¾"
Waist	22½"	23½"	24½"	26"	27½"	29"	31"	33"	35"
Hips	33½"	34½"	35½"	37"	38½"	40"	42"	44"	46"
Upperarm	9¾"	10"	10¼"	10½"	10¾"	11¼"	12"	12½"	13"
Wrist	5¼"	5½"	5½"	5½"	5¾"	6"	6"	6¼"	6¼"
Sleeve length	16¼"	16½"	16½"	16¾"	16¾"	17"	17"	17"	17¼"
Head circumference	21"	21½"	21¾"	22"	22"	22"	22½"	22½"	23"

WOMEN'S SIZES
5'4" to 5'6½". Fuller, more mature figure.

	Size									
	34	36	38	40	42	44	46	48	50	52
Approximate height	5'4½"	5'5"	5'5½"	5'6"	5'6½"	5'6½"	5'6½"	5'6½"	5'6½"	5'6½"
Approximate weight (lbs.)	144	159	173	189	204	219	233	248	262	277
Bust	38"	40"	42"	44"	46"	48"	50"	52"	54"	56"
Shoulder width	13½"	14"	14½"	15"	15½"	16"	16½"	17"	17½"	18"
Armhole depth	8"	8"	8¼"	8¼"	8¼"	8½"	8½"	8¾"	9"	9"
Raglan depth	9¼"	9¼"	9½"	9½"	9½"	9¾"	9¾"	10½"	10½"	10½"
Armhole to waist	7¾"	8"	8"	8¼"	8¼"	8¼"	8¼"	8¼"	8¼"	8¼"
Waist	30"	32"	34"	36½"	39"	41½"	44"	46½"	49"	51½"
Hips	39"	41"	43"	45"	47"	49"	51"	53"	55"	56"
Upperarm	12"	12½"	13¼"	14"	14¼"	15¼"	15¾"	16¼"	17"	17¼"
Wrist	5¾"	6"	6"	6¼"	6¼"	6½"	6½"	6½"	6¾"	6¾"
Sleeve length	16½"	16¾"	16¾"	16¾"	16¾"	16¾"	16¾"	16¾"	16¾"	16¾"
Head circumference	22"	22"	22½"	22½"	22½"	23"	23"	23"	23"	23"

WOMEN'S HALF SIZES
5'3½" and under. Medium to heavy frame. Shorter from shoulder to waist.

	Size							
	12½	14½	16½	18½	20½	22½	24½	26½
Approximate height	5'½"	5'1"	5'1½"	5'2"	5'2½"	5'3"	5'3½"	5'4"
Approximate weight (lbs.)	123	138	153	167	183	198	214	229
Bust	36"	38"	40"	42"	44"	46"	48"	50"
Shoulder width	13"	13½"	14"	14½"	15"	15½"	16"	16½"
Armhole depth	7½"	7½"	7¾"	8"	8"	8"	8¼"	8¼"
Raglan depth	9"	9"	9¼"	9½"	9½"	9½"	9½"	9½"
Armhole to waist	7"	7½"	7½"	7½"	7½"	8"	8"	8"
Waist	28"	30"	32"	34"	36½"	39"	41½"	44"
Upperarm	11½"	12"	12½"	13¼"	14"	14½"	15"	15¾"
Wrist	5½"	5¾"	6"	6"	6"	6¼"	6¼"	6½"
Sleeve length	15¼"	15½"	15½"	15¾"	15¾"	15¾"	15¾"	15¾"
Head circumference	22"	22"	22"	22"	22"	22"	23"	23"

MEN'S SIZES

Size

	Small		Medium		Large		Extra Large		
	34	36	38	40	42	44	46	48	50
Approximate height	5' 8"	5' 9"	5' 10"	5' 11"	6'	6'	6'	6'	6'
Approximate weight (lbs.)	123	137	152	170	190	210	230	250	270
Chest	34"	36"	38"	40"	42"	44"	46"	48"	50"
Shoulder width	15"	15½"	16"	16½"	17"	17½"	18"	18½"	19"
Armhole depth	7½"	7¾"	8"	8¼"	8½"	8¾"	9"	9¼"	9½"
Raglan depth	8¾"	9"	9½"	9¾"	10"	10¼"	10½"	10¾"	11"
Armhole to waist	8"	8"	8¼"	8¼"	8½"	8½"	8¾"	8¾"	9"
Waist	28"	30"	32"	34"	36"	39"	42"	44"	46"
Hips	35"	37"	39"	41"	43"	45"	47"	49"	51"
Upperarm	10½"	11"	11½"	12"	12½"	13"	13½"	14"	14½"
Wrist	6¼"	6½"	6¾"	7"	7¼"	7½"	7¾"	8"	8¼"
Sleeve length	18"	18¼"	18½"	18¾"	19"	19¼"	19½"	19¾"	20"
Head circumference	23"	23¼"	23½"	23¾"	24"	24¼"	24½"	24¾"	25"
*Sweater length to armhole	14"	14½"	15"	15½"	16"	16¼"	16½"	17"	17¼"

*This is an average sweater length, not a body measurement.

ACKNOWLEDGMENTS

Special thanks are due to:

All the knitters who make me grow by asking questions,

Mary Thomas, Ida Riley Duncan, and all the anonymous contributors at Mon Tricot who answered my questions when I didn't know whom to ask,

Mary-Ann Davis, for the impetus to get this onto paper and for stretching my limits,

Michelle Wipplinger, for the generous sharing of her knowledge and ideas when I was struggling to put color instincts into words,

Deb Robson, for soothing words when all seemed overwhelming,

Lee Anne Bowie, for her friendship,

and especially to my parents, Tom and Fina Michelson, whose love and support were crucial.

This book is dedicated to my children, Jody and Mari: dreams do come true!

Carmen Michelson

Special thanks to:

Carmen Michelson, whose knowledge of knitting made this book possible, the Seattle hand- and machine-knitting communities for their encouragement,

Marion and Peter Davis, Anna and Joseph Salata, four very special and talented people who instilled in me their love for handicrafts,

Jo-Ann Vucetich and Alma Schlieps, for their support,

and above all, my husband Armin Schlieps, whose patience and love were my bulwark during the years of work on this project.

Mary-Ann Davis

INDEX

Adjusted Shoulder Width Measurement 218, 221, 224

Alternate Round Neckline 119–20

Alternate Set-In Armhole shaping 79–80, 113, 195–96; method used to shape pocket opening 354

Aran sweaters, 380–81; test swatches for 40

argyle knitting 9

armhole shaping 34, 113; Alternate Set-In 79–80; for vests 107–11; Set-In/Semi-Raglan 80–82, 110–11; Set-In Standard 57–58, 61–62, 110; variation 63

armhole-to-waist measurement 34–35, 388

assembling a sweater 38, 361–63

asymmetrical: cardigan 143; necklines 115

Attached Hoods 319–25

back neckline 115; finishes 167, 281, 296; shaping 114, 140, 233

back yoke width measurement 34–35, 388

Band 282; depth 269; for Blunt V Neckline 289; for vest 107; narrow 270–72; on cardigan 144; picking up 268–69; ribbed 114; with insert 290; see also Butted Band, Decreased Band, Horizontal Band, Overlapped Band, Picked-Up Band, Traditional V Neckline Band, Vertical Band

basic: Dolmans 253; formulas 51–56; hood shapes 304; neckline shapes 116; sleeve 198

Basic T 209, 381, 383; knit horizontally 8, 88, 256; knit vertically 88, 255; Sleeves 246, 362; Yoke 86–88, 246

Bell Sleeve 205–06

beret 385–86

Bias Bind-Off 374

biasing 40, 361

bind-off 56, 115, 374

Bishop Sleeve 203–06

blocking 40–41, 360–61

Blouson Body 51, 65–66, 71

Blunt V Neckline 115, 122, 126, 281, 302, 327; Band for 289; Overlapped Band for 286–87

Boat Neckline 38, 88, 130–36, 275, 326; finishes 299–300

body length for Ts and Dolmans 253

body shapes and styles 57–113; see also Blouson Body, Bolero Jacket, Bust Darts, Cinched-Waist Body, Classic Body, Dart-Tapered Body, Double-Tapered Body, Enlarged Sweater Front, Extended Shoulder Shaping, Full-Fashioned Shoulder Shaping, Modified Raglan, Modified T Yoke, Reverse-Tapered Body, Round Yoke, Saddle Shoulder sweater, Shaped Yoke, Standard Raglan sweater, summer tops, Tapered Body

Bolero Jacket 141–42, 176

border: on Peter Pan Collar 280–81; stitches and patterns 5, 34, 130, 158, 165, 167, 197, 270, 275, 281, 325; test swatches for 39

bound-off stitches 365; see also bind-off

Box Cap 36, 80, 190, 218–21, 231

brioche stitches 270, 274

broad shoulders, fitting 82

brocade patterns 5

bust: Darts 36, 76–78; measurement 34–36; small 71

Butted: Band 295–96; Boat Neckline 130–31, 300

buttonholes 141–42, 300, 325–26, 375–77; for drawstring 209

buttons 276–77, 325; placement 334–37

Cable Cast-On 374

Cabled Decrease 372

cables 7–8, 40, 100, 270, 361, 381

Cap see Sleeve Caps; see also Basic T Sleeves, Box Cap, Classic Set-In Cap, Designer's Choice Cap, Expanded Cap, Folded T Sleeve, Gathered Cap, Modified Raglan, Modified Saddle Shoulder, Modified T Sleeve, Modified T Sleeve with Gathers or Pleats, Pleated Cap, Raglan sweaters, Saddle Band and Saddle Shoulder, Semi-Raglan Cap, Standard Raglan Cap, T Sleeve, T-Square Cap

Cap Sleeves 249–51

Cap Triangle 193–95

Cape Collar 272, 281, 300

Caps (hats) 383–86

Cardigans 141–88; buttonholes 142; charting 146–48; designing front finishes 144–45, 147, 149–75; Lapel Collar 186–87; necklines 115, 142–45; Non-Overlapping styles 176–77; Shawl Collar 177–88; styling 142; V-Neck 120, 141, 145, 161, 173, 177; variations 142–43, 147; Vest 107

casing for elastic 209

Cast-On, Cable 374

cast-on sequences 56

cat's paw hem 377

CB (Classic Body) 49, 63, 197

Chanel Jacket 141–42, 176–77

charted patterns 100

charting tools 44–45

chest: measurement 34–35, 388; small 71

children's garments 21, 37–38, 113, 120, 134, 255, 297; sizing 390–91

Cinched-Waist Body 36, 74, 142

circular knitting and needles 3–4, 38, 98, 255, 270, 381–83; circularly knit finishes 268; circularly knit V Bands 270

Classic Body and Classic Sweater 49, 57–63, 67, 71, 190, 193, 197, 199–200

Classic Set-In Cap 190, 193, 197, 199–200

cleaning 17–18

Collar 286; depth 269; double-thickness 269, 275, 279; horizontally worked 269; picking up 268–69; separately knit 276; shaped 276–77; vertically worked 269; see also Cape Collar, Cowl Collar, Foldover Collar, Lapel Collar, Peter Pan Collar, Picked-Up Shawl Collar, Reverse Taper Collar, Ruffled Collar, separate collar, Shawl Collar, Split Collar, Standard Collar, Stand-Up Collar, Wing Collar

color patterns 8, 380–83; seeding 382

Combination Seam 365–66

combinations of neckline finishes 300–01

combining: circular and flat knitting 11–13, 38; stitch patterns 10; yarns 20–21

comfort 257, 297, 382–83; see also warmth

commercial knitwear 104

construction of Designer's Choice Caps 229; of Lapel Collar Cardigan 186; of Modified Raglan 94; of Shawl Collar Cardigan 177–78; of Standard Raglan Sweater 94; of a tam 386; of a watch cap 384; see also assembling a sweater

converting fractions to decimals 44

corners, mitered 162, 296

Cowl Collar 269, 271, 274–76, 277, 282, 285, 300; as hood 275; for Boat Neckline 300; separate 275

Crewneck 98–99, 145, 270, 272, 275, 300

crochet finishes 114, 270, 299

cuff or cuff finish 34, 197

Curve Guide 258, 378–79; used to shape pocket openings 355

Curve Measurement 191

darts 75–78, 218, 221, 372
Dart-Tapered Body 75–76
decimals 44
decorative use: of decreases 92, 104, 368; of increases 211
Decreased Band 283–85, 296–97, 300
decreases 51–52, 100, 368–72; along side edges 52; as design element 92, 104, 368; for Full-Fashioned Shoulder Shaping 372; for Wide Band finishes 272–73; fullness 51; in ribbing 272
decreasing: for Round Yokes 99–104; needle size for neck finish 272–73; stitches for neck finish 272–73
deep neckline: Round 270–273; Square 127
Deep V Band with Collar 286
depth: of band or collar 269; of neckline 114
Designer's Choice Cap 36, 80, 190, 206, 214, 224–32; construction of 229; Knitting Guidelines 227
details, finishing 268–359
Dolmans 35–36, 56, 252, 257–67, 325, 374, 378; Body Width 253; measurements for 253; necklines for 254–55; shaping 56; sleeve length 253
double-breasted cardigan 141, 143
Double Decreases 370–72
Double-Tapered Body 36, 69–70
double-thickness bands and collars 269, 275, 279, 300
Doubled Bands 300, 366
Draped Neckline 136–40
drawstring 209
drop-shoulder sweater 86
duplicating a favorite neckline 114

ease 36–38, 189; for adult garments 37; for children's garments 37; for infants' garments 37; in examples 57
easing a seam 364
edges: Overlapped 276–77; smooth 374
Edging see Purl Welt Edging
elastic, casing for 209
elongated vertical buttonhole 375–77
Enhanced Decreases: Double 371; Single 369–70
Enlarged Sweater Front 36, 50, 63–65
enlarging pictures 46, 48
ethnic traditions 380–83
Expanded Cap Shaping 214
extended shoulder cap 224
Extended Shoulder Shaping 85–86
extension of front border for V Neckline 281
eyelet: buttonhole 375; row 377

facings and faced finishes 141, 165 ff., 167, 171, 270, 326–27, 332–34
fibers 14–16
figure faults 29, 35, 257
fine yarns 13–14, 79–80, 115
Finished Width of Sleeve Cap 192

finishes: combination necklines 300–02; faced 165 ff.; for Boat Necklines 299–300; for Hoods 303–04; for Round Necklines 270–81; for Square Necklines 295–98; for Ts and Dolmans 254; for V Necklines 281–95; Narrow Band 270–71; Neckline 268–302; neckline combinations 300–01; overlapped 269, 286–87, 290–91; Rolled 274; stitch patterns for 270; using stockinette stitch in 270
finishing details 268–359
fitting 29, 35–36, 82, 257; larger sizes 120
flaring techniques for Cowl Collars 274–75
flat knitting 3–4, 38, 381
Folded T Sleeve 249
Foldover Collar 282, 285, 300
formulas, basic 51–57; charting 57
fractions 44, 50
front finishes for cardigans 145, 149–88
Front Overlap Width 146, 177
front pockets 357–59
front yoke for Modified Raglan 98
Full-Fashioned Shoulder Shaping 104–07, 372
Full Sleeve 203–06, 211, 214; Lantern Sleeve 201–02; Leg o' Mutton Sleeve 206–09
fullness, increasing or decreasing 51
Funnel Sleeve 209, 211

garment: length to armhole 34–35; shaping 10–11; see also shaping
garter stitch 149, 153, 270, 296, 330
Gathered: Cap 35–36, 80, 189–90, 206, 209, 211–14; Overlapped Band 289–90; Sleeve 203–04
gathers formula 51–52
Gathers on T Sleeve 246
gauge 4, 21, 38, 51, 251, 274, 364; in examples 57
Gradual Flaring Cowl Collar 274–75
graph paper 44; see also knitters' graph paper
gusset 255, 257–58, 379

halter 113
hats 383–86
head measurements 302
Height of Sleeve Cap 192
hem(s) 130, 137, 154, 158, 169, 171, 197, 232, 254, 270, 366
High Round Neckline 117, 270, 274, 302, 366; finishes 300
hips, measurement 34–35, 388; wide 71
Hood(s) 268, 302–25, 378; Attached 319–25; basic shapes 304; Cowl Collar 275; finishes 304; measurements for 302; seams 365; Separate Rectangular 305–12; Separate T-Shaped 312–19
horizontal: Band 156–62; buttonhole 375; knitting 88, 251; Placket 328–29; Shawl Collar 293, 298; turning ridge 377; Woven Seam 365

horizontally knit: garments 251, 253, 255; collars 183–84, 169, 292–93, 298; Shawl Collars 183–84, 292–93, 298; Ts 88, 256
hourglass figure 36

immersion blocking 361
increases 366–67; decorative use of 211
increasing along side edges 52; fullness 51
Inserts 290, 294–95, 300, 302, 327; separate 302
Inset Pockets 348–59; on Seam Opening 355–59; with Curved Opening 354–55; with Horizontal Opening 348–50; with Slanted Opening 352–54

jackets 383; front edges 378; see also Bolero Jacket, Chanel Jacket, Lapel Jacket
joins 363–66

kangaroo pocket 344–45
Keyhole Openings and Plackets 115, 325–26, 328–34
knitters' graph paper 45–46, 51, 89, 95, 100, 115, 251, 258, 387
Knitting Guidelines for Designer's Choice Cap 227
knitting needles see needles and circular knitting and needles

lace patterns 6–7, 270, 274, 281, 377
Lantern Sleeve 51, 200–02, 209
Lapel: Collar 107, 145, 186–87; Jacket 184, 188
large: bust 36; midriff 36; sizes 120
Large Round Yoke 98–101, 102, 104
Leg o' Mutton Sleeve 206–09
Loose Inset Pocket with Horizontal Opening 350–51
Low Round Neckline 117

machine knitting 3, 269
marking edges of fabric 363–64
maternity wear 36, 71
Math Method 194–95
measurement: chart 388; string 33–35
measurements 33–35, 388; children's 390; for bust darts 76–77; for hats 383; for hoods 302; for Leg o' Mutton Sleeves 206; for neckline finishes 269; for pockets 344; for short sleeves 189; for summer tops 113; for Ts and Dolmans 253; for tams 385; juniors' 391; men's 393; misses' 392; standard 390–93; teens' 391; women's 392; women's half sizes 393
measuring the armhole curve 61; 191
medium neckline: Round 117, 302; Square 127
men's garments 141, 269, 325, 331–32, 334; sizing 393
Minimized Decreases: Double 370; Single 368
mitered corners 162, 296
Mock: Insert 294–96; Turtleneck 271, 274–77
Modified: Lantern Sleeve 201–02; Leg o' Mutton Sleeve 206–09; Raglan 95–98, 243–45; Saddle Shoulder

91–92, 235–38; T Sleeve with Gathers or Pleats 247–48; T Yoke and Sleeve 89–90, 209, 246–47
multiples 10

narrow: Band(s) 114, 120, 270–72, 300; shoulders 36; straps 113
neck-to-wrist measurement 34–35
necklines 34, 113–40; back shaping 140; bands 34, 107; cardigan 142–45; combinations 115, 300–01; decreasing 272–73; depth 114; duplicating 114; elastic 100; facing for back 167, 171; finishes 107, 268–302; openings 325; optional back shaping 233; shapes, basic 116; shaping 34, 113–40, 233, 268; variations 115–16, 121; width 61, 113–14; *see also* Alternate Round Neckline, Blunt V Neckline, Boat Necklines, Butted Boat Neckline, combinations of neckline finishes, Draped Neckline, Overlapped Boat Neckline, Round Neckline, Shaped Boat Neckline, Square Boat Neckline, Square Neckline, Traditional V Neckline, V Neckline, Wide V Neckline
needles and needle sizes 100–01, 182, 270, 272–75
Non-Overlapping Cardigan Styles 176–77
Notched Shawl Collar 184–85

One- and Two-Piece Garments 251–67, 325, 374
one-row stripes 9
open collar *see* Split Collar
Optional Back Neckline Shaping 233
overlap placement 337; width 146, 177
Overlapped Band 286–91; Gathered 289–90; paper trick 286; Pleated 290–91
overlapped: Boat Neckline 134–35; Edges 276–77; finishes 269
Overlapping Insert 327

Paper-and-Ruler Method 194
paper trick 286
parts of a sweater 34
Patch Pockets 344–47; with Side Hems 345–46
pattern repeat gauge 40
pattern stitches 41, 98, 275; matching 365–66
personal measurement chart 388
Peter Pan Collar 272, 280–81, 300
picked-up: Band 162; border 254; finish 135, 183, 268–69; Shawl Collar 276–77, 279
picking up stitches 156, 254, 268–69, 363–64
picot edging 377
picture knitting 46–48
Piping 137, 274, 297, 300, 327, 366
placement: of neckline on Ts and Dolmans 254; of stitch pattern for neck finishes 270, 283, 296
Plackets 38, 325–43; buttons on 335–37; Faced 332–34; Horizontal 328–29; Keyhole Openings 328–34; Raglan seam opening 340–43; Saddle Band overlap 337–38; Seam Openings 335–43; Self-Finished 329–32; Vertical 329–30

Pleated: Cap 36, 80, 189–90, 193, 206, 209, 214–18; Overlapped Band 290–91
pleats 230, 232, 364; on T Sleeve 246
Pockets 344–59, 364, 378; front 357–59; inset 348–59; measurements for 344; patch 344–47; pouch 344–45, 347, 364
Pouch Pocket 344–45, 347, 364
Purl Welt Edging 274, 297, 300

Quadruple Decreases 372

Raglan sweaters 35, 37, 40, 51, 325, 327, 381, 383; Armholes 52, 113; assembling 381; Caps 189, 239–45; cardigan 141; Modified Sleeve Cap 243–45; Modified Yoke 95–98; Plackets 340–43; Standard Sleeve Cap 92, 239, 241–42; Standard Yoke 92–95
raglan: depth measurement 34–35; Seam Opening Placket 340–43
Rectangular Hoods, Separate 305–12
reducing pictures 46, 48
Removable Insert 295
repeat and repeat gauge 10, 40
Reverse Taper Collar 290, 294
Reverse-Tapered Body 36, 69–74
rib tickler 113
ribbing 5, 34, 51, 113, 130, 151, 153, 197, 254, 270, 296, 361; at waist 74; decreasing in 272; in yoke 100; test swatches for 39
Rolled Collar and Finish 271, 274, 282–86, 295, 297, 299–300
Round Neckline 88, 98, 114–20, 186, 236–37, 269, 326–27; Alternate 119–20; Deep 273; finishes 270–81
round shoulders 82
Round Yoke 35, 37, 98–104, 380, 382; decreasing 104; for cardigan 141
row gauge 4, 39, 251
Ruffled Collar 281, 290, 294, 300

Saddle Band and Saddle Shoulder sweater 35, 89, 91–92, 189, 233, 235, 237, 325–26, 381; Box Cap 220; Cap 190, 193, 233–38; cardigan 141; Plackets 337–40; Yoke 89, 91–92
sawtooth edge 377
scaling a drawing to size 48
seam: allowances or stitches 38, 57, 114, 269; openings and plackets 325, 335–43
seams 4, 363–66; easing 364; knitted 364; woven 365–66
seed stitch 149, 153, 254, 270, 296, 330
Self-Finish 130; on Boat Neckline 299; on Placket 329–32; on Square Neckline 295–97; on V Neckline 281, 283
selvedge: seams 365; stitches 38
Semi-Raglan sweaters: Armhole Shaping 80–82, 85, 113; Armhole Shaping for vests 107–11; Sleeve and Cap 35, 80, 190, 193, 239–40; Yoke 239

separate collar 182, 275–76, 278, 300, 302; Cowl Collar 275, 302; Shawl Collar 182, 278
Separate Hood: Rectangular 305–12; T-Shaped Hood 312–19
Separate Insert 294, 302
Set-In Armhole Shaping 49, 57–63, 85, 113; Alternate 79–80; for vests 107–11; method used to shape pocket opening 354; Semi-Raglan 80–81; Standard 57–63
Set-In Sleeve and Sleeve Cap 35, 37, 80, 106, 189–200, 224; assembling 362; Box Cap 220
shallow neckline 56, 127
shaped: Boat Neckline 132, 135, 299–300; collar 276–77; Yoke 82–84
shapes, basic 3, 380
shaping 10–11, 31, 51, 57 ff., 372–74; Armhole 113; body and yoke 57 ff.; curved pocket openings 354–55; Expanded Cap 214; formulas 51–56; Full-Fashioned Shoulder 104–07; neckline 268; Optional Back Neckline 140; Round Yoke 99–103; short row 29–30, 372–74; shoulder 258; vest armhole 107–11
Shawl Collar 52, 114, 127, 143, 145, 177–85, 268, 271, 276–79, 290–93, 295, 297–98, 372; for cardigan 141, 177–85; for Square Neckline 297; for vest 107; Horizontal 183–84, 291–92, 298; Notched 184–85; Picked-Up 276–77, 279; Separate 182, 278; Standard Vertical 178–80, 185; Vertical 180–82, 185, 291–92, 298; Wide Vertical 180–82, 185
short rows 29–30, 76, 132, 135, 276, 300, 372–74
short sleeves 189
shoulder: pads 85, 222, 228, 231; seam openings 335–37
shoulder shaping 34, 88, 258; Extended 85–86; Full-Fashioned 104–07, 372; variation 63
Shoulder Width Measurement 34–36, 82, 218, 221, 224
shoulders 56; fitting 82, 85
Side *a, b, c* 193
side edges, increasing or decreasing along 52
Simple Patch Pocket 344–45
Single Decreases 368–70, 372
sizes *see* measurements
Sleeves 34; basic 198; ease 189; length for Ts and Dolmans 253; length measurement 34–35, 388; on Ts, Straight 255; on Ts, Tapered 256; short 189; *see also* Bell Sleeve, Bishop Sleeve, Cap Sleeves, Folded T Sleeve, Full Sleeve, Funnel Sleeve, Gathered Sleeve, Lantern Sleeve, Leg o' Mutton Sleeve, short sleeves, Straight Sleeve, Tapered Sleeve, T Sleeve
Sleeves and Sleeve Caps 189–251
Sleeve Caps 34, 52, 92, 95, 189–251; charting 61; Expanded Shaping 214; Finished Width 192; height of 192; Set-In 106, 189–200; Standard Raglan 92; tapering 195; Unfinished Width of 192–93; *see also* Box Cap, Classic Set-In Cap, Designer's Choice Cap, Expanded Cap Shaping, Gathered Cap, Pleated Cap, Raglan Caps, Saddle Band and Saddle Shoulder Cap, Semi-Raglan Cap, T-Square Cap

sleeve-to-sleeve knitting 251, 253, 255
slope formula 56
sloping shoulders 29
small bust or chest 71
Small Round Yoke 98–101, 103–04
Split Collar 270–71, 275–77
Square Boat Neckline 133, 135, 300
square inches of fabric in garment 42
Square Neckline 38, 115–16, 127–29, 133, 135, 269, 295–98, 327; finishes for 295–98
square shoulders 35
stable stitch patterns 270, 325, 330
Stand-Up Collar 300
standard: Armhole Shaping 57–58; Collar 272, 280, 282, 285, 300; graph paper 44; measurements and sample measurements 33, 290, 390–93; measurements for neckline finishes 269; Set-In Cap 80; Shoulder Shaping 49, 57–63; sizes 29, 390–93; Vertical Shawl Collar 178–80, 185
Standard Raglan sweater and Sleeve Cap 92–95, 239, 241–42; Yoke 92–95
Standard Saddle Shoulder sweater and Sleeve Cap 92, 233–35
Starting Number of Stitches 146
steam-iron blocking 361
steep shoulder slope 35, 85
stitch: gauge 39, 251; patterns 5–8, 10–13, 18–19, 26, 51, 249, 254, 270, 281, 380–83; ratios 45
stitches: picking up 156; useful 365–66
stooped shoulders 29
Straight Sleeve 209–10; on Ts 255
strapless top 113
straps, narrow 113
stripes 8, 21, 249, 365–66; one-row 9
Sudden Flaring Cowl Collar 274–75
summer tops 112–13
Sweatshirt-Style Pocket 344–45

T-Shaped Hoods, Separate 312–19
T-Shaped sweater 3, 35–37, 251–67, 325, 374, 380–82; Basic Yoke 86–88; Body Width 253; measurements for 25; Modified Yoke 89–90; necklines 254–55

T Sleeve, Basic 246–47; Bind-Off 246–48; Folded 249; Length 253; Modified 246; with Gathers or Pleats 246–47
T-Square Cap 190, 221–24, 228
taking measurements 33–35, 388
tam o' shanter 385–86
tank top 113
taper formula 52–55
tapered: Body 52, 67–68; Flaring Cowl Collar 274–75; Sleeve 57, 197–200, 209, 256; Square Neckline 129
tapering a Sleeve Cap 195
tapers, arranging 54; on draped neckline 138–39
test swatch 4–5, 38–41
textured stitches 381; stripes 8
tools for assembling sweaters 362; for charting 44–45
traditional: knitting 380–83; Turtleneck 274; V Neckline 120–25, 281, 286–87, 302
Triangle, Sleeve Cap 193–95
trick, paper 286
Triple Decreases 372
Ts see T-Shaped sweater
TS (Tapered Sleeve) 49, 197
turning ridges 167, 173, 377
Turtleneck 98–99, 117, 145, 268–69, 271, 274–75, 277, 285, 300
Typical Set-In Cap 190

Unfinished Width of Sleeve Cap 192–93
upperarm measurement 34–35, 388

V Band: circularly knit 270; with Collar 286
V Neckline 38, 51–52, 88, 114, 116, 120–26, 236–37, 269–70, 326, 364; Blunt 122, 126; cardigan 141, 145, 161, 173, 177; Decreased Band 300; finishes 281–95; Insert and Mock Insert 294; Self-Finished 281, 283; Traditional 120–25; variations 121; wide 125
variations of Box Cap 220; of Designer's Choice Cap 225; of Dolmans 251, 257, 265; of Hoods 303; of Leg o' Mutton Sleeves 208; of neckline finish combinations 301; of Plackets 326; of Pleated Caps 216; of Pockets 345, 348; of Round Neckline finishes 271

vertical: Band 141, 149–54; buttonholes 375–77; Dolmans 257–67; garment 251, 253; knitting 88; One-Piece Dolman 260–62; Placket 329–30; turning ridge 167, 173, 377; Two-Piece Dolman 258–59, 263; Woven Seam 365
Vertical Shawl Collar 291–92, 298, 365; Separate 182; Standard 178–80, 185; Wide 180–82, 185
vertically knit: collar 269; Dolman 56; garment 251, 253; Ts 88, 255–56
vest, armholes for 108–10, 364; neckline on 120

waist, fitted 74, 76
waist measurement 34–35, 388
warmth 268, 381–83
washing 17–18
watch cap, construction of 384
Welt Edging see Purl Welt Edging
wet-wrap blocking 361
wide: Band 114, 271–72; hips 36, 71; neckline 115; shoulders 35; V Neckline 125, 237; Vertical Shawl Collar 180–82
width of neckline 113
Wing Collar 272, 280, 282
women's garments 141, 269, 325, 330–33; sizing 392–93
wrapped short row 373
wrist measurement 34–35, 388
wrist-to-wrist see sleeve-to-sleeve knitting

yardage chart 389
yarn 13–23; biasing problems with 41; for cables 8; for lace 7; in slip-stitch patterns 8–9; in stranded-color knitting 9; not enough 43–44; requirements and selection 8–9, 13–23, 41–44, 389; too much 43; weight 274; yardage chart 389
yoke 34; classic 60; ribbed 100; width measurement 34–35, 82, 388; see also Basic T Yoke, Modified Raglan, Modified T Yoke, Round Yoke, Saddle Shoulder Yoke, Shaped Yoke, Standard Raglan Yoke